In the Company
of Educated Women

IN THE COMPANY OF
E·D·U·C·A·T·E·D
W·O·M·E·N

A History of Women and
Higher Education in America

BARBARA MILLER SOLOMON

Yale University Press · New Haven and London

Designed by Nancy Ovedovitz and set in Baskerville type, by Universal Printing Services, Inc. Printed in the United States of America by Vail-Ballou Press, Binghamton, New York.

Library of Congress Cataloging in Publication Data

Solomon, Barbara M., 1919–
  In the company of educated women.
  Bibliography: p.
  Includes index.
  1. Women—Education (Higher)—United States—History.
I. Title.
LC1752.S65   1985   376'.973   84–19681
ISBN 0–300–03314–1 (alk. paper)

10   9   8   7   6   5   4   3   2   1

In memory of my friend
Mary Flug Handlin
(1913–1976)

C·O·N·T·E·N·T·S

vii

I·L·L·U·S·T·R·A·T·I·O·N·S

Public parade for women's suffrage, Philadelphia, ca. 1913

Wellesley students boarding a train for New York City
for a weekend off campus

Pioneer in black women's education Lucy Slowe

Promoter of economic opportunities for women students
Lucy Ward Stebbins, 1941

Chorus line in *Making with the Maximum*, Smith College, 1943

College president and Office of Minority Affairs head
Mary McCleod Bethune

The first twelve women to enter Harvard Medical School, 1945

Sisters in Blackness at Spelman College in the 1960s

Student protest at Harvard commencement, 1971

Women's crew at the Head of the Charles Regatta,
Cambridge, Massachusetts, 1982

T·A·B·L·E·S

xi

A·C·K·N·O·W·L·E·D·G·M·E·N·T·S

During a long project the passage of time seems to go unnoticed until the end is in sight. Only then does one relive the stages that have been part of it. I have enjoyed many sources of support and cannot fully convey my appreciation in a few brief words.

Toward the end of a year as a fellow of the Charles Warren Center at Harvard (1968–69) I began a foray into women's history. But it was not until the award of a Guggenheim Fellowship in 1976–77 that I embarked on educational research at many colleges and universities. That year also, as a fellow of the Bunting Institute, I had an office at Radcliffe. There followed a summer sojourn at the Rockefeller Center in Bellagio, Italy, where I began writing. After that, I decided to extend my research further into the twentieth century, and research for this phase was supported by a grant in 1979–80 from the Andrew Mellon Foundation under the auspices of the Henry A. Murray Research Center, Radcliffe College. The Graduate Society of Harvard University in 1981 facilitated preparation of the manuscript.

The many hours spent in libraries across the country were enhanced by the cooperation of individuals too numerous to mention. However, I wish to thank librarians and archivists at Barnard, Boston University, Bryn Mawr, Cornell, Fisk, Mount Holyoke, Smith, Spelman, Stanford, Swarthmore, the University of California at Berkeley, the University of Chicago, the University of Wisconsin, Vassar, and Wellesley. I am indebted to the staffs of many libraries of Harvard University, particularly the Gutman Library and the University Archives. The reference department of Harvard College's Widener Library has been extraordinarily helpful, and especially Christina Haftmann of the Union Catalog desk. I also thank the entire staff of the Schlesinger Library and the Radcliffe College Archives; Karen Morgan, moreover, gave assistance well beyond the call of duty.

Many scholars shared ideas and material, including William Chafe, John Milton Cooper, Mary J. Oates, Barbara Page, Joel Richardson, Mary Ryan, Paula Fass, Gerda Lerner, Marcia Synnott, Lois Carr, Andrew Creeley, Geraldine Clifford, Anne Scott, Louise Young, Merze Tate, Charles Willie, John Hope Franklin, Kathryn Kish Sklar, Mary Kelley, Florence Howe, Barbara Sicherman, and the late Annette Baxter. K. Patricia Cross guided me in the literature of community colleges. Brunetta Wolfman, president of the Roxbury Community College, was very informative. Others who supplied information were Dr. Mary Eldred, Amelia Frye, Aurelia W. Franklin, Felicia L. Kaplan, Mina K. Curtiss, Elsie Lipset, Mickey and George Langstaff, Gene Dahmen, Lucy Somerville Howorth, Algie Newlin, and Nancy Randolph. Still others who helped are acknowledged in specific endnotes.

It was rewarding to have assistance from the following graduate students: Patricia Hill, Eugenia DelaMotte, Gail Richter, Janice Knight, Blanche Linden, Lynn Brickley, and Terry Epstein. Undergraduates who participated in the coding of questionnaires enlivened one summer and included Katherine Evans, Lisa Radetzsky, Chris Sailer, and Kate Silverman. Patricia Nolan not only coordinated the coders but contributed insightful analysis of the data. The computer study was aided by Girard Smitts's programming, Charles Grimshaw's advice, and Margaret Grimshaw's attentiveness.

Writing is a lonely process, but it was less so with this book because of the interest and encouragement of a wide array of individuals, colleagues, friends, and students. Oscar and Lilian Handlin read an early version. Carol Lasser and Susan Ware reacted to several drafts and their responses to the questions I raised made a profound difference.

In various typings of the manuscript, Patricia Denault and Anne Smith performed with dispatch. In winter and spring 1984 Miranda Cowley, Carla Harris, Alissa Land, and James Warner participated in typing and checking the manuscript, and Peggy Moldstad also gave thoughtfully of her time. In countless ways, Donna Brogan helped bring this work to fruition; she deserves special credit for preparation of the tables, but even more for her loyalty and enthusiasm, which never flagged.

I am also appreciative of Connie Griffin, who joined me in the final polishing of the text and provided sensitive editorial assistance. The manuscript benefited also from the meticulous scrutiny of Jean van Altena. Finally, Chuck Grench proved to be a most supportive editor, demanding but sympathetic.

Throughout this book the importance of family in furthering women's education emerges, and I cannot forget the passionate interest of my own parents where my education was concerned. Nor do I underestimate the contribution of my daughter Maida Solomon, whose encouragement and understanding have added precious meaning to this enterprise. And, as always, Peter Solomon remains faithful as critic and supporter.

I·N·T·R·O·D·U·C·T·I·O·N

Education, over the last two hundred years, has profoundly changed the contours of women's lives in America. While the impact of women's education has had revolutionary implications for the whole society, educated women have still not achieved equal status with men either within or outside the sphere of education. *In the Company of Educated Women* presents a historical overview of women's higher education and, at the same time, explores the paradoxes of this unfinished revolution.

This book is a history, not of institutions but of generations of women: those who hungered for education, those who fought for it, and those who took it for granted. In many contexts, women have been protagonists in a drama in which their own desires and efforts, as well as conditions beyond their control, contributed to a momentum for change.

Conceived as a narrative, this story has four themes: (1) women's struggles for access to institutions; (2) the dimensions of the collegiate experience; (3) the effects of education upon women's life choices; and (4) the uneasy connection between feminism and women's educational advancement. In exploring each of these themes, we see the interaction of women's aspirations with outside forces that both hindered and helped women in the sphere of higher education.

From the beginning of my research I sought connections between education and the extent of choice in women's lives. This probing brought me back to the colonial era, when neither the idea of personal choice nor the opportunity for formal education existed for women. I found myself asking why it was possible for women as a group to advance in the last two hundred years but not before. I subsequently saw women's aspiring to liberal arts study as the starting point of my work. Although social change was a constant in the American republic, women were expected to be the stable, unchanging element in a changing world. But the roles of women could not remain static, for both the demands of women themselves and the needs of a dynamic society necessitated their educational advancement.

The process of women's entry into higher education has been integrally linked with economic and social factors that have shaped American life. Among these, the impact of industrialization, the significant decline in fertility rates, and the introduction of formal schooling for youth, have all contributed to the release of women from expected societal roles. For women more than for men, education evoked opposition, because it gave women an identity outside the family. While the utility of educating women gradually gained acceptance, anxiety over their possible abandonment of traditional roles endured.

At every stage of their progress, individual women persisted in exploiting opportunities. This history reveals a dialectic between women's demands for education and the opposition they encountered. Public controversy over women's academic training surrounded each struggle for access, whether to an academy, college, or professional school. Yet advocacy grew from the late eighteenth century to the present, in large part because women's education proved advantageous to society. Significantly, women's special role as mothers of male citizens offered the first powerful rationale for some education. A similar logic gradually justified to religious leaders the function of women as schoolteachers. Finally, the republican ideal, apart from the practical needs of the society, gave philosophical recognition to the rights of individuals. Aspiring women eventually applied to themselves the Jeffersonian principle that each man should rise according to his abilities.

This social ideal became the instrument through which women in educated families first identified their own yearnings for education. Moreover, certain families increasingly understood the intellectual and practical value of education for their offspring, some more for sons, some more for daughters, and others for both. I emphasize that, whereas most students have come from a wide range of middle-class families, the college population has become increasingly diverse. What in the nineteenth century was an act of nonconformity became in the twentieth century a social necessity. Different ethnic, racial, religious, and social groups, as well as poorer students generally, did gain access to education. However slight at first, these gains affected not only particular individuals but also the expectations of unknown others.

The promises of an open America ultimately required public support of higher education in the United States. Women over time benefited from increasingly progressive attitudes. Support grew from modest beginnings in local communities to the state level and finally to the federal government. The innovative Morrill Land Grant legislation (1862) en-

couraged students of small means to work their way through college by
enrolling in schools that were virtually free. Scholarships, which students
would later take for granted, long remained insufficient, and it was not
until the 1960s that government aid reached many of the talented poor.
Women students have valued differently the elements common to
their education: the quests for knowledge, vocation, and identity apart
from family. Women entered diverse institutions, which changed academically within each period and offered many variations on the collegiate experience. But consistently, one generalization holds: coeducational schools made plain both directly and indirectly what could be
denied at women's colleges, that society attached greater importance to
men's achievements. Academic study became another way to reinforce
the differences between men's and women's lives; no woman could forget that she was in a man's world. Yet, despite this attitude, women
everywhere experienced intellectual awakenings at college. However
educators judged any particular curriculum, institutions at their best
enabled women to take themselves seriously.

Although the collegiate experience encompassed formal studies and
professorial influences, peer values proved to be the greatest influence
on undergraduates. Student perspectives are therefore a necessary complement to official views of higher education and its meaning. Group
identities developed in successive student generations, first among the
academy-educated and then still more among college women in the
nineteenth and twentieth centuries. Each generation confronted
changing ideals for their sex, whether they saw themselves as "true" or
"new" women. Educated women may not have been consciously trying
to redefine womanhood; yet all along their actions did extend its definitions. These women had rising expectations, and, inevitably, they experienced both internal and external conflicts in making life choices.

For all generations, after the uniquely privileged collegiate period
came the time of reckoning, publicly labeled "After College, What?".
Whatever the educated woman absorbed as an undergraduate, in adulthood she dealt with a central dilemma posed by the demands of society:
how to live up to the promise of her education and at the same time fulfill her female role. Experiences of the antebellum academy-educated
women foreshadowed those of college women later in the century, who
felt under stress from the competing claims of family, society, and self.
Early collegians knew that they had an obligation to marry and produce
their share of babies. Nonetheless, despite an occasional expression of
guilt, a considerable minority never married; such a decision proved to
be a more or less viable option for the educated woman. In addition, by
1920 other ways in which college-educated women differed from their
less educated sisters had become apparent. Those who married had

fewer children than other women of childbearing age. As the female college population expanded, however, marital patterns of the educated came to resemble more closely those of the uneducated. In fact, after World War II, most college as well as noncollege women married young, thereby contributing to the baby boom of the 1950s. Yet, in the 1970s, college women reverted to the older patterns by marrying at later ages or not at all.

More striking even than demographic shifts has been the steady expansion in gainful employment for college women at different points in their lives. By the 1920s there was a corps of professional women, and paid employment for the unmarried collegian was becoming a conventional option. At the same time a vanguard of college women combined marriage (and motherhood) with a job or career. Those educated in the late twentieth century no longer held the nineteenth-century middle-class ethos that a woman, single or married, should work only out of financial necessity. By the 1980s many women, married or single, made contributions to a whole range of occupations, from the traditionally female to the traditionally male.

Education has proven for some women to be a path of social mobility. Nonetheless, it is painfully evident that education does not necessarily hold for women the advantages it holds for men. Access to the most valued employment is just beginning. Overall, women in 1984 were earning only 62 cents for every dollar earned by men, and most women still could not expect financial remuneration commensurate with their educational level. But the limitations for a woman without an education are still more disturbing. Every thoughtful person must be concerned about the feminization of poverty; women make up almost 60 percent of America's poor, and these include not only young single mothers, but aging widows and retired workers as well.

The educated, regardless of background, are privileged. Yet generalizations about women's expectations and attitudes are misleading. Just as women acquire an education for different reasons, so their uses of it vary. Educated women have made individual choices at different times in their lives about the place of paid employment or voluntary activities. While committing themselves to family responsibilities, women have nevertheless held on to personal goals. Patterns differ as to how an individual adapts and yet sustains her ambition. Shifts can also be seen in how the generations have met this challenge.

College education, whatever its form, has always carried with it a consciousness of possibilities for women. The essence of a liberal education is learning to think for oneself. This experience has sometimes led to a further step: an embracing of feminism. Although a liberal education does not guarantee feminism (any more than its absence precludes it), education offers a process by which women can learn to value their own thinking and themselves. The definitions and implications of feminism of course have changed during the past two hundred years. Ironically, throughout this time, even though feminism has been one catalyst for women's education, academic institutions serving women have often tried to repress or ignore its messages. Nonetheless, educated women, whether they admit it or not, are beneficiaries of the feminist legacy. In periods of strong feminist consciousness the aspirations of individuals have been bolstered by a supportive environment; the presence of an active women's movement makes a profound difference in the lives of American women.

Achievements of the 1970s prompted the hope that women had reached a new threshhold of opportunity. The following years, however, have demanded closer examination and renewed questioning. The expanding company of educated women must still contend with the fear and ambivalence implicit in public attitudes and policies toward women's changing roles. To maintain and propel a momentum for equality, it is vital to understand the enduring complexities facing women, educated or not. *In the Company of Educated Women* aims to illuminate some of those complexities in the belief that the knowledge will strengthen future generations in taking the next steps toward true equality.

O·N·E

A Forbidden World

If you complain of neglect of Education in sons, What shall I say
with regard to daughters, who every day experience the want of it.
With regard to the Education of my own children, I find myself
soon out of my depth, and destitute and deficient
in every part of Education.
I most sincerely wish that some more liberal plan might
be laid and executed for the Benefit of the rising Generation, and
that our new constitution may be distinguished for Learning and
Virtue. If we mean to have Heroes, Statesmen and Philosophers, we
should have learned women. The world perhaps would laugh at me,
and accuse me of vanity, But you I know have a mind too enlarged
and liberal to disregard the Sentiment. If much depends as is allowed upon the early Education of youth and the first principals
which are instilld take the deepest root, great benefit must arise
from literary accomplishments in women.

Abigail Adams to John Adams, August 14, 1776
Adams Family Correspondence, ed. L. H. Butterfield et al., II, 94

Colonial Americans in the 1600s would have dismissed summarily the
notion of women attaining, or even wanting, a college education. Yet,
during the American Revolution, Abigail Adams not only suggested that
the new code of laws make provision for women to have some portion of
the liberal education, but she declared that the new society should make
a place for learned women. Fifteen years later a poem addressed "To a
Lady, Who Expressed a Desire of Seeing an University Established for
Women" began: "Deluded Maid, Thy Claim Forego." It was not accidental that such a bold claim was made in 1791, for educational aspirations
arose at that time out of vital developments in the transition from colonial to republican America. Social, economic, and intellectual changes
between the seventeenth and eighteenth centuries not only fanned the
political revolution, but also introduced new questions about the posi-

1

tion of women and their education. To appreciate the demands of the most forward-looking women (only a few), then, it is necessary to look back to the beginnings of American society.[1]

Usefulness was the measure of all learning, but many factors slowly affected the process of women's educational advance. All along women acquired specific knowledge as it related to their particular duties. Limitations on female education reflected the traditional view of women's place and abilities; it was assumed that women had smaller brains and weaker minds than men. At first there seemed no reason for any woman to acquire a formal liberal education.[2]

For most of those who settled in the wilderness of seventeenth-century America, book learning was a remote concern. Yet the leaders of the Massachusetts Bay settlement acknowledged the importance of liberal education with the founding of Harvard College in 1636. The next outpost of learning in the New World, William and Mary College, was established in Virginia in 1693, soon followed by Yale's opening in 1701. Seven more colleges were started between 1746 and 1776. These fledgling institutions provided students with a prescribed liberal course of study: initially ancient languages, mathematics, science, and philosophy, with rhetoric and belles lettres added later. College was beyond the reach of most men, for lack of social status, and of all women, by virtue of their sex. Collegiate education offered the cultural background considered essential for the careers of ministers, lawyers, doctors, and men of affairs. Although there were fewer than three thousand living college graduates in 1770, the bachelor's degree was the mark of distinction of potential leaders.[3]

One's place in the community determined one's specific instruction; most people received their education in apprenticeships, not at institutions. Women's roles were set from birth, their identities derived from family membership—as daughters, wives, and mothers—and functions performed within the family unit determined women's employment. Women shared family goals, and their household contributions were essential in promoting the well-being of families and communities. Marriage was the accepted state, and most women married between the ages of twenty and twenty-three (the average age for men was between twenty-five and twenty-eight). Women understood that their primary duty was to bear children; children could help in the labors of the farm and shop as well as in the operation of the household.[4]

A woman did not question her place; the husband was the family's head, children and bonded servants were in lower categories; the mother had full authority only in the father's absence. The wife was subordinate to her husband. Although the Protestant denominations made marriage a civil contract dependent on mutual consent, and colonial laws enforced the rights and responsibilities of both men and women, a wife was expected to accept her husband's authority. In practice not all colonial men applied the logic of family law autocratically. One Puritan wrote in memory of his deceased spouse: " 'Tis hard to tell, where love did bear such sway / Who was commanded or who did obey."[5]

In early seventeenth-century settlements, and thereafter in new rural ones, the family was the unit of economic production. Domestic labor consumed most of the waking hours of all females, who prepared or supervised the preparation of food, clothing, and household necessities. Their employment sometimes extended beyond traditional domestic labors. By the turn of the eighteenth century the growth of trade had widened the range of women's employment within family enterprises to include management of dry goods shops, tavern keeping, furniture making, printing, and publishing, among other activities. Women also took on full management of other family business during the absence of, or after the death of, a spouse; only a few, like the famous Dutch she-merchants, ran independent businesses. One exclusively female occupation until the late eighteenth century was midwifery, in which practitioners transmitted valued skills from one generation to the next, often from mother to daughter. However they worked, women's responsibilities were to help their families survive.[6]

Few women could be concerned with educational deprivation. Their expectations did not include education beyond what was required to fulfill their prescribed duties in a hierarchical society. The rudiments of education started in the family, and boys and girls were trained according to their stations in life. Instruction in domestic skills constituted the education common to all girls.

But in New England primarily, reading and writing became required in the training of the young. There parents were legally obliged to teach reading and writing to boys and at least reading to girls. Because some parents were too busy, or illiterate themselves, an older woman might take on the responsibility of teaching children their letters in her kitchen; thus began the dame schools. Only the most fortunate girls were taught to write. Even in New England only one-third of the women in the first generation of settlers were able to sign their names, and at the end of the colonial period, only fifty percent could do so, as opposed to eighty percent of the men. Yet compared to women in other parts of America (and Europe), New England's women were highly advanced.[7]

The demands of Puritan religion and Yankee commerce accelerated the growth of literacy; bible reading as a means of achieving piety was as important for females as males. Writing, a skill at first reserved for boys preparing for business, became an asset for girls in trading families. Daughters in educated families at the top of the social hierarchy in these communities benefited from informal exposure to liberal education. Favored daughters often discovered their intellectual powers in bible reading, private writing, and participation in prayer groups. But there were limits to public encouragement of female religious learning, since it was not meant to stimulate independent thinking. Most Protestant leaders held the view that women should be silent in church and subservient everywhere else. Anne Hutchinson's rise and fall in the early Massachusetts Bay Colony illustrates the vulnerability of a brilliant, pious woman who placed her own theological interpretations above those of the clergy. A learned reader of the bible, this mother of twelve and midwife held weekly meetings at her house to discuss the ministers' sermons. When Sister Anne's influence grew with young women of humble station and wives started bringing husbands to hear her commentary, the leaders of the community halted the talks. Hutchinson was inevitably excommunicated after two church trials; her interrogation turned into a persecution, making her an example to her women supporters.[8]

But after Anne Hutchinson was banished into the wilderness, other women, with varying degrees of discretion or rebellion, used religion as a way to communal leadership, not unlike ministers. The dignified private prayer meetings conducted by Esther Edwards Stoddard in the 1650s caused no stir, but the potential of prayer meetings for challenging a community reemerged in the Great Awakening and other revivals of the eighteenth century. When schoolteacher Sarah Osborne's large public prayer meetings attracted white, black, old, young, men, and women, a minister challenged her fitness for conducting a revival. But she had her answer: "Would you advise me to shut up my mouth and doors and creep into obscurity?"[9]

Among Protestants only the Quakers found scriptural justification for the calling of women as well as men to preach. Starting with wandering enthusiasts of the seventeenth century, and continuing in a lay ministry, women had a dominant place in the Meetings of Friends. In the eighteenth century women had charge of a separate subdivision of Meetings, where they provided counsel and supervision for other women.[10]

Although not all women had the same intensity in religious devotions, obviously, by the mid-eighteenth century female participation predominated in every religious group. As men turned to moneymaking or politics, women carried more responsibilities in church. Increasingly it appeared that men who were not ministers left religion along with domestic duties to women. Undoubtedly women made the most of this shift. But however much religion offered women opportunities for personal development and support for their hard lives, as an approach to education, it was indirect and incomplete.[11]

Shifts in religion and science, as well as in demography and the economy, converged with religious currents to make female education a matter of increasing interest at the upper levels of colonial societies. The

Newtonian scientific rationale (discussed in churches and colleges) placed God at a distance and gave human beings greater responsibility for their lives. Rationalism, like evangelism, emphasized the role of human will in the improvement of the individual. The Puritan Enlightenment philosopher John Locke envisaged the infant mind as an empty slate upon which ideas and sensations from the environment were impressed, thereby molding the individual's personality. Locke's psychology found no distinction in the mind by sex, and his psychology slowly undermined the assumption of the immutability of female inferiority.[12]

Locke's argument opened the way for innovative training of the young. One South Carolinian parent, for example, designed blocks for his children, and a Boston family had their African slave girl tutored with their own daughter and a son who was preparing for Harvard. Phillis Wheatley proved Locke's point by her precocity in learning languages and writing verse. Identifying herself as an Ethiopian in one poem, she addressed students of "the University of Cambridge in New England" aptly: "Improve your privileges while they stay." Wheatley absorbed the cultural values of her environment and spoke indirectly for its women, who were still left out of the collegiate world. The potentiality in women's education was no different from that in men's, at least theoretically. Education thus emerged as central in the shaping of human beings of either sex.[13]

Talented women were always reminded of the societal restraints on their learning, whether by fathers, husbands, or the community. Boston minister Benjamin Coleman, praising daughter Jane's verses, noted that "with the advantages of my Liberal Education at School and College . . . your genius in writing would have excelled mine." But by the mid-eighteenth century not much had changed from the 1650s, when poet Anne Bradstreet wrote "I am obnoxious to each carping tongue / Who says my hand a needle better fits."[14]

At first glance the career of the first female scientist in America appears to be the exception to the pattern of limited encouragement. Jane Colden, daughter of the distinguished botanist Cadwallader Colden, received unusual training from her father, who translated Linnaeus from the Latin for her use and imported botanical books for her instruction. In time Jane Colden produced her own catalogue of over three hundred plants and gained public recognition for her botanical discoveries. Yet, after her marriage at age thirty-five, she ceased her work. Was this her choice or not?[15]

On the whole reactions to educating daughters were mixed. Some parents recognized that education would provide a livelihood for a daughter who remained single; and indeed there was increasing evidence that some women, in certain communities that had a surplus of females, might never marry. Other parents, however, were more concerned with the marriageability of daughters than with their educational advancement. Above all, fear lingered that education might unfit a girl for her subservient role as a wife. Female education became the focus of a growing debate in books and magazines widely read by prosperous families in America as in England.

The vogue of the lady, as promoted in English advice literature, had a large impact on American parents intent on training girls to be polished but congenial, obedient as daughters and future wives. The significant hopes for women's learning in Enlightenment thought were ignored while criteria for gentility predominated. John Witherspoon, president of the College of New Jersey, in an anonymous essay advised college men to marry women of equal rank, pointing out that in cases of unequals marrying, men could rise to elegant habits more easily than women. Colonial Americans read George Savile's *The Lady's New Year's Gift, or Advice to a Daughter,* the Reverend James Fordyce's *Sermons to Young Women* and *Character and Conduct of the Female Sex,* and Dr. John Gregory's *A Father's Legacy to His Daughters.* These English writers insisted that women accept the inequalities between the sexes, and applauded softness, delicacy, and helplessness as female traits.[16]

In the same vein the novels of Samuel Richardson in the 1740s and 1750s addressed the issue of proper female behavior and offered what was seen as sensible advice. Richardson favored women's education to elevate female virtue. Thus, *Pamela* taught the lesson that the servant girl's preservation of her virginity won her marriage into the gentry, whereas *Clarissa* showed a proud heroine seduced because she did not obey her parents' rules, who had to die for her mistake. This fiction, like the domestic essays, discouraged too much book learning for women and too much independence. Even a group of English "learned" women writers known as Bluestockings maintained that moral instruction rather than serious study would usually suffice for their sex.[17]

For evidence that education need not ruin a woman for marriage, the example of Eliza Lucas Pinckney stands out. Eliza Lucas, about to marry Charles Pinckney in 1744 after an extraordinary youth in which she studied freely in the arts and sciences and made discoveries about indigo that served her father's business well, was reminded of her "place" as a female. She in turn reassured her parents that she would accept her husband's authority: "The acting out of my proper province and invading his would be an inexcusable breach of prudence, as his superior understanding (without any consideration) would point him to dictate and leave me nothing but the easy task of obeying." In recognizing her "proper province," Eliza spoke with full awareness, for even those with unusual educational advantages accepted the authority of fathers and husbands, thereby maintaining the division of the sexes, in theory if not always in practice.[18]

The turbulent 1760s and 1770s tested colonial women further in thought and action, and many did make unusual contributions to their families and society. But however ingenious self-educated women were, they still deferred to men. Keeping their sense of domestic priorities, they rarely questioned the female condition. Yet, in the 1760s, women entered the political arena in explicit ways and to varying extents absorbed the natural rights ideology of the impending American Revolution. Those on the patriot side developed boycott strategies—of tea and English cloth—that clearly depended on housewives' cooperation. The times made heavy demands on both sexes in such families to support the radical principles of the rights of man and the consent of the governed.

With the onset of the war women took on the responsibilities of men on farms and in the shops; as patriots or loyalists, females were disguised as soldiers, spies, and camp followers. Other women made group protests throughout the colonies and struggled to withstand attacks on both property and themselves. Others, like the Philadelphia women who organized a subscription campaign, raised funds. Of necessity, all coped both independently and jointly, in ways reminiscent of the pioneer generations. While the rhetoric of gentility still differentiated between the sexes, women performed in public and private spheres at the same time. This war, like all wars, heightened the importance of women; some overcame their lack of confidence during the long struggle. Moreover, those identified with the patriots discovered that the political ideology about the rights of man had meaning for the female sex. Only a very few women, however, left a record of their responses to these heady ideas and their import for women.[19]

In the unstable 1770s two privileged New England matrons pondered the conflicting views of female capacity in this time of increased activity. Mercy Otis Warren (1728–1814) and Abigail Smith Adams (1744–1818), growing up in prominent Massachusetts families, had always had access to books along with training in domestic skills. Mercy Otis, who adored her patriot brother James (he once asked, "Are not women born as free as men?"), married at the late age of twenty-six his Harvard classmate James Warren, a rising politician. Abigail Smith, daughter of a liberal Puritan minister, at nineteen married another ambitious Harvard man, John Adams. Both women, though elegant and fashionable, had strong religious convictions and subscribed to the virtues of delicacy and modesty. Yet, during the Revolution, each reexamined the tradition in which she had been brought up, while managing her absent husband's affairs and raising children. These experiences not only transformed their lives but gave them an understanding of what women could contribute to the new republic. The Adams–Warren correspondence has the quality of a dialogue on women's concerns. Both accepted as fundamental the limitations placed on women in their world.

As Warren reminded Adams, "Our weak and timid sex is only the Echo of the other, and like some pliant peace of Clock Work the springs of our soul move slow or more Rapidly."

Adams in turn explained to her brother that "the natural tenderness and Delicacy of our constitution, added to the many dangers we are subject to from your Sex, renders it impossible for a single Lady to travel without injury to her character."[20]

But these women, like others in the Revolution, were far from "pliant" in their thought and action in the emergency of war. Warren, writing under a pseudonym for local newspapers, achieved a quasi-career as a political satirist against the Tories. Her plays, published both anonymously and under a pseudonym, attacked the Boston Tories vitriolically. Because her talent as a versifier was well known locally, Dr. John Winthrop asked her to use her pen in a war campaign to tell fashionable ladies what not to buy. Warren was delighted to condemn in print what she called a Clarissa type of woman, unwilling "to check her wanton pride / And lay her female ornaments aside."[21]

Both Mercy Warren and Abigail Adams admired Catharine Macaulay, the radical author of *A History of England* (1763), who supported the cause of the American patriots. Mrs. Adams wanted to know what prompted Mrs. Macaulay to engage in the writing of history, a project "never before Exhibited to the publick by one of her own Sex and Country." Under Macaulay's influence Mercy Warren conceived her plan to write a history of the Revolution, living to complete it in 1805. Abigail Adams rejected literary ambitions for herself and never lost her sense of inferiority about her spelling and ignorance of Latin. Yet her letters, rather than Warren's plays and verse, have become the greater source in documenting signs of a dawning feminist consciousness that was expressed only privately.[22]

Abigail Adams welcomed every advance for women and foresaw more than could be realized in her lifetime. She urged her husband to "remember the ladies" in the new code of laws, to give married women protection from tyrannical husbands. As she pointed out the terrible deficiencies in female education at all levels, she finally made that significant request to her husband, that the new constitution "be distinguished for Learning and Virtue," and that "if we mean to have Heroes, Statesmen and Philosphers, we should have learned women." This awareness of education's value, rooted in the Enlightment faith in human potentiality, had feminist implications before there was a feminist ideology.[23]

A younger contemporary of similar background gave the reading public an explicit feminist argument for the education of women. The views of Judith Sargent Murray (1751–1820) reflected both personal and family experience. Daughter of an affluent shipowner in Glouces- ter, Massachusetts, who later lost his fortune, she started her self- education with her brother's college texts. She and her parents suffered social rebuffs in their community when they became Universalists, but her intellectual independence grew. She married at eighteen, was wid- owed at thirty-three, and then married the Reverend John Murray, leading exponent of Universalism. But her marital happiness with him did not bring financial security.[24]

Murray expressed in her writing an awareness of the trials of married women. Steeped in the tradition of the Bluestockings, she moved be- yond their conservatism in her plays and essays published between 1784 and 1794 under the pseudonym Constantia. Murray's essay "Equality of the Sexes," written in 1779 and published in 1790, portrayed vividly and with some bitterness the frustration of girls whose yearning for ad- vanced study, stimulated by the example of their brothers, was stopped short of fruition. In her vision liberal education would develop women's power to reason and to make judgments without stooping to pedantry. She had confidence that introducing women to liberal education would give them an intellectual "humility" different from that which ministers preached for females. Murray would teach women "to aspire . . . and . . . to estimate every accomplishment, according to its proper value."[25]

More than Mercy Warren and Abigail Adams, Judith Murray con- veyed the personal advantages of education. In an article entitled "Des- ultory Thoughts upon the Utility of Encouraging a Degree of Self- Complacency, Especially in Female Bosoms" (1784), young women were told not to underestimate themselves. Lack of self-respect led too many girls to "give themselves up to the first man who presents himself," be- cause they were afraid of becoming "old maids." (Was her advice a re- flection of her own experience?) Her counsel clearly contradicted that of the domestic advice books.[26]

Murray's *Gleaner* essays published in the early 1790s transcended the boundaries of her world in recognizing the need for training women to earn their own living. Although, like Mercy Warren and Abigail Adams, she was brought up with the values of gentility, she knew through per- sonal hardship that even women of her class might be forced to be self- supporting; education could provide independence for women in need, whether they were spinsters or widows or helping wives. Not all women in her social group would be able to marry, and Murray made a virtue of this necessity. She dared to suggest that girls should not be taught that marriage was the "summum bonum," the highest good, without which no woman could lead a life of dignity. Yet, even though she cited alternative benefits of liberal education for individual women, Murray, like Warren and Adams, always stressed the importance of women's duties as wives and mothers.[27]

Thoughtful women in the republic must have experienced agreeable shocks of recognition upon first reading *A Vindication of the Rights of Woman* by the radical Englishwoman Mary Wollstonecraft. What Mercy Warren, Abigail Adams, and Judith Murray conveyed with wit now took form as a direct feminist polemic. Writing during the French Revolution, Wollstonecraft saw connections between women's education and their advances in society. She delivered sharp attacks on all those who confined women's place and education, from the conservative English Bluestockings to the male prescriptive writers. Wollstonecraft condemned advocates of "ladylike" behavior, especially Rousseau, Fordyce, and Gregory, who considered females rather as women than "human creatures." Using Locke's psychology, she argued that women must be educated as rational creatures if they were to develop fully as human beings. Her plan for the national education of boys and girls together deliberately minimized gender differences imposed by society. Declaring that women's first duty was to themselves, she subsumed motherhood under citizenship and removed one boundary of woman's private sphere. The English feminist then demanded that women have representatives in the government, and that some enter the professions as doctors or nurses.[28]

While Warren, Adams, and Murray, like Wollstonecraft, believed that liberal education would not only enable a women better to perform the duties of wife and mother, but would also empower her to think for herself, the Americans were not ready to advocate specific careers for women. Even Judith Murray, who admired Shakespeare's Portia, did not suggest that women become doctors, lawyers, or politicians. By contrast, a younger Connecticut woman, Susan Bull Tracy, born in 1759, expressed solid agreement with "Miss W's idea, that women ought to learn certain professional business." Tracy asked, "Why not make surgeons and physicians of some?" This wife and mother of five, daughter of a schoolmaster and herself a teacher at age sixteen, was as liberal in real life as the fictional woman in Charles Brockden Brown's *Alcuin* who objected to the exclusion of women from law, medicine, and the ministry.[29]

The *Vindication* was widely discussed in America and was reprinted in Boston and Philadelphia in 1792 and 1794 respectively. Although it is difficult to determine the extent to which women actually read the book, vague references to its content and the author in private journals and letters abound. In a well-known tantalizing response, Philadelphia Quaker Elizabeth Sandwith Drinker wrote that "in very many of her sen-

timents, she, as some of our friends say, speaks my mind." Wollstonecraft's feminist ideas left their mark on many more individuals than acknowledged her publicly. Abigail Adams, when her husband joshed her
as a "real Wollstonecraft," retorted that he had much to learn from her.
Wollstonecraft precipitated an explosion of feminist consciousness in the
English-speaking world. Whether one agreed or disagreed with the *Vindication*, thinking about women would never be the same again.[30]

Nothing could have been further from the goals of the patriot (male)
generation than the promotion of women's rights and learned women.
The leaders did not want their wives and daughters to be intellectuals;
they, like other less educated Americans, feared the result of too much
learning for women. Although Franklin, Jefferson, and Adams had enjoyed the company of English Bluestockings and French *femmes savantes*,
these leaders retained a homegrown model of American womanhood.
They agreed with their South Carolinian colleague Henry Laurens who
sent his daughter Martha a pair of globes with the message: "When you
are measuring the surface of this world, remember that you are to act a
part on it, and think of a plumb pudding and other domestic duties."
These statesmen intended their daughters to be "notable" as housewives
upholding the colonial tradition of piety, modesty, frugality, and
fertility.[31]

The founders of the republic had the clear purpose of reordering society after the Revolution. The evolving national identity stimulated expectations for the whole society, but how women fared would depend on
how their needs fitted in with other concerns of the new nation. Political
leaders intent on creating a society different from the old colonial or European models made citizenship central but left women out of this fundamental category. The logic of the republican ideal created deep divisiveness about the slavery of black people but not about the ambiguous
position of free white women, who continued to derive their civil status
from that of their fathers and husbands.

From war's end in 1783 until ratification of the Constitution in 1789,
men of different political and religious persuasions worked to create a
legal foundation for the republic. The Constitution gave some men
more rights than others but gave none to women. Leaving to the states
decisions about voting, marriage, and divorce, the Constitution did not
interfere with local and sectional differences. While the states in general
ignored female status in their constitutional deliberations, there are a
few examples of local variations. Thus, the town of Northampton, in accepting the Massachusetts state constitution of 1790, justified the omis-
sion of women from the right to vote by referring to Locke's *Treatise on
Government* and the *Essex Result*. Apparently through oversight, New Jersey's 1787 law gave suffrage to "all inhabitants of the proper age and

property qualifications." Seventy-five women in Elizabeth seized the opportunity to vote for the town's state representative, and women also
voted throughout New Jersey in the 1800 presidential election. They
continued to vote until 1807, when an election fraud led to a new act
granting suffrage only to "free white male citizens twenty-one years of
age, worth fifty pounds proclamation money, clear estate." Women were
thus disqualified by virtue of their sex, irrespective of the status of their
families. The demands for free manhood suffrage would soon accentu-
ate the decline in political status of upper-class women relative to all
white men in this period.[32]

Not female suffrage but female education became linked with the republican ideal. Because the effectiveness of male suffrage required an
informed citizenry, some education for everyone became a necessity.
The promotion of literacy for the male majority and of liberal education
for future leaders gave new importance to education in the whole society. District and common schools would provide the elements of literacy
to expanding numbers, irrespective of class and sex. Further growth of
colleges (twenty-five by 1800) indicated public and parental support for
some higher learning. Republican wives and mothers gained a special
role in the creation of an informed citizenry. Though not citizens themselves, they would train their young male offspring for citizenship. In
1787 Benjamin Rush presented this social rationale explicitly in a public
address at a new school for girls, The Young Ladies Academy, in
Philadelphia. Rush maintained that the education of women was critical
to the well-being of the new nation, with emphasis on mothers' responsibilities for the early instruction of children. He assumed that the demands of business and politics in the republic would separate men and
women in their activities even more than in the past. The republican
wife, as her husband's representative, would therefore execute their
common decisions in bringing up the children and in imparting moral
and religious principles, as well as in managing the household. Thus
republican motherhood furnished a utilitarian motive for educating
women.[33]

The patriot generation did not suggest that females should have the
full liberal education offered to sons. Thomas Jefferson's liberalism in
promoting the education of socially mobile men of talent and abilities
did not apply to women; he was not interested in females' education beyond preparing them for their practical functions in the community. Yet
he made his own daughter's education somewhat more rigorous, with
reading in some of the best literature and the "graver sciences." Thus,
if she drew a "blockhead" for a husband (the chances, he said, were
"fourteen to one"), Martha would be intellectually equipped to head "a
little family of her own." Some parents in isolated communities saw util-

ity in daughters learning Latin, Greek, and Hebrew on the assumption that, as mothers, they would then be able to instruct their own sons in preparation for academy or college. By contrast, John Adams told daughter Nabby that "it is scarcely reputable for young ladies to understand Latin and Greek—French, my dear, French is the language next to English."[34]

Sometimes the matrons in educated families urged the younger females to combine intellectual with domestic duties. Mercy Warren told her nieces and other young friends that they should not read until they had taken care of their responsibilities "in the economy of domestic life." Murray's *Gleaner* essays laid out patterns for mothers and daughters to allow for both the essential "female administration" and the studies that could follow. Eliza Lucas Pinckney took equal pride in her daughter's Latin and in her management of the dairy.[35]

A few women in the early republic had unprecedented aspirations for their sex, which Susan Bull Tracy articulated: "The light of science, where it has only beamed on half a Nation (for women, naturally, have never partaken but of the reflected blaze) has shown us wonders." In the colonial era individuals had sought and gained education wherever they could, through the bible, ministers' sermons, religious meetings, family conversations, and books in private libraries. The revolution radically altered the lives of one generation, and it invested its hopes in the next. A Judith Murray or a Mary Wollstonecraft might inspire unknown young women. Another writer who signed herself as an "aging matron" in a Connecticut journal offered a challenge: "What would be the consequence if the doors of our seminaries were as effectually shut against the gentlemen, as they now are against the other sex; and colleges and superior schools of scientific improvement, were appropriately thrown open to the benefit of the female world . . . ?"[36]

The utility of full liberal education for women had still to be established. An idea had come into being, but to implement it would require preliminary stages. In the next half century circumstances would give some women the chance to prove their faith in women's educability, and the institutionalizing of women's education would advance.

T·W·O

Boring from Within:
A Beginning in the
Academies of the Republic

Female academies are everywhere establishing and right pleasant is
the appellation to my ear. . . . I expect to see our young women
forming a new era in female history.

Judith Murray, *The Gleaner* (1798) III, 188–89

The idea of a college for males will naturally be associated with that
of a seminary, instituted and endowed by the public; and the absur-
dity of sending ladies to college, may, at first thought, strike every
one, to whom this subject shall be proposed. I therefor hasten to
observe, that the seminary here recommended, will be as different
from those appropriated to the other sex, as the female character
and duties are from the male.

Emma Willard, *An Address to the Public* (1819), [2]–3

Educating women was one of many propositions receiving attention in
the new nation, and despite resistant publics the idea took hold with surprising rapidity. The years between 1790 and 1850 witnessed a remarkable growth in female schooling, and as a result the notion of collegiate
study moved from the realm of fantasy to that of real experimentation.
It was not the dreaming of privileged individuals, but the institutionalizing of education at many levels that unexpectedly produced opportunities for women. This profound shift developed from a convergence
of social, religious, political, and economic conditions which educators of
women exploited resourcefully. Female students gained a larger and
larger "portion" of the liberal education in varied institutions—academies, seminaries, and so-called colleges. In the longer perspective of history the struggles for this education recede; these were trial runs, which
by 1850 had laid a crucial foundation for women's higher education.

Such progress was not to be predicted at the end of the eighteenth century. In the new republic no agreement existed on a national design for education for male citizens, let alone females. When the American Philosophical Society sponsored an essay contest to enlist ideas for a unique American system of education, one prize-winner, Maryland clergyman and educator Samuel Knox, expressed a popular view when he proposed a public system of elementary schools open to boys and girls. However, the other prize-winner, Samuel H. Smith (president of Princeton), declined to include any discussion of female education in his plan, saying that there was too much "diversity of opinion" on the subject. Yet, in passing, he applauded the "improvement of women" and hinted that they should be educated. Not surprisingly, no national system of education was established, but local communities responded to the particular needs of their members.[1]

Although there was no uniformity in attitude or practice, a few colonial precedents did exist for the instruction of girls at elementary and secondary levels. The former had public and the latter private support: in different places some town schools, fashionable "adventure" schools, and a few more serious schools admitted women from the mid- to late eighteenth century. Academies instructing boys customarily offered both college preparatory and terminal studies. Because of its flexibility, the academy proved effective as the transitional institution where women had a formal introduction to liberal studies.[2]

Academies, chartered in the late eighteenth century by colonies and later by states, had some public support given in recognition of religious and educational goals validated by a supporting board of trustees. Immediately after the Revolution, a variety of academies grew at a great rate. A few admitted girls on an equal basis, whereas others let them use the same facilities at different hours. Timothy Dwight opened a coeducational academy at Greenfield Hill, Connecticut, in 1783. Later, as President of Yale, he wrote that it was "high time that women should be considered less as pretty and more as rational and immortal beings."[3]

Coeducational and single-sex patterns developed in different parts of the country following settlement. A number of schools appeared before 1800, but the largest expansion by far came between 1830 and 1850. At mid-century more than a quarter of a million students were enrolled in over 6,000 academies. However, it was in the separate female academy that, as Benjamin Rush had said they would, the values of women's liberal education prevailed.[4]

Several factors contributed to this advancement in the first sixty years of the republic. Above all, public opinion on female education grew increasingly favorable within the limits of utility to American society. The ideal of republican motherhood had provided the first rationale appropriate to the perceived need of raising virtuous citizens in the new na-

tion. A second impetus arose with the renewed religious fervor of the
Second Great Awakening that gripped much of the country from the
late 1790s to the 1850s. The ideal of the Christian wife, mother, and
teacher gave repeated urgency to women's education. Revivals promoted youthful conversions but also nurtured the individual's right to
choose church membership freely, as a matter of conscience. Thus the
female influence became even more critical than before in families,
communities, and churches. Republican and Christian rationales made a
formidable combination justifying the education of women.[5]

Although Protestant groups respected women's personal independence within certain contexts, for a time the potential connection between a woman's religion and her education on the one hand and female
rights on the other was denied. The simultaneous backlash against Mary
Wollstonecraft, the most conspicuous feminist of the eighteenth century, was no accident. Once it became known that this English radical
had borne a child out of wedlock, she became an easier target for those
who wanted to discredit her thinking. It was Hannah More, the conservative English author of evangelical moral tracts, rather than Wollstonecraft, who offered appropriate guidance for benevolent ends of female education in America and England.[6]

Educating women to be teachers became a respected element in the
good works and goals of all religious groups. The need to Christianize
western frontiers created both the demand for new schools and competition in their establishment. Sponsorship by particular Protestant
denominations—Congregationalists, Presbyterians, Unitarians, Methodists, Quakers, Baptists, and others—soared. Catholics just arriving also
planted a few academies as their stake in the New World. Irrespective of
theological differences, each group stressed activism by which to fulfill
the social missions demanded of women and men within their separate
spheres. Teaching became an important female mission.

Apart from public purposes for educating women, private concerns in
certain families directed females into the sphere of education both as
consumers—that is, students—and as wage-earners, or teachers. Demographic changes in the older sections of the country (except in the
South) created the problem for some parents of what to do with their
unmarried daughters. Where men were marrying later, or where men's
ventures west or to sea put women in the majority, many females had little chance of marrying. Their families understood the utilitarian advantages of educating such daughters, who as schoolteachers could support
themselves and alleviate financial pressures on the family. At the same
time industrialization in the Northeast altered the domestic functions of
young women within the family, by removing some tasks daughters had

performed in households; they thus became less housebound than their mothers.[7]

The changes in the economy affected the various social classes differently. The American girl at the upper levels spent more time socializing, giving the impression of independence and freedom noted by many observers, including Alexis de Tocqueville. Parents readily paid for the education of an indulged daughter in an academy as a way to keep her busy, under control, and, perhaps, make her more marriageable. By contrast, young women in the middling and poorer classes continued what had been domestic functions outside the home, in textile and other manufacturing industries, where they were able to earn their own money. With parental permission such young women could use their savings to start their education in local schools.[8]

Rising attendance of females in district schools also increased demands for elementary school teachers. Significantly, an informal, unplanned process evolved: girls not only attended district schools but taught in them; then some used the money they earned to attend academies, where they studied and taught. In time some opened schools of their own. Economic necessity, religious zeal, and intellectual curiosity drew women into schoolteaching. Extraordinary individuals of talent who combined these motives to a high degree had an unprecedented impact on the education of their sex. Although men like Joseph Emerson in Massachusetts, Noah Webster and Jedidiah Morse in Connecticut, and John Poor and Benjamin Rush in Pennsylvania supported female education, it was women who made the greater contribution in ensuring the permanence of female institutions and in raising their standards.[9]

New England produced the first array of great innovators: Sarah Pierce, Emma Willard, Catharine Beecher, Zilpah Grant, Mary Lyon, and Almira Phelps. In different personal and economic situations, each struggled to acquire an advanced education. Like many ambitious men who went to college and gained professional status, these women were socially mobile, "self-made" achievers within their communities. Each in her own way appeared to accept the social constraints placed on women and yet drew on Enlightenment republican thought and on evangelical sentiment to enlarge the scope of women's higher education. Women, pioneering in new roles, founded schools where the female student became the focus of academic purpose.[10]

Sarah Pierce's "respectable academy" in Litchfield, Connecticut, which started in 1791, only four years after the opening of the Young Ladies Academy in Philadelphia, served as one model. While upholding separate spheres for men and women, Sarah Pierce regarded her students as "rational beings" and stressed that both sexes needed "the discipline of the mind." Miss Pierce, recognizing the need for physical as well as mental development, required evening walks for all students. The school grew in numbers, drawing predominantly from the upper classes nationwide, and acquired its own buildings through the gifts of local supporters. Proximity to the Litchfield Law School, where eligible young men sought the company of Miss Pierce's girls and in many cases married them, also helped. As part of her long-range plan to expand and strengthen the curriculum, she paid for her nephew's tuition at Williams College so that he could teach more advanced subjects on his return. Sarah Pierce used Hannah More's texts to inspire benevolent endeavors in her students; many of these students later carried on Pierce's work as teachers. Moreover, her school became a flourishing business, which others would emulate. Perceptive educators after Sarah Pierce sought public financing such as legislatures and local government gave to academies for young men, believing that full acceptance of female education would not occur without guarantees of permanent institutions.[11]

Emma Hart Willard was the first to claim publicly that advanced education for women should not depend on individuals and chance circumstances. One of seventeen children in an economically hard-pressed family, she was taught first by her father, a bookish Yankee farmer and Revolutionary captain who never completed college. At fifteen she was intermittently a pupil and a teacher in district schools and for a short time attended a local academy. Self-supporting and enjoying the independence that teaching afforded her, she married John Willard, a doctor many years her senior. After his political and financial reverses in 1814, Emma started a family boarding school in their Vermont home. She was twenty-seven when she studied the mathematics and philosophy textbooks of a nephew attending Middlebury College. Admitting to herself the limitations of her academic background, she set out to design an original plan for women's education.[12]

The Willard Plan called for a liberal arts curriculum incorporating some essentials from men's colleges, but classes were to be taught by women exclusively. Willard's request rested on the cogent argument that the well-being of the republic demanded educated mothers. Though she had support from distinguished political leaders, the New York state legislature rejected the plan, whereupon Mrs. Willard published it at her own expense to keep its ideas before the public.[13]

She moved her family to Troy, New York, after merchants in the expanding city offered land for school buildings, and there Troy Seminary, started in 1821 without an endowment, became a flourishing institution owned and run by the Willard family for three generations. A younger sister, Almira Hart, who also studied and taught in a district school, joined Troy Seminary and ran it in 1831 during her sister's absence. Later, as Mrs. Almira Phelps, she became an important educator on her own, heading, among other schools, the Patapsco Institute in Maryland.[14]

Next to press the cause of a permanent female educational institution was Catharine Beecher, eldest daughter of the prominent Congregationalist Reverend Lyman Beecher. Although Catharine had led her class at Miss Pierce's and taught school in New London, she was indecisive about her vocation until the death of her fiancé, Yale professor Alexander Fisher. In reading his papers on mathematics, she discovered a level of intellectual discourse unknown to females and became determined both to pursue advanced study and to establish a women's seminary. In 1832 she rented a room for teaching above a harness shop in Hartford, Connecticut. With the assistance of her sister Mary, she made Hartford Seminary a spectacular success. In the first year nearly a hundred students attended, and a revival starting at the school spread to the town. Beecher proceeded with a plan to gain funding and, through the writer and former teacher Lydia Sigourney, met influential citizens and sought their support to gain substantial funding. When the plan received a limited response from leading men, Catharine Beecher shrewdly appealed to their wives at a prayer meeting in her home. In 1827 she raised almost $5,000 by selling stock subscriptions to the school, and by 1828 Hartford Female Seminary had its own building, eight teachers, and a number of trustees. Beecher had learned what support women could provide and, like Willard, depended on the largesse of the upper classes.[15]

By contrast, in a unique approach, two teachers from the hill country of western Massachusetts, Mary Lyon and Zilpah Grant, turned for support to their own "middling" class. Zilpah Grant, brought up by an impoverished widowed mother, had spent only a few weeks a year at a country school; yet, self-taught, at age fifteen she was teaching others during summer terms. In 1820, though twenty-five years old, she enrolled with permission from her mother and brother in the Reverend Joseph Emerson's school in Byfield, Massachusetts. To save money, she walked three days to reach the school. There, in 1821, she met another young woman of similar determination. Mary Lyon had kept house for her farmer brother and used her earnings of a dollar a week from him and other sums from district schoolteaching to attend Sanderson and Amherst academies and finally Byfield Female Academy.[16]

For both Grant and Lyon, studying with Joseph Emerson became the turning point in their intellectual and social development. This minister addressed women as the equals of men in intellectual capacity, and for students of Grant's and Lyon's caliber, he lectured on the philosophy of Jonathan Edwards and included other collegiate subjects. Emerson

noted in 1822 that the applications to his academy far exceeded his expectations; he gave credit to the many thousands of American mothers,
"impressed with the importance of knowledge, which they do not possess," who were "willing to rise up early, to sit up late, to eat the bread of
the most rigid economy, to exert themselves to the utmost, that their
daughters may be favored with the means of improvement." He predicted that the time was "not remote" when female institutions "very
greatly superior to the present" would be "as important as are now our
colleges for the education of our sons."[17]

Mary Lyon and Zilpah Grant absorbed this view and while teaching at
Adams and Ipswich seminaries sought community backing for an endowed institution. When their plan for a New England Female Seminary
for Teachers received no support, Mary Lyon traveled as far as western
New York and Detroit to talk with educators and women about her
ideas. Surer than ever of the validity of her own conception, she wrote to
her mother that "my heart has so yearned over the adult female youth,
in the common walks of life, that it has sometimes seemed as though a
fire were shut up in my bones." She resigned from Ipswich and in 1834
gathered a committee of male advisors who hired an agent to raise funds
for such a school.[18]

Fund-raising for Mount Holyoke revealed both negative and positive
community attitudes. At first the General Association of Congregational
Ministers of Massachusetts refused to endorse the plan; her minister
friends were willing to see in this refusal "the hand of the Lord." Mary
Lyon would not give up: "I may be fifty years in advance of the age, but
the work is of God and must surely go on." Ignoring opposition, she devised a fund-raising appeal directed to families in modest circumstances.
She won when poorer middle-class parents and women identified with
her goal. Significantly, the first thousand dollars for the seminary came
from women, including $259 from teachers and pupils at the Ipswich
Female Seminary, $475 from women in the town of Ipswich, and a wid-
ow's donation consisting of one-quarter of her means. In two years Mary
Lyon had $15,000 from the "Christian public," a sum almost four times
as great as those with which Willard and Beecher had started in the
1820s. Mount Holyoke's relatively ample endowment made it possible
for Lyon to keep her promise of low tuition for young women "fitting"
to be teachers but with little in the way of resources. In the end, three
towns competed for the seminary, and South Deerfield and Sunderland
lost to South Hadley. Mount Holyoke Seminary was chartered in 1836
and opened in 1837 with three buildings. A year later some of Mary
Lyon's supporters still had misgivings, but the experiment of Mount
Holyoke triumphed.[19]

Outside New England public support for female academies also grew in response to local situations. Formal education in the South (limited of course to whites) advanced more slowly, in part because of the greater devastation the region experienced during the revolutionary war. The absence of a system of public schooling meant that at first only elite southerners had access to education. The interest in schooling for girls in the South gained momentum with the recognition, however limited, of the need for a public school system. Moreover, the Second Great Awakening eventually precipitated an expansion of women's leadership in southern church organizations. The educated evangelical woman was recognized as an asset, whether as wife and mother, deaconness, lay exhorter, or missionary. As in the North, female academies drew on the precarious support of civic and business groups and on interested religious denominations, especially on Methodists and Baptists.[20]

It was assumed in the South, unlike the North in this period, that the well-bred female would not teach school; rather, her education should fit her to be a lady—polished, competent, and subservient. In the early decades southern parents frequently sent daughters north to school, but in the late antebellum period they preferred to educate them in their own region. The cotton boom made education feasible for socially mobile families, but the sectional strife over slavery intensified suspicions of northern institutions. Almira Phelps's Patapsco Institute, in the border state of Maryland, was one exception, remaining popular with southerners. Although southern schools were frequently family-owned, they were more often directed by ministers with the assistance of women teachers from the North. The great women innovators of academy education in New England and New York strengthened an existing pattern by sending their students to the South as teachers. As a result, the educational values of Emma Willard, Catharine Beecher, and Mary Lyon spread throughout the country.[21]

Troy, Hartford, and Mount Holyoke became prototypes for women's institutions in the Midwest and Far West as well as the South. Unexpectedly, a new model, for the joint education of the sexes, appeared in 1833 in a midwestern evangelical community. To its militant Christian founders, Oberlin College in Ohio was "God's College." Here men and women, white and black, were to be educated together to carry out God's cause on earth. Even though coeducation seemed an aberration to those who believed in maintaining the separate male and female spheres of society, Oberlin's academic community operated as a religious family in which both sexes retained their distinctive roles. Not all classes were joint; a less demanding literary course was usually taken by women, but it was still superior to that of most academies. Significantly, Oberlin had a Female Department, whose heads had trained in New England academies under Mary Lyon or Zilpah Grant. At first, Oberlin College stood alone in its limited coeducational form, but by mid-century similar schools had been founded in the Midwest.[22]

Academy expansion paralleled the large growth in men's colleges, many of which started as academies. Wherever some form of collegiate education was established for men, academy instruction for women was likely to appear. For different reasons, educators of women and men had special challenges in sustaining their institutions. This was a chaotic period of competition among men's colleges, for although increasing numbers of students attended, enrollments fluctuated frequently. In these decades liberal colleges for men were under attack either for retaining the traditional four-year curriculum or for introducing new subjects. Collegiate study included not only Latin, Greek, mathematics, physical sciences, and natural philosophy, but also rhetoric and sometimes modern languages. The requirement of the classical languages had long caused contention, with Benjamin Franklin and Benjamin Rush among the early opponents. The Yale Report of 1828 represented an effort to preserve the curricular tradition with some modifications. Brown, on the other hand, under Francis Wayland, offered in 1842 a more scientific education. Whatever the curriculum, the students often left without completing the degree. Riots, unrest, frequent faculty turnover, and constant shifts in direction were indicative of the instability of colleges in the first half of the nineteenth century.[23]

Although female seminary educators wanted to prove that their students were capable of mastering any course of study offered to young men, they were not overly impressed with the nonacademic aspects of life in the men's colleges, for many a young man left college "demoralized." Indeed, the women saw themselves as the more creative pedagogues and became convinced that men's colleges could learn much from female seminaries. Moreover, in 1832, Emma Willard confided to her brother that the troubled University of Vermont would do well to turn its buildings over to those who would make it a "Female University."[24]

Yet planning and implementing a more advanced curriculum at women's schools involved some similar kinds of trials, and some different ones, from those plaguing men's colleges. The three-year course at academies limited what could be accomplished. In addition, as at the men's institutions, many academy students left without completing the whole course. Keeping classrooms full made it difficult to maintain minimum age requirements for entrance, and these varied at different institutions: Troy, for example, established twelve, Hartford fourteen, and Mount Holyoke sixteen as the lowest age for attending. Above all, parental, communal, and even faculty views on appropriate subjects had to be considered. Educators had to move within the parameters of what could be accomplished without antagonizing their supporters.[25]

The study of ancient languages provoked strong opposition. Evangelical schools everywhere from Mount Holyoke in western Massachusetts to the Female Collegiate Institute in Georgetown, Kentucky, had difficulty introducing Greek and Latin; some schools could not countenance modern languages either. At the outset Oberlin College did not intend to instruct women in the dead languages, no doubt agreeing with the southern educator who warned against having students exposed to the "squabblings of heathen gods and goddesses" while they remained "ignorant of the character and attributes of the true God." Nonetheless, in time, the most advanced schools everywhere incorporated both Latin and French, and some offered Greek as an option. By the 1850s more schools took the highly progressive view of the Richmond Female Institute in Virginia, that "the fairer sex ought to enjoy advantages for liberal culture equal in grade to that afforded the other, assuming a position analogous to that which our noble state university does with regard to young men."[26]

Outstanding women's academies have not received enough credit for their innovative pedagogy in enlarging the range of subjects, especially in the sciences. In addition to offering chemistry and physics, many, like Patapsco, excelled in botany and geology. Relatively few provided courses in citizenship, but one instructor at the Elizabeth Academy in Mississippi, in 1825, used *The Federalist Papers* for her text. Mathematics, American history, and geography became part of the female academy curriculum. Hartford initiated calisthenics; its popularity fit with courses in physiology and hygiene at many schools. Troy's strengths also included fine arts, dancing, and music. Although ornamental studies in drawing, singing, and piano playing became conventional offerings, most academies, contrary to public opinion, did not give courses in housewifery or domestic science. Rhetoric, too, had great importance, for women learned to keep journals and write compositions and also studied the art of declamation before being allowed to use it in public.[27]

The best institutions offered, over decades, an increasingly substantial portion of the liberal studies provided at men's colleges. According to Thomas Woody's reliable study of catalogues, 107 women's schools operating between 1830 and 1870 covered most of the subjects taught in the junior and senior years at men's colleges. "Three out of five listed logic, nine out of ten offered chemistry and physics, and four out of five listed mental philosophy (psychology) and moral philosophy (mainly ethical)."[28]

The growth of academies reached a climax in the 1850s, when other relatively new institutions, such as the normal (teacher-training) schools and the public high schools, were emerging as educational alternatives in the North. Some of the most rigorous academies, especially in the Northeast, avoided the use of the term college and called themselves seminaries. Other institutions that combined secondary and collegiate types of programs freely adopted the name *college*; as a result, several claimed to be the first women's college. Georgia Female College, later renamed Wesleyan, was chartered by the state legislature in 1836 and opened in 1838. Despite its name, this pioneer institution resembled a superior academy more than a male college, regularly admitting twelve-year-olds. By contrast, Mary Sharp College in Winchester, Tennessee, founded in 1853, was a four-year, real college, whose curriculum stressed Latin, Greek, and higher mathematics.[29]

All schools depended primarily on the consumers who could afford to attend them. But some institutions served the needs of a more economically mixed student body. To cut costs, Oberlin experimented with manual labor, assigning field work to men and household tasks to women—although some men were allowed to bake bread, all women had to darn their male classmates' socks. Mount Holyoke provided a reduced tuition (two-thirds the cost of either Troy or Ipswich) by assigning domestic chores to everyone, faculty as well as students. Educators made concerted efforts to include ambitious young women who needed to be self-supporting. Mount Holyoke succeeded more than the others in giving opportunities to poorer Yankee girls in their twenties and thirties, more than one-third of whom came, as David Allmendinger shows, from families whose real estate in 1850 was valued at $2,000 or less.[30]

At the other end of the scale, Patapsco, which still attracted southern students in the 1840s, charged $170 a term and advertised single rooms. Catharine Beecher at the Hartford Seminary also catered to the daughters of the affluent, yet rationalized that she was preparing them for benevolent activities. At Troy, Emma Willard maintained a balance between the well-to-do and the less prosperous. Her revolving scholarship fund helped serious applicants who depended on their own savings from district schoolteaching and could not pay their way entirely. Willard, Grant, and Beecher all lent money for tuition to students who became teaching assistants. Other schools adopted similar patterns. Emily Chubbuck (later the popular writer Fanny Forrester), from a struggling family, pushed ahead through district schoolteaching with intermittent study; thereafter she taught composition at Utica Female Seminary in New York State, in return for the scholarship she received. The more prestigious the school, the more likely that some students earned their way.[31]

Wide variations among the academies reflected the attitudes of the teachers as well as their clienteles. Not all female educators had the hidden motive of adapting and improving on the curriculum of men's colleges. Those who did, however, followed in the tradition created by Willard, Beecher, Grant, Lyon, Phelps, and their disciples. More forward-looking educators were trying to create something new for American women: to instill aspirations for learning and to enlarge women's sphere of usefulness—to educate in the deepest sense. Because of their immediate influence on some students and indirect influence on others, the innovators of the first generation became representatives of a new professional, the female educator.

The thought, even more than the curriculum and the techniques of the first great female educators, shaped the spirit of women's education. These pioneering instructors attempted to balance their aspirations for students with society's claim of the traditional female sphere. None questioned the accepted Christian ideal of True Womanhood, summed up in the precepts of piety, purity, obedience, and domesticity. Knowng well that men feared that a woman of learning would get out of hand, they promised that students would not be spoiled for family duties. Among the values of these educators, piety came first, but learning was also essential.

Yet they entered fields previously closed to women and, by their own examples, contributed to the redefining of women's roles. They showed students that they were not stopped by lack of resources. They wrote textbooks when needed, kept studying themselves to become better teachers, and made teacher training one of their goals. It was evident that students had mixed motives for acquiring a liberal education. Learning, teacher training, religious vocation, and social status: each of these goals had appeal for some more than others. Fully aware of this diversity, educators deftly urged students to think about their futures consciously. Seeming contradictions thus appear in their advice. Beecher remarked that "a lady should study, not to *shine*, but to *act*," and Phelps urged: "Think what you would wish to be, and strive to render yourself such." Discreetly, educators instructed pupils to achieve as much as possible. Without repudiating women's place, they tested the limits to the acceptance of greater public responsibilities. As Willard explained, "I do not wish women to act out of their sphere; but it is time that modern improvement should reach their case and enlarge their sphere from the walls of their own houses to the limits of the school district."[32]

Even while urging caution to women with aspirations, they opened the way for them to take unconventional routes. Almira Phelps thus observed that "if genius, circumstance of fortune or the providence of God assigns" one "a more public and conspicuous station," a woman "ought cheerfully do all that her own powers, aided by the blessings of God, can achieve." As many students remembered, Mary Lyon directed them to "be willing to do anything and go anywhere for the good of others."[33]

Such wise teachers understood that women's decisions had consequences. They advised students who expected to marry differently from
those who would remain single. Marriage, they made clear, changed
women's options. Mary Lyon emphasized that, once married, "males
should go forward in all public duties, the female should go forward in
private duties with courage, patience, and submission. Men are to earn a
support, and the women to save." Zilpah Grant insisted that a woman
"yield cheerfully more than half to one who has an equal claim to herself," for, she explained, "where there are only two there can be no majority, and the supremacy must rest on one." But, as Grant herself observed, finding a man worthy of the deference of an educated woman
might be difficult, for, she warned, a woman "must see that she do[es]
not marry a man whom she cannot reverence."[34]

These educators would not have declared themselves feminists, although they defended women's rights to education, even as they
avoided the thorny political issue of slavery, and often opposed women's
suffrage. Nonetheless, they showed women students that they had both
a right and an obligation to take themselves seriously. Emma Willlard
had declared that in educating the female sex, the first object should not
be "to prepare to please the other" (shades of Mary Wollstonecraft
earlier and Simone de Beauvoir later). Moreover, she invoked Enlightenment principles to show that "reason and religion teach that we too
are primary existencies." Students who listened learned that education
was a life-long process that would not end when they left school. The
great female educators of the first generation were optimistic. They saw
themselves and their students as at the beginning of a long struggle and
counted on committed graduates to carry on the work of leading women
out of their inherited backwardness.[35]

T·H·R·E·E

The Utility of Their
Educations, 1800–1860

He [Horace Mann] will not help the cause of woman greatly, but his
efforts to educate her will do a greater work than he anticipates.
Prepare woman for duty and usefulness, and she will laugh at
any boundaries man may set for her.
Sarah Grimké, 1853
Quoted in Catherine H. Birney,
The Grimké Sisters (1885), 275

Between the 1790s and the 1850s the minority of females who acquired
a portion of the liberal education at academies, seminaries, and "colleges" became the vanguard of a new American type: the educated
woman. In this chapter we consider briefly the views of academy students and the impact of education on their lives. Available evidence
shows that these precollegiate groups dealt essentially with the problem
that later confronted college women: how to relate the purposes of liberal academic study to their duties as women.

These pathbreakers, set apart from the mass of their sex who were in
no position to acquire an education, shared the beliefs of other women
in their communities. They accepted the code of true womanhood, the
popular term invoking the ideal of the republican and Christian wife
and mother. Indeed, they intended to be the truest. But how students
utilized their education was determined by both this tradition and an
amalgam of personal needs, quests, and obligations discovered either at
school or afterward. In maturity their responses to the social and economic conditions modernizing America greatly broadened the defini-
tion of female usefulness. Despite their ambiguous social status in an increasingly democratic (male) society, the expectations of these women
rose. As a result of working in a range of activities, women began to trust
their own judgment. More and more they found themselves involved in

public controversy over the boundaries of woman's sphere.[1]

Academy students encountered the woman question in different forms throughout their schooling. From the outset their instruction depended on decisions about what women should study. Another central issue was the extent to which women should adopt the social traditions of male liberal education. The study of rhetoric, for example, had become part of the training of young men in colleges and academies. The introduction of this course in women's schools, however, produced an educational dilemma not easily resolved. While men were expected to declaim as preparation for public life, religious precepts held that women should remain silent in church and in mixed company. For most women in this period, the restriction was so ingrained that they were uncomfortable speaking in the presence of their male classmates. Thus, at Oberlin an experiment with a coeducational course in rhetoric ended when the women requested a return to separate classes.

The basic contradiction between women's education and their probable futures became obvious at their school commencements. Borrowing from college ceremonies for young men, women's academies held appropriate exercises. If ever a girl forgot her place, at graduation she was reminded, for usually young women were not allowed to read their parts at this public event; rather, their speeches were read by adult substitutes or were delivered personally at a private session.

Sometimes student speeches referred to the conflicts they felt in being female and students. A few expressed their resentment plainly, but most gave praise to woman's separate sphere. One speaker in 1793 mirrored the open mood of the early republic. Priscilla Mason, in her salutatorian oration at the Philadelphia Academy's commencement, declared bluntly: "They have denied women a liberal education and now if we should prove capable of speaking, where could we speak? The Church, the Bar, the Senate are closed against us. Who shut them? Man, Despotic Man." Miss Mason, in the vein of Mary Wollstonecraft, proposed that there be a place for women in the American Senate. Yet such tantalizing hints of rebellion were usually followed, as in this case, by the graduate's retreat to approval of the separate duties of men and women. In the 1800s, in keeping with the evangelical spirit, a graduate of Susanna Rowson's Academy upheld the moral suasion of women in the private sphere: "We are called upon to use our influence to the honour of God and the well-being of society, we are responsible for the use we make of our acknowledged power, wide is its extent, indefinite its effects, inestimable its importance. It involves not only the happiness of the present but the principles of a future generation." The obligations of educated, evangelical motherhood received awesome acceptance in this speech.[2]

Few women protested their exclusion from public speaking, for being an orator was an important expression of masculinity, associated with ministers, lawyers, and statesmen. The image of a female lecturer recalled the specters of Mary Wollstonecraft, Frances Wright, or Ernestine Rose—all foreigners, religious radicals, and champions of women's rights. The first American-born female to make public speeches was Maria Stewart, a free black woman who, in the early 1830s, advocated abolition and called on black people to educate themselves. Her speaking brought some disapproval, but she too could be dismissed as an outsider.

It was not until 1837 that two cultivated white women from a leading southern family, Sarah and Angelina Grimké, forced the issue of whether an intelligent, educated woman could address controversial social and political issues publicly. The sisters, who earlier had taught slave children and befriended black Quakers, now asserted that God had shown them that it was their duty to speak out against slavery. These evangelical rebels brought down the wrath of the Massachusetts Congregationalist clergy, whose Pastoral Letter reminded all females that "the power of woman is in her dependence." The Grimkés disagreed with prevailing scriptural interpretations and emphasized in their feminist tracts the evangelical belief of the equality of men and women in God's eyes. Sarah's *Letters on the Equality of the Sexes and the Condition of Woman* (1838) presented to thinking women in the northern and western states an extended, passionate discourse on the woman question.[3]

After the Grimkés' challenges the association of a "female public lecturer" with both abolition and woman's rights made most educators all the more adamant in opposing female public speaking in their schools. It was a rare school like Oread Institute in Worcester, Massachusetts, where students became abolitionists after the examples of their teachers. Yet at coeducational Oberlin, which admitted black students from the beginning and identified publicly with abolition, the faculty remained divided on whether to permit women to speak in public. Some women tried to persuade professors to let female students make speeches at commencement. Elizabeth Prall in 1841 pointed out that Queen Elizabeth could address audiences at Oxford, "while in liberty-loving America [woman] is not allowed to speak in her own tongue, among the populace, to defend her own rights." Afterward the ridicule of other students reduced Miss Prall to tears. Six years later Lucy Stone, an activist both for women's rights and abolition, took a more radical stand. Determined to be a public lecturer, she refused to write a commencement speech or to participate in the public exercises since she would not be allowed to read it. Not until 1857 would an Oberlin woman be permitted to read her part at the public commencement.[4]

Serious students were for the most part concerned with benefiting personally from the experiment of advanced female education.

Euphorsine Schmidt from New Orleans, while at Nazareth Academy in Kentucky, wrote home in 1850 about a classmate's attention to "painting and polish" but added: "As for myself, I do not learn polish, and am not much advanced in painting, as this year I apply myself a great deal to my studies, in order to graduate soon." Anna Gale, studying at the Greene Street School in Providence, Rhode Island, wrote in her journal in 1838 that teacher Margaret Fuller had assigned Dr. Wayland's text in moral philosophy in the hope that his thoughts would "take root sufficiently deep to produce one little thought of our own, something entirely original." The student then added: "We shall derive an advantage from this study." At Oberlin, student Mary Ann Adams extolled the opportunity for intellectual inquiry: "We are taught not only to fully appreciate the worth of an author but to think for ourselves upon the various subjects brought before us, and we do feel that this knowledge after which we are searching is of more value than the diamond which sparkles in the sands of India and the pearl in its ocean bed." She concluded that "the works we investigate are such as are calculated to furnish discipline of mind and a supply of rich thought."[5]

The thirst for learning among young female scholars was promoted in many cultural forums. Religious academies fostered academic excellence in addition to conversion and piety. Outside of these, students also heard and might absorb the more radical ideas aired by liberal ministers and lyceum speakers. The preaching of Unitarian William Ellery Channing, as well as of Congregationalist Lyman Beecher, emphasized personal will and human capacity to grow. Further, Ralph Waldo Emerson's lectures precipitated a new consciousness of human possibilities for young women as well as young men. In one talk on heroism (addressed mainly to young men), he observed incidentally the problem of young women's aspirations: "[Let] the maiden, with erect soul, walk serenely on her way, accept the hint of each new experience . . . the fair girl who repels interference by a decided and proud choice of influences, so careless of pleasing, so wilful and lofty, inspires every beholder with somewhat of her own nobleness." More than he intended, Emerson stimulated not only Harvard students but women still outside the college gates, with his disturbing message to trust thyself, "go alone."[6]

Individualism in old and new forms pressed the educated woman to be independent in seeking her own moral course. Independence was a double-edged ideal: while a young man was applauded, a young woman at best received ambivalent approval from family and society in her struggles to strike out on her own. How could she do this as a female and meet the requirements of the True Woman? To some extent answers lay in finding appropriate duties at different stages of her life cycle.

The introduction of education into a woman's life, combined with the needs of the changing society, altered her life pattern in a fundamental way] The period between girlhood and marriage began to represent a time in which female youth could pursue a variety of interests and employments. During this interval the academy-educated woman tested ideas first encountered in the course of her schooling. Some less-educated women also found a new period of semiautonomy: for the Yankee mill girl, a stint of factory work provided a time of economic and personal experimentation before marriage. Indeed, some mill workers saved money to attend Oberlin or Mount Holyoke. Thus a new period entered young women's lives, its form depending on social class. Regardless, being a student or working at some paid employment away from the parental home and familiar community enabled a woman to be on her own within recognized limits.[7]

Although marriage remained the ultimate goal for most women, these varied courses of action prolonged the period of youth. The heroine of a popular novel expressed an attitude of young women common to the time: "Let me follow my own volitions, for at least three or four years to come. . . . Let my mind soar unfettered to the heights where I wish to stand" before being "tempted to wear those bonds which, though covered with roses and seemingly light as air, must be stronger than steel, and heavier than iron." Female students, enamored of their new independence and influenced by their educators, deliberated more carefully before marrying. Their education and the opportunities it offered reinforced their sense of the seriousness of the marriage commitment.[8]

The effects of academy education that have been measured statistically do point to significant shifts in marriage patterns among the educated. Academy women of Mount Holyoke (1837–50) married later than others, and some not at all; the average age of marriage for graduates was twenty-seven, and the median age twenty-six, as compared to the median age of twenty-one for women in the general population. The education and employment intervals interrupted a woman's life cycle and delayed marriage (see table 4).[9]

Another striking difference emerged in the number of single educated women. Again during the first period at Mount Holyoke, 19 percent of the graduates never married; at Troy 16 percent of those graduating between 1821 and 1842 never married. Corresponding figures for the general population range from 6 to 13 percent, well below any of the above figures. The case of the female alumnae of coeducational Oberlin, however, provides a contrast. A small sample of forty Oberlin women showed that, of those attending in 1840, all but one were married by 1860. Yet, after 1860, marriage patterns at Oberlin slowly began to resemble those at other colleges in the latter part of the century.[10]

For those who deferred marriage, or indeed never married, education did make it possible to be self-supporting, to have, in Catharine Beecher's phrase, an "honorable independence," however meager. In encouraging all students to use wisely the time before marriage, educators knew that their counsel had special meaning for women who preferred not to marry.

Social class influenced the employment of educated young single women. In opposition to Catharine Beecher's advice that the daughters of the well-to-do should express their benevolence by "taking a school," affluent families often believed that a lady should not take a paid job. We do not know how many daughters followed the path of the heroine in Ida Norman who determined to teach even while she thought her family had "unbounded wealth." The author of this novel, educator Almira Phelps, conveyed the same sense of mission to her own students, much like the fictional Ida's teacher. In real life the wealthy girl might spend the time between school and marriage in benevolent activities. Elizabeth Cady Stanton, for one, relished the "first taste of liberty" after graduating from Troy. She used this time to visit and learn about the social reforms that would occupy her adult years. Angelina Grimké, however, in rebellion against her southern plantation family and culture, considered training to be a teacher under Catharine Beecher at Hartford Seminary, and her sister Sarah sought to train for the Quaker ministry.[11]

The many academy students who could not afford to be "ladies" usually embarked on schoolteaching. Both novices and those with some training gained advantages from the increasing demand for teachers and the lack of set structures in a field regarded as a vocation and not yet developed as a profession. Schoolteaching had little status at the time women began to enter it: men who lacked alternatives taught school, and some college youth might teach intermittently before turning to business or a profession. Yet only slowly were women accepted as teachers. Although they were seen as suitable instructors of small children, public prejudice kept them out of more advanced teaching in many places. In the early nineteenth century people doubted both women's ability to teach and the desirability of their leaving home to work. Families and school boards resisted boarding females out in the community, fearful that they required greater supervision than male teachers. Moreover, it was claimed that young women would not be able to control older boys in the classroom. But by the 1830s, a significant shift in rhetoric accompanied approval of female schoolteaching. Horace Mann cited woman's tenderness, gentility, and patience as qualities contributing to her success as a teacher—qualities usually associated with a good mother.[12]

Young women in the Northeast started making teaching a women's field. They were available to take the jobs that men increasingly left for better-paying jobs. Women then had the opportunity to meet both communal and personal needs. The numbers of female teachers at the elementary school level grew substantially until, by the late nineteenth century, they predominated. Only rarely did females receive even half of what their male counterparts earned: usually women's salaries approximated one-third of men's. Educators, school boards, and teachers alike discovered that the schoolmarm was, in Beecher's words, "the cheapest guardian and teacher of childhood."[13]

Under the influence of revivals at academies, many students made teaching their mission. Although there was often evangelical incentive, however, more fundamental was the financial return. Though the wages were low, they made a difference, whether used to supplement family income, for personal expenses, or saved for future education. For some, the thought of improving matrimonial chances by living in a new community was undoubtedly attractive, as many employers complained.

Yet teaching as a vocation proved more demanding and discouraging than many anticipated. Romantic notions of adventure and service evaporated in the face of reality. Young Almira Hart recorded in her journal in 1816: "But where is my fortitude? My removal to this place is the result of my own choice." Nonetheless, she stuck by her decision to teach, and in mid-life was a respected educator. One young Vermont woman, Arozina Perkins, trained at Johnson Academy, wrote in her diary in 1850 of the trials of teaching in a girls' academy in Iowa: "Many long, dreary weeks have passed, which I would forever forget. . . . Now I feel that I can go on calmly and hopefully again, yet with deep humility." Another pious young woman, Antoinette Brown, concluded: "God never made me for a schoolteacher." She sometimes wished her students were "mesmerized." Recalcitrant pupils, uncooperative parents, indifferent school boards, inhospitable communities, and general isolation made the job seem hopeless. In the face of such difficulties, it is not surprising that many left after a short tenure. Whereas only a small percentage of white women aged fifteen to sixty taught at any one time (2 percent in the 1840s), the turnover was so swift that, as Richard M. Bernard and Maris Vinovskis have noted insightfully: "For every woman standing at a chalkboard at a given time, there were a number of women who . . . had left the profession."[14]

Those who taught, including those who lasted only one or two years, found that achieving control over a classroom matured them. While away from home and family, the schoolteacher had to rely on her own judgment. As she became more independent, she gained self-respect.

The second generation of female educators included some who had impressive careers. Betsey Mix Cowles, for example, became superintendent in several schools in Ohio and administered the entire school system in one town. Anna Peck Sill, who founded Rockford Female

Seminary in Illinois on the Mount Holyoke model, expanded it to a four-year institution. A number of married women continued the pattern of operating schools with their husbands: an excellent seminary, Barhamville in Columbia, South Carolina, was directed by Troy graduate Julia Pierpont Marks and her husband Elias Marks.[15]

An ordinary teaching post did not always satisfy the consuming missionary purpose, and some sought alternative ways. These were women who went to teach Indians on the frontier or wanted to participate in a foreign mission.[16]

The single woman had special problems that restricted her choice of missionary activities. In spite of her desire for independence, the woman with religious zeal was usually enjoined to marry a minister. At first it was unacceptable for an unmarried woman to serve in dangerous places like Africa, India, or the Far East. Anne Hasseltine Judson, a recently married schoolteacher, had to get special permission from the American Board of Commissioners for Foreign Missions to allow her to accompany her husband Adoniram Judson to India. She was the first woman to leave America for duty in a foreign mission. Customarily the overburdened minister's wife did the teaching. Not until 1827, when Cynthia Farrar, already a mature educator, left to start schools in India, did the American Board grant a single woman permission to serve. It was still an exception when Mount Holyoke's Fidelia Fiske (with a strong recommendation from Mary Lyon) became a missionary overseas in 1844.[17]

The importance of schoolteaching as a base from which to move on to other employment or activity is well demonstrated by the figures in *Notable American Women*. Of these highest achievers, nearly half (46 percent) of those born between 1790 and 1830 taught school for some duration. Some left schoolteaching for radical endeavors at home. Susan B. Anthony and Abby Kelley (Foster), after the example of the Grimké sisters, became lecturers for abolition and temperance. Some women at Oberlin imitated Lucy Stone. Ironically, lecturing would become a viable means of support for educated women by the end of the nineteenth century. Antoinette Brown used schoolteaching to pay for her education at Oberlin and, despite the disapproval of the Oberlin faculty, was ordained as a Congregationalist minister in 1853.[18]

While teaching opened up to women before it became a profession, the field of medicine, in a new phase of its professionalism, continued to resist their overtures. A few hardy females nonetheless recognized the need for women physicians to concentrate on the health of women and children. Medical research in Europe in the early nineteenth century, notably the discovery of anesthesia, overturned traditional therapeutics and made medicine a more appealing occupation for women. But, even at a time when both medical study and licensing lacked uniform standards, no medical school was willing to admit women. It therefore became the moral mission of a few individuals to break this barrier. Two former schoolteachers, Harriot Hunt and Elizabeth Blackwell, managed, with difficulty, to acquire their first training through apprenticeships with sympathetic doctors. Despite a successful practice in Boston, Harriot Hunt's attempts to enter Harvard Medical School were repeatedly rejected. It is well known that Elizabeth Blackwell, after many refusals, was finally admitted to Geneva College Medical School. Later, she instituted separate medical training for women at her New York Infirmary for Women and Children. This school became the model for several similar institutions later in the century.[19]

Still, at mid-century, the medical profession remained a male preserve where few women ventured. Similarly, scholarly and literary work belonged in the male domain. At a time when men of letters could not count on public support, the idea of a woman of letters was a contradiction in terms. Nevertheless, several New England women aspired to think and write like the college-educated men they knew. Among those who shared the ideal of the "woman of genius," Margaret Fuller and Elizabeth Palmer Peabody edged into high literary company. What these academy- and family-educated women achieved while carrying heavy economic and domestic responsibilities was impressive. They developed their talents amid great insecurities but did not reach the level of creativity they aimed for. Neither received the constructive criticism that she needed for professional development, because male mentors and colleagues tended to regard them as assistants, translators, and conversationalists to great thinkers like Channing and Emerson. At the same time Fuller and Peabody were undoubtedly sustained by other women who looked to them for inspiration and gave them steadfast support. Educator Peabody, an early abolitionist, was the first woman publisher in America, and eventually the founder of the kindergarten movement in the United States. Literary and social critic Fuller was first an innovative teacher of girls and adult women and later a journalist for the *New York Herald Tribune* and its first foreign correspondent. Fuller's feminist essay "Woman in the Nineteenth Century" (1845) called for full choices in occupations for women: even let them "be sea captains if they will."[20]

Outside the rarefied sphere of high culture, the field of popular writing opened unexpectedly to women. Several economic and social factors produced a "damn mob of scribbling women," in Hawthorne's unpleasant phrase. Technological improvements in printing made books less expensive to produce; developments in transportation improved circulation and distribution; above all, the growth of literacy among women created both female authors and a readership for their works. By the 1850s, as academies increasingly emphasized composition writing, many a female student could imagine herself as an author. Soon popular writing followed teaching as woman's second "profession."[21]

Women gained paid and unpaid employment as essayists, editors, journalists, and fiction writers. But there was criticism of women writers. One who should have known better, Sarah J. Hale, editor of *The Ladies Magazine*, declared in 1828 that for a woman "to make a happy home for her husband and children" was "far more praiseworthy than to make a book." Individuals in fact wrote for a number of reasons: some desired to fill leisure time, while others hoped to earn some money to support failing parents or husbands and children. Some who left schoolteaching made writing a didactic mission[22]

As writers, women entered the business world by negotiating contracts, and the male-dominated publishing sphere by editing magazines. Evangelical publications had "editresses," and the Transcendentalists employed Margaret Fuller as editor of *The Dial*. Women's magazines multiplied, and in the 1840s and 1850s women worked on numerous publications like *Godey's*, *Graham's*, *Peterson's*, and *The Moral Advocate*. Remarkably, with some rapidity, women established themselves as participants in the writing profession.

Women writers of domestic fiction created an American version of the British didactic novel. Their stress on lofty moral purpose made the novels palatable to evangelical publics, and the role of author partially acceptable for women. Educator Susanna Rowson's best-seller *Charlotte Temple* (1794) foreshadowed the voluminous outpouring of domestic literature from the 1820s to the 1850s. These novels had tremendous appeal for middle-class women and for authors and readers trying to live up to the demands of True Womanhood while exploring new options. This body of work provides documentation of a spectrum of viewpoints about female roles and the limits of separate spheres.

Novels written by educators often dealt with the advances in and anxieties about female education. The woman teacher had "the power of awakening the ambition of her pupils" through "heroic and striking examples"; however, she also had the obligation to affirm the value of domesticity. Significantly, the outstanding teacher in Maria Cummins's *Mabel Vaughan* had not only "sound judgment and a highly cultivated intellect" but was accomplished "in every branch of housekeeping" as well. The authors gave qualified support to increasing opportunities for women. Mary Virginia Hawes Terhune, an opponent of women's rights, justified female education and training only in relation to domesticity, as preparation for homemaking or in case of family need for professional paid work.[23]

These authors, like their characters, had to reconcile their belief in domestic values with decisions to step beyond the conventional bound-

aries and become professionals. Grace Greenwood (a pseudonym for
Sarah Jane Clark Lippincott) admired the woman who risked the "vul-
gar cry of unfemininity" and "dares to live up to her own capacity—to be
an *individual,* and not a *thing,*" but advised an aspiring poet: "Never un-
sex yourself for greatness." Historian Mary Kelley has perceived correctly that these writers never came to terms with their new professional
status. Although they often suggested that single life could be "fulfilling," like other women, they still regarded marriage as woman's real
profession. Yet ambiguity about the rewards of marriage filtered into
their writing.[24]

In real life educated women were redefining the marital relationship.
Graduates of early nineteenth-century academies lived in a dynamic,
changing world. As professional white men competed for material gains
in the expanding but unstable economy, women accepted as their female
duty the obligation of providing husbands with a needed refuge from
the wider world. A wife at home was one measure of success and social
status. But since she was also the keeper of spiritual values in the family,
she was expected to temper her husband's drive for moneymaking. Indeed, an educated wife, it was presumed, would be able to manage these
sometimes contradictory roles. Increasingly, the professionally educated
man insisted that a bright, educated female would make the best of
wives, for she could use her learning and intelligence as a partner and
homemaker.

Nonetheless, although patriarchal assumptions predominated, a new
ideal of choice coexisted with the deeply ingrained traditional view of
marriage. Love and affection were not new expectations in marriage,
but a few bold voices now promoted the principle of equality within marriage. Margaret Fuller criticized "the present relation between the sexes"
in which "the woman does belong to the man, instead of forming a
whole with him." And Oberlin alumna Lucy Stone wrote to her friend
Antoinette Brown, still at Oberlin in 1850, deploring the "mere *thing* the
law makes of a married woman." Stone's later marriage to Henry Blackwell was a union that upheld in practice the ideal of equality: together,
from 1870 to 1893, they edited the *Woman's Journal* in Boston. Brown's
marriage to Blackwell also achieved an impressive degree of mutuality.
The Reverend Antoinette Brown Blackwell, as wife and mother, continued studying and writing and preached part-time.[25]

Both Stone and Blackwell found inspiration in the marriage of James
and Lucretia Mott. They were particularly impressed that Lucretia Mott
"preached while bringing up the family, being in perfect amity with her
husband who aided her in the care of the children." The Motts were also
a model for Mary Frame Myers and Owen Thomas, who embarked on
medical study together after the birth of their third child. Mary Thomas,

who intended that her husband and children should not "suffer for any comforts a wife and mother owed them," sewed clothes enough for eight or nine months before going alone to Western Reserve College in Ohio and then to the Pennsylvania Medical University in Philadelphia. During the Civil War both Mary and Owen Thomas served as doctors. Hannah E. Myers Longshore, Mary Thomas's half sister, repeated this pattern; at thirty-one this mother of two children enrolled in the Female Medical College of Pennsylvania and received her M.D. in 1851. She had a successful career as a private practitioner in Philadelphia and a congenial marriage with her teacher-husband Thomas Longshore.[26]

The role of minister's wife had traditionally been that of his helpmeet: entertaining visitors, keeping the household accounts, copying sermons, and serving the needs of the congregation when the minister was away. This role could extend even further in some evangelical partnerships. Under the influence of the Reverend Charles Finney, many wives of ministers conducted prayer meetings for women. Finney's first wife, Lydia Andrews, the first "editress" of *The Moral Advocate*, assumed the role of moral educator to the young and advisor to adult women quite separately from her husband. Moreover, the second Mrs. Finney, Elizabeth Atkinson, led prayer meetings in England jointly with her husband, and it was hard, some said, to distinguish who was the minister.[27]

Alumnae reports from Troy, Oberlin, and Mount Holyoke suggest the large extent to which wives of other professionals participated in their husbands' activities. In some cases women helped prepare briefs for lawyer-husbands or prepared translations of foreign literature. Clearly, some women enjoyed these cooperative ventures.[28]

In certain marriages, however, tensions increased as a result of the higher expectations women had for self, husband, and children. Personal relations could be hurt in marriages in which women as well as men earned money. More and more, women contributed to the economic support of their families when husbands failed in business or simply never could earn enough as ministers or farmers. Usually, however, the fact that the wife showed her competence by earning money did not in itself make for conflict; it was not the breadwinning, but the demands and expectations of the two individuals in the marriage that created the strains. If, as Jane Gray Swisshelm related, a wife had more education than her husband, conflicts emerged; she in fact gave up reading in order to lessen the contrast between herself and her "uncultivated husband."[29]

Many marriages failed to live up to either the new ideal of mutuality or the traditional form. Even in partnerships based on common interests, such as those between pairs of reformers, there was no guarantee of a happy marriage. As Julia Ward Howe and Elizabeth Cady Stanton discovered, after marriage their reform-minded husbands preferred old-fashioned, submissive wives. Harriet Beecher Stowe observed that "a large proportion of marriages have been contracted without any advised or rational effort."[30]

An advocate of liberal divorce, Elizabeth Cady Stanton went further in arguing before the 1861 New York state legislature that when marriage becomes "a mere outward tie . . . with every possible inequality of condition," it should be dissolved. But many women put up with unhappy marriages not only to avoid a public spectacle, but because they believed that they derived their primary identity and self-worth as wives and mothers. Few, even among women's rights advocates, favored as much liberalization of the divorce laws as Stanton proposed.[31]

Whatever their concepts of marriage or self, all women experienced the threat of frequent pregnancy resulting from the religious decree that a wife must always submit to her husband's will. Nonetheless, educated women tended to challenge this edict, and, although some husbands cooperated with their wives, this situation presented a major area of marital conflict. As always women dealt with the problem in a variety of ways, but denial of the "marital right" became one of the more common ways for women to assert some autonomy. Lucy Stone asked her three brothers bluntly whether one should have sexual relations unless one intended to have a baby. Angelina Grimké thought that one should have babies only once every three years. Harriet Beecher Stowe, after seven children, arranged frequent separations, under one pretext or another, from her husband Calvin. The national birthrate declined in these decades, as women and men either denied themselves regular sexual intercourse, or men practiced coitus interruptus. The problems caused by lack of access to birth control were universal.[32]

It was not that such women did not want children; in fact, as tensions increased over how to achieve mutuality in marriage, educated women, like their uneducated sisters, still found fulfillment in motherhood. The raising of children became the critical focus of family life, thereby escalating the importance of motherhood. The religious shift away from belief in original sin precipitated particular interest in the mother's part in shaping the character of the innocent young. Preparing children for conversion became a prominent activity of maternal associations in the 1820s and 1830s. Although the Reverend Horace Bushnell's popular text *Christian Nurture* (1847) opposed revivals as a means to conversion, it too stressed the importance of the mother's daily influence on the young child.[33]

The intense concern with the moral training of children soon expanded to a concern with the moral well-being of the whole society. Women who identified themselves as moral instructors in classrooms and homes extended their obligations beyond charities and Sunday schools to address problems of social deviance of their time, including prostitution and drinking. While still operating within the domestic female sphere, women entered the realm of public policy. In addition to prayer meetings in prisons, they proposed laws to close brothels. When men wanted to abandon the cause, women made moral reform a national movement. With their faith in human perfectibility, they promoted chastity for male college youth and, in sympathy with their "fallen sisters," worked to reclaim them. Under the direction of Lydia Andrews Finney, then wife of the president of Oberlin, male and female undergraduate moral reform societies were started. Moreover, three reformed prostitutes were brought to Oberlin for education and rehabilitation. Female educators took the lead in their communities as well as in academies and colleges. Significantly, the ambitious plans of the educated female leaders in the movement depended on networks of women who shared their values and gave them support. By mid-century the focus on moral reformation in temperance and prison work, as well as in the anti-prostitution effort, entered the concerns of wives, mothers, and daughters. These were aspects of social questions that women could not only understand but agree on.[34]

While female reformers often engaged in several of these activities, there were individuals in every organization who embraced more controversial problems. Some schoolteachers became staunch abolitionists. The proper Maria Weston Chapman, a former principal, headed the Massachusetts Anti-Slavery Association, backed by a coterie of Unitarian schoolteachers and writers. Outspoken academy graduates also ignored the neutral stands of the first generation of female educators and participated in anti-slavery societies. Two of Charles Finney's wives, Lydia Finney and Elizabeth Finney, worked in the Ohio organization.[35]

Black women had long worked for the elevation of their race in the option most available to them, that of schoolteaching. Over half the black women listed in *Notable American Women* between 1790 and 1870 taught school at some point in their lives. Their commitment to education necessarily drew many of them into the abolitionist societies, as a starting point to enlighten both white and black people. These strong individuals confronted prejudice, not only from the white community, but from blacks who felt that they were "stepping out" of place.

Maria Stewart pointed out that money used in African colonization efforts would be better spent on educating black Americans: "True friends of the Negro would build a college," she declared, and insisted that: "Before I go [back to Africa], the bayonet shall pierce me through." Sarah Douglass, a tireless anti-slavery leader, had opened her own school for blacks in Philadelphia in the 1820s. Later she taught at a school that

would become Cheney State College. In her work in the abolitionist societies in Philadelphia (one of which her mother had helped found),
Douglass associated with the Grimkés and became a lifelong friend of
Sarah. Her work and that of other black women was the beginning of a
long struggle for the elevation of their race.[36]

Some white women supported the educational goals of black women.
In 1831 in Canterbury, Connecticut, Quaker Prudence Crandall admitted a black girl to her school in order to prepare her to become a
teacher. When the community forced Crandall to close the school, she
attempted to open a black teacher-training school. Her work brought
support from abolitionists but violence in the town, and she was forced
to move.[37]

Female anti-slavery advocates ignored the boundaries of woman's domestic sphere. As in the moral reform cause, women carried on most of
their work independently of men. But even separate societies could not
forestall confrontation between tradition and transition in women's pursuits. In every reform activity women encountered disrespect for their
opinions and limits to their executive leadership. But experiences in the
anti-slavery cause finally sparked a small group of activists into furious
awareness of their unfair and unequal treatment. When in 1840 female-
elected representatives from American anti-slavery societies were refused seats at the International Anti-Slavery Convention in London, two
witnesses of this humiliation, Lucretia Mott and Elizabeth Cady Stanton,
resolved to form a society at home on women's behalf. The convention
they organized at Seneca Falls, New York, eight years later launched the
first women's movement in the United States.

Their Declaration of Sentiments in 1848, like its model, the Declaration of Independence, combined the moral fervor of reformers with the
Enlightenment commitment to human rights. The Seneca Falls Declaration summed up the accumulated legal, economic, social, and political
deprivations American women had suffered during sixty years of the republic. The convention demanded both an end to the deprivations of
the past and the enlargement of women's opportunities in the future.
Certain demands—recognition of married women in the law, a single
standard of morality for men and women, fair wages for gainfully employed women, and consideration of mothers as guardians of children
in cases of divorce and separation—addressed the needs of the widest
range of American women. More controversial claims included not only
female admission to men's colleges and professional schools, but suffrage as a right of female citizenship. Suffrage became a new symbol, the
political instrument through which the more farsighted of these women
believed that they could improve women's lives and make a better
world.[38]

Feminism and higher education were thus linked, but for most women liberal education took precedence over suffrage. Those who opposed making suffrage a symbol agreed on the necessity of full liberal and professional education for women equal to that offered white men. These mature wives and mothers valued what education they had had. In their own lifetime, education had already offered women possibilities for personal choice through earning a living as teachers and writers. Enlightened women had new perspectives about the limitations on their sex. Because of advances in female education from 1790 to 1850, the courageous saw beyond the existing boundaries of their sphere. The rising expectations of this small group signaled new directions for a future in which women, benefiting from education, would be as free as men to participate in the work of the world.

F·O·U·R

The Push into Higher Education

Our demand that Harvard and Yale Colleges should admit women, though not yielded, only waits for a little more time. And while they wait, numerous petty 'female colleges' have sprung into being, indicative of the justice of our claim that a college education should be granted to women. Not one of these female colleges . . . meets the demand of the age, and so will eventually perish. Oberlin and Antioch Colleges in Ohio . . . admit women on terms nearly equal with men.

Lucy Stone (address to the Seventh National Women's Rights Convention, New York City, November 25–26, 1856)

Lucy Stone, the first woman in Massachusetts to receive the A.B. degree (Oberlin, 1847) expressed the rising expectations of feminists and others who had longed to "go off with the boys to college." In the next fifty years, female higher education did become a "demand of the age." By 1900 women had access to widely varied institutions, though the oldest men's colleges remained off bounds. Coeducation ultimately became the dominant mode, as early feminists had hoped (see table 1) but women's colleges did not perish. In addition, coordinate female institutions founded next door to resistant male ones offered a compromise between single-sex and coeducational instruction. The varied options underscored the different perceptions of appropriate collegiate education for women in American society.[1]

Women's efforts alone did not end the old academic restrictions on their sex. From the onset of the Civil War to World War I, three critical forces contributed to women's advance into higher education. First, and of lasting importance, was the popularizing trend in public education, evident in the growth of common schools, high schools, and finally, colleges. Second was the more immediate impact of the Civil War and its

43

TABLE 1
Colleges Open to Men and Women 1870–1981

| Year | Number of institutions | Percentage distribution | | |
		Men only	Women only	Coeducational
1870	582	59	12	29
1890	1082	37	20	43
1910	1083	27	15	58
1930	1322	15	16	69
1957*	1326	13	13	74
1976*	1849	4	5	91
1981*	1928	3	5	92

Sources: Mabel Newcomer, *A Century of Higher Education for American Women* (New York, 1959), 37; and U.S. Department of Health, Education, and Welfare, National Center for Education Statistics, *Digest of Education Statistics*, 1976 and 1982.

*excludes nondegree granting institutions

aftermath, Reconstruction. Third, the ferment and expansion in university education generally throughout the period unexpectedly had reverberations for women's education. Yet setbacks always accompanied the progress, for skepticism lingered about the worth of educating women. Opponents still saw in female education a direct challenge to the traditional place of women in American society. To the participants—educators, supporters, and students—uncertainty and insecurity plagued each step, and the way seemed long. Thus in women's drive for acceptance in academia, their persistence made the difference in holding on to gains.

Since the founding of the republic, Americans had acknowledged, in principle anyway, the obligation to provide some educational opportunities for all citizens. By the mid-nineteenth century, increasing numbers of men and women from diverse backgrounds believed in some kind of education as the means to a better life for themselves or their children. Educational goals in the democracy ranged from literacy to technical training to study in "liberal" subjects. In 1862 Lincoln's signing of the Morrill Land Grant Act affirmed the importance of public higher education. This law to promote "the liberal and practical education of the industrial classes in the several pursuits and professions of life" made public lands available to states to endow colleges for instruction in agriculture and the mechanical arts. In addition, the second Morrill Act of 1890, which required federal allocations to be "fairly divided between Negroes and Whites," enlarged college clienteles. Although the legislation had not specifically referred to women, as old institutions were enlarged and new ones created, women gradually established their right to attend, with far-reaching consequences.[2]

The Civil War itself initiated new opportunities for women as a group, both in employment and in education. The question of whether an employed woman was stepping out of her domestic sphere became irrelevant in the face of an overwhelming need for labor. Because of the dearth of trained or untrained male personnel, the few women with any medical skills were welcome as nurses and doctors. Upper-class women with no previous organizational background joined in the work of the United States Sanitary Commission, collecting and distributing hospital supplies. As aides in hospitals and camps, women pursued voluntary activities on an unprecedented scale. Off the battlefield, too, women took over, especially in the beleaguered South where they managed family properties. In the North, women not only worked the farms but participated in the operation of factories. By 1870 nearly two million women were employed, in each of the 338 occupations listed in the United States census. This number accounted for "one woman in eight over ten years of age." Even though most of those employed were not in the professions, the figures included 525 women physicians, 67 ministers, and 5 lawyers. As substitutes for the generation of young men turned soldiers, women gained invaluable experiences, furthering their professional goals. They also developed new expectations.[3]

The forced reevaluation of society that accompanied the end of slavery logically extended to a reconsideration of the status of women. Reconstruction generated hope for educational advancement of women. During the war women had assumed places in the schools and colleges both as teachers and students, and their reputations in both roles had grown. Schoolteaching continued to provide women of all backgrounds with important ways to serve and to support themselves. The crucial need for schoolteachers visible in the antebellum decades now became even more pressing on several counts. Women with an evangelical missionary spirit found a new focus in educating men and women recently freed from slavery. Hundreds of black and thousands of northern white women were drawn first into the war zones and later into the desolate rural areas of the South. In addition, immigration to the United States accelerated, and settlement of the West expanded; urban and rural America thus required more schoolteachers. Practical considerations then justified women's education in the postwar world. Further, the loss of men during the war meant that a large proportion of native-born women could not expect to marry, and these women sought opportunities to support themselves.

For southern white women, whose personal and economic losses were

higher, opportunities for gainful employment were fewer. Until the advent
of a fully developed system of public education, such women had nowhere
to go for teacher training. In time a few privileged female leaders, with
support from farmers' organizations, gained state support for education.[4]

Advocacy for female education also had political dimensions. Male
abolitionists, having deserted the cause of women's suffrage to pursue
that of enfranchisement of black men, thereafter ardently backed the
collegiate education of women. These reformers, unwilling to jeopar-
dize black men's suffrage by linking it to women's, now looked upon education as a reward for women's contributions in the war. But suffragists
who had shelved their own cause to work for black emancipation were
bitterly disappointed by the passage of the fourteenth and fifteenth
amendments, which granted black men citizenship and right of suffrage
but deliberately excluded women. In the 1870s suffragists split into two
organizations, disagreeing over means and ends. But both the more ag-
gressive New York wing, headed by Elizabeth Cady Stanton and Susan B.
Anthony, and the more patient New England faction, led by Lucy Stone
and Julia Ward Howe, were united in calling for full female higher education. Simultaneously, the women's movement in the late nineteenth
century expanded outside the suffrage organizations to the burgeoning
women's clubs of the post–Civil War era: the Sorosis, the New England
Women's Club, the Association for the Advancement of Women, and
the Women's Christian Temperance Union, among others, all actively
supported female education. Literary and cultural leaders likened the
activities of their groups to those of women's colleges. Thus individuals
and organizations with varied social and political beliefs—from evangelical and liberal Protestant ministers and educators to business and
professional men to suffragists, former abolitionists, and anti-abolition-
ists—now agreed on the importance of higher education for women.[5]

Since it was obvious that relatively few women could afford a full liberal arts education, advocates of female education also favored intermediate institutions offering vocational or professional training.

Significantly, by 1890 more girls than boys were graduating from high
school. As economist Susan Carter explains, high school attendance gave
women access to better jobs, notably in schoolteaching. For similar reasons, normal schools also expanded greatly from their small antebellum
beginnings. The founding in 1884 of the exclusively white Mississippi
State Normal and Industrial School initiated a pattern soon followed by
Georgia, North Carolina, South Carolina, Oklahoma, and Texas. These
institutions provided a briefer and less expensive course of study than
that of colleges. Several female medical colleges opening at this time did
not require collegiate education for admission. Black as well as white
women enrolled, often in the same schools. Increasingly high schools

served two functions, that of providing an alternative to college education and that of offering preparation for it.[6]

Although men still outnumbered women in the colleges, the break-
through had occurred; in smaller but ever increasing numbers, girls
would slowly stream into the colleges, as more received preparatory
training. Increased need for teachers helped the whole process. The up-
surge in secondary school enrollments led to the expansion of normal
schools for teacher training. Moreover, some women combined training
and teaching before continuing on to further education, for although a
college degree was not required to teach, the advantage of a college education soon became apparent.

A variety of collegiate institutions grew in religiously, socially, and racially heterogeneous America. Between the 1850s and the 1870s several
models developed: the private women's college, the religiously oriented
coeducational college, the private coordinate women's college, the secular coeducational institution, both public and private, and the public
single-sex vocational institution. The precedent for women's colleges lay
in antebellum seminaries, that for coeducational schools in the Oberlin
model. The privately sponsored coordinate female college attached to an
institution for male students offered a solution that avoided coeducation.
Nonetheless, coeducation became dominant in public and private universities in the 1870s, and new universities thereafter took coeducation
for granted. Only in the South was single-sex education the norm in public institutions for white women. The variations in these educational models made sense pragmatically, and each type appropriately served the
educational values of its supporters. But founders and early advocates
could not anticipate the ways in which these institutions would grow.

The one place where women had a guaranteed welcome was at a wom-
en's college. Although feminists regarded the early female college as
second-best, for a long time this institution had more public appeal because it upheld the separate female sphere. Four-year women's colleges
appeared in different parts of the country in the 1850s and did not last.
But four schools opening in the North in the post–Civil War decades—
Vassar in 1865, Wellesley and Smith in 1875, and Bryn Mawr in 1884
—became national institutions. The evolution of this group of colleges
had a far-reaching impact on both coeducational and single-sex institutions throughout the country. These women's colleges were founded by
religiously motivated individuals. Three of the benefactors—Matthew
Vassar, Henry Fowle Durant, and Sophia Smith—endowed institutions
on the Mount Holyoke seminary model, and the fourth, Joseph Taylor,
bequeathed an endowment for a conservative Quaker institution for
women. In their inception, Vassar, Wellesley, Smith, and Bryn Mawr re-
affirmed the purposes of the old seminaries to produce Christian

women better prepared to assume their duties in the domestic sphere, as wives and mothers, and only if need be, as schoolteachers.

Plans for Vassar College in New York State, the first large endowed collegiate institution for women, took shape when Milo Jewett, head of Judson Female Academy in Alabama, persuaded a retired brewer, Matthew Vassar, to provide the money in 1857. Vassar, an English immigrant, self-made, self-taught, and a devout Baptist, had a practical bent: he wanted to make women better teachers. The philanthropist was so pleased with his idea that he wrote in his diary, "the founder of Vassar College and President Lincoln—Two Noble Emancipists—one of Woman—[the other of] The Negro."[7]

With a similar sense of making history, Wellesley's founder, Henry Fowle Durant, a converted lay preacher (Harvard graduate, former lawyer, and businessman) collaborated with his wife Pauline to provide women with "opportunities for education equivalent to those usually provided in colleges for young men." As a trustee of Mount Holyoke Seminary, Durant saw hundreds of young women turned away; his school would be another for "the glory of God." To help in his moral and educational crusade, he selected Jane Howard, a Mount Holyoke graduate, to be the nominal president, but he really ran the school himself. At chapel Durant told the students that "the higher Education of Women is one of the great world battle-cries for freedom: for right against might. It is the cry of the oppressed slave. It is the assertion of absolute equality. The war is sacred, because it is the war of Christ." Both Vassar and Durant made a virtue of having few or no men on their faculties, presumably to provide employment for well-trained women scholars, but also because of the economic advantage of employing lower-paid female instructors.[8]

The third benefactor was Sophia Smith, an aging single woman with a fortune and no heirs, who had considered endowing a college for women as early as 1861 but was dissuaded by the presidents of Amherst, Harvard, Williams, and Yale. By 1868 her plan was approved by two Amherst professors, William Taylor and Julius Seelye, and the Reverend John Morton Green, whose wife had attended Mount Holyoke Seminary. The pious Sophia Smith sounded moderately feminist in articulating her purpose: "It is my opinion that by the higher and more thoroughly Christian education of women, what are called their 'wrongs' will be redressed, their wages will be adjusted, their weight of influence in reforming the evils of society will be greatly increased as teachers, as writers, as mothers, as members of society, their power for good will be incalculably enlarged." But disappointingly, the college named for Sophia Smith (unlike Wellesley, which started the same year) appointed only male presidents for almost a century.[9]

The fourth in this group of women's colleges, Bryn Mawr, established in 1884, benefited from the experiences of its predecessors. Joseph Taylor, an Orthodox Quaker doctor and businessman, bequeathed his fortune to establish a women's school to be the counterpart of Haverford College. Though Taylor urged the preparation of Quaker "teachers of a high order," he emphasized that "should they become mothers," they would "train infant minds and give direction to character and make the home the center of interest and attraction." The trustees of the College agreed with the donor's purposes, but the dean and second president, M. Carey Thomas, changed the emphasis from moral discipline to academic rigor. Thomas, an early graduate of Cornell and a feminist, after visiting major eastern colleges for men and women, observed with disapproval that some women teachers at Wellesley, Smith, and Mount Holyoke had never had a single college course; she resolved to make Bryn Mawr the equal of the best men's colleges.[10]

Leaders in the four colleges were very conscious of the inadequacies of the first candidates. Vassar and Wellesley started with preparatory departments because so many applicants had insufficient preparation. Smith and Bryn Mawr took pride in establishing more stringent admissions requirements, but without preparatory departments had difficulty adhering to their standards. Similarly, some outstanding seminaries, including Mount Holyoke, Mills, and Rockford, were qualified to be rechartered as colleges in the 1880s.

Institutional developments took longer in the South, where several older seminaries gradually became rigorous colleges. Representative of these were Mary Baldwin in Virginia, Judson in Alabama, and Agnes Scott in Georgia. Two new schools that opened as colleges became academically prestigious. The Women's College of Baltimore, sponsored by the Methodist Conference in 1884 and inspired by developments at nearby Johns Hopkins University, is better known as Goucher College. The other college with high intellectual standards was Randolph-Macon College for Women in Virginia under Presbyterian sponsorship, the academic mate of the men's college of that name.[11]

Women's colleges everywhere adhered to the religious ideal of virtuous, True Womanhood, but within its framework extended woman's sphere beyond the familial roles. Smith's president L. Clark Seelye expressed well the potentialities for their common ideal of the educated woman in the 1890s: "The college is not intended to fit woman for any particular sphere or profession but to develop by the most carefully devised means all her intellectual capacities, so that she may be a more perfect woman in any position."[12]

Protestant lay and clerical leaders had contributed to an array of nonsectarian colleges. At the same time Catholic interest in higher education for women was just beginning. Influenced by the existing female college model, Catholics started their own colleges for women just before 1900. Catholic colleges for men had been established much earlier, and by 1860 there were already eighty-four such institutions. Although education of women had trailed, a groundwork had been laid in the form of convent schools and female seminaries. Finally, in 1895, when the Catholic University of America refused to admit women, the first Catholic women's colleges opened: the College of Notre Dame in Maryland, founded in 1896, and Trinity College, set up in Washington near the Catholic University of America in 1897. These schools, according to historian Edward Power, stressed "religious rather than academic ideals," but they, like Bryn Mawr and Goucher, were stimulated by the proximity of Johns Hopkins. Catholic institutions did not offer the option of coeducation until later. For any conservative group uncertain of the effects of education on women, the separate women's college seemed the safest route.[13]

The development of the women's college did not hold back coeducation everywhere, since economy necessitated joint instruction in many communities. Small religious colleges on the Oberlin model continued to take root, especially in the Midwest in the 1840s and 1850s and in the black South in the late 1860s. The boards of such institutions found it less expensive, and therefore desirable, to maintain one school rather than separate schools for men and women. Perhaps more important, they justified coeducation in ethical and religious terms of the equality of souls, male and female. The many institutions established in this way included Knox in Illinois, Antioch in Ohio, and Bates in Maine (open to blacks as well as women). Blacks started Wilberforce in Ohio, but Fisk, Howard, and other predominantly black schools were founded by white missionary societies. Oberlin graduates made up a large part of the teaching force, especially in the black colleges. In most instances, coeducation did not mean that all classes were joint; as at Oberlin, they were often separate. Moreover, women usually did not take the full liberal arts course but were assigned instead to a separate female department.[14]

Social and economic factors, combined with religious convictions, had various effects on the development of coeducation in different groups. The history of Quaker higher education provides contradictory examples. Quakers had always educated boys and girls together at the elementary and secondary levels. Yet Haverford, their first liberal arts college (started by affluent Orthodox Quakers in 1834) was all male. By contrast, the founding of Swarthmore College, in 1864, after long years of planning, reflected the vision of the Hicksite branch of Quakers in Baltimore and Philadelphia. Swarthmore supporters included outright feminists like Lucretia Mott and her daughter Anna Hooper, as well as more conservative female sponsors. From the outset equal numbers of men and women participated on the board of managers. Swarthmore founders, influenced by Oberlin, made their college a family community; men and women in training their minds also prepared for their separate spheres. Nonetheless, the founders stated with considerable frankness that women should have training for self-support in order to avoid misguided marriages. Swarthmore became the model for later Quaker colleges that developed out of academies like Guilford in Greensboro, North Carolina, and Earlham in Indiana.[15]

It was a religiously sponsored new school that finally brought coeducation to Massachusetts. The establishment of Boston University in 1873, with its admission of women to every department, represented the religious and feminist ideals of its Methodist founders. The first president, William Fairfield Warren, optimistically announced that the new College of Liberal Arts "welcomes women not merely to the bench of the pupil, but also to the chair of the professor." This was the only college in the Commonwealth of Massachusetts open to women; soon it offered women undergraduate, graduate, and professional training. Moreover, to create a pool of qualified applicants, Warren, with the support of leading Boston women, also fought for a public college preparatory school in Boston. The resulting Girls' Latin School has prepared girls for liberal arts colleges since 1878. Warren's commitment to coeducation at all levels places him among exceptional male educators of the era.[16]

In the same years academic leaders in the elite schools were absorbed with new questions arising from the revolutionary growth of scientific knowledge. A new breed of educator, of whom Harvard president Charles W. Eliot was representative, set out to transform their colleges into research universities. In their great visions there was no place for women. Yet even these educators were forced to address women's demands.[17]

The beginning of Cornell University exemplified the mixture of old and new ideals represented in one institution. For some old-timers Cornell symbolized the agricultural and industrial pursuits of the self-made citizen. The idea for a People's College for men and women in central New York State originated in the early fifties. The school's founders, Ezra Cornell and Henry Sage, expected women as well as men to share in the training at their school. Yet its chartering in 1865 did not mention women. The first president, Yale graduate Andrew Dixon White, was a freethinker in religion and was liberal in his attitude toward the admission of blacks and women, but he wanted to preside over a research university. As a result, he stalled on the admission of women, and in 1868 Cornell opened with more than four hundred students from many walks of life, all of whom were men.[18]

The arrival of a young woman a few years later with a state scholarship in hand forced a change. Jenny Spencer's admission related to the peculiar conditions of the institution's funding. Ezra Cornell's money was only one of the financial resources. The rest of its support came from New York State and from the Morrill Land Grant Act; thus the leaders of Cornell could not deny Spencer entrance. Even after women were included, however, White, anxious and defensive, assured friends of Cornell that no "flippant and worthless 'boarding school misses' " would be admitted. Primary concern for the male students is reflected in his statement that "this university must not only make scholars; it has a higher duty; it must make men—men manly, earnest, and of good general culture."[19]

Jenny Spencer's coup at Cornell foreshadowed other confrontations over coeducation in the 1870s at many public institutions. These schools lacked the unifying religious principles that justified women's admission to the private evangelical colleges. Each community responded idiosyncratically to the controversies over coeducation. The refusal of the City College of New York, established in 1847, to admit women contributed to the creation in 1870 of the normal school for women that later became Hunter College. In the early years, from 1839 to 1917, women were prohibited from entering the municipally controlled universities of Toledo and Louisville, Kentucky, and Charleston, South Carolina. In contrast, Cincinnati founded a municipal university in 1870, with free tuition and coeducation to "open the door of higher education to hundreds . . . who are now hopelessly excluded from the same" in order to create "an aristocracy of intellect and cultivation." From its inception more than half the University of Cincinnati student body was female; in 1900 women comprised 80.8 percent of students in the collegiate course. Here women obtained their goal, but only after determined efforts to do so.[20]

The most conspicuous conflicts occurred in state universities, where opposition to coeducation spread like a fever from one campus to another. In spite of the fact that several had declared their intention to permit coeducation before the Civil War, only the University of Iowa did so. This institution opened in 1855 with both male and female students. Three years later, however, new managers adopted a resolution "excluding females from the University after the close of the term." The board was overruled, but the clause was indicative of the tensions accompanying women's admission. Several other universities acknowledged the growing public demands for admission of women but did not act. In 1857 the regents of the University of Wisconsin noted the success of women in secondary schools and colleges but concluded that "public sentiment in Wisconsin is not yet ripe for dispensing with separate female schools."[21]

Yet most state institutions (except in the South) discovered that they could not delay the admission of women. The female presence was not a legal requirement under the Morrill Land Grant Act, but neither did the act specifically exclude women. While individuals of feminist persuasion campaigned for the educational rights of women as citizens, presidents and deans felt conflicting pressures from their different constituencies. Women's demands for admission to schools receiving state funds eventually turned the tide in one public institution after another.

The first thirty women at the University of Wisconsin in 1863 entered the Normal Department for teacher training. With fewer men attending during the Civil War, the women were allowed to take other college courses as well, though they were not allowed to sit down until all male students were seated. After the war, in 1867, coeducation was abruptly eliminated, and the Female College was established. Four years later the regents gave women the option of attending coeducational or segregated classes. Women boycotted the Female College, joined the men in classes, and reestablished coeducation in 1873. John Bascom, appointed president in 1874, solidified coeducation at Wisconsin.[22]

Although at the University of Missouri women made their way from the Normal School to a few classes in the college, their acceptance was greatly restricted. It was 1871 before women were admitted to all classes, and even later before they had full use of the library and permission to attend chapel with the men. In one administration they were "marched to class" with teachers as guards at the front and rear. In another, uniforms were made compulsory in order to distinguish female students from other women in the town. The resistance of Southerners in the town made itself felt in the peculiarly military supervision of the first coeds.[23]

The acceptance of women at the University of Michigan also came in 1870, long after the first demands, which were made during the 1850s. For two decades faculty members and presidents resisted the persistent clamor of young women teachers, taxpaying parents, and feminists of both sexes. Although the original charter of the university called for a female department, no money had ever been appropriated, and the regents persisted in denying the applicatons of women. Coeducation at Michigan succeeded only after the resignation of the implacable President Henry Tappan and after women had raised $100,000 with which to back up their lobbying. Finally, in the administration of James Angell, Michigan became one of the most desirable academic places for women to study.

The first eight state universities to accept women were Iowa (1855), Wisconsin (1867), Kansas, Indiana, Minnesota (1869), Missouri, Michigan, and California (1870). Of these, California, Iowa, Kansas, and Minnesota admitted women only from the home state.[24]

Southern universities had a different history, with only seven admitting females by 1912, but educated women in local communities managed to find alternatives. Annie C. Peyton's agitation in Mississippi in 1879–80 resulted in the opening in 1885 of the first state-supported separate institution for women—Mississippi State College for Women (originally called the Collegiate Institute). This school became a model for other states of the region.[25]

The elite private institutions for men—Harvard, Yale, Princeton, and others—despite the predictions of Lucy Stone, long remained closed to women. Yet they did not wholly escape the demands for coeducation and made various compromises. Yale bypassed the question for undergraduates but admitted women to graduate programs in the 1890s. Princeton agreed to a coordinate arrangement with nearby Evelyn College, a women's school that soon folded. Plans for coeducation at the University of Pennsylvania did not materialize for fifty years, despite money for women's education given by philanthropist Joseph Bennett in 1883.[26]

When President Thomas Hill was asked in 1868 by Vassar professor Maria Mitchell how long it would be before Harvard College admitted women, he answered that it would take place within twenty years. The demand was not new, but in the 1870s many wives, sisters, and daughters of Harvard alumni and faculty joined those demanding a Harvard education for women. Advocates included suffragists, anti-suffragists, and former abolitionists. Young women studying in academies in Cambridge, Boston, and outlying towns had begun to present themselves to Harvard professors for private instruction. Neither the opening of Boston University nor the founding of Wellesley College satisfied women who wanted to have a Harvard education. Hill's successor, Charles W. Eliot, inherited the question of coeducation and, in a public debate with abolitionist Wendell Phillips, argued against it. In 1874, in response to increasing pressure from women's groups like the Women's Education Association of Boston, the Harvard Corporation offered examinations to women, graded by Harvard professors (following the pattern of British institutions).[27]

It was a Cambridge couple, schoolmaster Arthur Gilman and his wife Stella, who, with their daughter in mind, worked out a collegiate plan with a few professors to provide a full course of liberal studies for young women, even though it did not lead to a degree. Unofficially, President Eliot permitted moonlighting by his faculty for the instruction of twenty-seven "Harvard girls." The success of the "Harvard Annex" led to the incorporation of the Society for the Collegiate Instruction of Women in 1882, with Elizabeth Carey Agassiz as president and William Byerly as chairman of the board. In 1892 hopes rose that women would be admitted to Harvard for the A.B. degree. Eliot's suggestion that the women raise $250,000 in order to make possible their inclusion in the school was taken up by Alice Freeman Palmer and others, who accomplished this goal. However, the Harvard Corporation refused the money and denied women admission; clearly, coeducation was too great a risk.

After this serious setback the undaunted determination of Mrs. Agassiz and her friends at the university brought the chartering of Radcliffe College in 1894 as a degree-granting institution to offer the equivalent of a Harvard degree; the corporation, though unwilling to give women its A.B., agreed to serve as "Visitors" and to let Harvard's president countersign Radcliffe diplomas. Both alumnae of the Collegiate Society and feminists in Boston were outraged by this compromise.[28]

Mounting efforts for the admission of women to Columbia in New York City encountered opposition similar to that at Harvard. Although President Frederick Barnard was convinced that women could not get the best education at a female college, his faculty objected to full coeducation. As at Harvard, the first compromise was to let women take Columbia examinations without hearing the professors' lectures. When this arrangement brought protests, Columbia trustees finally agreed to a female annex. Barnard College began in 1889, with Columbia faculty serving as professors and the corporation as "Visitors." The academic status, like that of Radcliffe, derived from its connection with a prestigious male institution. But over the years one essential difference developed in that Barnard gained the right to recruit its own faculty. Radcliffe women were not awarded Harvard A.B.s until 1965, and the first women undergraduates were not admitted to Columbia until 1983; but Barnard still maintained a separate existence.

Elsewhere a variety of coordinate colleges were founded as a way of avoiding coeducation. Flora Mather College was started so that Adelbert College, of Western Reserve University, could become an all-male school, reversing its coeducational beginnings. President Hiram C. Haydn claimed that the "demand for separate education is one of the late growths of civilization and the advance of wealth," a luxury that did not exist under frontier conditions. Brown University also worked out an arrangement for women that allowed the faculty to instruct women separately at Pembroke College, a coordinate unit. Jackson College of Tufts University and the Women's College of Rochester University were other coordinate educational arrangements by schools that began as coeducational and subsequently sought segregation by sex. Yet other institutions failed at working out compromises due to their ambivalent attitudes toward higher education for women. Welseyan in Connecticut, for example, was at first all male, then coeducational, than all male in 1912, and finally in 1970 again admitted women.[30]

Schools in the South had to deal with these same issues, and there were fewer successes for women. The establishment of Sophie Newcomb as an affiliate of Tulane University in New Orleans represented an unusual innovative pattern. Newcomb, founded by the legacy of philanthropist Josephine Louise Le Monnier Newcomb, was considered a department of Tulane, even though it had its own faculty, who gave separate instruction. But women in most southern states (a majority among high school graduates) had fewer opportunities unless they went to another part of the United States. As late as 1910 the state of Virginia had four state-supported colleges—William and Mary, Washington and Lee, the University of Virginia, and Virginia Military Institute—none of which admitted women, although as early as 1880 the faculty at the University of Virginia had recommended their admission to the college. Campaigns to admit women met with defeat and with the prophecy that co-education produced a type of woman from whom "we devoutly pray to be spared": boisterous and bold. The next attempt, that of a women's committee organized by Mary Munford, between 1910 and 1920 produced five bills at the legislature. But it was not until 1970 that women gained admission to the University of Virginia.[31]

Even though the educability of women was obvious in the 1870s, new arguments emerged from scientific thinking to endanger female higher education. Darwinian evolution relegated women to a permanently inferior condition, physically and mentally. In this view, women were too far behind men in human evolution ever to catch up; moreover, some doctors declared it was harmful for them to try.[32]

The most famous attack came from Dr. Edward Clarke's *Sex in Education* (1873). This retired Harvard Medical School professor was alarmed by the increasing presence of women in high schools, normal schools, and colleges. Moreover, as he knew, women were demanding entrance to the university's medical school and divinity school, as well as to the undergraduate college. After studying the cases of seven Vassar students, Clarke concluded that if women used up their "limited energy" on studying, they would endanger their "female apparatus." Although a girl could study and learn, Clarke noted, she could not "do all this, and retain uninjured health and a future secure from neuralgia, uterine disease, hysteria, and other derangements of the nervous system." The risks were great for any individual female. This medical verdict put the stamp of scientific truth on the ancient suspicion that the female brain and body could not survive book learning. What made Clarke's arguments most compelling was his separation of women's education from women's rights. It was not a matter of what was right or wrong for the individual, he maintained, but what was good for society that mattered; clearly, women needed to save their energies to fulfill their biological function as childbearers.[33]

Widely read and discussed, *Sex in Education*, which went through seventeen printings, captured the attention of the educated public. Although female students at Michigan ridiculed the book, prominent advocates and educators of women, including Julia Ward Howe, Mary Peabody Mann, Caroline Dall, Thomas Wentworth Higginson, John Bascom, and Abby May, responded seriously with examples to refute Clarke. Others assumed that until many more women went to college, the validity of Clarke's hypotheses could not be fairly tested. His attack reinforced the determination of educators to make the college woman a healthy specimen, conspicuous for her vigor in mind and body.[34]

Women doctors and social scientists followed the lives of the early women graduates carefully. Dr. Mary Putnam Jacobi's essay "The Question of Rest for Women During Menstruation," which won Harvard's Boylston Prize in 1876, was one of many studies made to disprove Clarke's contentions. In addition, in 1885, a special committee of the Association of Collegiate Alumnae surveyed 1,290 graduates to produce a report on health statistics. The analysis did not gloss over the fact that 19.58 percent of these alumnae admitted deterioration of health in college, while 21.13 percent reported improvement. But the report emphasized intelligently that many factors contributed to the poor health of all Americans and not only that of college women. These factors included family constitution, public hygiene, "the rapid discovery of inventions which . . . put a severe pressure upon the mental power of men and women," the "social customs of modern life," and even the "climatic effects" of the American environment.[35]

But the excitement over Clarke's warnings subsided quite swiftly. A survey of coeducational institutions in 1885 emphasized the positive effects of coeducation on the scholarship and "manners and morals" of both male and female students. Acceptance of coeducation rose in the next decade, and the 1890s saw the establishment of two major universities that admitted female students from the start. The opening in October 1892 of the Baptist- and Rockefeller-sponsored University of Chicago was a landmark in the history of coeducation. The exuberant young president, William R. Harper, envisaged a free, open, academic environment and recruited women as undergraduates, graduates, and faculty members. To implement his plans, he appointed Alice Freeman Palmer, formerly president of Wellesley, to be dean of women and Marion Talbot to be assistant dean. Similarly, the opening of Stanford in 1887 and its reestablishment in 1892, with a place for women apparently secured in its charter, affirmed faith in coeducation. President Daniel Gilman of Johns Hopkins (which did not admit women) hailed women's advance in the various institutions as one of the great and "remarkable" changes of the era and praised the way each community had resolved its problems through single-sex, coordinate, and coeducational institutions. Women had arrived to stay in the colleges.[36]

Between 1870 and 1900 the number of females enrolled in institutions of higher learning multiplied almost eightfold, from eleven to eighty-five thousand. This increase was more rapid than that for males, and the number of women as a percentage of all students rose from 21 percent to at least 35 percent in this time. After the 1870s the majority of women enrolled in coeducational institutions, and by 1900 there were more than twice as many women in these than in the separate women's colleges. Between 1902 and 1912 the explosion in female enrollments in coeducational institutions precipitated yet another round in the cycle of criticism.[37]

The very success of collegiate education for women induced strong waves of reaction. Rising numbers again brought into question full coeducation. The new fear was that women would take over the colleges. Chicago, Stanford, California, Wisconsin, Boston University, and even Oberlin had qualms; the impact on male enrollments was the central issue, and complaints by some male students were noted. Academic achievement was held against females when they surpassed males in either sheer numbers or academic honors. Faculty members echoed the views of disgruntled, or perhaps envious, male students and charged that women interfered with male academic performance.[38]

The University of Chicago, originally so proud of its commitment to women, became a storm center of controversy in 1902. Within one decade of its opening, the percentage of women rose from 24 to 52 percent, and between 1892 and 1902 women received a majority (56.3 percent) of the Phi Beta Kappa awards. An alarmed President Harper, speaking for the majority of the faculty and undoubtedly for most of the male students, sought retreat from full coeducation. When he announced the organization of a women's union to promote the interests of female students in December 1901, he also claimed not to know the "exact nature" of coeducation and "limitations that attend it." Obliquely Harper conveyed concern with its effects on male students. His solution was to halt the trend by segregating undergraduate classes wherever numbers warranted.[39]

Backers of this move looked nostalgically at the eastern private women's colleges, but the proposal violated the university's statutory guarantee of study on equal terms and caused a "civil war" within the university. Alumnae ardently protested against these schemes that were calculated to change their alma mater. One of the most eloquent, Madeleine Wallin, warned that such a step could undermine the opportunities for women at the university. She opposed Harper's proposal as a "halfway method" that would "only lead to self-consciousness and exaggeration of sex differences." A minority of the Chicago faculty, led by young John Dewey and Dean Marion Talbot, also upheld full coeducation. For them, segregation of the sexes was an "un-American, anti-democratic, and reactionary policy." To socially aware members of the university, the repudiation of women's rights to take the same classes as men represented a backward trend.[40]

The faculty liberals lost, and separate classes for freshman and sophomores, in the so-called junior college, were established at Chicago in 1902. But within five years the policy lapsed, because the arrangement was costly and a bureaucratic nuisance.

Notice of the harmful effects of coeducation reached beyond Chicago. Educators elsewhere resorted to segregation of classes when their universities encountered enrollment "problems" of the type seen at Chicago. A similar situation existed at Stanford, with 102 men and 98 women graduating in 1901. There, too, women received a higher number of awards and honors, which worried leaders. In 1908 President David Starr Jordan tried an organizational maneuver similar to that adopted at Chicago, to eliminate women from some liberal arts courses; he proposed the establishment of a junior college division within the university as a way to eliminate "immature students," especially from the freshman and sophomore classes. Jordan's proposal followed earlier rulings by Jane Stanford and others that had already diminished women's enrollment. Jane Stanford, who controlled institutional policy after her husband's death, ignored the university statute requiring "equal advantages in the University to both sexes" and set a limit of five hundred as the maximum number of women permitted to be enrolled at any one time. Later, in 1904, Stanford alumni and alumnae settled on yet another restriction—a ratio of three males to each female student. This ratio was not overturned until 1933.[41]

Neighboring University of California followed these developments with concern for its own female population, which was growing rapidly and was expected to swell even more with disappointed Stanford applicants. President Benjamin Wheeler decided to handle the increase by establishing junior colleges all over the state, for women were "more likely [than men] to remain at home and attend the junior college" on the West Coast. Similarly Boston University, which had offered equality for men and women, also had qualms as women flooded into the school. Its administrators publicized a movement to attract more men, and a professor's will endowed scholarships "for men only." Thereafter women were less welcome than before but at least remained regular students in the university.[42]

A more blatant reversal of policy at the University of Wisconsin in 1907 projected a return to segregated classes reminiscent of the Female College of Liberal Arts. The percentage of women had risen from 40 percent in the 1890s to 50 percent in 1906. After a decline of 10 percent in the male student population, President Charles Richard Van Hise asserted that the growing number of women was "undoubtedly pushing the men out" of the College of Liberal Arts due to "natural segregative laws." He suggested segregating sections of a number of courses, especially psychology and hygiene. Separate history quiz sections already existed, and Professor McGilvary advocated a separate ethics course for men. Van Hise no longer fully upheld the ideal of the state university whose "gates are opened to all of both sexes who possess sufficient intellectual endowment."[43]

Wisconsin critics of coeducation referred, very inaccurately, to the early years of the university as a time when a few women made "scarcely more disturbance than . . . a considerable group of Japanese, Chinese, and Filipinos." This xenophobic comparison did not go unnoticed by 275 irate alumnae, who signed a militant protest against Van Hise's effort to stem "the feminine equivalent to the yellow peril in education." Feminist alumna Helen Remington Olin rallied the opposition to this revolutionary step with her pamphlet "Shall Wisconsin University Remain a Co-Educational Institution?" She maintained that if men were to be "enticed" into the humanities, the university should entice women into the professions at public expense, with separate law, medicine, pharmacy, and agriculture schools. Women, Olin insisted, must have the same undergraduate education as men to prepare equally for graduate study. With support from alumnus Senator Robert La Follette, the alumnae won the battle, and thereafter the place of women in the integrated College of Liberal Arts remained intact.[44]

At this stage of coeducation, educators sought to explain how men and women chose their courses when they were permitted electives. President Van Hise developed a "sex repulsion" theory—that as soon as one sex dominated numerically, fear of competition drove the other out. Thus professors in classics and philosophy, as well as political science, attributed the lower enrollment of men in their courses to the overwhelming presence of women. The female student became the scapegoat for faculty frustration in a time of transition when the release of students from a required, set curriculum gave professors and administrators less control over students' academic direction.[45]

The investigation of behavioral differences also produced an opposing theory, namely, that of sex attraction. G. Stanley Hall's major study of adolescence, in 1904, analyzed the development of sexual urges at puberty and further testified separating the sexes at college. Moreover, Hall had an intense hostility to intellectually aspiring women. They would, he predicted, "become functionally castrated, unwilling to accept the limitations of married life," and resentful when called upon to perform "the functions peculiar to their sex."[46]

The latest objections to women in higher education attested to their successes as students. For centuries there had been the question of females' educability; in the 1870s objections centered on the issue of their health. By the 1900s, psychological emphasis on male and female academic interests posed additional threats to equality in women's education. Women, charged with sex repulsion and sex attraction, both of which interfered with the holy process of educating the future leaders (males) of the country, simply could not win. They either drove men out of the classroom, or they attracted them into it and then distracted them too much. The best solution was to have women attend their own schools.[47]

Some academic men had never lost the feeling that separate colleges were more desirable educationally and socially, and they did not hesitate to say so. Others, after initially supporting the idea of joint instruction, reversed themselves and wanted to retreat back to segregated classes. Coeducation then became, in the minds of many, second-best, whether due to the exaggerated threat of feminization, a concern for scholarly standards, dislike of female students or their often superior performance, or the belief that women became "mannish" when studying with males. By the same token, supporters of women's colleges, in claiming that better women came out of all-female colleges, expressed an elitist preference for females educated apart from males. Since most women could not afford to attend the expensive women's colleges, advocacy for single-sex colleges had a tinge of class bias. Not everyone, however, lost sight of the ideal of equal education. Educators like James Angell of Michigan and John Bascom of Wisconsin always supported coeducation, while some leading female educators saw separate instruction as a necessary but temporary stage in the process of attaining full, equal, joint education.[48]

Whatever form the argument took, the essential point always resurfaced, that the value of educating women was less than that of educating men in American society. Yet the historical paradox remained that women's access to the colleges progressed steadily. The period between the 1870s and the 1910s witnesssed an extraordinary movement of women taking advantage of new opportunities not always designed for them. Whatever the hardships for individuals, whatever the attitudes toward them, whether openly hostile or subtly ambivalent, women as a group stayed on the academic scene and by their faith and tenacity created collegiate patterns for future generations. Access to diverse institutions served the various needs of women students. The next chapters focus on who they were, what they sought, and what they gained.

F·I·V·E

Who Went to College?

To resist the demand that women are making for education is
a hopeless task.

Henry Adams, unsigned review of Edward Clarke's *Sex in
Education* (1874), quoted in Eugenia Kaledin, *The Education of
Mrs. Henry Adams* (1981), 137

The first women to make their way into institutions of higher learning
let their fervor and determination be known to all. Opponents were
waging a losing battle in the 1870s for no discouragements stopped the
rising tide of female students in the next half century. Despite the end-
less discussions about college education for women, more and more parents and daughters became convinced of its desirability. The early collegians formed a small but growing nucleus of ambitious women. It did
not take long for the news of the practical and intellectual benefits of
higher education to reach others. The female proportion of the total
college population rose from 21.0 percent in 1870 to 39.6 percent in
1910 and 47.3 percent in 1920, as shown in table 2. Of course, this remarkable growth occurred at a time when most Americans did not receive even a high school diploma, so that although almost as many
women as men became collegians by the end of the period, as individuals
they were rarities among the nation's youth.[1]

For every woman who aspired to a place in higher education, there
were many more in her social group who did not. In 1870, the percentage of college women among those eighteen to twenty-one years of age
was only 0.7 percent; by 1900 it has increased to 2.8 percent, and by
1920 to 7.6 percent, as shown in table 3. Nevertheless, although the proportion remained small, the increase had social significance. In the
course of this period, the denigration of college as an option for women
evaporated, and its desirability became established. In this chapter we

WHO WENT TO COLLEGE?

TABLE 2
Women Enrolled in Institutions of Higher Education, 1870–1980

Year	Number of women enrolled (thousands)	Percentage of all students enrolled
1870	11	21.0
1880	40	33.4
1890	56	35.9
1900	85	36.8
1910	140	39.6
1920	283	47.3
1930	481	43.7
1940	601	40.2
1950	806	30.2
1960	1,223	37.9
1970	2,884	41.9
1975	3,847	45.4
1980	5,694	51.8

Sources: Mabel Newcomer, *A Century of Higher Education for American Women* (New York, 1959), 46. U.S. Bureau of the Census, National Center for Education Statistics, *Digest of Education Statistics* (Washington, D.C., 1980, 1982, 1983).

will look at which women went to college from the Civil War to World War I and at the various supports some had and others devised to gain the prized liberal arts education.[2]

The early females who contended for places in collegiate institutions wanted that education passionately. But they needed encouragement at a time when their objective defied convention. Nothing was more crucial among the factors accelerating women's advance into academic institutions than family support. Ordinarily the aspiring young woman had to take the initiative with the family in negotiating her educational future: her parents were unlikely to pressure her to continue her schooling. The decision was a major one in most families. Assent depended on available financial resources and recognition of the value of a college education for the particular daughter. It was assumed unquestioningly that once permission was granted, a daughter would attend the school of her parents' choice. In some cases, parents had the money but did not want a girl to go to college; others with a strong interest in educating their daughter simply could not afford to send her or could not spare her from the home.

For the poorest Americans, college was out of the question and beyond expectation. Yet the availability of money did not make college a given in families that discounted either the intellectual or economic ad-

TABLE 3

College Women as a Percentage of Young Women in
the United States, 1870–1980*

Year	College women compared to 18–21-year-old women	College women compared to 18–24-year-old women
1870	0.7	—
1880	1.9	—
1890	2.2	—
1900	2.8	—
1910	3.8	—
1920	7.6	—
1930	10.5	5.7
1940	12.2	7.1
1950	17.9	9.9
1960	—	15.4
1970	—	23.5
1975	—	27.7
1980	—	37.9

Sources: Mabel Newcomer, *A Century of Higher Education for American Women* (New York, 1959), 46. U.S. Bureau of the Census, National Center for Education Statistics, *Digest of Education Statistics*, 1962, 1971, 1976, 1982.

*Mabel Newcomer in computing percentages for the years 1870–1950, assumed that the overwhelming majority of college women were between eighteen and twenty-one years of age. In fact, while the majority of college women in the mid- and late-twentieth century were between these ages, almost an equal proportion were outside this age category (for example, in 1980, 34.3 percent of college students were twenty-five or older—most of these, women). In order to bring Newcomer's table more in line with the actual situation, I have adjusted the age group by which we define "college women" to include eighteen- to twenty-four-year-olds, believing that this cohort better represents the bulk of female enrollments.

vantages for their daughters. The established eastern elites—Boston Brahmins, Philadelphia Main Liners, and Hudson Valley New Yorkers—preferred to educate daughters privately at home, in boarding school, and through travel abroad. New rich millionaires obsessed with making good marriages for their daughters imitated the patterns of the older families, dismissing college as preparation for women who had no option but to be schoolteachers. Both sets of families prepared daughters for a life of leisure, not work.

The female collegians, instead, came from a range of families within the broad and expanding middle class. Heads of these families included those in the professions (doctors, ministers, lawyers, professors, and teachers), those in business (manufacturers, proprietors, and tradesmen), and still others in agriculture. What distinguished a large proportion of the fathers was their economic and social mobility; they were achievers in professional and business enterprises. Often brought up in the antebellum tradition of intellectual and social reform, they viewed college education for both sexes as the path to a fuller life, intellectually, socially, and economically. Thus, parents in certain kinds of families were increasingly receptive to the female college experiment, and some were determined to make it available to ambitious daughters.

Among interested parents, it was easier for some than for others to afford this undertaking. An Association of Collegiate Alumnae study of 3,636 women who graduated from 22 colleges between 1869 and 1898 documents family income levels for female graduates. At a time when the average income for a U.S. family of four increased from $680 in 1869 to $830 in 1890, the average annual income of the families of these college graduates was $2,042. Yet this should not obscure the fact that for most of these families, financing a college education was a difficult task. More than 34 percent of the women surveyed were from families whose annual incomes were below $1,200. These families were not the poorest members of American society, nor were they the wealthiest; only 7.3 percent came from families with incomes over $10,000 a year.[3]

Paying for college took extensive planning except for the most affluent. On the average in 1890, teachers earned $250 per year, ministers $900, physicians $1,200. Male college professors earned $1,200–1,500 in 1905. To any of these, the $350 (tuition, room, and board) required annually to send a girl to Wellesley College was hardly affordable.[4]

Many factors, including the tuition and locality of the school as well as the income and situation of the family, affected women's efforts to reach college. Institutional costs varied greatly. Tuition at the University of Illinois in 1868 was $20; at Boston University in 1873 it was $60. Was the school a public one with low tuition ($30), like Michigan, or a private one like Smith, where tuition was $100 in 1905? College expenses rose over this period. By 1908, Mount Holyoke charged $350 a year for tuition and board, and by 1917 Cornell students paid $150. Tuitions also varied by region; though expensive schools were found in every section of the country, more of the costly ones were in the Northeast. Throughout this period most families cut costs by sending their children to schools near home or in the same state, eliminating or at least reducing expenses for room, board, and transportation. As in the 1980s, sending a girl to school meant making choices: choices as to what would be given up, how much money would be saved, what school it would be, and what standard of living parents and students would enjoy.[5]

Willing parents managed in a myriad of ways to provide college educations for their daughters. Income and cost figures alone do not convey how they did this. Occasionally assistance from an interested relative, family friend, or local patron in the community substituted for the parents' support and enabled young people to obtain a college education. An aunt subsidized the daughter of Elizabeth Cady and Henry Stanton at Vassar (though the girl, Harriet, preferred Cornell). In other families, the problems of dependent relatives highlighted the importance of collegiate training. Although William Breckinridge, lawyer and onetime congressman, earned more than $5,000 a year in the 1880s, he was burdened with responsibilities for the many members of his large southern family. He wanted daughter Sophonisba to attend Wellesley where he expected her to prepare to be a self-supporting adult.[6]

In established families, economic reverses sometimes operated to allow a daughter to go in new academic directions. The failure of Montgomery Hamilton's wholesale grocery partnership in 1885 confirmed for his wife and four daughters the value of economic independence achieved through academic and professional training. Michigan-trained Alice became a doctor, Bryn Mawr graduates Edith and Margaret became educators, and Nora found her metier as an artist. When Alice Duer's banker-father lost his fortune in the 1893 economic depression, he granted her request to enter Barnard College (with the help of a scholarship). Even successful fathers like Solomon Comstock (a railroad lawyer) and William Moller, (a hardware retailer) justified their daughters' educations as investments in case of financial crises. Ada L. Comstock became a college president, and Lillian Moller (Gilbreth) a pioneer industrial engineer.[7]

These and other parents increasingly identified with their daughters' quest for intellectual as well as economic independence. In the vanguard of collegiate women, families of "educated ancestry" were a distinctive element: fathers were often college or professionally educated and mothers academy graduates. Some mothers had taught school before marriage and instilled the habit of family reading. One or both parents might have been social reformers, former abolitionists, and women's rights proponents. For such parents, education approximated a religion, a means toward the improvement of self and society. For many of their daughters and sons, college became a logical step in their intellectual and social advancement. There was no question that Edith and Grace Abbott were headed for college in the 1890s. Their Quaker mother, Elizabeth Griffin Abbott, a graduate of Rockford Seminary and Lombard University in Illinois, had been a school principal and an advocate of abolition and women's rights. Their father, public-minded lawyer Othman Abbott, onetime lieutenant governor of Nebraska, shared his wife's feminist ideals. Although the combined effects of a Nebraska drought and the depression of 1893 delayed Edith's entrance to college, she received her A.B. from the University of Nebraska in 1901. In the interval she had taught at a high school and studied during the summers.[8]

A rarity even among intellectual families, Marion Talbot was trained from infancy to be a candidate for the female collegiate experience. Father Israel Tisdale Talbot, a Harvard graduate, homeopathic doctor, and the first dean of the School of Medicine at Boston University, and mother Emily Fairbanks Talbot, a former schoolteacher and health reformer, both worked actively for the higher education of Boston women. Young Marion, prepared at home and at school, entered Boston University in the 1870s and fulfilled her mother's dreams. She became not only a college woman, but an influential educator as dean of women at the University of Chicago.[9]

Some daughters of educated families had an easier time than others in gaining permission. Two famous examples, those of Florence Kelley (social analyst) and M. Carey Thomas (college president), provide different versions of the family's role in a daughter's decision. Both the Kelleys and the Thomases were well-to-do, practicing Quakers. Older women in these families had already exhibited strength and formidable social convictions. Florence's grandmother, Sarah Pugh, a friend of women's rights leader Lucretia Mott, taught school until she was fifty, then retired to devote herself to abolition; the family physician was the pioneer Dr. Hannah Longshore, already mentioned in chapter three. Young Florence Kelley read the works of Channing and Emerson in her father's library. He, William "Pig-Iron" Kelley, was a self-made man who sent his sons to the University of Pennsylvania, and as a supporter of women's rights, he took pride in Florence's entering Cornell in 1876.[10]

In contrast, M. Carey Thomas had difficulty getting permission from her affluent father, a Johns Hopkins trustee who was committed to higher education for men. "Minnie," however, had strong, self-reliant relatives in her mother and her aunt, the preacher Hannah Whitall Smith. As an adolescent, Minnie had long dreamed of going to Vassar. But her boarding school teacher Jenny Slocum told her to aim for Cornell, the better school. Although Minnie's father resisted the initial pleading of his daughter, after much weeping by mother and daughter, he gave in. Both parents accompanied the young woman to Cornell for her entrance examinations. She recorded in her diary that "last night [father] said to me, 'Well, Minnie, I am proud of thee, but this university is an awful place to swallow thee up.' " Thomas's father thus revealed his deep involvement with his daughter's education.[11]

The influence of mothers extended beyond convincing obdurate fathers to relent. Mothers' encouragement and confidence helped daughters to pursue their collegiate interests. A mother's support might relate to her own difficult life or thwarted ambitions. Some had been widowed early, and others had endured marriages to weak men and wanted better lives for their daughters. Willa Cather's mother headed a family that moved from Virginia to Nebraska to overcome economic reverses. Willa adored her unsuccessful father, but it was her mother who insisted that this talented young woman and future novelist enter the University of Nebraska in 1891. Similarly in the 1880s and 1890s, the widowed mothers of Virginia Gildersleeve (Barnard dean), Vida Scudder (Wellesley professor), Hilda Smith (Bryn Mawr dean), Mary Austin (writer), and Elizabeth Wallace (Chicago professor of English) pushed their sometimes hesitant daughters into college. Many of these widows, living on fixed or declining incomes, realized the economic value of an education.[12]

In the earlier part of the period more of these mothers were academy graduates; by the latter part some were themselves college graduates who had married and raised daughters. Flavia Camp (Canfield), a student at Wisconsin in the 1860s, approved when her daughter, future writer Dorothy Canfield (Fisher), entered Ohio State University, from which she graduated in 1899. The daughters of Beatrice Fulton, an 1882 Vassar graduate, attended the same school; one is better known as Ruth Benedict, the anthropologist. The numbers of mothers and daughters with common dedication to collegiate education increased over the period from 1870 to 1920.[13]

Sisters in educated families provided a source of support to each other. Within a family one sister might start the younger ones on the college trail; Jane Addams's three older sisters preceded her to Rockford Seminary. Yet not all sisters followed each other to college; many chose to stay at home. At a time when there was no pressure to attend, parents were comforted to have some daughters remain with them. These siblings admired their sister the college woman and rejoiced at her accomplishments but carried the domestic responsibilities she had left.[14]

Farm daughters formed another contingent of the first college women. Their families viewed education as a way out of the constrictions, isolation, and poverty of rural life. It was not always easy for farm families to part with these daughters any more than it was with sons, but farming students came to college in steady proportions during the period. An 1898 survey by Charles Kendall Adams, president of Wisconsin, found that almost 22 percent of the students at the Colleges of Letters and Science and Engineering were children of farmers. A similar poll conducted at Michigan in 1902 revealed the same proportion of farmers among the parents of students. Economic risks and the low social prestige of farming motivated many sons to gain university training in the professions of law and medicine. The goals for women were not as clearly defined, but they too sought educational alternatives to life on the homestead. Acquiring a college education proved a long and arduous process for students who had to take time off to earn money through teaching or other employment. It took Jenny Field, an 1879 graduate, ten years to complete her degree at Wisconsin because of several interruptions of schoolteaching to meet her expenses. She was valedictorian, a popular member of her class, and a future leader in the Association of Collegiate Alumnae.[15]

Alice Freeman (Palmer) provides another example of struggle and achievement in a "middling" family. Alice's father had left farming in New York State and was studying medicine. It was hard for his wife, a former schoolteacher, to make ends meet. Alice's request to attend college surprised her parents. They initially resisted, until Alice convinced them that she would repay her debts to them and see her brothers and sisters through college. Both parents then became very interested in Alice's education and passed up nearby schools to send her to the Univesity of Michigan in 1872. Alice became president of Wellesley in 1882.[16]

Although some farm women had the psychological support of parents, others did not. Two who rebelled against their stubborn fathers' opposition were Carrie Lane (Chapman Catt) and Anna Howard Shaw, both future suffrage leaders. Carrie Lane fought to be allowed to attend high school in a town away from the family farm and later, stimulated by her teachers, continued at Iowa State College, earning her way, still without parental approval. Anna Howard Shaw entered Albion College at age twenty-six with the encouragement of her former high school principal but despite her family's opposition. She subsequently became the only female to graduate in her class at the Boston University divinity school (1878) and from the medical school (1886) as well.[17]

Farm women who did not acquire a college education often understood the value of it. As twenty-five-year-old Rena Rietveld (Verduin), an unmarried Dutch immigrant with only a fifth-grade education, told a debating society in 1907: "I did not get up here to show how much I know, but how little I know, and so try to prove that women should have higher education. Through an education, girls are enabled to become self-supporting and acquainted with the ways of the world. Through an education girls learn to earn a livelihood and are not so liable to throw themselves away in marriage on some worthless man." And a Tennessee farm woman in 1915 called for female education as "the first thing needed, education of every kind. Not simply agricultural education . . . I mean the education that unfastens doors and opens up vistas; the educa-

tion that includes travel, college, acquaintance with people of culture;
the education that makes one forget the drudgery of today in the hope
of tomorrow."[18]

For the more fortunate rural woman and others, an important source
of inspiration and psychological support came from teachers. Some
young women, native white as well as black and daughters of foreign-
born, first heard of college possibilities from an instructor. A college-
educated high school teacher increasingly directed students to her alma
mater. Instructors who recognized intellectual promise inspired more
students to continue their education than we shall ever know.

Teachers also served as models of independence for women whose
families either could not afford a college education or were unwilling to
provide it. Even more than in the first half of the nineteenth century,
schoolteaching offered employment opportunities for women in the
burgeoning high schools. Women (as well as men) who earned their way
through college by teaching tended to be past adolescence, because of
frequent interruptions in their formal education. It was not uncommon
for women in their twenties and thirties to enroll at new instititions,
where there was no established clientele. In the 1870s and 1880s
Wellesley and Smith had such contingents. At Stanford, also, the first
women were generally more mature: only one-third (34 percent) of the
female students between 1891 and 1900 were below age twenty. But, as
institutions became better established and had more applicants, admissions policies shifted so as to favor younger undergraduates. In Stanford's second decade (1901–1910), teenagers comprised slightly over
half the female student body. A similar trend occurred at the University
of Chicago and many other institutions. At Radcliffe the average age of
women graduates in 1890–1900 was twenty-nine, but in the 1920s the
graduating age dropped to a little over twenty-one and a half. At most
institutions irregularities in age patterns of undergraduates virtually disappeared in the second and third decades of the twentieth century.[19]

Although the age of self-supporting college women declined over the
period, the acceptability of working one's way through college increased
at all institutions. Deans' reports and college guides implied that at both
public and private schools—for example, the universities of California,
Minnesota, Wisconsin, and Iowa; Northwestern, Chicago, and Boston
University—the numbers of women making personal contributions to
their support grew between 1900 and 1919. Dean Lucy Stebbins of the
University of California was one educator calling attention to the needs
of "self-help" women.[20]

While some women from more comfortable families helped out by
earning pocket money, other supported themselves completely. One
Minnesota girl earned her way by washing dishes. Her accounts show

that she spent $22.75 in 1904 and went home with $1.10 surplus. Clara Beyer, daughter of a Danish immigrant, showed how far intelligence and energy could carry a student. At California, Berkeley in 1915, she worked in canneries, packed fruit, and waitressed for her room and board. She received both her B.A. and M.A. and went on to become a social analyst in the federal government. Deans, impressed with students' contributions small and large, insisted that there was no stigma attached to employment during college. Thus far we lack sufficient student voices to test the claim.[21]

Although public attitudes toward paid work for students were mixed, undergraduates increasingly sought termtime jobs. Expensive private women's institutions like Wellesley and Smith publicized the fact that women could earn their way through their schools. After 1910, many colleges established appointment bureaus for those seeking jobs during the school year and summers, as well as after graduation.

Still, the women who worked during college were overshadowed by the presence of those that did not have to. A significant shift in attitudes toward college-going was under way among wealthier families. In the economic prosperity of the decades preceding World War I, upper-middle-class parents found college a convenient parking place for adolescent daughters; only the old elites continued to keep their daughters out. Well-to-do mothers and fathers often insisted that a daughter go to their alma mater, be it a state college or private university. Thus both private and public institutions had increasingly affluent student bodies.[22]

The predominance of moneyed collegians concerned educators on all campuses. Administrators, especially at expensive schools, worried that these institutions were becoming havens for the privileged. In an effort to attract poorer students, they analyzed undergraduate budgets and published their findings. In 1906–07 the annual budgets of Wellesley women ranged from $500 to over $1,200. No woman there could manage on less than $350 annually. In 1915 Smith students' budgets varied from $350 to $1,850 a year, whereas in 1916–17 Berkeley women spent between $91.98 and $495 for college expenses.[23]

The focus on student budgets reflected a general interest in the financing of college education. In 1917 deans at California, Berkeley, and Smith College emphasized the need for more financial support for students. No college woman (or man) could count on scholarships or loans. The idea of financial aid for all who qualify did not exist. Education between 1870 and 1920 was a privilege for the fortunate or a reward to be earned through one's own efforts.[24]

The limited institutional support reflected the historical evolution. The small colonial colleges had helped a few poor scholars, who thus be-

came rare models of Jefferson's republican ideal that every man should
have the opportunity to develop his natural talents, whatever his social
and economic origins. The growth of public education in the first half of
the nineteenth century provided an opportunity to apply and strengthened the egalitarian belief that industrious women as well as men should
have access to appropriate education at the polity's expense. But educators and institutions had different views on how to apply the democratic
ideal to education. At the outset, educators construed this principle narrowly, fostering the talents of young men with whom they identified.
Colleges did not have sufficient funds to look beyond familiar types and
thus did little to open the way for many able individuals, men and
women.[25]

In addition to institutional policies, there were other obstacles in
financing female education. Raising scholarship money for women was
even more difficult than for men since not all publics were persuaded of
the value of educating females. Neither the newly established women's
colleges nor the coeducational schools could afford to be generous with
their limited funds. Exceptional institutions like Boston University in the
1870s and the University of Chicago in the 1890s opened with equal
amounts of money available to both sexes, but in general, more scholarships were available to men than to women. In 1906, there were two
hundred scholarships for men at Tulane and nine for women at its female coordinate Sophie Newcomb. As late as 1918–19, Stanford had
only three scholarships open to women.[26]

The relatively few women who did receive aid were usually chosen by
the president or dean of the college. Donors also might set the criteria
and even select the recipient. Most colleges, though nonsectarian, had
associations with specific denominations. At Bryn Mawr twelve original
awards were reserved for members of the Society of Friends. Ministers'
daughters frequently received awards at Wellesley and Mount Holyoke.
Missionaries' daughters paid reduced tuition. Scholarships were customarily given to students who seemed especially deserving to educators or
belonged to a particular group providing the money. At Wisconsin the
John A. Johnson scholarships (established in 1876), open to men and
women, were reserved for students of Scandinavian origin, and initially
recipients had to speak one of the Scandinavian languages fluently. The
scholarship carried a grant of $50 for each academic year, and it was ex-
pected that the recipient would repay the money when he or she could
afford to.[27]

The Scandinavian donation followed the native tradition of private
aid. In the older parts of the country, voluntary beneficiary societies had
earlier in the century provided small loans to male students not sufficiently financed by other sources. Women's clubs in many social and eth-

nic groups continued the pattern of extending loans and scholarships to promising female students of their kind. Notable among these was the Massachusetts Society for the University Education of Women (MSUEW), started by friends of Boston University. Shortly before World War I another group of noncollege Bostonians established the Women's Scholarship Association and raised their first money to create a loan fund for Jewish girls at Radcliffe. The money such groups could provide was small, for their members had little themselves.

These women's organizations were careful with their money. The MSUEW made loans only to women who had proven themselves worthy of such funds, and "not for the comforts of life but to maintain existence. Applicants frequently live in the humblest way, cooking their own meals, teaching night schools, copying, working in restaurants and stores, or in a dozen ways that a determined girl can find." With this frugal attitude, the MSUEW assisted ninety-five young women at various New England colleges between 1877 and 1897. Before long, female undergraduates and alumnae also formed societies to reduce the burdens of their self-supporting classmates. Student aid societies made gifts, such as beds, as well as loans to reduce residential costs. As these societies acquired additional funds, they proved more flexible and generous than the earlier beneficiary ones.[28]

At the institutional level, the idea of providing generous scholarships to ease the way for students of limited means developed slowly. No scholarship was sufficient to allow a student without other support to attend college. In 1891 Alice Hayes, a writer in *The North American Review*, attacked the social inequalities in the university system. She published the results of her survey of the "pecuniary aid" available to female students at leading colleges, including Boston, Cornell, California, Kansas, Michigan, Syracuse, Wesleyan, Wisconsin, Bryn Mawr, Smith, Vassar, Wellesley, and the "Harvard Annex." The answer to the question posed in her study "Can a Poor Girl Go to College?" was emphatically no. Hayes found that the sums given were so small that recipients had to be students "who have almost adequate private resources."[29]

The usual scholarship recipient was unlikely to become very comfortable on the small sums provided. A rare answer to Hayes's call for scholarships was the announcement by the *Ladies Home Journal* in March 1890 of a contest that offered a four-year college education at Vassar, Wellesley, or Smith, all expenses paid, to the girl who sold the most subscriptions (over a thousand) for the magazine. The *Journal*, taking note of the "thousands of mothers and fathers" who desired a college education for their daughters, declared that although there were a "thousand and one advantages which a college education means for a girl," often "the desire is there, but not the means."[30]

The sparseness of scholarship awards reflected in part administrators' ambivalence toward financial aid. Was the scholarship a form of charity or an award of honor? Would the recipient become spoiled and feel freer not to study? Common wisdom held that any worthy indigent person should have to struggle to get ahead and not have life made too easy. Like other educators, Vassar professor Maria Mitchell favored loans over scholarships, so that students would cultivate "the habit of earning money."[31]

Few scholarship donors had both the resources and breadth of vision of former schoolteacher Phoebe Apperson Hearst. In 1891, in contrast to the New England do-gooders who collected small sums and distributed them with Yankee frugality, she gave the University of California $1,500 for "worthy young women and needy." In 1895 there were more than fifty applicants. Accordingly, the committee on scholarships asked her to reduce the amount per student from $300 to $200; but she refused, saying that she felt that "three hundred dollars is quite enough to pay a girl's living expenses, pay for books, etc. The idea was to give it to those who could not possibly go the University without this fund, and if we are to make it necessary for them to secure part of the amount, we might be debarring some of the most deserving." Thus Mrs. Hearst extended the range of scholarship recipients to include those who had no resources.[32]

Understandably, schools were reluctant to take risks with limited funds and preferred to offer aid to those who had already proved themselves academically. As a Smith College dean wrote: "On one point we are all agreed, and that is the necessity of offering aid only to those students who are making a fair record in their classes. It would be of no service to the college or to the individual to use funds to keep here students who are mentally unequal to the demands of college." The issue of scholarships for freshmen presented administrators with difficult choices. On the one hand, they recognized that scholarship awards to freshmen could bring to college "students of ability who might otherwise never have had the courage to come." On the other hand, they realized that a grant to an untried freshman deprived a qualified upper-class student of needed support. On the whole, administrators made conservative judgments and excluded freshmen from scholarship competition, thereby eliminating some of the neediest applicants. By 1920, however, some schools had modified this practice.[33]

Always the demand for scholarships outstripped their availability. Students saw loans as a useful alternative. In 1915 a writer for the Association of Collegiate Alumnae noted that more women were borrowing money, motivated by the sense that investment in a college education was worth a struggle, whatever the cost. There was greater recognition of the need for scholarships and loans by the end of the period, and the availability of both improved steadily. Scholarships remained small, but by 1920 some schools had a few special grants that covered the entire tuition. Institutions that made awards to 6 percent of their students in 1900 advanced to aid between 20 and 25 percent by 1920. Although these increases were encouraging, they seem insignificant compared with financial aid in the 1980s, when schools help 60 to 70 percent of their students. By later standards, support for both females and males in the early 1900s was low at all types of institutions. Even the oldest schools were not sufficiently endowed to extend funding further. Not until the federal government made a commitment to higher education would colleges be able to seek out undiscovered talent among poor Americans.[34]

Although many American youth of the early 1900s had no sense of the growing educational possibilities, individuals from a widening range of groups found their way to college. They too might have been held back by financial considerations or social prejudice, but they were not. The expanding college population numbered more students from ethnically and racially diverse groups: these newcomers were of varied economic means, from middling to well-to-do. They might be daughters of proprietors, shopkeepers, artisans, doctors, lawyers, manufacturers, or farmers. The sons often entered first, but the daughters were never far behind. They, like the first collegians, frequently came from socially mobile families. The mothers or fathers might lack schooling, but they placed extraordinary faith in it for their children.[35]

Again, for newer collegians, as for those of earlier generations, decisions regarding their education involved the whole family. Novelist Fannie Hurst's Bavarian-born parents refused their daughter's request to attend Vassar or Smith and sent her to nearby Washington University in St. Louis so that she could live at home. It was an elementary schoolteacher in Boston, who persuaded Israel Antin to keep his precocious daughter Mary in school rather than pull her out to work in a factory. Antin later wrote of her childhood in *From Plotzk to Boston* (1899). In these instances, as in others, young women had to have ability and personal drive, as well as a little luck, to acquire a college education.[36]

Daughters of immigrants pioneered as firsts in their families whether they funded their own college education or had parental support. These women stood as models of possibility for others of similar background. One young woman of Bohemian parentage, a graduate of a state university, had her picture in Emily Balch's study *Our Slavic Fellow Citizens*. This farmer's daughter was ahead of the large number of families who would not gain a "fair chance of education and advance" until the next generation. Similarly, the autobiographical writings of Mary Antin and Anzia Yezierska inspired many unknown women.[37]

More and more in the first decades of the twentieth century, the daughters of the foreign-born were coming to college. A dean's report at Boston University in 1907 applauded scholarship applicants from the "newer elements in the population" who demonstrated as much "un-selfishness and heroism" as the "scions of earlier New England stock." The Immigration Commission's report of 1911 found that of all female students at sixty-three colleges across the country, 23.8 percent had im-migrant parents, only slightly lower than the percentage for men (25.8).[38]

The same report noted that blacks, another group on the academic fringe, comprised only 0.3 percent of the female student population. This abysmally low figure reveals how difficult it was for black women to enter a liberal arts college. Because most of their parents were too poor, and because most schools did not want them, fewer black women gained any higher education. Those that did usually received teacher or indus-trial training. Black colleges had few women in the liberal arts course throughout the period. In 1892 Fisk enrolled twelve women, but Howard University had none. The black college woman was the excep-tion of exceptions. It was the traditional pattern of self-support through schoolteaching and domestic employment that eventually brought her into the college ranks. A distinguished black educator, Anna Julia Cooper, exemplified this pattern. After marriage and divorce, she earned her Oberlin B.A. in 1884 and took her master's in 1887. Cooper estimated that in 1891 there were thirty black college women in the United States. In a feminist tone, she urged that "money be raised and scholarships be founded in our colleges and universities for self-supporting worthy young women, to offset and balance the aid that can always be found for boys who will take theology."[39]

Cooper's alma mater, Oberlin, had led the way from the 1860s, graduating the first black women: Mary Jane Patterson in 1862, Fanny Jackson (Coppin) in 1865, and Mary Church (Terrell) in 1884, among others. From the turn of the century, Wellesley, Smith, and Radcliffe had a few black graduates. Other predominantly white institutions like Vassar, Mount Holyoke, and Bryn Mawr, hardly welcomed black stu-dents. As a Mount Holyoke dean wrote privately in 1913: "We do not in-tend to receive negro students at Mount Holyoke College. . . . If a negro student were to present herself now, I hardly know what course would seem best, as we have a much larger percentage of southern girls than was the case a few years ago." One well-to-do black parent arranged with difficulty the admission of his daughter Jessie Fauset to Cornell in 1905. A Phi Beta Kappa graduate, Jessie later became a teacher, novelist, and editor. Black women who made it to college had to have significant fam-ily or teacher support to overcome strong social prejudice.[40]

Compared with the college population of the 1870s, that of the early twentieth century was diverse. In the nineteenth century going to college had been an unusual and complicated choice for native white women. By 1900 these female collegians were no longer regarded as social rebels. Aspiring outsiders from black and foreign-born families still found the route difficult, but they were building for later generations. Now collegiate education appealed to women of many backgrounds. While popular magazines featured the glamor of college life, guidebooks helped parents and daughters choose the right school. By World War I college was a very important option to provide a daughter with in some circles, and outside these circles, it was something to aspire to.[41]

S·I·X

Women and the
Modernizing of Liberal
Education, 1860–1920

Men cry out against women's extravagance and trifling, yet they are
the first to condemn the opening of paths to her: her education
will not necessarily prevent her from properly filling her sphere in
domestic life. If she knows fire burns, why bread rises, is it incompat-
ible with her making fires or good bread?

Josephine Lindley, *Echo* 1 (1871), in William W. Ferrier, *Origin and
Development of the University of California* (Berkeley, 1930), 332–33

Never having seen or met a college woman before becoming one
myself, the whole experience was a great adventure—like traveling
through a wonderful country which had never been described or
pictured to me.

Annie Jump Cannon, Wellesley, '84, quoted by Margaret Mayo,
Harvard Magazine 83 (1981), 34

Between 1860 and 1920, going to college became an accepted part of
growing up for women in certain social groups, as it was for men. Female collegians arrived in appreciable numbers at a pivotal time of modernization in higher learning. It was a period of great confusion and
creativity for colleges and universities trying to incorporate new fields of
knowledge into the study of liberal arts and sciences. Women and their
educators were uncertain about what defined a full liberal arts education
as well as what should be the ultimate goals of a liberally educated
woman. Even though women and men shared common elements in this
liberal education, the female academic experience evolved with important differences.

In this chapter we will consider the changing curriculum and its impact on women as undergraduates. Several questions are pertinent:
What did women study? How did they respond to the courses? How did
the female presence affect the modernization of liberal education? And

to what extent did academic studies encourage women's sense of professional purpose? We explore these knotty questions in two contexts: the formal course curriculum and the exposure of students to intellectual issues confronting the larger society.

Although considerable disagreements emerged about what was essential for female students, defining a liberal arts education for men had already become a problematic issue. As we have seen, earlier in the century the classical curriculum (Greek, Latin, mathematics, philosophy, science, and English) had come under attack from faculty and students. In the 1860s and 1870s scientific studies of evolution, beginning with Charles Darwin's *Origin of the Species* (1859), further strained the limits of the traditional course of study. Innovative educators intent upon enlarging the curriculum had to determine what the essential elements should be in a modern liberal education. In an expanded curriculum, what would be the criteria to mark an educated man or woman?[1]

During this crisis of curricular redefinition, students were introduced to a widening range of subjects that became part of a greatly enlarged liberal arts study. By 1900 everything, from manual labor and calisthenics to engineering and home economics, competed with classics, philosophy, and sociology in the academic marketplace and vied for recognition as legitimate subjects in a liberal education. Between 1870 and 1915, at various schools, both monumental and incremental changes were made in the college curriculum. Under Charles Eliot's leadership, Harvard's approach was the most radical, gradually allowing students to choose all courses under the elective system, with only English composition required. Very few colleges went as far as that, though Stanford, Columbia, Indiana, and Cornell came close. Elsewhere, the pattern of discarding the old curriculum in favor of a modified elective program took hold more slowly.[2]

In theory, electives had two purpooses. First, they were to stimulate professors to conduct original investigation and to teach new subjects; second, to encourage students to take initiative in developing their own interests. Eliot assumed that secondary schools would train students properly so that they could profit from intellectual independence at college. In reality, however, students were generally not well prepared. But colleges soon permitted a measure of electives for other reasons.[3]

During the first part of this period, between 1860 and 1900, colleges could not be too choosy in their admissions because of a relative scarcity of male or female applicants. Even after 1900, when greater numbers applied, competition still caused them to admit many with varying levels of preparation and to offer greater flexibility in academic programs.

Electives became the means by which colleges accommodated the students' diverse academic needs, some of which related to their level of preparation, others to their future expectations. Those who knew they must prepare to earn a living selected courses largely on the basis of anticipated post-college employment. Some male youths resisted studying Greek or Latin since they did not intend to become lawyers or ministers.

The early women's colleges, which began before the elective principle became widely accepted, were reluctant to dispense with the classical curriculum. As Mabel Newcomer has pointed out, they rationalized that female educability must first be tested in the traditional course of study. In addition, for a while their faculties could not offer the range of courses provided at established men's colleges and growing research universities. Thus women's colleges approached curricular decisions cautiously. Yet the frequency with which exceptions were made resulted in the awarding of different kinds of degrees to certify what level of study had been reached. The variety of undergraduate degrees, from A.B. to B.S. to Ph.B. (bachelor of arts to bachelor of science to bachelor of philosophy), indicated that students had completed different programs; in some Greek or Latin might be minimal or even nonexistent. Such programs at first allowed little room for electives, though modern languages were sometimes permitted as substitutes for ancient ones.[4]

Starting later, in 1884, Bryn Mawr, more innovative from its opening, adopted the Johns Hopkins Group Plan, which permitted a judicious use of electives. The plan had four elements: a core of required courses, a choice of sequences comprising a major area of study, a limited choice of electives for a distribution requirement, and finally a few completely free electives. The majors usually combined two or more subjects, such as history and political science, or Greek and Latin. Most liberal arts colleges in the 1890s offered courses of study according to group plans. By 1910 the most advanced white women's colleges in the South, including Salem, Judson, Wesleyan, Sophie Newcomb, Goucher, Agnes Scott, and Randolph-Macon Women's College, had also reached this level of curricular development.[5]

Women's academic options at coeducational colleges varied greatly in this period. As we have noted, coeducational religious colleges in the early years did not necessarily offer the same instruction to men and women; now institutions faced more complex decisions about the joint instruction of the sexes. Liberal arts undergraduate programs, whether in the evangelical schools or the university colleges, had to compete with professional schools in attracting men, who often bypassed the undergraduate degree. Curriculum became the battleground for faculty contests over student enrollments.

Women were not seen as an asset in this competition for male students. Although they demonstrated excellence in every field, their predominance in certain courses precipitated outcries against the "feminization" of the disciplines involved. Classics professors lacking large male enrollments were dismayed at the large proportion of female students in their field. In 1910 no one remembered that educators in the previous century thought women were incapable of learning Greek and Latin.

The concept of feminization expressed the judgment that unless men enrolled in a course or program in substantial numbers, the subject was devalued. When women rather than men chose English or modern languages, the notion of inherent sex tendencies was invented to explain the choices. Studies of electives and majors at both single-sex and coeducational institutions sometimes corroborated such differences by gender. In fact these patterns of selection did not rest on "sex tendencies" as claimed, but on the uses students could make of these studies and on personal interests. Generalization about inherent sex differences in course selection was based on simplistic impressions. In the early part of the period the limited electives could not prove any point. The programs varied from school to school and changed over the course of time. Terminology also confuses the later observer. At Wisconsin from 1875 to 1880, for example, students had three options: ancient classical course, general science, and modern classical course. The first had prerequisites in Latin and Greek and was least often chosen by women; the general science included English courses and was the most popular with women. Later, however, when the English and general science components were separated, more women than men chose the modern classical, which then offered the English course.[6]

Some reviews of male and female class enrollments showed similarity in course selections. Dean Marion Talbot's analysis of undergraduate preferences at the University of Chicago in 1902 indicated that the gender differences were popularly exaggerated and not what might have been expected. For example, more women than men took physiology courses; equal proportions of both sexes studied philosophy; and a surprisingly large percentage (16 percent) of the female undergraduates took mathematics beyond the required course, despite "the current statement that women have no aptitude for Mathematics." Similarly, at Boston University during the same period, male-female differences in some departments were slight; 9 percent and 4.3 percent of the women students chose mathematics and history respectively, as compared with 11.4 percent and 5.4 percent of the men. Evidently, the interests of men and women were sometimes closer to one another than was generally recognized.[7]

Students' choice of electives reflected not only vocational and personal interests, but intellectual experimenting. Both sexes were attracted to new viewpoints in the social science courses that replaced the old moral philosophy course in college after college. In place of this course that had covered religion, philosophy, and current events were courses in economics, sociology, philosophy, psychology, history, and government. From the 1890s on, at both women's colleges and coeducational colleges, a significant proportion of the courses students chose were in these developing fields of the social sciences. Some attributed this trend to women's interest in social problems and the new social work field in which such studies as economics and sociology were useful.[8]

The University of California enrollments provide an interesting case history indicative of the breadth of women's interests. The Berkeley data showed a preponderance of women in liberal arts programs but dominance of men in the professional schools and in departments like agriculture, commerce, mechanics, mining, civil engineering, and chemistry. Both sexes gravitated to fields that served vocational needs. Women could find employment most easily in teaching, which utilized their liberal arts courses; men had access to more varied employments (which they often preferred to schoolteaching). Although not every female student expected to support herself, many did, at least temporarily. A study of undergraduates at the University of Minnesota in 1912 showed both sexes equally certain of their vocational motives when they entered college. Professor Caroline Latimer at Goucher wrote perceptively of the value of electives for the young woman who knew that she must "in the near future look entirely to herself for support." The more certain a student was that she would teach, the more carefully she would select her courses to fit herself for that vocation. Alumna Helen Olin pointed out that women at Wisconsin found it advisable to prepare two specialties, like Latin and German, to ensure finding a job. Thus, women students choosing to study what interested them were often consciously seeking practical vocational training at the same time.[9]

Academic interests at women's colleges illustrate the weakness of the notion of sex tendencies. The issue of gender differences in course selection did not apply at these schools. Here students took as required, or selected when made optional, courses in all disciplines. The older women's colleges promoted the study of Greek, Latin, and mathematics but emphasized the importance of the sciences; thus, when electives were limited, all students had exposure to elementary sciences. Moreover, when students were allowed to choose electives, many continued in advanced science classes. Vassar statistics in the early part of the period show strength, not only in classics, but also in the sciences. These schools developed academic distinction in one or two of the natural sciences: astronomy and physics at Vassar; mathematics and geology at Bryn Mawr; chemistry and zoology at Mount Holyoke; botany and psychology at Wellesley; and anthropology at Barnard. Margaret Rossiter has shown that of 439 female scientists listed in the first three editions of *Men of Sci-*

ence (1906, 1910, 1921), a surprisingly large proportion—41 percent—graduated from women's colleges.[10]

Although this achievement in the sciences still held in the early twentieth century, elite women's colleges (like comparable schools for men) were increasingly emphasizing cultural studies. An important curricular development occurred in the burgeoning humanistic disciplines. At prestigious single-sex liberal arts colleges, some students devoted a large part of their four years of undergraudate study to courses associated with the liberal culture. Areas like literature, foreign languages, and fine arts had broad appeal at women's colleges as well as at comparable men's schools. Yet this change in the academic climate had different implications for women and men students. Obviously these humanistic studies did not deter men from making professional choices after college. Every male student knew that the liberal education started him on the path to a future in a profession or business or public life. What had always been an implicit expectation, the clear end to which this male education was the means, developed into open professionalism in this period. Yet for women, who now had a stake in the outcome of new approaches to liberal education, ambiguity prevailed. Liberal culture for women was held up as learning for its own sake, detached from professional motives. Most educators grappling with curricular problems had in mind the educated man; to them, the educated woman was an enigma. Her presence raised separate questions: Should her education be the same as that of a man? Why or why not? How did her abilities and interests compare with those of men? Conflicts over the purposes of liberal education for women imposed constraints and pressures on the woman student as to whether or not she should aspire to a profession. Beneath this ambiguity lay the assumption that women would eventually marry and bear children and thus "waste" advanced education.

Female collegians (unlike male) were caught between the attraction of using their education in professional ways and keeping in mind that a woman's usefulness was not equated with professionalism. Educators of women invoked the old seminary precept that liberal education would enable women to deal with any circumstances that life brought forth but was not intended to train them for any particular situation. Yet scientific developments in the increasingly industrialized society not only created new demands for the university training of professional men but generated needs in service fields that trained women could fill. Despite the emerging opportunities, women's progression in academic studies continued to reflect the divided sentiment about the goals of female education.

The persistent denial of the need for professionalism implied that college women who had the option should retreat into the private domestic sphere. Significantly, Mary Van Kleeck (Smith 1904), a social analyst who conducted a census of college women in 1915, criticized the eastern women's colleges for "disclaiming any intention to give professional or vocational training." Still more pointed, in 1918, Mabel L. Robinson's "Curriculum of the Woman's College," based on information from Radcliffe, Barnard, Wellesley, Smith, and Mount Holyoke (but not Bryn Mawr) concluded that, "in the efforts to realize the ideals of general culture and an all-round existence, the college girl dissipates her energies." Concerned that female students did not plan their studies with Eliot's "life-career motive" in mind, Robinson noted that women needed guidance in the selection of electives and exposure to vocational fields from the sophomore year on so that they could make intelligent choices.[11]

Yet even at these women's colleges, despite their avowed antiprofessionalism, the broadening curriculum, with its variety of electives, did at times provide vocational opportunities for female students. Faculty members at Wellesley occasionally introduced professionally oriented courses, in pedagogy and premedical studies, for example. In 1905 Barnard made its first preprofessional arrangement when it admitted for two years students who then transferred to Teachers College; later it permitted some students to take courses at Columbia's School of Journalism. Mount Holyoke introduced courses in both journalism and pedagogy. A sociology course at Bryn Mawr on charities and correction introduced a social workers' type of course that became common in the 1900s. At Wellesley president Caroline Hazard welcomed economics as a field of study, noting that "women have not had the business training their brothers have inherited, and now that women are called upon to take a more important place in the active world, it is most important that the usual business principles which are imbibed by men should be carefully instilled into the minds of girls." But she did not elaborate on the use to which women should put such training. In fact, only a rare educator like M. Carey Thomas steadfastly regarded liberal arts study for women as not only essential but also preliminary to graduate or professional training. Of Bryn Mawr women she declared, "Our failures only marry." Her vision for women paralleled that of Charles Eliot for men, and both were elitist.[12]

In part the inconsistent views of women's educators related to the fact that they aimed to meet the needs of different segments of the college population. In the late nineteenth century, what few women undergraduates there were, were serious, some with very strong, if vague, aspirations to do something important with their education. A larger segment consisted of earnest, hardworking individuals who expected to teach or intended to seek other employment. Later in the period, however, these types were joined by others who appeared to be adrift; often from well-to-do families, their presence on campuses baffled educators. Sizable numbers of such women students prompted some educators to conclude that there should be a female collegiate curriculum that prepared women for their future lives as wives, mothers, and homemakers.

Most institutions, both coeducational and women's colleges, included domestic studies as part of the female collegiate course. Only the oldest eastern women's colleges self-consciously avoided the issue. To them, such studies were a waste of the precious undergraduate years. Domestic science courses such as those being offered at Cornell and the University of Illinois in the 1880s constituted a step backward into the kitchen. But in the 1900s home economics gained a solid place as an academic offering.[13]

Ironically it was a Vassar graduate, Ellen Swallow (Richards), who impressed both educators and students with the scientific aspects of home economics. Richards, the first female graduate student in chemistry at the Massachusetts Institute of Technology, contributed to scientific work on nutrition and eventually developed the field of household sanitation. She became the center of a group of advocates who held the annual Lake Placid conferences on home economics starting in 1899; their efforts culminated in 1908 in the founding of the American Home Economics Association, of which Richards was the first president. Home economics included a diverse range of subject matter unified by the focus on the home; the various branches of the field were aspects of applied sciences based on the knowledge of chemistry and economics. Dean Marion Talbot (one of Richards's graduate students) founded the program at Chicago; in her report to the president in 1903, she predicted that "as soon as Home Economics can be developed so as to have real educational as well as practical value, it will be given a place among the new social sciences as honorable as that which Political Economy or the Science of Government occupies."[14]

Though Talbot's vision was not fully realized, home economics with its varied specializations became a popular subject at many colleges, from California, Illinois, Chicago, Wisconsin, and Cornell to Goucher and other southern schools, white and black. In 1916 Professor Alexis Lange at California argued pointedly that every college woman should learn home economics for "even the first degree, that of liberal arts, should be not only for fitness, but also for fitness for something." Judging by the development of home economics in many public and private coeducational institutions in the 1900s and 1910s, women students agreed. In the *Stanford Sequoia* for May 1909, an alumna presented the case for the college's preparing women for domesticity. "Homemaking," she said, would become "the business" of the majority of Stanford alumnae.

Their higher education demanded "household economics, sanitation, child culture, and a knowledge of the laws of organic life." Clearly the growth of home economics derived from the interest of students as well as of female and male professors who developed the curriculum in a variety of dimensions—scientific, social, economic, and domestic. Whether it was the main focus or an elective, it flourished as more students took it of their own volition.[15]

Significantly, despite its traditional associations with private homemaking, home economics became an important source of female employment. During World War I graduates of advanced programs rose in the labor force. In this era of increasing professionalism, home economics provided a new occupational specialty for high school teachers, urban social workers, and college professors. Among the many success stories, a particularly appealing one is that of Agnes Fay Morgan, daughter of Irish immigrants. She went to Vassar on a full scholarship from a private source, then transferred to the University of Chicago, receiving a B.S. in 1904, an M.S. the next year, and a Ph.D. in 1914. Home economics was one of the few fields in which professorships were often filled by women; Agnes Fay Morgan taught nutrition at the University of California.[16]

For all the constructive contributions of the field, however, opponents were justified in asserting that home economics, household administration, and domestic science were all terms which focused on education for housewifery. Isabel Bevier, herself a well-known professional in the field, ended her book *Home Economics in Education* (1924) with a reassurance that the evident exodus of women from the homes "is only a passing phase." She wrote: "The age-old instincts will bring the same woman back to the home . . . and give to the new home and through it to the nation's life moral sanity, mental poise, devotion to child and family life, and those spiritual elements which have ever constituted her best contribution."[17]

Despite the opportunities for academic employment in home economics, this option posed a genuine threat to female academics. Individuals were too often shunted into that department of their institutions rather than being allowed to assume faculty standing in the disciplines in which they were trained. The professional career of Florence Robinson illustrates the point well. Robinson, a Wisconsin graduate with a Ph.D. in American history, could get a job only in home economics at Beloit College. She never lost her bitterness, and in her will established a professorship in history at Wisconsin reserved for a woman. Robinson further specified that the designated professor could never serve tea at faculty functions. It was no coincidence that a study in 1911 showed that 60 percent of women professors in coeducational schools were in home economics.[18]

Another understandable concern of feminist educators was that home economics might draw women students away from other disciplines and slow the process of attaining educational and intellectual equality. Yet there was a demand for such programs, and they provided employment on a long-term as well as a short-term basis. The accomplishments of students and faculty in this field should not be denigrated; nor should students' choices be summarily criticized without a full appreciation of their reasons, both vocational and societal, for choosing home economics. Although on an elementary level home economics did focus on courses in cooking and sewing, at advanced levels innovative advocates stressed its social and scientific implications. In urban communities applications to nutrition and diet helped social workers dealing with poor, immigrant, and black families. Home economics had even more relevance for agricultural and farming communities. The Smith-Lever Act in 1914 made available appropriations for home economics extension courses.

Home economics (and other social sciences), in the hands of imaginative professors, foreshadowed women's studies courses. At the University of Chicago Sophonisba Breckinridge's course entitled "The Legal and Economic Position of Women" studied the roles of women in the family as well as in industry and the professions. Courses in economics, sociology, and anthropology could also focus on these themes. Emily Greene Balch's Wellesley course on consumerism compared the incomes and budgets of middle- and working-class women; the syllabus included Charlotte Perkins Gilman's feminist *Women and Economics*. At Goucher Dr. Lillian Welsh introduced public health and hygiene courses, and Professor Mary Williams gave a course on the history of the women's rights movement. A social economist at the University of Washington in 1911, Theresa McMahon, taught an array of courses on women and economics, including "Women in Business and Industry" and "Vocational Opportunities for Women in the Pacific Northwest." Moreover, her advocacy of unionism emphasized the needs of working women. These courses in several disciplines addressing issues of particular relevance to women transcended a narrowly domestic focus.[19]

Women, whether as students, teachers, or scholars, were a part of the intellectual and social processes that modernized higher education. Certainly the evolving academic curriculum would have been less rich without the female presence. Though a minority in the professorial ranks, some women scholars explored new ways of teaching and thinking in the humanities, the social sciences, and the sciences. Students' understanding of the liberal arts curriculum depended not only on the formal content of the courses but on their teachers' presentation as well. Women students absorbed faculty attitudes toward education of females and toward intellectual and social problems of the larger society. College teaching itself changed drastically over the period. The controlled dull recitation format was supplanted in part by lectures and group seminars, both of which made the classroom a forum for the ideas of the professor. Although students were still captive audiences, they found lectures preferable to sessions that required memorization. Furthermore, strictly academic learning represented only one dimension of liberal studies; the student was influenced as well by what she heard out of the classroom from professors and administrators. Educators involved in the intellectual and ethical crises of the era challenged students' perspectives on public issues. Equally important, faculty expectations for their female students could either strengthen or diminish a young woman's aspirations.

At the beginning of the period the professoriat itself was small and uneven in academic background. By the 1900s, however, faculty who had gained advanced training either in Europe or in the United States were transmitting their own intellectual excitement to students. Undergraduates' letters home conveyed enthusiasm generated by particular professors; in later recollections it was the personality or style of a favorite professor that had created lasting impressions. Among the faculty members admired were George Howison (philosophy) at California, Herbert Mills (economics) at Vassar, George Lyman Kittredge (English) at Radcliffe, John Dewey (psychology) at Chicago, Mary Calkins (psychology and philosophy) at Wellesley, Jessica Peixotto (economics) at California, Berkeley, and Margery Bailey (English) at Stanford. This small sampling suggests the popularity of English and the social science fields but does not distinguish between those professors who were histrionic lecturers and those who offered demanding courses. Both types had appeal for different students. At all institutions, courses in themselves ranged from the rigorous to the "snap course."[20]

For the fortunate student a faculty member might have profound impact, setting her on an intellectual course for life. Both male and female professors, whatever their principles on women's advancement, became mentors to the brilliant female. Some male professors gave scholarly guidance despite their general reservations about feminism. Franklin Giddings, who steered Emily Greene Balch into sociology at Bryn Mawr and later shaped Elsie Clews's graduate plans at Columbia, was the same man who stated in a baccalaureate sermon at Bryn Mawr that the social order demanded the subordination of women.[21]

But even though some men pushed individuals to achieve, others, like Woodrow Wilson at Bryn Mawr, were embarrassed to be teaching women. Of course, female students did not always know that they were not being taken seriously. At Smith College a young professsor joked with a female colleague about a student whose uncle had scolded her for not taking an American history course. Dr. Charles Hazen continued, "I didn't tell her that Uncle Tom was a brute to want a pretty girl like her to understand politics . . . but I wanted to." Occasionally, an educator's opinion of the inferior status of female students was made clear. One of Berkeley's most popular instructors, Professor Charles Gayley, asked the female coeds to drop his Great Books course so that the men "for whom the course had been specially designed" might feel more comfortable enrolling. Still, the women were not as naive as they may have appeared to professors who showed interest in male students and simply tolerated females. Lucy Salmon recalled that her classmates in the 1870s gained from professors who did not believe in them, not "inspiration," but rather "courage" to disprove the doubts.[22]

For some female students in both women's colleges and coeductional schools, the presence of female faculty had even greater impact. In fact, the faculty–student relationships among women seemed much stronger than among men. Especially in the residential women's colleges, female faculty were more accessible than in the coeducational schools, and more opportunity existed for informal communication between students and teachers not much older than themselves. Professors often had places at the same dining table as the undergraduates and invited favorites for tea. Aware of the many difficulties confronting aspiring females, women faculty took especial care to encourage talented girls in serious study.[23]

Maria Mitchell, professor of astronomy at Vassar, had extraordinary impact in urging students in the 1870s and 1880s not to let criticism swerve them from their scholarly course. Mitchell ultimately selected her successor, Mary Whiting, from among her students—and Whiting in turn selected hers. As Margaret Rossiter noted, Vassar's astronomy professors were all "students and grandstudents" of Maria Mitchell until 1932. Similarly, Florence Bascom, professor of geology at Bryn Mawr, selected as protégées Julia Gardner, Anna Isabel Jonas, and Eleanora Bliss Knopf, all of whom became distinguished geologists.[24]

Over the period the female community of undergraduates and professors at women's colleges offered a pattern that coeducational institutions imitated in part. Women administrators in the largely male milieus adapted the standard of the private women's colleges through the encouragement of separate group endeavors. Yet in one important respect the female faculty at women's schools were of limited inspiration as models for some female students, since it was only single academic women who had access to teaching posts at women's colleges. These institutions failed to provide a different model—that of a married woman professor. By contrast, the few faculty women who held posts in coeducational institutions were sometimes married and often combined teaching and student advising responsibilities as deans.[25]

Yet at coeducational schools most undergraduates did not question the overwhelming male dominance of faculties. When young men at Boston University in the 1880s expressed shock at the idea of having a "lady professor," female classmates responded that they were quite content with male professors. In 1894, however, an articulate Berkeley undergraduate, Katharine C. Felton, protested publicly the absence of women on the faculty after twenty-five years of coeducation: "It is not right . . . that one woman, simply because she is a woman, should be deprived of the opportunity of pursuing the student's life and of supporting herself at the same time." Felton asserted that the presence of female faculty would be "an incentive" affecting all students "indirectly."[26]

In the long run, students respected most the faculty members, both male and female, who forced them to do superior work. Some instructors inspired awe and others terror, but their standards became those of the students. After receiving Smith professor Mary Jordan's scathing criticisms, for example, they would not countenance sloppiness in their writing. Of course, such experiences were painful to vulnerable students still unsure of their abilities. At Michigan in 1875, Lucy Salmon, in a letter to her mother, despaired over her part in a debate in the American history class. In a panic over this public speaking ordeal, she was grateful for the first time that a long skirt hid her shaking knees. Yet she also understood the value of this exercise, and afterward as a professor perpetuated the practice at Vassar College, where for forty years she taught history seminars that shook up her students.[27]

The able student developing a critical mind through liberal studies utilized this training to weigh religious, social, and intellectual questions that impinged in or out of the classroom. Throughout the period, colleges gained a reputation as hotbeds of radicalism on one issue or another. Indeed, students were introduced to unsettling ideas—evolution, socialism, anarchism—and as a result, some questioned the most fundamental principles upon which they had been raised.

In the late nineteenth century it was not uncommon for college women, like men, to experience crises of religious faith, exacerbated by challenges from the new scientific thought. In the antebellum college, science had had an accepted place in the liberal arts curriculum, without posing a threat to religion. Studying botany, chemistry, or physics had not destroyed religious faith when the subjects taught were placed securely in God's universe. Darwinism, however, in defining man merely as a highly evolved organism, seemed to eliminate the spiritual element and obscure the influence of the Creator. Even before there were formal courses on evolution, students, like their professors, were discussing its meaning. They read the works of atheist Robert Ingersoll as well as popularized accounts of evolution by Edward Yeomans and others; Wisconsin's undergraduate newspaper, the *University Press*, even published excerpts from Darwin's *Descent of Man* as early as 1871 and republished pro-evolution articles from magazines like *Appleton's Journal.*[28]

College presidents and professors insisted that religion had a firm place in their schools. John Bascom at Wisconsin, David Starr Jordan at Stanford, and Harris Wilder at Smith presented reassuring versions of evolution. Along with John Fiske, who popularized the subject on the public lecture circuit, these teachers stressed the compatibility of Christianity and Darwinism. To some observers, by the 1900s, the popularity of these courses indicated that evolution was not a threat to faith; to others, the fears remained that science was assuming preeminence over religion in the colleges.[29]

To students reexamining their personal religious beliefs, college introduced a variety of speculative ideas which either produced the feared effect of leading students to abandon the family faith, or led eventually to a renewal of faith. Those who were already in rebellion against the religious indoctrination of their elders welcomed liberalizing approaches. Carrie Lane (Chapman Catt) found that at Iowa State Agricultural College in 1877 she was not alone in her thinking, and she, like her professors, chose to become an evolutionist. At Cornell in the 1880s M. Carey Thomas spurned the conservative Quakerism of her parents and later regarded herself as a rationalist Godwinian. Emily Balch at Bryn Mawr and Jane Addams at Rockford read widely and talked evolution with professors and friends, but each in her own independent way eventually affirmed her personal faith. Most students worked their way through the conflicts and accepted some form of religious belief, though not necessarily a traditional one.[30]

By the 1890s, as evolution gradually became comfortably incorporated into liberal Protestant thinking, students looked outward and invoked social ethics to give purpose to their lives. The "social question" more often than the religious one engrossed college women. Under the influence of some professors, they then asked whether the principles of laissez-faire and the survival of the fittest could suffice to maintain American democracy with its deepening divisions between rich and poor that resulted from industrial capitalism. A minority of professors, such as E. A. Ross at Stanford and Edward Bemis at Chicago, lost jobs for their public opposition to business monopoly. Meanwhile, Professors Emily Balch at Wellesley, Jessica Peixotto at California, and Theresa McMahon at Washington taught the "isms," from trade unionism and consumerism to socialism (not excluding Karl Marx's views). Still, in economics and sociology courses, as in courses on philosophy, aesthetics, English literature, and history, the aim remained to instill moral purpose.[31]

A Radcliffe student in Harvard professor Charles Eliot Norton's Dante course recalled "his precepts on the relation of learning to life." Implied or stated in this teaching was the quest for solutions to intellectual and social dilemmas of American society. For small groups of students and professors in the freest academic institutions, the aesthetic impulse provided yet another complement to religion or moralism as a guiding principle for the liberal education. A Wellesley graduate of 1908 remembered two concepts from her courses in economics and literature: the "altruistic" and the "aesthetic," both of which stayed with her for life.[32]

Religious faiths absorbed intellectual ideals from the secular ferment. Moreover, evangelical revivals petered out at colleges by the end of the nineteenth century. The public claim that students were being lost to traditional forms gained credence with student resistance to required chapel-going, among the young men first, but among women as well. Each college community took its stand on chapel attendance in accordance with the perceived wishes of its supporters. Universities like Cornell, Harvard, and Wisconsin were the first to remove the requirement, in the 1880s. Chicago, however, after making chapel optional, was forced to reinstate it (though only weekly); this rule lasted from 1896 to 1927. Similarly, for a longer time, other schools of evangelical origin, both coeducational and single-sex, retained compulsory chapel as well as bible study. Vassar, founded by Baptists, did not drop the chapel requirement until 1926. Although Wellesley made chapel voluntary in 1900, it kept the required bible course until 1968. Whether or not chapel was compulsory, its exercises, as at Smith and Wellesley, increasingly became popular assemblies, imparting nonsectarian harmony in the college. The practice of religion itself became a matter of private rather than institutional concern.[33]

The explosion of scientific knowledge throughout the period eroded the social unity that these colleges had taken for granted. With the traditional curriculum fragmented and religion no longer the central force in most Protestant colleges, educators could not rely on the old traditional supports to provide cohesiveness in their communities. In compensating for these losses, they relied on "character" as a common value for their students.

The concept of the "whole woman" (and "whole man") served as the common ideal for collegians. In their roles as authorities, educators made out of every student activity an opportunity to instill ethical purpose. Physical, intellectual, and moral elements were accorded equal importance in the life of the well-rounded college man or woman. Just as gender stereotyping characterized the modern liberal arts curriculum, so did the concept of wholeness affirm the principle of separate female and male spheres. The majority of women did not question the feminization of studies and professional occcupations; moreover, they fully embraced the goals of well-roundedness. In the world of peers, however, students dealt with these issues and questions in their own ways, and all along women undergraduates discovered both feminine and feminist implications in their education.[34]

S·E·V·E·N

Dimensions of the
Collegiate Experience

College is such a grand place and there are such noble girls here that
I am beginning already to dread the breaking up in '76.

Lucy Salmon to her stepmother, December 1, 1873, University of
Michigan, Lucy Salmon Papers, Vassar College

To the masculine coeds, greeting. . . . We do not make our advent
with the idea of 'raising the tone of the University,' or taming with
gentle presence our brother of the book. Not at all. We come to
study, to learn, to enjoy, to meet the nicest men, to take a degree and
to go forth prepared for work, in or out of the home, as
Providence decrees.

The Occident, November 1, 1900, University of California

What did it mean to be a college woman? Each, during four or more
years, had a unique experience with many layers of meaning—intellectual, social, and personal—only in part shared by classmates. Individuals
placed different weight on what they wanted from college—intellectual
stimulus, pre-professional training, or social community. College
women appeared to each other in many guises: the lady scholar, the cu-
rious thinker, the cultivated dilettante, the "pelican" (older schoolmarm), the effervescent flirt, the "butterfly," the all-American girl, the
earnest "dig," and the striving outsider from an immigrant or black family. Three elements interacted in college life: formal studies, informal association with faculty and administrators, and relations with peers. The
classroom remained the sphere of authority and the peer group that of
relative autonomy. The undergraduate adventure with its trials and
pleasures gave college women a sense of personal identity and a group

94

spirit that transcended the purely academic aspect. But at the same time their involvement in myriad activities kept students constantly aware of their responsibilities as liberally educated women.

This undertaking meant leaving the familiar ground of home to venture forth, psychologically if not always geographically. Most students still felt an involvement with parents and other kin, and families became loyal, concerned audiences following daughters' encounters in the collegiate world. Students, in letters written home, shared anxieties about failing. Fathers wrote back reassuringly that the worried daughter would make it, that "blues" were natural for a while. Or parents praised their offspring for their academic progress, anticipating the fine jobs they would have as teachers. Yet, in this intense period of personal growth, students questioned family values and absorbed new viewpoints from professors and other students. While family attitudes still affected the young women, the separate, exclusive environment of the college dominated their thinking and daily life.[1]

Afterward the individual's collegiate experience took on a mythical quality perpetuated in collective memories. Female collegians from the Civil War to World War I identified themselves as three generations, defined, not demographically, but by what they had shared as undergraduates, by the issues that had challenged them as students. The college woman of the first generation (1860s to 1880s) knew she was a pioneer enlarging the female sphere, but she still defined herself as a "true woman," pure and pious at least, if not always obedient and domestic. The collegian of the second generation (1890s to 1900s), still pioneering, had a more expansive spirit; mentally and physically vigorous like a Gibson girl, she called herself a "new woman." The third generation (1910s to 1920) introduced a more sophisticated "new woman"; responsive to the Progressive causes of social reform but also flouting conventional mores, she foreshadowed the flapper of the twenties. These stereotypes, while not applicable to all college women in a generation, highlight significant developments in their attitudes toward the expanding roles of educated women. Significantly, despite their differences, the women of these three generations felt linked in the common enterprise of being "college-bred."

First-generation college women were forthrightly serious; single-minded and conscientious, they hid neither purposefulness nor anxiety. In contrast, the women of the second and third generations let themselves appear to be at college for the "pursuit of happiness." They presented themselves deliberately in different modes, depending on the circumstances. A Wellesley alumna, class of 1907, wrote, "Outwardly bubbling though I appeared, I was in fact essentially serious. . . . For instance, being required to read some Thomas Hardy and George

Meredith and Henry James for my English major, that winter and the following summer vacation I gulped their works pretty nearly in toto." A Cornell graduate in the class of 1910, Esther Cloudman Dunn, elaborated on this state of mind. "If we mentioned study it was only to be funny about it . . . to assert that we hadn't cracked a book this term. All this was not hypocrisy; it was urbanity. . . . Living in layers of alternate seriousness and noisy surface is one of the delights of college. . . . The light-hearted intervals fool the outsiders, the professors and parents, the lookers-on." By the second generation, college women had become confusing to educators. Though the individual often had high expectations for herself, the college woman was often something of a puzzle to those who watched over her.[2]

At some schools the unsettled patterns of grading generated ambiguity in student responses to studying. For much of the period students at women's colleges were not informed of grades as long as they were passing. As early as 1877 a Smith student objected privately; she missed "the incentive that the system of marking supplied [in high school]. . . . The vague idea of some indefinite future culture is hardly enough to make me sit down and study Greek verbs when I have a chance to go boating instead." In 1897 some Wellesley students campaigned to know their grades, insisting that "the rivalry which exists in high schools on account of marks would hardly be likely to arise among college women, who may be supposed to have arrived at a point of view where it is realized that each student's work is individual, and stands or falls by its own merits." At the other extreme, Stanford in the 1890s changed its original gradeless policy to one of public posting of all students' grades, known in the slang of the day as "the bawl-out." Although educators at women's colleges hoped to avoid the competitiveness of male institutions, students at most schools were receiving letter grades by 1912. No doubt the earlier protectiveness of female students ended also because the incentive of grades could be used to push the unstudious, whose numbers grew with the larger student bodies.[3]

In the exhilarating and demanding collegiate arena, where students discovered what their talents were, what they were capable of, and what others expected of them, the most precious part of the experience became sharing discoveries and growing together. Undergraduates, amid the array of intellectual and social stimuli bombarding them in and outside the classroom, found a powerful source of self-education in relating to one another. Just as the original decision to attend college tested a woman's courage or independence, so succeeding as one among many became an integral part of that test. Only one's classmates could fully appreciate what it meant to join this venture. Peers understood well the mixture of serious and frivolous desires that motivated each during this crucial period of growing up.

The variety of collegiate environs, whether rural, urban, or in-between, was striking. Dormitory residents, boarders with private families, and commuters alike expressed loyalty and enthusiasm for their institutions, whatever the setting; they made the most of their schools, as this Radcliffe College song indicates:

> Oh Wellesley has a campus to wake the muses' lyre
> The beauties of Northampton a poet could inspire
> And spring is sweet at Vassar when trees are in the bud
> But I sing of Radcliffe College in the midst of Cambridge mud.[4]

The urban scene provided exciting cultural opportunities, contact with city life, people, and social realities. By contrast, the isolation of rural colleges made students restive and eager for interludes away from this contained world. Schools located near railroads had a distinct advantage. Weekly outings to restaurants, theaters, operas, and other cultural events, for those who could afford them, brought needed balance to the preciousness of college life. But those who did not attend the expensive rural retreats glamorized campuses where girls skated on ponds and rode horses on wooded trails. Country-club styles (reported in *Scribner's* and *The Ladies Home Journal*) characterized the fun of college girls. Absorption in eating, preparing Welsh rabbit or making fudge, giving tea parties—these became rituals of female friendship. Although most undergraduates did not have a leisurely residential college life, this pattern represented the real thing, the ultimate for a college woman.[5]

Many colleges could not require on-campus residence because they lacked dormitories. At state institutions like the University of California, half the students lived at home, and another portion in boarding houses or with relatives. Similarly at Radcliffe, where the first dormitory was built in 1905, at least half the students were not housed by the college, and some had room-and-board jobs with local families. Boston University's student body was also one of commuters. Only the most expensive women's colleges became solidly residential, but by 1920 a few had established cooperative houses to bring students earning their way into closer connection with the idealized residential community of women.

College represented a social microcosm where students not only studied but learned to live and work together in a community. Individuals, in personal relationships and private peer groups as well as public organizations, actively pursued the goals of the well-rounded life. Undergraduates, like adult women in American society, became indefatigable joiners. In large part collegiate interests and activities related directly to the mental, moral, and physical excellence being emphasized by authorities. Yet some students, more in each generation, addressed personal and social issues that took them beyond the confines of the protected collegiate world. Significantly, each endeavor also nurtured the ideals of female friendship.

Growth of peer groups affected the social and political structure of college life and promoted the stereotypes that graduates held. The undergraduate world was a controlling force on student development. Those in the second and third generations especially made it appear that nothing mattered as much as the approval of their peers. The future economist Mabel Newcomer, a smart young woman at Stanford (class of 1914), admitted later, "I cared more for the approval of classmates than professors." Although students wanted faculty encouragement, the opinion of peers was more influential. Classmates expresssed themselves directly and indirectly and left no aspect of life free from judgment. For all their contact with the home community and the larger world, being young together created bonds that removed college girls from adults.[6]

Female undergraduates had been brought up with a sense of womanliness that regarded female friendship as one of the agreeable pleasures of human association. William Alger's popular *Friendships of Women* (1873), written in praise of women's friendships, was published at the peak of public approval of this ideal. It was natural and desirable for a girl to have an intimate friend and to form with one or two others a "bunch" or "coterie," the little crowd of peers who knew each other's deepest thoughts and feelings. The members of the clique gave each other respect and affection akin to love, as well as encouragement in their new adventure. Women's friendships became central to the undergraduate experience, with more similarities than differences from institution to institution.[7]

Living arrangements greatly influenced the modes of personal relationships, but in all collegiate environments such friendships grew spontaneously and received encouragement as consistent with the functioning of women's separate sphere. Those who enjoyed dormitory life pitied girls who lived off campus. A Smith instructor wrote to her mother in 1894: "Those poor outsiders—unless they board in a place where there are a good many other college girls—they lose half of what they came to college for." At institutions where women were in residence, whether eastern and southern women's colleges or Sage Hall at Cornell or the Beatrice at Chicago, close friendships flourished more readily than where students rushed from home to class; yet the many who traveled to school (as from New Hampshire towns to Boston or from San Francisco to Berkeley), had their special friends and often de-

scribed themselves as a "railroad riding fraternity." Although young
women might cultivate many friends, for some it was only one friendship that counted then or afterward; the friend might be found in the
classroom or boarding house as well as in the dormitory.[8]

Students at residential women's colleges especially liked the separateness of girls studying and playing together. Laura Scales, Smith College,
'02, recounted later: "College life absorbed us. To be the peer of hundreds of girls from everywhere, to have much always to do, and some-
one to do it with, to row on Paradise, have tea at a faculty house, walk in
the meadows among the sentinel corn shoots, spend a night on Mt.
Holyoke, following Jenny Lind, to welcome one's 'beaux' to Whately
Glen for the junior prom picnic, on a warm evening to grab the front
seat of the open trolley to Williamsburg and back, to have for background the life and past of the world, to open one's heart to a friend—
this, for a girl in 1901, was college life, meaningful—challenging." Thus
in 1896 one Smith undergraduate, Marguerite Wells, organized a five-
day walk in the Berkshire Hills. Without self-consciousness she inferred
that Massachusetts country people stared "indulgently" at this odd
group in their short skirts: "We were girls doing a novel thing, and more
than all, we were happy, most palpably happy girls." Many college
women of the first two generations preferred "the segregation of girls,"
like one Minnesota student who transferred to Smith in 1895. In ex-
tolling "the richness of girl companions," Ada Comstock typified young
women of this period who felt more comfortable with members of their
own sex and who gladly deferred or limited dating with boys. Moreover,
those who dealt with boys in a coeducational environment, when looking
back, placed the highest value on their friendships with other women.[9]

Both single-sex and coeducational milieus provided a range of opportunities for female friendships to develop into primary sexual relationships. The erotic component in these friendships varied greatly.
For most of this period openness about such "romantic friendships"
stemmed from the belief that these relationships were part of growing
up. Everyone at home knew about schoolgirl "crushes" on women
teachers or older students; the collegiate environment, with its Victorian
restrictions limiting association with men, produced an intensified version known as "smashing." College women of the first two generations
were particularly susceptible. Women's campuses facilitated "smashing,"
with its rituals of courting a special friend; flowers, poems, gifts, and
missives accompanied declarations of affection and love of the kind usually associated with male-female relations. Some experimented with female lovemaking but also had male suitors, became engaged, and eventually married. Others who acted out romances with female friends,
however, were not interested in relationships with men. Of these, some

women found lifelong loves with whom they would share their post-college years. Of the individuals who appear to have been celibate in college (not engaged in a "smash" with a special friend), many, in the decades after graduation, found intimate female companions and settled into permanent relationships. These were common enough in New England to acquire the name "Boston marriage." On college campuses pairing among women professors also became a familiar pattern.[10]

Generally undergraduates did not question the propriety of such intimacy among their professors or themselves. Yet in the 1880s there was some concern on the part of faculty and administrators in women's colleges about the psychological effects of "smashing" on rejected students. Discreet discussion, however, did not suggest that smashing was an abnormality. It is easier to generalize than to be specific on the nature of these relationships, because the relative openness about women's friendships had disappeared by 1920. During the homophobic reaction that followed, the women who had had primary relationships with other women usually destroyed personal evidence such as letters and diaries. But undergraduates in the three generations' continued to accept and respect love between women, even though student interest in heterosexual relationships was becoming more freely expressed than earlier and would soon dominate on all campuses.

It was not accidental that women at all types of institutions identified more with each other than with male students. Opportunities for socializing with men had clear limits. Single-sex colleges in the beginning permitted only remote acquaintance with young men, sometimes limiting callers to relatives (it is said that brothers grew in number). Even when this extreme isolation diminished, occasions when men were allowed on campuses were either formal events or, when informal, still very tightly structured. Only in the 1900s did women's colleges begin to respond to students' increasingly open interest in the opposite sex and allow girls to enjoy "beaux" albeit in chaperoned company.

Yet contrary to popular opinion, the patterns of coeducation in the late nineteenth and early twentieth century did not permit free association of the sexes outside the classroom. Students were always under strict surveillance especially at religiously sponsored institutions such as Oberlin, Swarthmore, and Fisk. Although boys and girls often sat at the same dining tables, they lived in completely segregated dormitories and were heavily chaperoned in their limited social intercourse. At Swarthmore, for example, women were not allowed to visit the west end of campus (the male domain) at any time without a chaperone and were not permitted to use the tennis courts (located in that area) except at designated times. Despite these restrictions the diary of a coed at Swarthmore in 1902 showed her hoping that a particular young man would escort her from the dining room. Behind the required decorum a female student might muse about a particular young man. Still, as at women's colleges, Victorian prudery long governed the rules at coeducational religious colleges; some retained social restrictions with few modifications even after World War I.[11]

By contrast, the openly secular public and private coeducational colleges and universities, though they started with the same conservative codes of behavior, had to compromise sooner to meet the demands of young Americans for more social freedom. Between 1905 and 1910 the greater expression of interest in the opposite sex among students challenged the rules for strict separation of college men and women. An advisor to women at Boston University in 1908 accepted new trends by agreeing to a certain degree of permissiveness. "Girls may flirt if they choose and have any number of friends of the opposite sex—anything short of engagement. To become engaged interferes with their work." Obviously some heterosexual romances were brewing in the colleges, where men and women, sharing experiences, were attracted to each other. Short stories in college magazines by both men and women revealed ambivalence and latent preoccupation with sex. The lack of social ease was reflected in doomed love stories, and the awkward ways student characters tried to impress one another.[12]

For both men and women the new vogue of social dancing in the twentieth century offered an escape from the uncertainties that plagued their relations. Ballroom dancing epitomized a basic change in social mores for college as well as noncollege youth. Earlier, in the 1870s and 1880s, many young women did not know how to dance (as a Wisconsin coed admitted), for in some families dancing was still forbidden as one of the sinful temptations of the flesh. But at the turn of the century and in the fifteen years before World War I, long-held social standards of Victorian Americans were being challenged. Not only dancing, but soon driving in cars and drinking, would signal the flaunting of the old restrictions. Young working women (immigrants and daughters of the foreign-born) sought dance halls, and upper-class ladies waltzed at balls.

College women, particularly at single-sex schools, were restrained longer from fully participating in the dance vogue. Yet they found a way to enjoy this pastime; they danced with each other after dinner nightly. Even formal dances took place at these colleges without men. On the few occasions when men were allowed, Mount Holyoke and others decreed, as late as 1907, that the couples must *walk* rather than dance around the floor. Male guests referred to these festivities as the "eight-mile walk." This pattern ended abruptly at Smith College, where couples spontaneously performed "the forbidden waltz" one evening in 1897, and by 1913 college men and women everywhere danced together regularly.

Then college authorities had to judge which dance steps should be permitted. While the turkey trot was banned at Barnard College in 1915, the tango was forbidden at Illinois, Wisconsin, and Iowa. But Chicago had already allowed the tango in 1912 to the horror of a male graduate student who identified himself as "a Southerner"; this "wriggling," he predicted, would soon lead to a nervous breakdown for an "innocent girl." Energetic Clara Beyer (University of California '17) recalled at age eighty-nine, "I was a great dancer." In the same era, dance as an art form, as expressed in Isadora Duncan's sensuous performances, both startled and fascinated many Americans. No more could college women be stopped from all kinds of dancing.[13]

Administrators' preoccupation with how much or what dances to allow reflected deeper concerns about male–female relationships. "Promiscuous" dancing was feared as a prelude to uncontrolled sexual activity. In the 1900s educators, faced with growing publicity over prostitution and the dangers of venereal disease, felt obligated to enlighten their naive students of both sexes. More likely than not, a woman came to college in the nineteenth century without knowing "the facts of life," especially if she grew up in an urban milieu. In the 1900s the hygiene lecture or course (separate for men and women) became one means of disseminating a mild brand of sex education. By the third generation, then, college women were increasingly exploring heterosexual relationships.[14]

Beyond these concerns, women in the three generations found that coeducational institutions provided a more complex milieu than that of women's colleges. The initial presence of a small number of females did not change the maleness of the atmosphere, nor did the presence of a mass of women later produce an integrated community of both sexes. Apart from personal boy–girl relationships, females at coeducational schools had a variety of associations with male students, whose attitudes ranged from distant and hostile to very friendly. The "coed" often remained a second-class citizen, for male attitudes depended on the mores of the particular institution. M. Carey Thomas at Cornell wrote home in 1875 of her embarrassment in passing by scores of men on the steps of the buildings, saying, "There is much that is very hard for a lady in a mixed university and I would not subject any girl to it unless she were determined to have it." Yet she did not regret attending, for she was of the first generation, which either tolerated whatever hardships they encountered in the process of breaking barriers or accepted inequities and exclusions as part of the old tradition of men and women acting in separate spheres. Lillian Moller at California in 1900, after earning a Phi Beta Kappa academic record, was denied election; girls, she was told, did not need this honor that made such a difference to a boy's future.

An underlying problem persisted at the mixed schools—especially at the more secularized ones—in that women's interests and affairs developed separately and did not have comparable importance in the collegiate community.[15]

Not surprisingly, for a variety of reasons, college women as well as men preferred separate activities. Whether women joined together as a defense against the hostilities of their male classmates or as a natural preference for segregated bonding, they needed institutional support as well as student interest. Thus the University of Chicago women in the first ten years benefited from the efforts of two extraordinary administrators, Alice Freeman Palmer and Marion Talbot, who helped shape female group patterns in the mode of Wellesley College. At most coeducational schools, such as Stanford, California at Berkeley, and Cornell, it took a long time for women students to gain strong advocates within the administration. Female coeds over the three generations developed the kind of solidarity that students took for granted at single-sex institutions. By 1910 the organizing of separate women's activities had advanced; many schools had plans for women's centers that would serve as oases on male-dominated campuses.[16]

The logic of separate spheres easily applied to athletics, where physical differences required separate activities. At college the goals of the womanly woman and the manly man included physical fitness. Advocacy of physical exercise took hold during the first generation, with doctors and educators observing both the dyspeptic tendencies of the young educated male and the chronic weaknesses of the female participant. Athletics fulfilled the educators' commitment to make college women stronger and healthier and thus disprove the warnings of opponents of higher education for women. The positive results were noted at a 1915 conference on "The Relation of Health to the Woman Movement," where Stanford physician Dr. Clelia Mosher declared: "The day of the type of woman who is all spirit, a burning flame consuming her misused body, is passing. What we need are women no less fine and womanly, but with beautiful perfect bodies, a suitable receptacle for their equally beautiful souls, who look sanely out on life with steady nerves and clear vision." The Promotion of sports occurred at all colleges, and females like males gladly played. Several factors explain the surge in popularity of sports among students. In the wider world also, athletic ability figured in a new image of the natural woman. Like other middle- and upper-class women, those in college imitated the styles of the Gibson girl. Familiar to everyone, this belle of Charles Gibson's sketches appeared in all the magazines. She was a tall, commanding woman in her shirtwaist and skirt; in constant motion, she was seen playing tennis, croquet, and other games, but not working.[17]

In addition, for female collegians, physical exercise became a symbol of "emancipated womanhood." The bicycling craze from the 1880s on challenged them to overcome personal inhibitions as well as disapproval of relatives. The successful natural woman both played and watched sports, from basketball and hockey to tennis and swimming. Her prowess in athletics enhanced the appeal of the college woman.

Yet the development of women's sports occurred more slowly at coeducational schools, where money for facilities and equipment was not made available at first. Although Cornell pioneered in athletics for men, the women's gymnasium in Sage Hall housed only a piano in Florence Kelley's college years, the 1870s. At state schools like California at Berkeley, it required the philanthropy of a Phoebe Hearst to provide a women's gymnasium in the 1890s. Women also confronted the problem of whether males should be their coaches or should even watch them play. At women's institutions spectators and participants formed a harmonious whole; at mixed schools women's activities did not attract the same attention as the men's, yet the coeds were expected to support the male contests. At the University of Chicago a young woman commented in her diary on the rah-rah side of collegiate life. Although she had heard President Harper talk about the aims of the school that day, all she could remember was the discussion before the football game about the college (should it be "Chicago!" or "Chica—go!"?).[18]

Women educators applauded organized physical exercise and permitted mildly competitive games. By contrast, too often men's athletics reached a frenetic feverish pitch, and winning the game superseded all other interests. A male writer in *The Occident*, a student weekly at Berkeley, criticized his peers for appearing indifferent to anything but football and other games. Women played to win in organized sports but without the impassioned absorption that carried away the men. For them athletics provided a satisfying alternative to studies and a means of increasing their self-confidence. A Michigan coed wrote home that she and a friend were "taking good exercise every day by playing ball." She added the justification, "We study so much better for it."[19]

Mary Dewson, later a leading New Deal Democrat, relished intercollegiate tennis matches; Louise Pound, University of Nebraska, '92, a future botanist, as well as Alice Paul, Swarthmore, '02, the well-known ERA champion, starred in basketball. Such collegians, feminists in the making, took satisfaction in fulfilling the ideal of a healthy mind in a healthy body. Moreover, their participation in sports afforded communal recreation more democratic than other forms of socializing, for in team sports it was athletic skill and not social reputation that brought respect and acceptance among classmates.

In addition to athletics, students voluntarily pursued a variety of interests. College women became avid joiners. Associating with others took many forms, ranging from the purely social and cultural to the creative and including religious and service organizations and eventually a few political ones. Associations began with literary clubs in which students elected members for sociability as well as cultural exchange. Debating, dramatics, and journalistic endeavors also attracted students who harbored secret ambitions to be writers, poets, actresses, or journalists.[20]

Female literary societies in the 1870s and 1880s imitated the male tradition with Greek letter names: Castalia at Wisconsin, Gamma Delta at Boston University, Phi Sigma at Wellesley typified the burgeoning literary groups. Debating clubs, long popular among college men, also proved of value to women. The Boston University debating club (male) welcomed their few female peers in the 1870s, but most women learned how to speak in public and argue cogently in separate debating clubs. College magazines and newspapers gave many their creative initiations; authors Zona Gale at the University of Wisconsin and Willa Cather at the University of Nebraska contributed to school periodicals. Poet Marianne Moore recalled later that at Bryn Mawr in 1909 she had had "no literary plans," but that "I was interested in the undergraduate monthly magazine, and to my surprise (I wrote one or two little things for it) the editors elected me to the board." Coeducational newspapers did not intentionally recruit women editors. When *The Californian* appointed a Women's Editor, as "self-protection," it assured readers that "if we see any chance of a woman becoming editor we will dismiss every woman on the staff." Yet other ventures at Berkeley made a place for women. *The Occident*, a literary weekly, published a few pieces by female writers and also put out a women's issue. On this campus, evidently, male students did not agree on the role of women in their enterprises.[21]

Popularity of college theatricals in the 1890s signaled another reversal of puritanical middle-class mores. As recently as the 1870s at Mount Holyoke, both theatergoing and card playing had been banned. To many students at colleges across the country, playwriting and acting now became "the thing to do," a means for expressing one's opinions. At Berkeley in 1911, Christina Krysto sketched the campus rivalries between the sexes in her successful play *The Infernal Masculine*; her motivation was the repayment of "the unchivalrous men who had tried to debar the women students from the A.S.U.C. early in the year." Acting careers, however, were still not considered respectable by the parents of undergraduates. Furthermore, theatrical productions were strictly supervised. At coeducational schools faculty advisors or deans or their representatives sat in on rehearsals, and at most women's colleges women playing male parts were not allowed to wear trousers. In 1910 the student council at Barnard voted not to allow men to attend college theatrical productions. Still, graduates of Radcliffe, Bryn Mawr, and many other colleges remembered being stagestruck in the 1900s.[22]

While athletics and theatricals brought students together both as participants and audiences, thereby unifying the collegiate community, certain organizations addressed the needs of particular religious constituencies. The oldest of these, the Young Women's Christian Association, became a major source of strength and influence among white and black Protestants. Initially their religious activities included missionary societies, prayer meetings, and bible study groups; later social work dominated. As expected, at evangelical colleges (both single-sex and coeducational) the YWCAs attracted a large share of students, but significantly at public and private secular institutions they flourished as well: at Agnes Scott, Randolph-Macon, and Spelman, as well as Chicago, Stanford, and California, for example.[23]

Paralleling the Protestant associations, the first Catholic Club was founded at the University of Wisconsin in 1883, and others appeared by the turn of the century. The Menorah societies for Jewish students came later (originating at Harvard in 1906). Such voluntary gatherings gave students the chance to explore questions of faith and affirm their religious identities in the pluralistic collegiate world. Protestant, Catholic, and Jewish organizations could strengthen group loyalties without interfering with other interests of their students. These societies were instituted to provide support for those conscious of being a minority, offering them friendship, recreation, and affirmation of faith. A California, Berkeley, alumna remembered chapel at Newman Hall as "an oasis in a desert of loneliness." Far from promoting divisiveness, religious-sponsored clubs supported intergroup relations, encouraging members' participation in service projects that involved interfaith and even interracial relations.[24]

Other organizations, however, had to deal with the collegiate community's internal conflicts. The pluralism of the campuses created a need for undergraduate leadership through self-government associations. Indeed, through these, students were enjoined to set standards for their peers. Student government associations were established at different times at the various institutions. Bryn Mawr included this innovation from the outset; for most men's colleges at that time, such organizations were considered too risky (though Amherst's also started in the 1880s). Class elections and assembly meetings also gave women an education in organization, leadership, working together, and articulating their views. This form of political involvement was a new experience for women. It took longer to achieve on coeducational campuses, where women were long excluded from men's organizations. The development of separate women's student associations at these schools was therefore necessary and, when attained, represented a major accomplishment. The governing organizations gradually filled another purpose: that of negotiating, almost bargaining, with the college on behalf of their peer constituencies. On many issues—drinking, dancing, motoring, leaving campus, and other restrictions—such associations served as agents through which compromises could be reached.[25]

The flowering of extracurricular associations on campus had mixed impact, however. On the positive side, it fostered the growth of individual talents, skills, and leadership, but on the negative side, selectivity in clubs necessarily left some students out. The extent to which the associations were truly democratic varied; not everyone was treated exactly alike. Some students discovered that whatever talents or skills they possessed, their religious, ethnic, or racial identities either kept them on the fringes or barred them from particular activities. A 1910 alumna qualified her denial of discrimination at Wellesley, for "no matter what their popularity or ability, Jewesses were never elected to high office either in class or general student organizations."[26]

The growth of sororities over the period illustrates well the mixed purposes and results of organized social groups. Sororities (sometimes known as fraternities or by a particular club name) were originally founded as secret societies to affirm the ties of friendship. Gradually, however, they took over public functions, and, to varying extents, became influential forces on many campuses. Thus at California, Berkeley, where college housing was almost nonexistent, the sororities functioned as select dormitories. In addition, especially at coeducational schools, they provided institutional group support for young women. Administrators, early wary of the political power of these societies as a competing authority, at first tried to halt their development. In time, though, they found it useful to enlist sorority leaders along with those of student government, to control social behavior on campus. Some schools, like Stanford, Chicago, and California, did not permit students to start a chapter unless their grades were respectable (dean's list in many instances) and even so they were required to indicate their intended plans and activities. Sororities gained status from overseeing the members and helping them maintain good grades.[27]

Some educators and students opposed sororities because their presence promoted exclusivity. Membership in sororities was based, not only on personal congeniality, but on the individual's ability to share expenses as well. Students outside sororities contributed to perpetuating them by too often believing that they were being left out of something valuable. Novels of college life document the consuming importance of acceptance in these clubs. The heroine in Dorothy Canfield Fisher's *The Bent Twig* (1915), at first not admitted to a "swell" club because of her family's lack of prestige, later found herself among the chosen because of her fencing achievements. Now she experienced "that breathless whirl of one engagement after another . . . one of the oddest developments of the academic life." The relatively happy ending of *The Bent Twig* belied the humiliations of students left out of these clubs.[28]

On some campuses student leaders recognized the inconsistencies between their democratic beliefs and maintenance of exclusive clubs. At Wellesley the "agitation" began with "radicals" in 1907 and 1908 and reached a climax in student protest in 1909. Sarah Baxter declared in the *Wellesley College News* that improvement was not the solution and demanded abolition of these clubs. "The Society Question," as it was known, perturbed so many that a Society Congress was established in 1910 to deal with the issue. As one participant, Professor Katharine Coman, stated, "A college community should be an intellectual democracy." It was clear that the snobbishness of the secret societies contradicted that ideal, but at the end of the Congress deliberations the societies were not abolished. Instead, as a compromise, membership lists were placed under a supervisory committee, and all students were free to indicate their interest in applying.[29]

Despite years of protest, more than one-third of the students belonged to fraternities at Barnard College in 1912. However, student council leader Freda Kirchwey, '15, challenged their existence. An investigation committee "decided that the evils of fraternities as they are presently organized . . . outweigh the advantages; that these organizations often cause snobbishness by overemphasizing lines of social cleavage, especially race lines." The issues deplored at Wellesley were criticized here—"rushing" and "secrecy," for example. Similarly, the positive social ends were recognized, those of cultivating "congenial, intimate friendships." But the results of the discussions at Barnard differed from those at Wellesley, and the Faculty Committee on Student Organizations took steps that culminated in the "phasing out" of sororities. In the histories of the college, prejudices against outsiders were fully acknowledged.[30]

At other campuses signs of discrimination against outsiders were also overt. At Oberlin, students like Anna Cooper, who lived with a professor's family in the 1860s, and Mary Church (Terrell), who associated closely with the local black community and had good white friends, were shielded in part from the hurts arising in integrated dormitories. During the late 1880s, however, as the abolitionist tradition eroded, black Oberlin students had a more difficult time; their presence in the dormitories exacerbated the tensions. By 1913 white students were refusing to sit at the same dining tables with black classmates, and for a while officials permitted segregated seating. Eventually, student committees and the Women's Senate cooperated to provide fair room assignments for black students but were met with protests by many white students. Similar prejudice was evident elsewhere. When Ida Jackson went from the South to the University of California after studying at Rust College, a coed black school, she found that her classmates pretended she was not sitting next to them. One of eight black students at Berkeley in 1920, she helped organize the first black sorority there. When the picture of this group was left out of the *Blue and Gold* class yearbook, Ida Jackson felt firsthand the pain and bewilderment of being an outsider at the university.[31]

Yet the quality of the collegiate experience for outsiders remains difficult to judge. Black or white, they often hid their sense of rejection. Two Catholic students at Berkeley, hearing offensive comments on their religion in a lecture, resented the slurs but discussed the matter only with their family. Usually it was only in retrospect that the "successful" outsider revealed feelings repressed earlier. On certain campuses the rare black like Charlotte Atwood, Wellesley '03, may have enjoyed full acceptance—in the 1903 yearbook "Lotte" as listed as a debater and member of the basketball team—but again, this impression is incomplete without knowledge of her personal relationships.[32]

Outsiders—Catholic, Jewish, "colored," or immigrant—absorbed slights and insults but were not altogether discouraged by peer ignorance and snobbery. They saw these as temporary problems that would be overcome eventually through education. Indeed, a growing minority of privileged undergraduates felt a responsibility to surmount social prejudices on and off campuses. Experience at settlement houses was the catalyst stirring many individuals.

In the late 1880s interests of pioneering social scientists converged with the idealism of new graduates, and among these women and men the settlement idea took hold. Settlements satisfied students' needs to apply the study of social ethics to the real world. College friends independently chose to live in small groups in the slums of different American cities (Chicago, New York, and Boston were among the first). The common goal was to reduce the distance between rich and poor by living as neighbors among urban dwellers. Settlements were to be focal points where the two poles of society would meet and forge a better understanding of one another. Also for the residents the "college settlements" (the original name) had an appeal similar to that of a dormitory.[33]

What started as an experiment to satisfy the personal needs of certain privileged youth grew into a public force for social change. A Smith graduate of 1884 spoke for the rest when she declared: "We, the first generation of college women . . . represent a new factor in the social order. . . . Our lives are in our hands." Vida Scudder expressed the exhilaration of college women assuming the obligation to serve and improve society, but it was her contemporary, Jane Addams, who wrote perceptively that this endeavor of college women would be of greater benefit to those "who do it" than to those they helped. At every stage, Addams was the creative leader of the movement, which expanded from six neighborhood settlements in 1891 to more than a hundred in 1900 and more than four hundred throughout the country in 1920. Although college men participated all along as founders, residents, and undergraduate volunteers, the enduring impact of the movement came from college women. The first generation gave it continuous leadership, while women undergraduates of the second and third generatons turned to the settlements for enlightening field work.[34]

The impact of settlement experience on students varied greatly. Both as undergraduates and graduates college women explored new questions and sought new solutions for the improvement of the lives of "the other half." At Vassar and Wellesley some students brought the settlement idea to the campus by organizing clubs to provide education and recreation for young women who worked as domestics. There, in cooperation with the YWCAS, undergraduates offered them instruction in gymnastics, dancing, singing, and elocution. The programs also included arithmetic, history, and stenography. According to student reports, college maids availed themselves of this instruction. It would be more illuminating, however, to know what the recipients of this education said among themselves.[35]

Neither courses in sociology and social ethics nor attendance at social settlements guaranteed that students or professors would succeed in removing the "blinders of a special point of view" (Wellesley professor Emily Balch's eloquent phrase) that kept them from understanding outsiders, whether poor or well-to-do. Some retained patronizing airs and felt a sense of superiority to those they helped. One Vassar student did not want to give music lessons to "the stupid Norwegian" maid. A Radcliffe undergraduate wrote to her mother about motoring in a Cadillac with friends to the mill town of Lawrence to observe the sights. Yet her classmate reported in the school magazine that "these people," however dependent, were no "different" as human beings. The more sensitive discovered in the effort to cross social lines—religious, racial, and ethnic—that "the others" had much to teach the insiders. Some, like Dr. Alice Hamilton, who lived in Hull House, were genuinely touched by the settlement experience. She observed that "education and culture have little to do with real wisdom."[36]

Some students working at YWCAS and settlements became politicized. Studying and observing the problem of urban poverty convinced them of the urgent need to improve the living and working conditions of poor

Americans, especially of women and children. Would not this goal be achieved sooner if women could vote and apply political pressure for legislation? Such reasoning advanced the cause of women's suffrage among the reform-minded.

Yet the issue of women's right to vote divided the three college generations to an extent incomprehensible to later collegians. Those attending college in the 1870s believed in a woman's right to higher education and understood that this education should provide economic independence, at least for the single woman. Yet many could not accept the next, more critical demand of the women's movement, for suffrage. At this time giving women the vote was associated with free love, socialism, and the "de-sexing" of women. Ironically, while suffragists worked for women's higher education, and some faculty members openly endorsed women's enfranchisement, college administrators discouraged discussion. A few schools, like Vassar, even forbade public meetings on the question. Although many students preferred to ignore the issue and others remained neutral, with each generation the pro-suffrage minority became stronger. At the same time, as a reaction to this trend, anti-suffrage views became more articulate. Between the 1870s and 1910s student interest grew with advances in the organized suffrage movement in the society as a whole.[37]

The first and second generations of college women, however they viewed the woman question initially, gained exposure to elements of feminism. The early pro-suffrage ranks included those who had grown up in women's rights families: for example, Harriet Stanton (daughter of Elizabeth Cady Stanton) at Vassar and Alice Stone Blackwell (daughter of Lucy Stone) at Boston University proselytized openly at college. Equally important, their numbers included instinctive rebels who chafed against public restrictions. When a Harvard professor in 1895 assigned to his Radcliffe class a daily theme on the enfranchisement of women, two nonconformists wrote in its favor (out of almost seventy students): Maud Wood (Park) and her friend Inez Haynes, '98. Together they organized in 1900 the first chapter of the College Equal Suffrage League, the purpose of which was to promote "intelligent" interest in the subject. By 1912 the National College Equal Suffrage League represented a network of chapters on many campuses. It had the personal and financial backing of older suffrage leaders, college women of the first and second generations who saw the undergraduates of the third as a potential constituency.[38]

By the 1910s, in contrast to the 1870s, it was increasingly difficult for colleges to ignore the subject. Speakers from England and America, both pro- and anti-, addressed students on and off campuses, particularly in states where suffrage amendments were under consideration. At

the University of Minnesota a strong undergraduate suffrage club cooperated with a local women's suffrage group. In the state of California,
the issue was so charged from 1907 to 1910 (the suffrage amendment
would pass in 1911) that students at Berkeley sometimes heard in a
single week both pro- and anti-suffrage lectures. The Massachusetts Association Opposed to the Further Extension of Suffrage to Women
sponsored a 1910 essay contest on "The Case Against Woman Suffrage"
at local colleges. Suffrage leader Dr. Anna Howard Shaw, invited to lecture at the convention of the Virginia Equal Suffrage Association in
1912, also appeared at Randolph-Macon College to enlist student support. Between 1905 and 1915 Maud Wood Park lectured at campuses
across the country, despite inhospitable receptions from administrations
in the early years. The College Equal Suffrage League encouraged de-
bates and circulated books on suffrage in a traveling feminist library.
Thus, for those students who were receptive college had become a forum for the exchange of pro- and anti-suffrage views.[39]

Pockets of opposition and advocacy emerged in unexpected places.
Most women's colleges, for example, were not potent breeding grounds
for the cause. Mount Holyoke president Mary Woolley was a known suffragist, but her student body as of 1907 still had not followed her lead.
At Wellesley, although Helen Paul (sister of the militant Alice Paul)
rallied her roommate, Myra Morgan (McNally), and a small group of
friends, they did not convince the majority. Despite an energetic campaign with speakers from the College Equal Suffrage League, in February 1911 a college poll showed that more students were against suffrage
than for it; moreover, a large proportion took no position. Yet the Catholic Student Association of America, in a few issues of *The Catholic Student* (1909–16), featured articles in support of women's suffrage; one
stated that "Catholic women can best prepare themselves by working for
its arrival." Although most black men stood with white men in opposition to women's suffrage, the importance of the vote for black women
received emphasis in DuBois's *Crisis* magazine. Here, in a 1912 report on
"A Woman's Suffrage Symposium," Adelia Hunt Logan wrote that "colored women feel keenly that they may help in civic betterment, and that
their broadened interest in matters of good government may arouse the
colored brother, who for various reasons has become too indifferent to
his duties of citizenship." On the issue of suffrage, as on other controversial matters, educated women did not form a monolithic group.[40]

The organized public movement for suffrage made more headway
from 1915 on, and undergraduate suffrage clubs flourished on campuses from Hunter in New York to Randolph-Macon in Lynchburg,
Virginia, to Sophie Newcomb in New Orleans. Even at Vassar, where in
1909 student leader Inez Milholland had to hold clandestine meetings in

a nearby cemetery (managing to enlist two-thirds of the students in a suffrage club), the new president in 1915 added his support. College women, black and white, carrying banners from many institutions, including Howard, Swarthmore, as well as the women's colleges, marched with other suffragists in parades in Washington and New York in 1913 and afterwards.[41]

Both anti- and pro-suffrage arguments were presented in political terms. Both positions rested in part on expediency. According to opponents, women were already adequately represented in the political process by men; as a group, women were still uneducated and therefore unfit to assume voting responsibility for themselves. When women throughout the population were better educated, the argument ran, they would receive the vote. Above all, anti-suffragists claimed that women had more influence on politics in a nonpartisan role. Such opposition to female suffrage had an anti-democratic, elitist bias against the proper extension of American rights to women as a group and to special subgroups. Student anti-suffragists reflected the attitudes of older, upper-class opponents: neither had confidence in the ability of blacks and immigrants to use the vote. Above all, female opponents of women's suffrage were afraid of social change that might affect their privileged position as a class and their traditional roles as women. Perhaps others feared being accused of man-hating. Many who would not espouse suffrage expressed a preference for gradualism, deferring activism to the vague future.

Advocates of women's suffrage used a different argument, also from expediency. It was said that women workers in industry and schoolteachers needed the vote to ensure protection for themselves in the laws. Pro-suffragists also identified women's enfranchisement with the American democratic system; they noted the inconsistency between the national ideal of equality and the exclusion of one half of the population from voting. Essentially, they favored the predicted effect of suffrage in broadening women's participation in the polity. At Radcliffe in 1911, a pro-suffrage writer, Lorna Birtwell, declared that women needed suffrage "now," in order to begin to regard themselves as "political persons."[42]

The Oberlin Suffrage Club described a range of attitudes among their female classmates, from the "frankly ignorant" at one extreme to the "indifferent, timid, and conservative" at the other. In between there were three important shadings of opinion: "One [type] in a state of suspended judgment, the second, who found the weight of evidence moved them to the negative, and the intelligent who, after careful consideration, found that the weight of evidence moved them to the affirmative." Strikingly, these collegians learned not only to tolerate but to respect classmates' differing views when arrived at after serious consideration.[43]

With considerable open-mindedness, a *Radcliffe Magazine* editorial (1914) praised the growth of three political clubs—the Socialist, the Suffrage, and the Anti-Suffrage—for their existence indicated that students "unsatisfied with a merely academic horizon are looking out with a sense of the allegiance which an energetic younger generation should feel toward the larger movements for social betterment that are to be their inheritance." A Hunter College student made the point compellingly in the college newspaper on October 27, 1915: "Girls at Hunter, Woman suffrage is a matter of vital importance for all of us. It can't be expected that all believe in it, but let us, each one, look into the matter. Let us study this movement, let us take a lively interest in the doings of our country, and let us individually do all we can for a higher standard in this great democratic country.[44]

A wise educator declared in 1910 that the college woman was "not typically anything but she represents all modern interests." While higher education had certain predictable and identifiable influences on various aspects of women's lives, the way an individual reacted to the collegiate experience depended on many variables, including temperament, aspirations (or lack thereof), time and place of matriculation, and economic and social needs.

To varying extents, each student was affected by the esprit of her college generation. The first generation, though more restricted in choice of studies as well as in recreation, had a strong sense of purpose. The second and third gained confidence from the broadening of academic and social choices. The shift in standards for personal behavior over three generations was part of the moving away from the Victorian to the modern sense of womanhood. Despite the preoccupation of the first and second generations with the female world and the attractions of the third generation to the world of men, all felt connected both as collegians and by a common belief in the worth of women. However they differed intellectually or socially, they shared respect for the trained mind. In their whirl of studies and activities, undergraduates agreed that they had responsibilities to think, act, and contribute as adults, not only within their families but in the larger society.[45]

Feminist and abolitionist Lucy Stone worked her way through school, receiving an A.B. from Oberlin in 1847 at the age of twenty-nine. As wife and mother she kept her own name, and in her career as lecturer and journalist she led the women's movement in New England until her death in 1893. Courtesy of Oberlin College Archives.

Antoinette Brown (Blackwell), a graduate of the literary course at Oberlin in 1847, completed the theological course in 1850 and, though denied its degree, was ordained as a Congregationalist minister in 1853. As wife of Samuel Blackwell and mother of seven, she preached in Unitarian churches, wrote philosophical and feminist works, and urged other women to combine marriage with employment outside the home. Courtesy of Oberlin College Archives.

Mary Eliza Church (Terrell), who graduated from Oberlin in 1884 and was an activist for both black civil rights and women's suffrage, served as president of the National Association of Colored Women from 1896 to 1901. As wife and mother she promoted educational and community work among black Americans. Courtesy of Oberlin College Archives.

Anna Julia Haywood Cooper was already married and divorced when she received her Oberlin degree in 1884. An educator of distinction at segregated schools in Washington, D.C., and author of *A Voice from the South by a Black Woman of the South* (1892), she linked advancement of black people with equality of women. Courtesy of Oberlin College Archives.

Sophonisba Breckinridge, who graduated from Wellesley in 1888, was the first woman to pass the bar exam in Kentucky, in the 1890s. She received a Ph.D. in political science from the University of Chicago in 1901 and pioneered as a social analyst, combining research and teaching in the Department of Household Administration at the University of Chicago and at the Chicago School of Civics and Philanthropy, later named The Chicago School of Social Service Administration. Courtesy of Wellesley College Archives.

Marion Talbot worked at the University of Chicago between 1892 and 1925, first as dean of undergraduate women and then as dean of women for the whole university. A graduate of Boston University in 1880 and a student of Ellen Richards at the Massachusetts Institute of Technology, she developed a program in sanitary science at the University of Chicago. Both as an administrator and as an academic she had great influence. Courtesy of the University of Chicago Archives.

In Atlanta, Georgia, the first graduates of Spelman Seminary in 1887 were eager for learning and for practical skills. They included Ella N. Barksdale, Clara A. Howard, Lou E. Mitchell, Adeline J. Smith, Sallie B. Waugh, and Ella L. Williams, all of whom became teachers after graduation. Courtesy of Spelman College Archives.

This picture of interested participants at Wellesley's chemistry laboratory is representative of women's colleges, where study in the sciences was encouraged. Courtesy of Wellesley College Archives.

Bicycling, despite the disapproval of conservatives, became an accepted sport for college women. Shown here is the Wellesley

One of four Smith students who appeared in short skirts in public during a five-day walk in the Berkshire Hills in 1895. Courtesy of Smith College Archives.

Studying in the protected library at Radcliffe's Fay House in 1897 was a treat. Courtesy of Radcliffe College Archives.

Maud Wood (Park), Radcliffe 1898, was a founder of the College Equal Suffrage League in 1900 and lobbied for the Nineteenth Amendment, starting in 1916. She became the first president of the National League of Women Voters in 1920. Courtesy of Radcliffe College Archives.

Women wore formal attire while walking to class and observing the cadets' drill on campus at coeducational University of California, Berkeley, ca. 1900. Courtesy of the University of California Archives.

Lugenia Hope was one of the few black faculty members at Spelman Seminary, where she taught millinery classes from 1904 to 1912. These classes appealed to students for both personal and vocational reasons. Wife of John Hope, Moorhead's president, Lugenia was also a community leader and a founder of the Neighborhood Union. Courtesy of Spelman College Archives.

Composer Mabel Daniels and author Rebecca Hooper Eastman acted in their joint work entitled *A Copper Complication*, which was put on for the Radcliffe Glee Club in 1900. Since trousers were forbidden to Radcliffe students, a long overcoat was worn to portray the male character. Courtesy of Radcliffe College Archives.

Coeducational instruction in typing and stenography flourished in 1906 at the Montpelier Seminary in Vermont. Teacher Gladys Sanders, a seminary graduate of 1899, later graduated from the University of Colorado Law School. From the Archives of Vermont College of Norwich University.

Lucy Sprague (Mitchell), a 1900 Radcliffe graduate, was appointed the first dean of women and an assistant professor of English at the University of California, Berkeley, in 1906. After marriage she specialized in childhood education. The Bureau of Educational Experiments that she started in 1916 in New York City later became the Bank Street College of Education. Courtesy of University of California Archives.

BOSTON POST, MONDAY, JUNE 26, 1911

Radcliffe Girls Warned to
Stay at Their Own Firesides

Bishop Lawrence Tells Them to Uplift Those at Home Rather Than the Down-Trodden Outside

SOME OF THE RADCLIFFE SENIORS ON THEIR WAY TO SHEPARD MEMORIAL CHURCH TO LISTEN TO THEIR BACCALAUREATE ADDRESS

In Massachusetts, long a center of anti- as well as pro-suffrage activism, college women became the concern of conservatives. The bishop's advice in 1911 pleased the Harvard-Radcliffe establishment. Courtesy of Radcliffe College Archives.

The increasing momentum for women's suffrage was manifest in public parades in which college women carried the banners of their schools, as in Philadelphia ca. 1913. Courtesy of Wellesley College Archives.

Boarding a train bound for New York City in 1924, affluent Wellesley students enjoyed weekends off campus. Courtesy of Wellesley College Archives.

Lucy Slowe, dean of women at Howard
University from 1922 to 1937 and professor of English and education, was herself a
Howard graduate of 1908. She earned an
M.A. from Columbia University in English
and taught in high schools before becoming
a college dean. From 1923 to 1929, as the
first president of the National Association
of College Women, the black counterpart
of the American Association of University
Women, she was innovative in promoting
high academic and social standards in black
women's education. Courtesy of Bethune
Museum and Archives.

Lucy Ward Stebbins, Radcliffe 1902, dean of women
at the University of California, Berkeley, from 1912
to 1941 and professor of social economics from 1923,
explored many avenues to further economic opportunities for women students. She had a particular
concern for those who were self-supporting. Courtesy
of the University of California Archives.

The chorus line in *Making with the Maximum*, Smith College theatrical of 1943, had as its leader Nancy Davis, who ended her acting career when she married Ronald Reagan. Courtesy of Smith College Archives.

By 1940 Mary McCleod Bethune achieved a distinguished career as founder of the Daytona Normal and Industrial Institute, president of its succcessor, Bethune-Cookman College, and president of the National Council of Negro Women. She headed the Office of Minority Affairs in the National Youth Administration during the New Deal. Photograph by Griffith J. Davis. Courtesy of Bethune Museum and Archives.

The first twelve women to enter Harvard Medical School, in September 1945, were, front row, Ladislas Dolores Wojcik, from Simmons College; Doris Ruth Rubin, Wellesley College; Edith Ann Schwartz, Radcliffe and University of Wisconsin; Martha Joan Kern Caires, Radcliffe; Marjorie Jane Kirk, Bryn Mawr and Radcliffe; and second row, JoAnn Tanner, University of California; Shirley Marilyn Gallup, Brown University; Edith Louise Stone, Smith College; Marcia Laura Gordon, Radcliffe; Dora Benedict, Stanford, Bryn Mawr, and University of Chicago; Raquel Eidelman, Tufts and Harvard School of Public Health; Idolene Hegeman, Bennington College. Courtesy of Harvard Medical School Archives.

Sisters in Blackness was the name of a club formed at Spelman College in the late 1960s. Members, shown here with clenched fists, identified with both female solidarity and civil rights. Some left college for full-time activism; others were jailed along with college men for their public stands. Courtesy of Spelman College Archives.

In 1971, at the second Harvard commencement of which Radcliffe seniors were a part, many protested against the unequal admissions of women as undergraduates. At the time the admissions ratio of men to women was still four to one. Courtesy of Radcliffe College Archives.

Women athletes benefited from the higher expectations that accompanied the feminist movement. Coeds regularly participate in the Head of the Charles Regatta in Cambridge, Massachusetts. Photograph by Jane Reed.

E·I·G·H·T

After College, What?

You know I am very anxious to go away to study [medicine] . . . but
I am trying to be contented and happy . . . but I do not keep always
patient. . . . I am learning everything about housekeeping and
sewing. Mother is a New Englander and has taught me that no true
woman should be ignorant of the way a household should be carried
on . . . though why a woman who intends to be a doctor should know
how to do everything that occurs in a household, anymore than a
man who is also a physician should need to know how to plan and
build a house for his family like a common carpenter—is a
distinction I cannot appreciate.

Emma——to Julia M. Pease, fall 1875, quoted by Nancy N. Barker
in *Vassar Alumnae Magazine* 47, p. 28

Strong, indeed, is the girl who can decide within herself where duty
lies, and follow that decision against the combined forces which hold
her back.

Charlotte Perkins Gilman, in *The Home*, 1903; 1972 ed., 268

The college woman knew that higher education had given her unusual
advantages, and at the end of the four years she wondered even more
than her male counterpart how she would prove her worth as an educated adult. At college she had accepted a double-edged message, to be
useful and to be womanly. Only later did she wonder whether she could
meet both the traditional expectations inherent in being a woman and
the new obligations introduced by her collegiate experience. In this
chapter we consider the complex attitudes and changing responses of
educated women from 1870 to 1920, of the three generations, dealing
with the critical question: after college, what?

Various forces acted upon each student to affect her post-college
choices. Options for the single woman differed from those available to

the married woman. No longer was life predetermined as a simple transition from daughter to wife to mother. Not surprisingly, in the years immediately after graduation, many women seemed to drift while deferring long-range decisions. What a young woman did in the post-college period often formed another separate, significant interval before she settled into a permanent pattern. Female graduates, exploring many avenues, often went through an apprentice stage of adulthood before they committed themselves to particular life courses.

Undergraduate experience had strengthened the college woman's sense of independence, allowing her to think of herself as an individual who should not be forced into any pattern unless she wanted it. At the same time, for this new woman as for the rest of her sex, the age-old traditions still applied, and biological functions directed her to prescribed roles. Despite her education, she knew she was expected to show that she was fit for her duties as a woman—that is, as a wife and mother.

At the Rockford commencement in 1881, young Jane Addams pictured the college woman engaged in thought in the nursery: "Let her not sit and dreamily watch her child, let her work her way to a sentient idea that shall sway and enoble those around her. All that subtle force among women that is now dream fancy, might be changed into creative genius." Marion Talbot, in her graduating address at Boston University in 1880, envisaged the same kind of future for her generation: "At the side of man she stands, ready to do not a man's work in a manly way, but a woman's in a womanly way." A quarter of a century later, in 1905, a class president at Goucher College echoed these sentiments, stating that the "highest aim" of college women was to participate in society as "womanly" women.[1]

Graduating seniors in the first two generations did not question the belief that they should contain their ambitions within the boundaries of domesticity. Yet even while these students paid homage to motherhood, new opportunities arising from social and economic developments in their lifetime forced educated women to redefine their options, though not without a struggle. The graduate felt acutely the interplay of pressures imposed by what her family expected and what college education represented to her.

The enormous variety of experiences women had in college challenged their notions of the female role and capacity. Yet for many, an important determinant of post-college direction remained parental demands. The "family claim," as Jane Addams described it, referred to the tradition that an unmarried adult daughter's first obligation was to her parents. Thus, most collegians expected to return from college and resume responsibilities in the home, to be dutiful and charming until they married. While conventional parents in all social groups did uphold the "family claim," certain educated parents did not impede their daughters' aspirations. Families who respected their daughters' academic achievements and saw that these girls might not marry for whatever personal reasons gave them strong encouragement to explore alternatives. Such parents, like their daughters, regarded professional or graduate training in the same light as they had undergraduate study—as a substantial investment and a significant choice. No doubt, the awareness of precarious finances in these middle- and upper-class families strengthened their liberal attitudes toward women's employment.[2]

In this postgraduate apprentice stage of adulthood, then, college women faced both private questions of identity and the competing influences of family and college. Moreover, many of the new graduates did not know what they really wanted to do even when they were permitted choices. In this period they tried a number of different activities. Some stayed at home, some took paid jobs, volunteered in charities and settlements, studied or travelled; some combined a variety of these choices.

Increasingly, in the three generations, a major crisis involved the issue of holding a job, whether paid or unpaid. Notable was the emerging desire of the economically comfortable alumna to seek an occupation outside her parents' home; this approach affirmed a new attitude toward work derived from education. In middle- and upper-class families employment outside the home, unless there was financial justification, was regarded as a repudiation of the domestic role. In some circles even unpaid volunteer work brought social disapproval.

Throughout this period the issue of paid work created conflicts in families when daughters asserted economic independence for women as their right. Their stand was buttressed by many feminist writers, including Charlotte Perkins Gilman and Olive Schreiner. Various types of educated daughters confronted parents with the new views of work. Socially mobile parents of the middle-class above all others believed that being a lady required staying out of the work force. Thus Oberlin graduate Mary Church's well-to-do black father forbade her to take a teaching job, but she, being a spirited, educated woman, overturned his decision.[3]

Over the course of two and a half decades the emphasis college women placed on work grew. In 1898 Helen Starrett, educator and author, in her pamphlet *After College, What?* urged parents to let their daughters take paid jobs if they so wished, and she reiterated the same point in 1905. By 1920, educators would note that students expected to prepare themselves for "a definite profession, something that would link them to a larger life."[4]

At college, women of different social backgrounds had found emotional satisfaction as well as practical advantage in earning money. For the self-supporting student, such employment was a necessity during and after college, while for the well-to-do it was a new idea. For comfortable but ambivalent alumnae, payment for work became a further step in validating the desire to hold a job after college. The desire for independence and for experience in the real world drew such students into the marketplace. Privileged by education and stimulated by experiences away from home, these women sought ways to test themselves.

For most graduates paid occupation would prove to be a temporary interval, for they did not intend to reject matrimony permanently. Still others, who were uneasy with young men, preferred not to marry. They used the traditional rationale of needing to help support the family to justify what was, in reality, a desire for economic independence. Sophonisba Breckinridge and Mary Dewson, graduates of Wellesley in the 1880s and 1890s respectively, typified those who never married and who justified taking paid jobs as a means of relieving their genteel but financially pressed families. In fact, the economic motive did not fully explain their choices, for these ambitious women wanted to serve society and to achieve personal distinction; they succeeded in becoming professional leaders in social reform and creating nontraditional life patterns.

The earliest college women assumed that they had to make a definitive choice between marriage and its obligations, and vocation or career with its commitments, yet uncertainty plagued young women who did not fit neatly into one particular channel. Madeleine Wallin, speaking of herself and other graduate students at the University of Chicago, wrote in 1894: "They are just as much in earnest about their aims and career as they are about marriage. . . . They don't know which they want, and they are trying the first one that comes until they can decide. They don't make an ironclad resolution about either one." Those who experimented in this interval did not always end up where they started.[5]

Wallin, after teaching at Smith College, did not finish her Ph.D.; instead she married a journalist and had two children. Some single women said that they did not rule out marriage as a deliberate decision, but that it never happened. Others rejected offers of marriage, committing themselves to careers.[6]

College education made it possible for a woman to approach singlehood in a new way. Even a conservative educator like Vassar's president John Raymond told students that "if any love literature or art better than married life, that woman should be free to choose." This liberal idea that a woman should have a choice not to marry reflected the feminist view of John Stuart Mill. Women who remained single traced paths in unfamiliar territory. At the outset it could not have been easy for the educated spinster of the first college generation to create a niche for herself as an independent person outside her family of origin. In the

1870s she was still expected to live with her parents or siblings, even
though feminists like E. D. Sewall were defending the right of a single
woman to have a home and garden of her own. Single women in the
next two generations had a wider range of choices afforded, not only because of economic self-support, but also by increasing social acceptance
of highly educated adult unmarrieds. Women's colleges, for example,
became domestic havens for the single women who became professors
and deans in residence. By 1900 settlement houses in all the major cities
provided congenial alternatives for women who earlier had been limited
to boarding with respectable families. Sometimes private women's clubs
also provided residences for professional women.[7]

Certainly many college women married later than noncollege women,
some graduates did not marry at all, and others formed long-term "marriages" with other women. Thus each graduate developed as an individual. Whether she married or not, however, helped to determine the
larger trends of her group measured over time. Surveys in the late nineteenth and early twentieth centuries charted demographic patterns of
college women in marriage (see table 4). The surveys also recorded
changing patterns in childbearing and in voluntary and paid employment outside the home.[8]

The declining birthrate in the nineteenth century had long perturbed
social observers, and the surveys give some credence to those who associated women's higher education with the increasing proportion of single
women in American society. Just as Anne Scott's study of Troy Seminary graduates from 1833 to 1872 showed significant percentages remaining unwed in the antebellum decades, so Mary Van Kleeck's analysis of college women (as of 1915) revealed even higher percentages of
unmarrieds in the college generations. Her study, based on information
from eight women's and one coeducational college (Cornell), showed
that only 39.1 percent of the 16,739 alumnae had married. Another interested observer, Helen Olin, found that only 41.3 percent of
Wisconsin graduates from 1869 to 1906 had married by 1907. National
statistics for the general population differed substantially from these
percentages for college women: in the population as a whole, over 90
percent married at some point in their lives, according to census figures
from 1890 and 1910.[9]

Statistics suggesting that less than 50 percent of college women married, along with their further tendency, once married, to have fewer
children, fueled public cries of "race suicide." It was argued that if
native-born college-bred women did not marry and have sufficient babies, the children of immigrants would soon supplant the older American stock. In the same vein psychologist G. Stanley Hall blamed college
men and the colleges that educated them for the related "bachelor prob-

TABLE 4
Marriage Rates of Alumnae at Selected Schools by Graduating Class Cohort, 1820–1930

Troy Seminary		Oberlin		Mount Holyoke		Vassar		Radcliffe	
Years	%	Years	%	Years	%	Years	%	Years	%
1821–32	87								
1833–42	83	1837–46	97.5						
1843–52	80	1847–56	80.6						
1853–62	79	1857–66	77.8	pre–1864	77.5				
1863–72	75	1867–76	68.3	1864–73	72.1	1867–71	61.9		
		1877–86	69.1	1874–83	57.1	1872–81	54.3		
		1887–96	60.9	1884–93	78.2	1882–91	55.8	1883–90	40.9
		1897–1906	52.6	1894–1903	52.0	1892–1901	56.5	1891–1900	51.3
		1907–16	59.5	1904–13	52.0	1902–11	60.6	1901–10	51.1
		1917–21	43.7	1917–21	50.0	1912–21	75.0	1911–20	49.6
				1922–26	60.6				

University of Michigan		Bryn Mawr		Wellesley		ACA census		Van Kleeck Census of nine colleges	
Years	%	Years	%	Years	%	Years	%	Years	%
						1869–78	55.4	pre–1880	57.4
1889–93	55	1889–93	43	1884–93	49	1879–88	50.3	1880–90	53.0
1894–1903	52	1894–1903	47	1893–1903	52	1889–98	22.5	1890–1900	50.2
1904–08	52	1904–08	44	1900–09	68.3			1900–10	46.6
1909–18	60	1909–18	67	1910–19	75.3				
				1920–29	83.3				

Sources

Sophia Meranski, "A Census of Mount Holyoke College Alumnae," *Mount Holyoke Alumnae Quarterly* 8, 3 (October 1924), 149–59.

Ann Miller, ed., *A College in Dispersion: Women of Bryn Mawr, 1896–1975* (Bryn Mawr, Pa., 1976), 105.

Mabel Newcomer, *A Century of Higher Education for American Women* (Washington, D.C., 1959), 212.

Hélène Kazanjian Sargeant, "Genus: Alumnae, Species: Wellesley," *Wellesley Alumnae Magazine* 49, 1 (November 1964), 13.

Anne Firor Scott, "The Ever Widening Circle: The Diffusion of Feminist Values from the Troy Female Seminary, 1822–1872," in *History of Education Quarterly* 28 (Spring 1979), 16.

Barbara M. Solomon, *Radcliffe Alumnae Information, 1928.* Unpublished analysis of responses to questionnaire.

Mount Holyoke College Alumnae Census (revised). Prepared by The Class in Statistics under the direction of Ruth Olmsted Trux. Mount Holyoke College, Department of Economics and Sociology, January 1937.

Association of Collegiate Alumnae, *A Preliminary Statistical Study of College Graduates* (Bryn Mawr, Pa., 1917), 121.

Roberta Frankfort, *Collegiate Women: Domesticity and Career in Turn-of-the-Century America* (New York, 1977), 56, 57, 112, 113.

Louis D. Hartson, "The Occupations of the Oberlin Alumnae," *Oberlin Alumni Magazine* 23, 4 (January 1927), 12.

Mary Van Kleeck, "A Census of College Women," *Journal of the Association of Collegiate Alumnae* 11 (May 1918), 577.

lem." Between 21 and 26 percent of the graduates of Yale and Harvard, for example, remained bachelors from the late 1870s to the 1890s. Nonetheless, advocates of women's higher education felt defensive. Smith College professor Charles Emerick, in 1909, published an article on "College Women and Race Suicide" which emphasized that college women came predominantly from professional white families, a group that tended both to marry in lower proportions and to have fewer children than other Americans. Emerick and other sympathetic analysts, eager to separate marriage rates and education, noted that the type of educated girl who did not marry would probably have stayed single even if she had not attended college.[10]

In general, studies of college alumnae used data describing recent graduates; many of the then single women would marry later. Thus an Association of Collegiate Alumnae report on more than thirty-six hundred college women in 1900 found that 31.1 percent of the graduates were married, as opposed to 46.1 percent of their noncollege sisters, but that many of the alumnae had been out of college for only a relatively short period, from two to ten years. Of those women who graduated between 1869 and 1879, 55.4 percent were married, while 50.3 percent of those graduating between 1879 and and 1888 and only 22.5 percent between 1888 and 1898 had married. Similarly, the national statistics on marriage rates exaggerated the differences between college and noncollege women, since the "never married" among college women were found primarily in cohorts above age forty, often above age sixty, whereas the age of the graduates to whom these women were compared was sometimes below forty.[11]

In fact, the majority of college women did marry, but later than most of the noneducated. When, in 1890, the median age at first marriage for women in the United States was twenty-two, that of women graduates was considerably higher. Thus, in the ACA survey of twenty-two institutions, the median age of marriage was over twenty-five; at the largely single-sex eastern schools, though, the figure tended to be higher than at the western ones. Significantly, however, after the mid-1890s, not only did the proportion of students marrying steadily increase, but the average age at marriage declined. In the twentieth century alumnae were progressively more youthful brides. If this tendency lasted, then, as a 1924 study of Vassar women suggested, college girls would resemble more and more "the typical rather than the exceptional members of their social group."[12]

Once allowances were made for the inevitable differences in marriage rates at the historic start of the collegiate "experiment," sympathetic investigators predicted that the patterns for college women would converge with those of the middle-class population of American women.

And later studies confirm these predictions. For example, a study of Wellesley alumnae reported increases in the marriage rate for every decade of the twentieth century; whereas prior to 1900, 58.2 percent married, by the 1940s 92 percent were marrying. And in terms of age, over 60 percent of the women attending Wellesley before the turn of the century married after thirty, whereas within half a century, nearly half married before age twenty-three. At all institutions, the trend after 1910 edged toward younger marriages.[13]

Although over time the majority of college women married, a substantial minority remained single, particularly in the first two generations. All lived through the post-college search for direction, but the permanent lifestyles that they developed as married or single women diverged in basic ways. We will consider the patterns of the two groups separately before addressing the ways in which their ultimate aims converged.

After marriage, what? became a new question with its own dilemmas. Although college women increasingly asserted their right to paid employment before marriage, most continued to believe that they should stay at home afterward. For some the roles of wife and mother offered ample satisfaction, but others sought alternatives that incorporated their past interests. The married defined their usefulness in traditional ways, often identifying their husbands' expectations as their own. Some wives collaborated with spouses in professional or business enterprises. Such partnerships won the approval of Charles W. Eliot, long a skeptic on women's higher education, who now concluded that educated women made "splendid assistants" to their husbands. Of course, the satisfactions in this role depended on the quality of one's contribution: whether academic expertise or merely emotional support was offered. Women like Elinor Stimson (Wellesley, '06) and Ellis Abbott (Smith, '09) who married writers Van Wyck Brooks and Ring Lardner, respectively, submerged their own literary ambitions in their husbands' careers. Some women bloomed in complementary roles, others did not. Ten years out of Wellesley in 1912, one graduate described her "contented family" with a professional lawyer-husband and two children. To the readers of the *Woman's Home Companion*, she presented a picture of the model wife, graciously entertaining her husband's friends, knowledgeable about public affairs, and busily engaged in social activities. She and her friends, "the girls," were just "average specimens," she concluded. Yet not all alumnae sounded as content in class reunion reports. Others, particularly those with small children, expressed guilt that they were not doing enough with their education. Elsie Frederickson, a Smith graduate of 1912, said: "And while I am ready to admit that I have an awfully good time with my nice husband and my little house and my silver and my funny daughters, I feel like a hopeless slacker all the time."[14]

Many of these women looked beyond their homes for ways to extend their usefulness. Before marriage they had worked either at a paid job or in some benevolent or cultural undertaking. As wives and mothers they still felt a need for extradomestic activities. But if such commitments had created problems for the college graduate before she married, afterward her dilemmas increased.

Commitments outside the home brought disapproval if they took too much time away from a woman's domestic duties. Even so, precedents existed for some measure of voluntary activity. Many an educated woman found an outlet for her need to serve and to enjoy the company of other women, as she had at college, in volunteer groups, both small and large. Historically voluntarism had long provided the means for women to initiate good works and cultural improvements in their local communities. Women's clubs had a phenomenal growth at every level of society in the same period in which collegiate education for women was taking root. Both the leisured lady and the working girl became joiners. The focus mirrored the concerns of the larger society, and clubs ranged from religious, charitable, and social reform organizations to horticultural, literary, dramatic, and sporting groups. The three college generations used the traditional, relatively acceptable route of voluntarism as a vehicle for expanding their interests and for involving themselves in current social, cultural or political issues.[15]

The college-educated contributed to different types of organizations, some relating to their religious or ethnic origins, others to their educated background. While the Protestant, Catholic, Jewish, and black associations were not limited to the college-educated, leadership in these groups increasingly devolved upon graduates. In addition, these women promoted professional and alumnae organizations based on their educational identities.

With the exception of certain esoteric clubs for amateur lady scholars, most of the proliferating societies were motivated by a concern to improve family life. In their group enterprises the women sought knowledge of the right way to live and intended to use the knowledge to improve and change deteriorating conditions in the family and in the society. Most women, like Vassar graduate Julia Lathrop '80, head of the Children's Bureau in 1912, regarded motherhood as a profession in which college graduates should excel; they could use what they had learned in chemistry and psychology courses in homemaking and child-raising. Educated women sought scientific expertise on how to overcome the social ills affecting family life. Scholarly books by G. Stanley Hall and popularizations such as Elizabeth Harrison's *A Study of Child Nature from the Kindergarten Standpoint* (1891) stressed the importance of a mother's education in training her offspring. Yet some women went beyond this, working to make improved domesticity the basis for educational and social improvement of individuals, families, and of the whole American society. In addition to the mothers' clubs that mushroomed at this time, social reform organizations like the Women's Christian Temperance Union, founded in 1873 (with a constituency of three million by 1915), as well as benevolent societies like the women's foreign missionary movement, attracted many educated women.[16]

The turn of the century witnessed great changes in the structure of extradomestic activities—changes that paradoxically reduced the scope of the married woman's participation. The new academic social sciences permeated the voluntarism of the educated woman, with profound consequences. Just as undergraduate participation in YWCAS, settlements, and other associations had taught college women to value professional methods, so after college they attached a sense of superiority to conducting their various clubs and societies in a professional manner. These married women liked to identify themselves as professionals, because the term conveyed a sense of expertise that enhanced even voluntary positions.

In this period the professionalizing of attitudes and methods in fieldwork and social investigations reshaped the traditional forms of social service. Service remained the unifying principle in the activities of all educated women. Yet, while commitments might be demanding regardless of whether or not they included financial remuneration, a schism developed between paid and unpaid workers. Tensions arising out of the development of professionalism in service fields altered the contributions that married and single women could make. As social work became a professional career demanding a full-time commitment, it was considered antithetical to marriage. The special responsiblities of a wife-mother with children at home presumably placed limits on her extradomestic activities. In contrast, the social activist who was single, widowed, or married but childless could assume larger commitments to serve society. Thus the singles became more respected in professional roles. Emily Balch noted in 1915 that "single and relatively independent women . . . permanently and professionally occupied, free to risk their living for a cause they believe in," were bringing about reforms to improve the lives of industrial working women. Leaders like Jane Addams at Hull House, Margaret Dreier Robins in the Woman's Trade Union League, or Grace Dodge in the New York Young Woman's Christian Association were the quintessential professional volunteers; they showed extraordinary commitment to their careers but skirted the issue of payment for their work.[17]

At the start of the period Mary Morton Kehew, head of the Women's Educational and Industrial Union in Boston in 1873, represented such a model. She and others of this type had money of their own or were partially financed by friends. But Frances Willard foreshadowed a new pattern. Willard had to be self-supporting, and after leaving her deanship at Evanston College for Ladies, she served first as secretary of the Women's Christian Temperance Union, then held other paid posts before becoming the WCTU's national head.[18]

Professional attitudes and expertise characterized women's leadership in a wide range of initially voluntary undertakings. Yet the lines between voluntarism and professionalism became increasingly blurred. Gradually many service groups that had relied predominantly on unpaid volunteers moved to paid staffs. The goal of "efficiency" determined the removal of volunteers in many agencies. Karen Blair, in *The Clubwoman as Feminist*, notes that at the Women's Educational and Industrial Union in Boston, twenty paid staff members supplanted the corps of volunteers in 1905. Professionalization of the American women's foreign missionary movement also led to the gradual replacement of the volunteer by the professional. Patricia Hill's study of this movement shows that missionary social work became a paid career option when its college-trained leaders succeeded in introducing "science" into the methods of missionary endeavors. Voluntarism for women did not end when certain aspects became professionalized. Some women both held a paid job and participated in a voluntary endeavor. In addition, whatever a woman was doing, professional, paid employment did not preclude her interest in serving as a volunteer in an organization that commanded her interest and sympathy.[19]

The last phase of the suffrage movement exemplifies how professionals and volunteers participated effectively to bring about the passage of the Nineteenth Amendment. The leaders introduced professional standards to develop more efficient lines of organization. In state after state the college-educated took the initiative. Montana gave women the vote in 1912 and elected suffragist Jeanette Rankin to be the first woman in the United States Congress in 1916. Even in resistant Mississippi, Nellie Nugent Somerville, a participant in the movement since 1897 and a vice-president of the National American Woman's Suffrage Association in 1915, had her supporters: in 1923 she would become the first woman to be elected to the state legislature. Above all, the national campaigns had professional direction, evidenced in Carrie Chapman Catt's 'brilliant "winning plan" and the effective congressional lobbying of Maud Wood Park and Helen Hamilton Gardener, as well as in the shrewdly planned tactics of violence of the young militants Alice Paul and Lucy Burns. These political innovators were generally unencumbered by family. The widowed, divorced, or childless could devote their lives full-time to the cause. Some received salaries paid by rich suffragists, while others, like Alice Paul, did not need the recompense. These women were professionals in competence and commitment. Their victory in 1920 was a credit to the skill and dedication of leaders and volunteers, who together exploited the favorable climate of wartime. The suffrage movement demonstrated the commitment to social activism and usefulness that characterized the employment, both paid and unpaid, of so many women graduates.[20]

Yet, even as the serious volunteer absorbed professional attitudes, ambiguity about the differences between volunteers and professionals created lasting tensions. The demand for trained "experts" in social service enterprises increasingly removed the most critical elements of the work from the domain of the (often married) volunteer worker. Thus, while professionalism attracted all educated women to various organizations and forms of employment, it gave single women in particular opportunities to go even further in paid careers. Although the options of both single and married women were growing in this period, those for the married ones were far more limited. Nonetheless, the large majority of college graduates did hold paid jobs at some point in their lives. Financial necessity, the ideal of independence, and individual vision were all factors contributing to the decisions made by educated women to enter the work force.

The college woman had fewer alternatives than the college man, even though advances in academic and technological fields increased the number of openings. The expanding female labor force included immigrant factory workers, domestic servants, and semiskilled clerical workers; the college woman was only one of many types seeking employment. Furthermore, the increasing number of high school graduates introduced a labor supply of females whose availability facilitated the entrance of women into several occupations. Opportunities for women were not growing in the same ways in every field (see table 5). So-called semiprofessions, including social work and librarianship, as well as older occupations such as teaching and nursing, were most often filled by women, some better paid than others; consequently they came to be known as feminized occupations. The use of the prefix "semi" denigrates these fields as less demanding, less permanent, and more appropriate for women than the prestigious ones reserved for men. Still, the "semi" professional fields were perceived as continuing and updating the female tradition of service to society.[21]

College women did not enter all these fields to the same extent: they were least interested in nursing and entered library and social work less often than teaching. Graduates continued to ignore the overtures of the nursing profession except during World War I, when four hundred Vassar students, for example, committed themselves to nursing for the

TABLE 5

Women in Selected Professional Occupations, 1910–82,
as a Percentage of all Workers in Those Fields

Occupation	1910	1920	1930	1940	1950	1960	1970	1982
Lawyers	1.0	1.4	2.1	2.4	3.5	3.5	4.7	14.0
Physicians	6.0	5.0	4.0	4.6	6.1	6.8	8.9	14.3
Nurses	93.0	96.0	98.0	98.0	98.0	97.0	97.4	95.6
Social workers	52.0	62.0	68.0	67.0	66.0	57.0	62.8	66.4
Librarians	79.0	88.0	91.0	89.0	89.0	85.0	82.0	83.4

Sources: Nancy Woloch, *Women and the American Experience* (New York, 1984), 546. Woloch cites as her sources: Cynthia Fuchs Epstein, *Woman's Place: Options and Limits in Professional Careers* (Berkeley, 1970). *Employment and Earnings*, Bureau of Labor Statistics, U.S. Department of Labor, January 1983. *The Female-Male Earnings Gap: A Review of Employment and Earnings Issues*, report 673, Bureau of Labor Statistics, U.S. Department of Labor, September 1982. *1970 Census of Population: Detailed Characteristics, United States Summary*, Bureau of the Census, U.S. Department of Commerce.

duration of the war, only to drop out by half after the armistice. Nor did social work as a paid occupation compete with teaching; college settlement fellowships were necessary to recruit to the field graduates who needed to earn a salary. And although an exceptional few pursued the most demanding work in the arts and sciences, most college women entered schoolteaching. Although the 1910 census showed that only 5.9 percent of women gainfully employed in the United States were teachers, the percentage of college women who were included in that group was considerably higher.[22]

The ACA study of thirty-five hundred graduates from 1869 to 1898 showed that 72.4 percent had taught. Mary Van Kleeck's study of over sixteen thousand college graduates (as of 1915) indicated that an even higher proportion, 83.5 percent of those working, were teachers, a number representing fully 58 percent of the total sample. Significantly, teaching has functioned as an intermediate or final step in the careers of distinguished female achievers; among the 1,359 individuals included in *Notable American Women* (I–III) many engaged in teaching either permanently or for a period. Over 17 percent of the subjects born between 1850 and 1909 were teachers throughout most of their lives. Another quarter of the group (25.2 percent) taught at some point during their lifetimes. These statistics demonstrate the importance of teaching for women as a route to advancement. Studies of individual colleges also substantiate the importance of the teaching option for college women. Consistently, surveys conducted at private women's colleges, at coeducational institutions like Oberlin, and at state universities confirm that education surpassed by far any other professional field employing women. Recent investigations into the untapped history of black women reveal that for this group of Americans, also, teaching proved of great consequence for their advancement and achievement. Although their numbers are small, of the black women born between 1850 and 1900 who are listed in *Notable American Women*, over half (57 percent) taught at some point in their lives.[23]

Why did the college woman still turn to what had become the most traditional option? Those who had enjoyed studying often wanted to teach; it was a way to continue to study while earning a living. Moreover, in this field not known for high salaries, many jobs still paid better than those in other semiprofessions that also required further training; in many areas it was still possible to teach without certification. Those with higher expectations for careers, however, balked at the inevitability of this course. Early Bryn Mawr graduate student Lucy Salmon advised undergraduate Emily Balch (class of '89) to try other options first unless she had a real vocation for teaching. Bryn Mawr president M. Carey Thomas agreed that the availability of teaching jobs should not preclude women's experimenting in other fields. On the economic level it could not be denied that teaching offered a reliable means of earning a living, but, as Sophonisba Breckinridge noted bitterly in 1914, for all the so-called feminization of the teaching profession, the public school systems were run by men—as superintendents and high school principals—with only an occasional female in a post of authority. Individuals reacted pragmatically to the advantages and disadvantages of schoolteaching as a vocation.

While educated women of the higher social levels resented the constraints teaching put on women of ability, for other women it became a vehicle for upward social mobility. It represented an improvement over what their mothers could do to earn a living, a welcome alternative to working in other women's kitchens and laundries or in mills and factories. Daughters in black and immigrant families found schoolteaching to be an advance on the occupational ladder. Moreover, black women in the South could not take many teaching jobs for granted in the 1900s. There was a long struggle before they replaced white women as teachers, even in segregated schools. As in the past, schoolteaching served many functions for educated women.[24]

By 1920 women were participating at many levels in a variety of undertakings. Females with talent in the arts increasingly asserted themselves. Writing, the secret ambition of many collegians, became one of the more acceptable and appealing ways of earning a living. The market for popular works expanded. Moreover, the authors included conscious artists. Although of the illustrious, Edith Wharton was not college-bred, several eminent writers got their start as undergraduates: Gertrude Stein at Radcliffe, Willa Cather at the University of Nebraska, Marianne Moore at Bryn Mawr, Babette Deutsch at Barnard, and Edna St. Vincent Millay and Muriel Rukeyser at Vassar. These and others, including Zona Gale at Wisconsin, Geneviève Taggard at California, and Louise Bogan at Boston University, served apprenticeships on student newspapers or literary magazines.[25]

Magazine writing and editing provided additional opportunities for the educated woman. As in the nineteenth century both popular and serious female writers found a large audience among middle-class women: specialized magazines, from the religious to the suffragist to the anti-suffragist, catered to their interests and also gave employment to other women. Magazines like *The Ladies Home Journal, Ladies Home Companion* from the 1890s, and *Good Housekeeping* in the 1910s expanded openings on their staffs. Throughout the period from the 1870s to 1930, *The Women's Journal*, edited by Lucy Stone and then by daughter Alice Stone Blackwell (both with Henry Blackwell's collaboration), employed many women. To a lesser extent periodicals from *McClure's* to *Harper's* made use of the talents of collegians like Ida Tarbell, Willa Cather, and Agnes Rogers. Yet the field of newspaper journalism proved harder to enter. In the whole country by 1886 only about five hundred women were involved in the editing of newspapers, and in 1888 some two hundred were employed on New York City newspapers. In a period when middle-class parents objected to daughters' frequenting business offices, few penetrated the newspaper precincts. City rooms still fell in the category of sordid places, appropriate for men only. William Randolph's Hearst's star female reporter, Adela Rogers St. Johns, in 1914 described the city room as "a fire trap. A test tube for breeding tuberculosis germs." Journalism remained predominantly male; though a few glamorous female newspaper reporters gained slots, they often had to write women's columns. Journalism held fascination, but as of 1920 its promise was yet to be realized.[26]

Some graduates looked to the performing arts for careers. Although most actresses still came from theatrical middle-class and poorer families, an occasional stagestruck collegian found her way from the college stage to legitimate theater. Radcliffe's Josephine Sherwood Hull acquired fame on Broadway, and Beulah Marie Dix became a Hollywood playwright. At the end of this period, in 1920, some sought positions as theatrical producers.[27]

In the business corporations there was no place for women at either the middle range or the top. Only under unusual circumstances in a family enterprise would a woman wield much power or influence. A few white and black women showed their capacity for entrepreneurship, however, in businesses of their own or advertising agencies that catered to female consumers or real estate ventures. Book learning was not a necessary ingredient for their successes. Throughout the period college women interested in business most often took the route of private secretary, court reporter, or accountant. In the 1910s increasing numbers of women learned typing and acquired stenographic skills after graduation so that they could take secretarial positions, though as late as the start of World War I, conservative parents and businessmen objected to having women on the office staff. But, as in other fields in which women were willing to work for less their numbers grew.[28]

It is hard for late twentieth-century women to appreciate the novelty and glamor that being a secretary once held for college as well as high school graduates. Some preferred typing to teaching as short-term employment, particularly as teacher certification requirements expanded and eventually made a post-college year of training mandatory for public schoolteaching. The pre–World War I generations looked upon these jobs as new, exciting employment options, and the establishment of Katharine Gibbs and other genteel schools offering post-college courses gave social approval to this type of employment. As a result, for a long time sought-after secretarial jobs did not become available to those of lower social status, including Jewish and black women.

At the other end of the scale, the most prestigious professions—the ministry, medicine, law, and academia—while not literally closed to women, remained supremely male strongholds. In the sphere of religion, unusual dissenters of one sort or another had from colonial times revealed their potentiality for leadership. Still, in the 1880s as in earlier times, a woman might lead in the creation of a new religious group—Mary Baker Eddy in founding Christian Science, for example—but women rarely became members of the ordained clergy. Only in a few denominations—Congregationalist, Methodist, and Quaker—did a minority become preachers. Unswerving purposefulness and spiritual intensity were needed to overcome the prejudices against female ministers, and among the early college women only a few stayed exclusively with this calling. Antoinette Brown Blackwell, Olympia Brown, and Anna Howard Shaw—all became better known as leaders in the women's movement.[29]

Feminist incentives strengthened women's resolve to end their exclusion from the fields of law and medicine. Changes in legal education facilitated their entry somewhat. Although lawyering had the most masculine connotations, those who wanted to improve women's status knew that they must begin with the laws. Women in lawyers' families had long read law books and had been encouraged by fathers, husbands, or brothers to master the material. It was one thing to read in the family setting, but another to become a student at an institution.

Between 1870 and 1920 law schools gradually replaced the apprenticeship system of training in a lawyer's office. Although a college degree was not required for admission to every law school, many women studying law did in fact have undergraduate degrees. St. Louis University in 1869 was the first school to admit students irrespective of sex, and Ada Kapley became the first female in the country to receive a law degree, from Union College of Law in 1870. Not unexpectedly, women encountered opposition to their entrance to law schools. The familiar pattern of institutional doors slowly opening was enacted at Michigan (1870), Yale (1886), Cornell (1887), New York University (1891), and Stanford (1895). Only at Howard University in Washington, D.C. (1896), could both black and white women enroll. Notable among those schools excluding women were Columbia, Harvard, Georgetown, and the University of Virginia. There was one other institutional route, however, for ambitious individuals, including immigrant sons and daughters who could pursue the study of law part-time, at night. Portia Law School in Boston and Cambridge Law School were established in 1915 as separate night schools for women. It was unlikely that this kind of institution received many college graduates.[30]

Yet graduation from law school was only one hurdle, women discovered; passing the bar exams and practicing law did not always follow. Different states at different times acceded to women's demands to practice. By 1920 anyone with proper credentials could, theoretically, become a lawyer; yet women still constituted only 1.4 percent of lawyers in the United States. Most women lawyers either joined fathers' or husbands' offices, and the woman who practiced law independently was relatively rare. Some women who collaborated thus were outstanding: Belle LaFollette, for example, wrote one of the most important briefs her husband presented to the Supreme Court. And even if they did not practice, women lawyers like Florence Kelley, Gail Laughlin, Crystal Eastman, and Alice Paul, often used their expertise as leaders in women's organizations, to encourage women's professional advancement.[31]

Historically, women's access to the medical profession developed differently. By 1870 the earlier efforts to establish a place for women in medicine had produced visible results. To younger women the careers of the well-known pioneers Elizabeth Blackwell (single) and Mary Putnam Jacobi (married) represented, not only service, but power and freedom to educated women. The woman doctor was personally independent while she improved the health of women and children. The medical profession attracted such aspirants as Jane Addams and

Gertrude Stein, both of whom eventually dropped out, and distinguished scientists like Alice Hamilton and Florence Sabin, who achieved renown in medical research.[32]

The late nineteenth century witnessed a rise in the number of women doctors, from less than twenty-five hundred in 1880 to at least nine thousand in 1910. Dr. Martha Eliot, Radcliffe '13, Johns Hopkins '21, remembered so many women doctors practicing in Boston during her childhood that she saw nothing unusual about planning to become a doctor. In the 1900s 25 percent of all women physicians in the country were located in Boston, where they comprised 13.7 percent of the city's doctors. But the peak of 6 percent of all doctors in the United States, reached in 1910, was not sustained. This trend stopped short early in the twentieth century for complex reasons. The mid-nineties saw the opening to women of regular medical schools like Michigan and Johns Hopkins, and gradually the "irregular" medical schools—homeopathic, eclectic, and physiomedical—began to close; many of these were women's medical colleges, and all contained large numbers of female students. By 1894, 66.4 percent of female medical students attended regular medical schools. However, the place for women in the university medical schools were far fewer than those available earlier in separate women's schools, and the proportion of female students began dropping. Whereas women in the regular medical schools sometimes comprised as much as 10 percent of their class in the 1880s and 1890s, by 1910 their proportion was usually half that. Mary Walsh's *Doctors Wanted: No Women Need Apply* argues that fluctuations in female enrollments depended on restrictive medical school policies.[33]

While it is clear that medical schools controlled women's admission, both directly and indirectly, the issue of discrimination is complicated by Regina Morantz's discovery that fewer women applied to medical schools in the latter part of the period. What explains this decline? Why did fewer women proportionately aspire to be doctors? As the medical profession advanced, the image of the male doctor as an expert was exalted, and fewer young women saw themselves functioning in this male preserve. In addition, with women no longer the special clientele of female doctors (as they had been in the late nineteenth century), women's work in the profession was less clearly defined. By 1920 even the most determined women were confronting both old and and new problems in becoming part of the medical profession. Opposition from the male establishment never lessened. The increasing prestige of the field for men reinforced the subjective and objective barriers impeding women physicians. As in law, women with a professional degree encountered further obstacles to practice. In 1920 the American Medical Association directory listed only 40 out of 482 general hospitals that included women on their staffs. Women's struggles for acceptance, repeated at every level of training, from school to internship to hospital staff, underscore the continuous male resistance to women in medicine. Those women who succeeded in becoming doctors made a courageous commitment and, contrary to public impression and claims of the male medical establishment, used their professional training even if they married. A substantial minority of women doctors (25 to 33 percent) combined medical careers with marriage.[34]

Throughout the period the college-bred found in graduate liberal arts study a new professional alternative. The first to seek the degree of doc-

TABLE 6

Trends in Academic Degrees and Faculty Employment, 1870–1980

Year	Percentage of women as undergraduates	Percentage of women with bachelor's or first professional degree	Percentage of women with doctorates	Percentage of women as faculty
1870	21	15	0	12
1880	32	19	6	36
1890	35	17	1	20
1900	35	19	6	20
1910	39	25	11	20
1920	47	34	15	26
1930	43	40	18	27
1940	40	41	13	28
1950	31	24	10	25
1960	36	35	10	22
1970	41	41	13	25
1971	42	42	14	22
1972	42	42	16	22
1973	43	42	18	23
1974	45	42	19	24
1975	45	43	21	24
1976	45	44	23	24
1977	48	44	24	25
1978	49	45	26	—
1979	—	46	28	26
1980	51	47	30	26

Sources: Patricia A. Graham, "Expansion and Exclusion: A History of Women in American Higher Education," *Signs: Journal of Women in Culture and Society* 3 (Summer 1978); U.S. Department of Health, Education, and Welfare, National Center for Education Statistics, *Digest of Education Statistics* 1980, 1982. Mabel Newcomer, *A Century of Higher Education for American Women* (New York, 1959), 46.

tor of philosophy met instant opposition from institutions—academic skeptics asked what possible use a Ph.D. would be to a woman. If the answer was vague in 1870, by 1920 recipients of the degree had fully demonstrated their professionalism. Determination and sacrifice led to partial triumphs for some women even before the ultimate grudging acceptance on the part of institutions still in need of graduate students (see table 6).

The undergraduate woman began collegiate study at the time when the Ph.D. was appearing dimly on the academic horizon. The first American degree was awarded to a man at Yale in 1862. It was not long before Boston University, in 1877, bestowed the first degree on a woman, Helen Magill, an alumna of Swarthmore. In 1880 Cornell, Syracuse, and the University of Pennsylvania each awarded one doctoral degree to a woman, and by the end of the century 228 women and 2,372 men had received doctorates.[35]

Between 1870 and 1920 women received little active, direct institutional encouragement to embark on graduate study, yet they found ways to make this precious education a reality. Some of the same women who fought their way into college struggled later for admittance to graduate school. Undoubtedly the challenge of crossing another barrier had its appeal. Women's colleges, still establishing credentials, were less prepared to offer advanced study; only Bryn Mawr, at the insistence of then dean M. Carey Thomas, included a Ph.D. program from the beginning in 1885. In the 1890s, however, because of pressure from a few women who were studying informally with sympathetic mentors, most major American universities, with some conspicuous exceptions, admitted women as doctoral candidates. Yale and Pennsylvania became coeducational at the graduate level rather than the undergraduate by design. Columbia relented in 1900, but faculties could still restrict women's access. Harvard, rather than be coerced into granting its Ph.D. to women, made sure that Radcliffe College gave the Ph.D. degree in 1902. Johns Hopkins's capitulation came in 1907, but Princeton and the University of Virginia, among a few others, remained closed to women until 1970.

Interestingly, when the sphere of graduate study was most limited, in the 1880s and 1890s, some aspirants, undaunted, applied to European centers of learning. Whereas in the United States male academics feared women's access would downgrade the option for men, German universities placed restrictions on women to protect the large numbers of men attending. American women pushed their way first into the Swiss University at Zurich and with considerably more difficulty enrolled at some German institutions where they startled skeptics with brilliant academic performances. Such women could not be written off as dilettantes. Margaret Rossiter, in her comprehensive study of women scientists, points out that Americans' battles for degrees had facilitated university access for German women by 1910.[36]

In the United States a vigorous minority of college women made opportunities for themselves at a time when graduate education at research universities was transforming academia. To a considerable extent a love of learning motivated the first female doctoral students to prolong their period of study—especially when parents agreed to pay for it. As with early undergraduate enrollments, an understanding parent might foster a young woman's aspirations. Helen Magill (White), a member of the first graduating class at Swarthmore (where her father was president), had strong family support. Mary Calkins, whose educated parents gave her every advantage, did her undergraduate work in classics at Smith and afterward, with her father's encouragement, became a tutor in Greek at Wellesley. After studying at Harvard under William James, Josiah Royce, and Hugo Münsterberg, she passed the Ph.D. examination with distinction in 1895. Still, Harvard refused to grant her the degree, and Calkins ten years later rejected the sop of a retroactive Radcliffe degree. At Johns Hopkins others met similar rebuffs, from M. Carey Thomas's not being permitted to attend graduate school to Christine Ladd-Franklin's not being awarded the Ph.D. she had earned in psychology to Florence Bascom's being awarded a degree in geology as an "exception." After the first inroads, the process by which the select few went from undergraduate to graduate study gained momentum in the twentieth century. Strengthened above all by achievements in college and supported by one another, these collegians formed a tiny female graduate subculture in pursuing the Ph.D. Those described here became distinguished scholars or educators.[37]

From the 1880s the Association of College Alumnae, founded by early graduates, became a major support for the new academic women. Some also had encouragement from professors, both male and female, although this influence on students was either fortuitous or consciously selective. Women professors did not see themselves as models for all students. Rather, they recognized individuals in whom they saw promise as potential teachers, would-be scientists, and future historians, social reformers, and writers. Fundamentally, faculty members were not accustomed to regarding women students as potential scholars.

At both women's colleges and coeducational instititutions, some professors urged graduate study for the individual of exceptional ability and promise. After all, in this period of academic transition relatively few males of outstanding ability chose academic paths to success. Nonetheless the professors who accepted women students and believed in their potentiality for scholarship did not assume they had the same professional goals as men. The academic woman still seemed an anomaly.

No one knew how far she could advance. Only a few professional women like M. Carey Thomas were convinced that educators must work to "make it possible for the few women of creative and constructive genius born in any generation to join the few men of genius in their generation in the service of their common race."[38]

Although some ambitious women had financial as well as psychological support, some did not; the ACA and other advocates of women in academia acknowledged the paucity of fellowships, which limited the number of women who could realistically expect to earn a Ph.D. Some brilliant students had to spend long years earning money to pay for this costly period of study. Cornell gave the first fellowship to a woman in 1884, but females were generally ineligible for most graduate fellowships open to men. The eventual establishment of fellowships usually offered only partial assistance to women. Generous fellowships to women and men at Chicago accompanied the opening of the university, but the good example did not last in the 1900s. At most coeducational schools, Wisconsin and Columbia, for example, fellowships were unequally distributed, with the proportion allotted to women changing and usually declining over time. At Columbia, the best fellowships (of $650, at a time when a year's full-time study cost about $600) were reserved exclusively for men, and out of thirty-two scholarships of $150, women could apply for only four. The women's colleges set up alternative fellowships (Bryn Mawr established a traveling fellowship for study abroad, of which Emily Greene Balch was the initial recipient in 1889). However, despite the efforts of the ACA and its successor, the American Association of University Women (AAUW), which raised money for fellowships, women were not provided with the same level of support that men enjoyed in this period. In a 1924 study of almost sixteen hundred Ph.D.s, Emilie Hutchinson described the sacrifices made by many women in combining graduate study with part-time and even full-time teaching and other forms of employment. Although nearly 70 percent had received scholarships or fellowships, the amount of the stipends never covered expenses.[39]

Several persons, notably physiologist Ida Hyde and biologist Nettie Stevens, achieved extraordinary success, becoming scholars despite great social and economic disadvantages. Both lacked family support of any kind but earned a living and saved money to begin college at a late age. Jobs ranging from domestic to factory worker to hatmaker to schoolteacher carried some of these women to institutional recognition and the full realization of their potential.[40]

Still others from disadvantaged groups had no institutional encouragement. Although Jessie Fauset, a black undergraduate at Cornell, was elected to Phi Beta Kappa in 1905, her classics professor discouraged her from graduate study, stating bluntly that she would not be able to use the training. Later Fauset received an M.A. in French literature from the University of Pennsylvania. In 1921 the first doctorates were finally awarded to three black women: Georgiana Simpson (University of Chicago), Sadie Tanner Mossell (University of Pennsylvania), and Eva B. Dykes (Radcliffe).[41]

By then the number of female Ph.D.'s had soared; in the 1920s and 1930s it would reach a peak of approximately 15 or 16 percent, with some variations in different fields. The Ph.D. was becoming, for women as for men, a form of certification for academic teachers and thus a professional asset. In a 1924 survey many women cited vocational motives for acquiring the degree.

The proportion of female Ph.D. holders in languages and literature declined after the turn of the century from nearly one-half to around one-quarter, whereas the number of Ph.D.'s in the natural sciences and mathematics rose slowly over the same time. Margaret Rossiter has shown that even though more women received degrees in the humanities and social sciences, a considerably greater proportion of women Ph.D.'s in the sciences (in fields ranging from botany and zoology to psychology and anthropology) achieved distinction as scholars. In this period of academic ferment, individuals explored frontiers of knowledge in new and old disciplines. Classical studies in the established field of philology and the new one of archaeology shaped the work of outstanding scholars like Abby Leach (who became the first woman president of the American Philological Association in 1889), Grace Harriet Macurdy, Mary Hamilton Swindler, and Lily Ross Taylor. Professors Myra Reynolds and Alice Snyder were literary scholars, and Vassar graduate Constance Rourke became a literary critic and explorer of American popular culture. Psychology, sociology, economics, and applied chemistry in home economics became fields in which women found varying ways to get a foothold in the academic world.[42]

The exceptional contributions of a few women were made in the face of circumscribed opportunities. By the end of the period their acceptance as members of faculty in coeducational institutions remained problematic. One self-supporting student, Lois Kimball Matthews, who earned her way through Stanford by schoolteaching and followed her Wisconsin mentor, Professor Frederick Jackson Turner, to Harvard, eventually wrote a brilliant thesis, earning a Radcliffe Ph.D. Although her book *The Expansion of New England* (1909) became a classic in the history of the American West, she ended up as dean of women at the University of Wisconsin and did not continue as a historian. As we have seen, others were channeled into the home economics departments of their institutions regardless of their graduate training.[43]

Most Ph.D. holders who realized professional goals remained single.

Of the two hundred and twenty-nine women who received the doctorate in the nineteenth century, only sixteen were married at the time the degree was conferred. Three-quarters of the roughly sixteen hundred women in the AAUW sample, which covered the period up until 1924, were unmarried, divorced, or separated. Furthermore, whereas more female Ph.D. students began marrying, only one-tenth, which represented one-half of those married, combined marriage and career in the mid-1920s. Married academic women received no support in the prewar period when women's colleges gave opportunities only to the single woman. The first award of an AAUW fellowship to a married woman in 1929 marked a real change.[44]

Investing in female scholars seemed a great risk to the academic establishment. Regardless of a woman's intellect and dedication, the expectation that a female's training would be lost upon marriage impeded the expansion of opportunities. Nor did most women question the underlying assumption that matrimony would, and should, abrogate academic commitment, thereby ending a promising career. But whereas some potential scholars turned down fellowship offers in favor of marriage proposals, some potential brides turned down grooms in favor of pursuing careers. Each recognized the limitations placed on her future and chose accordingly. But only for the relatively few women trained at the highest level did work become the means to public advancement in a profession or scholarly field and to self-fulfillment.[45]

Professional women knew that they were atypical of their sex and tended to view their professionalism as an "experiment" with existing limitations and an uncertain future. They operated under considerable disadvantages compared to men in their fields. In all professions, the work women did became "women's work," and the term always had negative overtones. Those women with the most status suffered from devaluation of their research, just as did other members of their sex in feminized positions such as teachers, secretaries, and librarians. Not surprisingly, some women wondered whether they were most useful in paid endeavors; professional goals evoked ambivalent feelings in them. While for men the pattern of extending educational years for professional training after college became conventional after 1910, for women the decision to attend a liberal arts college and to continue with further education involving long years of expense and commitment usually meant having to delay or renounce the option of marriage. As going to college became an acceptable way to spend four late adolescent years for the middle-class girl, so the notion of continuing in professional training became the nonconforming act of a few women.

All professional women—doctors, lawyers, and academics—knew that they were only at the beginning of a trial, with a long way to go before acceptance in the public, the man's, world. Thus they still identified with other women less fortunate than themselves. Edith Abbott noted in 1918 that "the efforts of the professional woman to realize a new ideal of pecuniary independence" constituted "a social revolution" that the "woman of the working classes" was not part of; the working-class woman's situation was one in which no "measure of opportunity" had come about, for her situation was "very much as her great grandmother left it." Abbott spoke as a scholar in the social sciences, a long-time resident of Hull House, and a founder of the Chicago School of Social Work. Whether working as professionals or volunteers, educated women focused most on what they knew best—the woman's world and its problems. Middle-class women who held paid jobs and women active in voluntary work moved in two separate worlds; most still worked with other women in the public sectors of the economy and in their clubs and associations. Thus, they had ample opportunity to reflect on the problem of work and family from the female perspective.[46]

The first World War interrupted the segregated patterns of women's employment at all levels. Those who had experienced limitations as professionals gained renewed hope from the acceptance of all women in the crisis. Yet the war also brought educated women into conflict with each other and with men. Jane Addams, Emily Balch, Crystal Eastman, and others spoke for an important minority who opposed the war and worked for an early peace. By contrast, many suffragists like Harriet Stanton Blatch welcomed the event as an opportunity to prove their patriotism and demonstrate women's capabilities. With the United States' declaration of war in 1917, college presidents made it easy for women students to take leaves to work for the war, as nurses and farmers, while the men went to the front.[47]

The opportunities for educated women in the war paralleled the advances of women factory workers. For a short period it seemed as though the separateness of the spheres was dissolving as women became welders and streetcar conductors at home, and telephone operators, nurses, and YWCA volunteers overseas. This war, like others, gave professional women more openings in government, business, and universities. Home economists gave valuable service to the nation. Dr. Alice Hamilton's expertise in toxicology made her indispensable, and as a result of her work she was appointed the first woman faculty member at the Harvard School of Medicine.[48]

The contribution of women at every level, as volunteers, professionals, farmers, industrial workers, and teachers, rose as the twentieth century unfolded. Women working for pay and for the love of service proved the capacity of their sex to accomplish many things and contribute as citizens to the growth of the nation.

From the Civil War to World War I the new college women demonstrated the usefulness of their education. As wives, mothers, professionals, and volunteers, they had a sense of purpose that carried them into diverse associations. They welcomed and sustained the growing company of educated women in careers, occupations, voluntary causes, and recreation. Responding to the unsettling changes in American society in the course of their lives, they saw more education as the means of furthering their goals of service to American society and for the advancement of their sex. Participation in World War I and the passage of the Nineteenth Amendment seemed to augur other successes in the future. Their contributions on behalf of many groups placed them beyond the private, family-oriented arena to which females had formerly been relegated. In 1920 they anticipated an era in which women would be at the center to shape a new world. In their view, the promise of the educated woman had just begun.

N·I·N·E

The Collegiate Education of Women: Its Plural Strands, 1920–1940

No one would wish a college to be homogeneous in
the wealth or race or social status of the families of its students;
but a certain homogeneity in aims, aspirations, and intellectual
ability in the student group has value in the education
which the College offers.

Ada L. Comstock, president of Radcliffe College,
Annual Report, 1927

In the aftermath of World War I, young people swept into the colleges, and with the force of an unexpected whirlwind a new era in higher education began. Women participated fully in this rush to academia (see table 2). Wartime achievements of an older generation not only demonstrated the utility of women's education but served as a call to younger women to take advantage of expanded opportunities. For more and more women and men of various racial, ethnic, and religious backgrounds, going to college became a necessary prelude to a successful life. Although overall, collegians remained predominantly white and Protestant, growing numbers of blacks, Catholics, and Jews came as well. The significant rise in numbers encouraged the growth of institutions for particular groups. Moreover, the numbers and variety of collegians precipitated new reviews of the liberal education. What purpose did it serve to so many newcomers? Which Americans would benefit from it? How could a common liberal education be preserved and advanced by which to identify the educated? And once again the corollary question arose: should women's education be the same as men's?

In this chapter we consider the impact of widening institutional access for women in a dynamic period spanning the prosperous twenties and struggling thirties. Educational pluralism shaped the expectations and experiences of female students at diverse institutions. All colleges, while serving particular clienteles, responded to the standards set by the most prestigious institutions and coped with the conflicting pressures of assimilation and separatism in higher education. Balancing these concerns would have different implications for women than for men.

College gained even more importance for both female and male youth in this period. It has often been noted that the percentage of women in the total college enrollments peaked in 1920 at 47.3 percent; thereafter, the proportion of women students declined, to 43.7 percent in 1929–30 and 40.2 percent in 1939–40. Nevertheless, although the overall percentage of women dropped during the Depression, their absolute numbers rose; and included among these were more individuals from different ethnic and religious groups. In 1919–20, of the approximately 600,000 students enrolled in the country's colleges, 283,000 were women; ten years later, in 1930, women comprised 480,000 of the 1,100,000 college students; and by 1940, college students numbered 1,500,000, of whom 601,000 were women. Moreover, the percentage of American women between the ages of eighteen and twenty-one who entered college doubled between 1910 and 1920, from 3.8 percent to 7.6 percent; by 1930 college women comprised 10.5 percent of the eighteen- to twenty-one-year-olds, and even during the Depression their proportion increased, to 12.2 percent by 1940 (see tables 2 and 3).[1]

Not all institutions welcomed the influx. State and city colleges, supported by the government and taxpayers, absorbed the bulk of the huge increases in enrollment of both sexes in the 1920s. Coeducational schools west of the Mississippi sustained enrollments in the thousands, transforming these schools into modern big-time universities. Their scale contrasted markedly with that of the largest private colleges. While racial, ethnic, and religious diversity enlarged the college population as a whole, plural strands did not characterize some schools. But public institutions, to a varying extent, mirrored the ethnic composition of their communities. In addition, private as well as public urban institutions received more local applicants from religious, ethnic, and racial minorities. Colleges like Boston University and Radcliffe in Boston, Barnard in New York, and Goucher in Baltimore enrolled greater numbers of such students because they could live at home. Outstanding in this respect was Hunter College in New York City, a public, free institution where black, Catholic, Protestant, and Jewish undergraduates mingled. After Oberlin and Kansas State, Hunter, with 2–3 percent of its students black in the 1930s, may have admitted more black women than any school that was not designated as a black college.[2]

Educators at the older institutions were perturbed, not only by the numbers going to college, but also by the ethnic diversity of new students. The older, more secure private colleges devised policies of selectivity to restrict the access of any group that in their view would alter the traditional social composition. Most educators believed that they must preserve the so-called Anglo-Saxon superiority of their colleges and used the popular scientific theory of inherent racial differences to justify their intent.[3]

Jewish applicants became the most conspicuous target. They did not have the opportunity to attend schools of their own and applied to all mainstream institutions, public and private. The emerging presence of Jewish male students had already been noted by the 1910s, and in the 1920s and 1930s prestigious colleges were determined to control their numbers. Not only did Columbia, Harvard, Yale, Princeton, Dartmouth, and Amherst, for example, aim to restrict access of Jewish students, but comparable women's colleges harbored similar inclinations. Privately administrators referred to the "Jewish problem," by which they meant the large number of qualified women (as well as men) applicants in this group. Each college's admissions policy was made arbitrarily, based on the availability of other applicants. In 1937 five eastern women's colleges exchanged information on their admissions policies, as shown in table 7A. Table 7B shows that Radcliffe admitted a larger proportion than the others. Nevertheless, despite tacit or overt restrictions, the numbers of Jewish women rose at all types of colleges.[4]

Catholic students also entered local public and private nonsectarian institutions; despite the old prejudices against their religion, they now became the most acceptable of the newcomers. Their numbers varied, depending on the regional options. In Boston for example, socially mobile Irish Catholics had already trickled into Boston University, Radcliffe, and Simmons College before there was a local Catholic college for women. Catholics had made their way into state universities as well, especially in the Mid- and Far West.[5]

Far smaller was the presence of black students in the predominantly white colleges. Raymond Wolters has noted that, in 1927, of the more than thirteen thousand black college students in the United States, approximately fifteen hundred attended such institutions; only at Oberlin did blacks constitute as much as 4 percent of the student body. In 1926, W. E. B. DuBois, reviewing the situation, commented on the scant admissions of black females to the elite schools: "Vassar had graduated but one Negro student and did not know it at the time. Bryn Mawr and Barnard have tried desperately to exclude them. Radcliffe, Wellesley, and Smith have treated them with tolerance and even cordiality. Many small institutions or institutions with one or two Negro students have been gracious and kind toward them, particularly in the Middle West. But on the whole, the attitude of northern institutions is one which varies from tolerance to active hostility." Policies that restricted or

TABLE 7A
Percentage of Jewish Students Enrolled at
Five Eastern Women's Colleges, 1936–38[a]

	1936–37	1937–38
Mount Holyoke	6.5	7.4
Wellesley	9.0	9.4
Vassar	9.4	10.3
Smith	10.0	12.9
Radcliffe	24.8	16.5

[a]In 1937–38, "Bryn Mawr reports that it has no Jewish problem—of this year's freshman class, 6.0 percent are Jewish."

TABLE 7B
Radcliffe Freshman Admissions, 1934–37

	1934–35	1935–36	1936–37	1937–38
Total number of applicants	264	296	310	351
Number of Jewish applicants	not indicated	not indicated	79	86
Total admissions	198	203	205	200
Jewish admissions	35	42	51	33
Percentage Jewish admissions	17.7	20.7	24.8	16.5

Source: This chart is based on information in a file entitled "Admissions, the Jewish Problem," November 1, 1937, in the Ada L. Comstock Papers, Radcliffe College.

denied access to blacks were not always stated publicly, as they sometimes were for Jewish students, and proved in fact more rigid. Established institutions did not expect black students to apply, and only a rare one did.[6]

Most women students attended predominantly white, coeducational institutions, although some enrolled in women's colleges. But in this period options for Catholic women expanded through the development of separate Catholic women's colleges. Moreover, black women enrolled not only in the older, coeducational black colleges, but also in two rising distinctive black women's colleges. Black and Catholic women had far greater options than had previously been provided by mainstream educational institutions.

Private black colleges (except Wilberforce) were started by white missionaries in the 1860s and 1870s. These schools, like many predominantly white institutions, opened with preparatory departments and slowly developed collegiate programs. Among black liberal arts colleges, Fisk in Nashville, Tennessee, and Howard University in Washington, D.C., represented the best academically; other schools also offered some college work. From the outset, most black institutions were coeducational, for their communities could not afford the luxury of single-sex schools. The two separate institutions for women that emerged had the backing of northern women's philanthropic and religious organizations. Spelman, in Atlanta, Georgia, moved from female seminary to collegiate status in 1925, and Bennett, in Greensboro, North Carolina, originally a coeducational school, became a women's college in 1926.

Before World War I, the numbers of females enrolled in black colleges were small, for more women took a teacher-training course than a liberal arts degree. Significant increases occurred in the 1920s, however, and during the 1930s women became the majority in black colleges. But educational statistics from 1929 showed women already in the majority at some black colleges. Even during the Depression, black women knew that degrees would guarantee them jobs as teachers at segregated schools, while the utility of degrees for black men was more doubtful. In 1939–40 women numbered 21,418 at black institutions, compared with 16,311 men.[7]

It was in the 1920s also that acceptance of collegiate education for women became more widespread among Catholics. Women's colleges met the increased demand, in response not only to the Church's preference for separation of the sexes, but to the reluctance of Catholic men's colleges to adopt coeducation. Educators had observed a trend of Catholic attendance at nonsectarian private and public colleges and decided to promote their own institutions to instill Catholic Christian values. By 1915 Catholic women's colleges that had begun as seminaries included St. Catherine in St. Paul, St. Theresa in Winona, St. Benedict in St. Joseph, St. Scholasticus in Duluth, all in Minnesota, and Manhattanville of the Sacred Heart in New York City. Other institutions started as colleges, namely, Trinity in Washington, D.C., in 1899, and Emmanuel and Regis in the Boston area, in 1919 and 1927 respectively. Chicago and its suburbs became another center for a cluster of institutions that included Rosary, Xavier, Barat, and Mundelein. The number of Catholic women's colleges grew from only 14 in 1915 to 37 in 1925 and 116 by 1955.[8]

The growth of these colleges marked social and economic advances of Catholic families, more of whom were in a position to encourage the education of their daughters. Suitable instruction in a protective setting appealed to the well-to-do and those especially pious. While some Catholic parents stressed education's economic and vocational advantages and urged daughters to enter established secular colleges, many wealthier families placed their girls at Catholic institutions like residential Manhattanville.

Not only did student populations in black and Catholic schools comprise different socioeconomic elements, all schools began to see a greater variety within the college community. Attendance at a particular institution did not necessarily indicate a student's social status. By the 1920s one variant of the American myth of success applied to needy aspiring college youth, female as well as male, for although such students were still relatively few in the college population, their presence made a difference—to the colleges as well as the larger society.

Certainly the very poor had no access to college, but cost discouraged attendance by many middle-class Americans as well. However, both upwardly mobile and established sons as well as daughters attended both public and private schools. Nonetheless, data collected by O. Edgar Reynolds in 1923 showed that, as in the preceding period, the median family income of women attending private, nonsectarian women's colleges ($5,140) was considerably higher than that of women in state universities ($3,349). Moreover, the families of those attending nonstate coeducational institutions had a slightly lower median income ($3,091).[9]

Although more families in the 1920s could spare daughters to go to college, inflation did affect the ability of many to sustain this financial commitment; the crash of 1929 and the onset of the Great Depression extended the hardships to far more. Helen Goetsch's analysis of gifted Milwaukee high school students in 1937 and 1939, for example, indicated that the median parental income for those planning to attend college full-time was $1,988.46—far less than Reynolds's figure for the average income of college families in the mid-1920s.[10]

At a time when the majority of American youths could not go to college, those who made it from poor families, as in earlier decades, had psychological support from parents or teachers or both. Immigrant and native black parents often gave the essential encouragement to daughters as well as sons to gain collegiate education. Thus, one woman recalled: "My father made tremendous sacrifices for me to go to college. He was an Irish immigrant (with a salary of $125 a month), and, like most Europeans, he thought education was the answer." Similarly, a daughter of a Japanese immigrant family in California said: "My father felt a powerful need to educate his children and was always willing to give us a lot of time to study although he had to work even harder on our strawberry farm."[11]

Some black parents left the South for New York City, where daughters could attend Hunter College. Likewise, the mother of future high school supervisor Ida Jackson had moved her family to California because she wanted her children to have access to better education. Not only parents but extended families cooperated to promote the education of black women; relatives often boarded female students whose immediate families lived too far away from a college.[12]

The devastating economic disaster of the thirties did not make the problems of staying in college any more difficult for black students than they had already been. One women student remembered: "I didn't feel any great contrast. . . . We didn't have much to begin with so we didn't have much to lose."[13]

Indeed, most families of black students were far from wealthy, as shown both by income figures and by analysis of the occupations of their fathers. A study of over five thousand black collegians graduating in the early 1930s indicated that 48 percent had fathers who worked at unskilled jobs—as compared to the 4.7 percent in Reynolds's predominantly white sample. A study of the black collegians at Howard University in 1929 found that their median family income ($1,560) was only about one-half that of white students in comparable institutions. Black parents made great sacrifices, it is clear, to send their children to college, often spending close to one-third of the entire family income. As one analyst observed, it is "an enigma" how some black students managed to stay in school.[14]

Over the period increasing numbers of white as well as black students had to contribute to the payment of their college expenses. Although more men than women worked either part- or full-time, the growing trend of "self-help" students included females. This proportion became a significant element in the college-going population. The College Club of St. Louis, a branch of the American Association of University Women, in a 1923 study covering 170 colleges and universities, found that 15 percent of the students of private women's colleges contributed something to their support while at college. Reynolds's study confirmed these findings.[15]

However, in Reynolds's study a higher proportion of female students contributing to their expenses were found at state universities and nonstate coeducational colleges, 32 and 40 percent respectively. Women attending coeducational colleges were particularly dependent on their own resources, with 6 percent supporting themselves completely. There were regional differences in the numbers in the broad category of self-supporting students; more of them attended western colleges and fewer the southern white schools. A more comprehensive report in 1929 provided information about "self-help" students in every state, including responses from 763 colleges and universities. Walter Greenleaf's results reinforced Reynolds's earlier study, and while proportions did not change in the five years spanning the two studies, larger enrollments included more students who earned their way.[16]

Although Greenleaf concluded that being a self-help student no longer detracted from the social status of the individual, this view seems problematic, especially for the 1920s. Such students earned money in libraries, administrative offices, and in summers at camps and restaurants. Many worked in private homes for room and board, in child-care, and also grading papers and doing clerical work. All agreed they would do this over again. One wonders what one Wellesley student really felt when she laundered by hand the silk underwear of her classmates for forty cents an hour. This girl reported to Greenleaf: "Since the self-help girl always does some of her own laundry it pays well for a girl to do the laundry for two."[17]

Still, self-support became an accepted social fact for more and more women as well as men. Patterns established in the 1920s became commoner in the next decade, when many more families suffered economic reverses in the Great Depression. Students from formerly wealthy or comfortable families sought jobs in order to stay in college. A greater awareness of economic needs of the diverse portions of the college population impelled educators to gain public and institutional support for talented students of limited means through scholarships and loans. But institutions alone could not meet the growing needs of the students.

The federal government finally responded with an innovative approach. The National Youth Administration spent over $93 million to assist over six hundred and twenty thousand college students between 1935 and 1943. Even though this program did not satisfy the needs of all students requiring aid—only about one out of eight students was helped—the NYA helped 450,000 in 1936–37, of whom 45 percent were women. Grants and work–study funds, which averaged $15–16 per month, went further at the state schools where tuition might be as low as $25 than at Vassar or Wellesley, which charged $1,000 for tuition, room, and board. Daughters of professional families who had been brought up with the expectation of going to college were among those not able to proceed without scholarships and self-help. Kirsten Vandenberg found her way from a junior college to the University of Chicago with a scholarship renewable with a certain grade point average. Because she was working so hard at four or five jobs, she did not get the grades. It was an NYA grant that saved her college education.[18]

Although black families did not make financial gains in the thirties, some of their sons and daughters benefited from the work–study funds that the NYA made available. Fittingly a key figure in seeing that black students received a fairer share of the NYA funds was Mary McLeod

Bethune. Born into a southern rural family, she had scholarships and parental encouragement for her own education in private black schools. She founded the Daytona Normal and Industrial Institute, which became Bethune-Cookman College in 1929, and her reputation for leadership in black women's education brought her to the attention of Eleanor Roosevelt who arranged her appointment to the National Advisory Committee of the NYA. Eventually she became the director of Negro affairs in the NYA and used her influence to expand the participation of black youth in school aid programs. In the seven years of the agency, 4,118 blacks received a total of $609,930.[19]

Even though too many talented individuals were still left out, in the 1920s and 1930s, college did become more accessible to highly motivated youth from various backgrounds. But, it was undeniable that the better-off and the wealthy had visible advantages at college. Even prior to the decade of the Depression (1929–39), however, many Americans remained skeptical about what so many young people would do with a college education and how the economy could support this influx. Amid confused perceptions of the changes in academia, reviews of the purposes of higher education again mounted. Educators, confronted not only with heterogeneity but also with masses, continued to disagree on how to define liberal arts education. By 1920 the academic pendulum had moved away from the permissiveness of electives to a tightening of course structures. Harvard's new president, A. Lawrence Lowell, in the 1910's, laid this groundwork by reintroducing requirements to bring greater depth and breadth to undergraduate study. The movement to reinvigorate the humanist liberal education launched a new school, Reed College in Oregon, in 1911; Wisconsin established in 1917 its Experimental College, to be a community of learning; and in 1920 Columbia was the first to institute a formal general education program, soon adopted elsewhere. In the twenties selective honors programs, like coeducational Swarthmore's, promoted academic rigor for qualified students.[20]

Elite colleges became pacesetters, introducing experiments such as tutorial, independent study, reading period, junior year abroad, and freshman orientation. Midway through this period, in 1931, Vassar's president Henry McCracken unabashedly singled out the eastern Seven Sister women's colleges for their "steady raising of standards in teaching and learning"; their departments of classics, history, modern languages, and fine arts ranked in reputation with those of comparable men's schools. In the 1930s, educators at elite schools, influenced by University of Chicago president Robert Hutchins and educators' expert Abraham Flexner, denigrated vocationalism as mere "triviality" in the classroom.[21]

Not all institutions conformed to the standards of Harvard, Columbia, or Chicago, however; coeducational Antioch redesigned its curriculum to combine liberal study and vocationalism. In a five-year program students alternated terms of study with periods of off-campus employment. Nevertheless, at all institutions, the old questions persisted about the connections between vocational and professional goals and undergraduate education. Advocates of women's education continued to tackle their special curricular problems. A few experimental colleges for women established in this period, including Bennington, Sarah Lawrence, and Stephens (a junior college), focused on the arts. Such schools catered to affluent students. In the 1920s traditionalists, like Radcliffe's president Ada Comstock, avowed that the liberal education produced a "trained intelligence," and that women (like men) could easily acquire technical and professional training later. But other arguments gained momentum among educators who insisted that women's lifelong domestic responsibilities be addressed in their undergraduate education. Clara Brown in 1930 observed cogently that all women, professional or not, married or not, will be "maintaining homes or apartments" and "need some training in homemaking that the liberal arts colleges are not giving." Ahead of her time, Brown also pushed for the recognition that "home-making is a man's problem as well as a woman's."[22]

Controversies intensified the ways to integrate women's undergraduate study with their future roles as wives and mothers. Women's colleges everywhere found students interested in practical courses in psychology, family life, mental hygiene, and educational pedagogy. Such courses fit the old double purpose of preparing students who would go on to teach but also equipping them as future mothers. Vassar went the furthest in establishing the interdisciplinary major of euthenics. Although few students majored in it, many sampled its courses. Domestic relevance reached absurd levels when some educators tried to codify every subject in the curriculum to fit the peculiar needs of female students, as if to guarantee that all would acquire knowledge solely for the purpose of domesticity. One Smith student objected, "I study chemistry because I want *chemistry*. . . . I must have all that I can get. . . . Of course I'm interested in the chemistry of nutrition—but in an entirely different way." Although feminist Ethel Puffer Howes, as director of the Institute for the Coordination of Women's Interests, had a theoretical conception of how to incorporate women's perspectives into every college course, she was not able to implement her ideas. Thus, what might have become women's studies did not develop in the 1920s and 1930s.[23]

Many women of all backgrounds could not attend college without taking into account what they would do afterward; they knew that they had to be gainfully employed. Even the elite women's colleges had to acknowledge the practical interests of their students by active promotion of vocational bureaus (which they had already started before World War I). There were real differences, however, in the ways that institutions approached these concerns. In contrast to the prestigious women's colleges, public state universities, as well as black and Catholic colleges, openly emphasized vocational preparation.

The dean of women's report of the University of California in 1930 took into account different vocational incentives. It was not a minority of females, Lucy Stebbins stressed, but a majority who sought guidance "in the choice of a calling." These she categorized as: first, those who had to be self-supporting and possibly support others; second, those whose parents expected to be repaid for their educational expenses but were free of further financial demands; third, those who felt that earning money was a sign of usefulness; and fourth and finally, those seeking outlets for their special talents and abilities. Stebbins believed that the wise direction of all these types was not "hostile to fine scholarship." Her balanced perceptions of the economic as well as social motives of women at a large public state university had relevance to groups at other colleges.[24]

Black and Catholic educators had their own problems to resolve on the issue of vocationalism. From the turn of the century Booker T. Washington and W. E. B. DuBois had clashed over the competing values of liberal arts and technical subjects for black men and women. Washington at Tuskegee Institute implemented industrial education, making it the predominant pattern at schools for blacks, whereas DuBois upheld classical liberal arts education for the "talented tenth." To DuBois, with his B.A. from Fisk and Ph.D. from Harvard, pursuit of liberal arts studies symbolized essential aspirations for black men and women.

Prior to World War I, few black institutions offered a full liberal arts program, and those that did had only a handful of college-level students. Most black women studying beyond the elementary level took industrial courses at colleges or other schools. They learned specific skills—domestic, nursing, sewing, hatmaking, printing—but along with these classes took some liberal arts courses, including English, music, and bible study. The growing enrollment of women at black colleges coincided with the academic advancement of these institutions. Increasingly females entered the more advanced colleges like coeducational Howard and Fisk, the rising women's institutions of Spelman and Bennett, and others less advanced. Throughout the period educators who shared DuBois' view campaigned to raise the standards of female collegiate education. Such groups as the National Association of College Women and the National Council of Negro Women were committed to improving the academic quality of black institutions.[25]

Lucy Slowe, dean of women at Howard (1922–1937), in touch with deans at older colleges, pushed for increases in the number of liberal arts courses in order to "lessen rather than perpetuate the cultural isolation" of the black college-bred woman. Slowe urged the introduction of courses in political science, economics, sociology, and psychology. In the pattern of white women educators of the early twentieth century, she saw liberal education as a way to develop both individuality and the capacity for community leadership among young women. Slowe was one of several black women educators who, while seeking to enlarge offerings in liberal arts courses, did not make false dichotomies between learning and utility. Despite the focus on the liberal arts offerings, training in vocational skills was not abandoned.[26]

The development of the two women's colleges, Spelman and Bennett, exemplifies the balance sought. In 1881 two white teachers, Sophia Packard and Harriet Giles, had brought books and bibles to Atlanta to start Spelman Female Seminary. During Florence Read's presidency (1927–53) Spelman matured into a full-fledged liberal arts college. Of great importance for its academic growth, Spelman in 1929 gained official affiliation with the Atlanta University group (Morehouse College, Clarke, Morris Brown, and Atlanta University). Spelman students thus enjoyed the intellectual and social advantages of a coordinate college. Atlanta's president John Hope promoted a more demanding curriculum and encouraged activities in the creative arts. Yet, with the expansion of the academic offerings in the 1930s and 1940s, Spelman, like the older eastern women's colleges, successfully instituted some of the newer "practical" kinds of programs including child psychology and music. The training of a "lady" was inculcated with a down-to-earth view of the future of these women students.[27]

Black Bennett (Greensboro, North Carolina), had become a school for women in 1926. Although it offered a blend of liberal arts and teacher education, under the direction of Dr. David Jones, it committed itself to what he called a "functional" education for black women. Jones, an extraordinary leader in interracial organizations, saw women as especially handicapped, "first as members of an ethnic group which is relatively isolated and, in a sense, lives in two worlds—America and Negro America; second, as the brunt of social attitudes and traditions, resulting directly from the process of cultural lag, which have exerted a retarding influence on the complete emancipation of women." David Jones, like Lucy Slowe, acknowledged that black women had to surmount double barriers of sex and color. Jones made it his mission to provide education that equipped "the black student both to live within the limitations imposed by virtue of her color," and "to enable her to transcend the racial boundaries and to reach beyond these limitations in an endeavor to obtain the satisfactions and privileges of the wider life which the color line seeks to deny; and finally it will prepare her to fulfill the role which society has assigned her by virtue of her sex." Bennett students not only studied nutrition, consumer education, family life, sociology, and psychology, but traditional cultural subjects as well. Bennett combined intellectual ideals with practical necessities.[28]

Willa Player, a member of the faculty and later Bennett's president, made an illuminating study of the responses of graduates and undergraduates to the curriculum. In the early 1940s former students were asked if college had helped them advance, and 80 percent agreed that it had. Yet nearly 82 percent of the alumnae respondents thought that there should be still more courses on earning a living, and the vast majority also favored more teaching focused on the changing status of Negro women (84.4 percent), Negro history (68 percent), and ways to deal with prejudice (90 percent). At the same time, nearly two-thirds also believed that the college should teach more creative arts courses (64.5 percent). Administrators concluded that "topics related to Negro life in America and to earning a living seemed of signal importance" and revised the curriculum to include child health, home economics, and fieldwork in nearby rural communities.[29]

Black educators faced painful dilemmas in training students without raising their expectations beyond levels permitted by the larger white society. On the one hand a college woman should not be trained for positions she could not hold, on the other she should be equipped to earn a living in more than one occupation. Significantly more and more black educators transmitted the importance of aspirations even while they emphasized realistic preparation for black women.

Like the black colleges Catholic institutions served a variety of students. Catholic faculties conceived the liberal arts program as religious, intellectual, and vocational. Just as the nineteenth-century Protestant seminaries and women's colleges started with a religious purpose, so Catholic educators intended religion to be the foundation upon which the curriculum was built; liberal arts studies must be "permeated with the principles and traditions of Roman Catholicism."[30]

Catholic women's colleges, like black colleges, had modest beginnings and only gradually achieved full academic programs in the liberal arts. These schools also recognized that practicality as well as piety must shape the curriculum. The vocational concerns of Catholic students justified the growth of separate institutions. By 1920 entrance into schoolteaching required more advanced schooling, which many obtained at public and private nonsectarian colleges as well as at Catholic ones. Competition from secular colleges undoubtedly stimulated the expansion of Catholic colleges. Moreover, by the 1930s, when sisters did not constitute sufficient staff, the demand for lay teachers in Catholic elementary and high schools added another teaching option.[31]

The vision and caring of a few farsighted women educators and of unusual church leaders produced distinctive results at some Catholic institutions. Advancement of these institutions emerged only after considerable struggle and controversy about the values of a liberal education for Catholic women. Leadership in some orders of women religious, in conjunction with that of individual cardinals, had a significant impact on broadening education at various institutions. There was no consensus on Catholic women's education; even within the same communities liberal as well as conservative viewpoints existed. The progressive cardinals John Ireland and John Spalding espoused the principle of equal rights in education for both sexes. As early as 1903 Spalding argued that the "primary aim [of education] is not to make a good wife and mother, any more than it is to make a good husband and father. The educational ideal is human perfection, perfect manhood, and perfect womanhood. . . . Woman's sphere lies wherever she can live nobly and do useful work. The career open to ability applies to her not less than to men. . . . It is good to have a strong and enlightened mind; therefore it is good for a woman to have such a mind."[32]

Two kinds of traditionalists challenged these liberal positions. One group favoring liberal arts education for Catholic women emphasized intellectual training to make "a well-bred woman"—that is, a lady who would spread culture in her home. Another group, more conservative, who agreed to some education for women, proposed making the same subjects less rigorous for girls than for boys. Even more negative was the opinion of Katherine Conway, an editor of the *Boston Pilot* in 1893, that the majority of Catholic women would never need an education. She, being single and a professional woman, however, saw herself as an exception.[33]

Women religious who shared Spalding's and Ireland's vision of equality in liberal arts education persisted in remodeling Catholic women's academies into real colleges in the years before World War I. Their diplomatic, patient efforts to successfully raise the standards recall the earlier struggles of Mary Lyon and others at New England's Protestant female academies and colleges. Educators like Sisters Mary Molloy, Antonia McHugh, and Madeleine Ingraham did not settle for promoting finishing schools to make proper ladies. Such women saw their institutions as responding to multiple needs.[34]

At the National Catholic Educational Association meeting in 1917, Molloy spoke out on behalf of the aspirations of college women. She demanded that Catholic colleges train those who wanted to specialize academically in any field, from higher mathematics to medicine. Asking both the all-male clergy "who rule the NCEA" and the women religious "to take their task seriously," Molloy declared, "that undoubtedly eighty out of a hundred girls find their places in the home. With college graduates, however, it is different. Only 33 percent find their place in the home. Can we at the present ignore tha claims of the 67 percent who may wish to pursue work other than that bearing directly on the home? Women are restless in this generation. They are taking their places side by side with men in political, sociological, and pedagogical fields. If a young woman wishes to become a specialist in higher mathematics, in the classics, or in history or sociology, is her ambition legitimate?" She insisted that it was, and that the Catholic curriculum accommodate such ambition. Of her own students at St. Theresa's in Minnesota, Molloy insisted that "there is not a single student in the institution who does not know what she is going to do." She expected her students to teach in the public high schools and sent many of them on for advanced degrees. Molloy recognized that not all female students would marry, and for those who did not, she demanded excellence of training in work "other than that bearing directly on the home."[35]

Nearby St. Catherine's brought its students new expectations as well, but significantly, in contrast to what was going on at St. Theresa's, graduates of St. Catherine's did not consider doctors, lawyers, and professors as career prototypes. One famous alumna, Abigail McCarthy, recalled: "We came out prepared for a world of specialization, prepared professionally to be journalists, writers, teachers, social workers, musicians, technicians, librarians."[36]

Boston was one of the latecomers to Catholic higher education for women, probably because of the conservative leadership of Cardinal William O'Connell. Emmanuel, the first Catholic women's college in New England, made the liberal arts curriculum primary, stressing theology, philosophy, and psychology. Yet this framework made room for "practical" training. Dean Madeleine Ingraham saw her mandate as the education of Catholic women in "liberal and useful arts and sciences." As in the nonsectarian women's colleges, the liberal arts course justified educating women by preparing them to be teachers, then extended the vocation to economics, nursing, and social work. Yet, as at the elite white and the most advanced black colleges, the best Catholic colleges made an overt and unapologetic commitment to the liberal arts curriculum. Thus, the College of Notre Dame denied credit for home economics, and Emmanuel refused to open a nursing school. Emmanuel wanted to prepare its students for professional graduate programs other than those traditionally assigned to women, such as home economics, nursing, library science, and teaching. Instead, Emmanuel became an innovative institution where the liberal arts curriculum gave women the intellectual background prerequisite to study at professional schools in medicine, law, and business. As Ann Drinan, class of 1935, explained, the liberal arts provided a foundation for entry into traditionally male-dominated professions: "There is much talk of careers for women, but in the average college class how many girls are going to be lawyers, doctors, or business executives? Though only a very small percentage of them . . . it is far better to have a liberal arts course first." Ann Drinan was a woman who would have pleased feminist educator M. Carey Thomas.[37]

In the Catholic structure, then, there was room for a college that, while taking into account the vocational needs of its students, provided a strong liberal arts program. Other schools within the parochial system, such as secretarial junior colleges and nursing colleges, had the necessary vocational programs, freeing flagship colleges like Emmanuel to serve those desiring a liberal arts education.

Even though so many students in the new institutions, as well as some in the old, would need to earn a living, it was still assumed that marriage would ultimately replace paid work for most. In this context vocationalism filled only temporary rather than lifetime needs. Serving society as educated wives and mothers remained the educators' ideal for even the newest collegians; regardless of the probable futures of these students the nineteenth-century feminine ideal remained the desired end. It was up to the various colleges to transmit the traditional values of genteel ladyhood, which meant abiding by a code of personal retrait and service to others. Educators of women committed to academic and ethical standards had a common worry: Would their young women live up to these intellectual and social expectations? Students' resistance to authority, a social phenomenon increasingly apparent after World War I, left in doubt their understanding of liberal education. As young men and women at all kinds of institutions declared their independence of the directives of an older generation, a new question was posed: did college life represent vocation for all? or vacation for some? The explosion of youth culture in the twenties and thirties left the answers uncertain for a time.[38]

T·E·N

The First Modern College Women: Their Expectations in the 1920s and 1930s

"No one understands the problem of the younger generation, then, because there is no one problem to understand. You cannot heap us all together and announce that in some total we constitute a problem. We are not one single problem. We are a multitude of problems all different. Petting, necking, call it what you will, is a personal affair, participated in by two individuals with two unique personalities, and it is hardly more fair to generalize about it than it is possible to

"A Flapper Has the Last Word," *The Woman Citizen* 12 (June 1927)

Youth was *the* social problem of the 1920s and 1930s, and the college woman of the interwar period was a distinct part of it. Students were aware of their importance as the "younger generation," the object of much media attention. The college woman of these years inherited the educational and feminist traditions already established. She could not help but be aware of the fact of her new, full citizenship, won for her by the previous generation.

Youth culture that had existed on a smaller scale before the war now became a major social phenomenon separating college students from adults. The college woman had more in common with the college man, who, since the nineteenth century, had asserted his independence from the generation of his educators. Female youth found their own way of identifying themselves, but not without conflicts.[1]

Earlier the predominant college model had been the "new woman" of serious intent, self-reliant, free to achieve and to serve. By the 1910s the female collegian, without ignoring the needs of society, tried to combine old and new values. The 1920s marked a new vogue for the college girl who entered school in the age of the flapper.

Not all flappers went to college, but flapperdom invaded the campus

157

as well as the whole of American society. The physical image of the flap-per, made famous by John Held's drawings, presented a hipless, bosom-less figure with bobbed hair, her long legs accentuated by short skirts. The modern figure lacked the force and grace of the Gibson girl. The flapper looked tomboyish, yet she had sex appeal: the IT of movie star Clara Bow. The flapper was the girl who left her corset in the powder room of the Ritz hotel, the girl who danced the Charleston. What did these capers mean? How deep was the flapper's rebellion?[2]

The preoccupation with these images suggests deep levels of public anxiety toward the changing roles and life-styles of American women, with anti-feminist implications. It was an attack on the perceived inde-pendence and freedom of the post-suffrage woman. The flapper was strong as well as self-centered. She was the woman who liked men but would not be controlled by any man. Zelda Fitzgerald expressed the complexities underlying the flapper stereotype—an ideal with a feminist overtone, stressing the independence, honesty, and integrity of women. "The best flapper," Fitzgerald wrote, "is resilient emotionally and coura-geous morally. You always know what she thinks, but she does all her feeling alone." Clarence Dane, author of the popular play *Bill of Di-vorcement*, articulated the fear of such independence. He asked, "What kind of grandmothers will our present day *masterful* flappers make? (em-phasis mine). Accustomed as they are to their own way, will they be con-tent in 1960 to let themselves be overruled by fresh young things?[3]

At every college presidents and deans found themselves bedeviled and challenged by external expressions of the flapper personality: the young woman bobbed her hair, powdered her nose, and wore lipstick as bra-zenly as Joan Crawford. Yet appearances misled older observers. Even more than earlier collegians, flappers tended to conceal their personal intentions. Peer groups at all schools were of two minds in both resisting and accepting the standards set for them. Students did not abandon the compulsion to behave correctly, to be ladylike, though they insisted on their individuality. Every college woman felt pulls in her experience, "a desire to dash in three or four ways," Marita Bonner, Radcliffe '23, re-called two years after graduating. The effort to be well-rounded became a quest for experience. As the boundaries of college life expanded, it be-came hard to judge what was most important to young women deter-mined not to miss anything. Did they know better than their educators where they were headed? At no time could anyone be sure.[4]

Although the decade of the emancipated flapper ended with the onset of the Depression, her successor in the soberer thirties shared similar quests. Tensions over whether to be a "lady" or a flapper existed; yet, how to sustain loyalty to one's heritage while developing one's individu-ality became another concern. Those being educated were still being taught that they had an obligation to serve society. But many students balked at making commitments while in college, even though they knew that in the future they would. Those who could afford it, and they were in the majority, sometimes acted as if college were a four-year moratorium from real life. Some girls in their exuberance seemed openly to defy the purposes of their educators. White educators had long deplored the presence of fun-loving, undirected, "aimless" girls. Black dean Lucy Slowe now discerned two types among her students: the serious and the frivolous. In certain moods many of them agreed with Slowe that students' "infancy should not be prolonged by the college, but they should be taught to think and to act while there, in order that when they leave they may be ready to assume the responsibilities which life, whether they will it or not, will place on their shoulders." Yet the young did not allow this message to interfere with their day-to-day activities. Libertarian in spirit, students wanted no restrictions on their lives.[5]

Rebelliousness typified each particular peer culture; students resisted any interference with personal and recreational aspects of college life. Restrictions on students—involving clothes, dating, sports, drinking, smoking, and the like—could precipitate turbulent responses. In 1919 at Syracuse University, two thousand students went on strike and "rampaged through buildings when the administration denied them a holiday to celebrate an athletic victory." In 1923, at the University of Wisconsin, female students held a mass protest against chaperone requirements.[6]

As before, parents expected colleges to keep young people within the accepted boundaries of morality. Some colleges instituted formal dress codes, and others had regulations on proper appearance, in an effort to uphold earlier standards. Black and Catholic schools required simple dress to promote a ladylike appearance. Not only the more permissive private urban colleges like Radcliffe, but also sororities at public state institutions like the University of Nebraska asked students to wear hats and gloves to class; the purpose was in part to prevent students from drawing unfavorable attention to themselves and thereby to the college. In addition, such dress codes were thought to obliterate social distinctions between rich and poor. Students were to be seen and not heard, by being as inconspicuous as possible when they were off campus, to let their gentility and respectability shine.[7]

Catholic and black schools demanded the strictest behavior both on and off the campus. Catholic schools extended their supervision and rules to the hours that students were not on campus. The discipline of women at black colleges reflected a special determination to obliterate a presumed inherited taint of impurity often associated with the female slave in the minds of black men. Parents approved of this strictness. For women, as well as men, breaking rules, even minor ones, could result in expulsion. But W. E. B. DuBois objected and publicized what Fisk matron Abigail Jackson wrote about "the girls' " reactions to the various rules and regulations. She said that while they might have put up with not talking to boys on campus and not being allowed to dance, it was too much to have to "keep on wearing cotton stockings and gingham aprons." At Fisk women were finally allowed to select their own hats— within certain guidelines, however.[8]

Black and Catholic colleges were the most set on reinforcing older moral standards. Shielding their students from the most flamboyant behavior that disturbed many public and private institutions, administrators meant to prove the excellence of their students academically and socially, but they were always conscious of their position as "outsiders" in coping with the larger world. Yet students saw themselves as living in an era of new freedom in which they would uphold residual, though "morally" correct, ideals on the one hand, while adapting to changing times and entering the mainstream on the other.

Dancing had been a major symptom of rebellion before World War I, but for the college man and woman, dancing to the jazz of the twenties and swinging bands of the thirties was an accepted vogue. Yet, to beleaguered administrators, dancing to jazz and swing bands seemed tame compared to the problems posed by liquor. The prevalence of illegal drinking during Prohibition now demoralized the larger coeducational campuses. Excesses were associated with male students, but drinking had obvious dangers for women. To a young man and his flapper companion, having a gin flask or going to a speakeasy was proof of a daring nature. At the University of Wisconsin, two thousand women promised not to attend any gathering where men were drinking. Yet a California alumna of the class of '27 later recalled that "drinking was our way of social life. More often than not our dates carried flasks, or a bottle of booze in a brown paper bag."[9]

How pervasive drinking was among women is difficult to determine. During the twenties social drinking gradually became more common. The tradition of temperance may have restricted the extent to which some women inbibed, but others, rebelling against their families, became heavy drinkers. With the repeal of Prohibition in 1933, social drinking became conventional, although there were those who disapproved. At the opening of a new dormitory at Radcliffe in 1938, older alumnae objected to serving sherry to undergraduates, and therefore the reception was dry.

Smoking precipitated another trial for administrators. No longer was a cigarette the stamp of a prostitute, but rather a symbol of female liberation glamorized in movies and advertising. Some parents disagreed;

one father said that "a woman who smokes would do anything." Whether to permit the female student to smoke or not became a major area of contention. When the student government at Mount Holyoke abolished rules on smoking, President Mary Woolley reinstituted them. To the surprise of the head of the student government at Wellesley, who presented student demands on smoking, President Ellen Pendleton almost burst into tears, saying: "You girls are never satisfied." At Bryn Mawr, President Marion Park, herself a former head of student government, finally acknowledged that the college's ban did not fit the times. Other schools allowed smoking in restricted areas. But even as one women's college after another relaxed its rules, Catholic colleges retained their strictness. When it was rumored that an Emmanuel student had been seen smoking in Harvard Square, she was called in and threatened with loss of her scholarship.[10]

Yet the overreaction on the smoking issue masked deeper concerns over the changing ideals of womanhood. Beneath the efforts to maintain standards of decorum lay a sense of needing to uphold morals in the face of changing relations between young men and women. While there had been increasing awareness since the turn of the century that the sexual behavior of Americans was changing, the war made these changes more pronounced. Starting in the 1920s relationships between young men and women on the campuses were markedly different from those of past generations. College women had new attitudes toward heterosexual companionship. No longer were such interests something to be shy about, something to be concealed. Whereas in the late nineteenth century female collegians had been fulfilled by their relationships with "girls, girls, girls," it was boys, boys, boys who most appealed to the college women of the new generation (see chapter seven). They were beneficiaries not only of the earlier women's movement, but also of the sexual revolution that had overturned Victorian patterns of courtship. Unlike their mothers and grandmothers, they began dating in high school and looked forward to continuing at college. For these young women the sexual revolution had become a reality.[11]

In addition to the loosening of traditional strictures on heterosexual relationships came greater opportunities for sex play. With the growing popularity and availability of automobiles, the "backseat" provided a place for intimacy beyond the purview of chaperones. Many young women engaged in heavy petting but went no further for fear of pregnancy. Even the more sophisticated knew little about contraceptives. Though often ignorant about sexual intercourse, college women began to anticipate learning about it out of curiosity or desire or both. In general they were not promiscuous. They were more likely to engage in sexual relations with a fiancé. Permissive tendencies in sexual mores, however, did gain some ground. The flappers and the post-flappers wanted both sex and marriage. Dorothy Dunbar Bromley's and Florence Britten's *Youth and Sex*, a 1938 study of 1,364 college students, found that one-half of the males and one-fourth of the females had had premarital sex.[12]

Government publications showing the effects of syphilis resulted in further efforts to improve sex education in college hygiene courses. Students were warned of the dangers of promiscuity or casualness in sexual relations. The ignorance of women students received special attention from the YWCA, whose workers joined women physicians and administrators to give campus talks on everything from reproductive knowledge, to "the importance of general good health to normal sexual experience," to "problems" such as masturbation and homosexuality.[13]

Media popularization of Freud's ideas stimulated interest among educated middle-class Americans. Although psychoanalysis was not yet a dominant mode of therapy, women (as well as men) needed only to read magazines to learn about the importance of the sexual drive in human development. College women agreed, but their interest in sex and marriage caused consternation among older educators and advocates of female emancipation. Leaders like Jane Addams and Charlotte Perkins Gilman were disappointed. Was not the college woman overemphasizing sexuality and once again succumbing to social pressures to fulfill the traditional stereotype of womanhood?[14]

Whether or not a young woman actually had sex, she had a stronger sense that she would be unfulfilled as a woman without sexual relations with men. Moreover, the implication that heterosexual relationships were essential to a healthy life placed limits on women's friendships. Increasingly, women distanced themselves from female intimacy, now viewed as "abnormal." In the 1930s not only might a girl be expelled for staying out all night with a man, but she might also be asked to leave for having too "intense" a relationship with another woman.[15]

Nevertheless, friendships between women were still important. A graduate of the University of California recalled with pleasure the weekly occasions where, "dressed to the teeth in obligatory hat and gloves (cloche hats tightly hugging our ears, waistlines tightly hugging our rears) we would meet our girl friends under the clock at St. Francis in a routine almost as prescribed as a minuet." On a deeper level, Mary McCarthy's novel *The Group* provides a brilliant, realistic portrayal of the interactions of a 1930s Vassar clique. Members of *The Group* are critical of one another but very loyal; an unexpected test of their friendships emerges when they discover that one of their leaders was, and had always been, "a Lesbian." McCarthy, historically authentic, conveys perceptively the bewilderment and confusion of these young women whose generation, unlike their predecessors', had been taught that there were limits on female friendships; yet their loyalty to their friend supersedes the growing taboo on love between women.[16]

Students had mixed perceptions of what they wanted to control in their lives. Whether native, daughters of the foreign-born, or black, all newcomers had more complicated identity crises. Those who were the first in their families to attend college especially appreciated the advantages they gained. But the experience often proved an uprooting, a removal from the world of family and kin and their ways. And the conflicts over whether or how much to conform varied, depending on whether one was at a school predominantly for one's own kind. Black, Catholic, and Jewish students felt the pressures differently. Individuals wanted to prove themselves academically and socially, but simple conformity or social acceptance might involve rejection of one's family or group values: ignoring religious observances or dietary restrictions for Catholics or Jews, for example. In any case the pressure to conform forced individuals to make painful decisions. Black women had special conflicts over assimilating white values. For many, entering college brought isolation in the new world and remoteness from the old. Radcliffe graduate Marita Bonner conveys the unique position in which black college women found themselves, "All your life you have heard of the debt you owe 'Your People' because you have managed to have things they have not largely had." Resistance was expressed toward one's inherited duty, as well as to pressures to conform in the new environment. However much a student might wish for assimilation, she often felt resentment at having to deny some part of her origins.[17]

Each of the varied collegiate milieus had its advantages and disadvantages. Women who attended schools with only members of their own religious or racial or ethnic group had the security that came from being among familiar contemporaries. As their parents intended, they were protected from influences that threatened their family's beliefs. By contrast, all minorities, whether well-to-do or not, experienced some degree of rejection as strangers or outsiders in old established institutions.

The experiences of the few black students entering mainstream colleges ranged from abysmal treatment in extracurricular activities to some acceptance as interesting outsiders. Writer Zora Hurston, older than most undergraduates and a much-touted stranger at Barnard College, described what it meant for her to be a student there: "Beside the waters of the Hudson, I feel my race." In contrast, when she "sauntered" in Harlem she felt: "At certain times I have no race, I am *me*." Edythe Hargrave, a student at a midwestern college in the late thirties, achieved academic excellence but did not gain the acceptance she deserved. She too wanted to gain respect, "not because I am a Negro doing well but because I am another student of this university." Though athletics and dances brought her the greatest misery, she remembered why she was in school and added: "Well, I am keeping my head up. I am going forward."[18]

Black students were not the only ones affected by the tensions of assimilation. In the autobiographical novel *Bread Givers*, Anzia Yezierska spoke of the difficulties facing other groups. One of Yezierska's characters, a college-educated Jewish immigrant, cried out, "I can't live in the Old World and I'm yet too green for the new. I don't belong to those who gave me birth or to those with whom I was educated." Jewish students then, as earlier, experienced various forms of anti-Semitism; ironically those from well-established families felt the snubs most acutely. One talented freshman at Swarthmore, not elected to a sorority, transferred to Radcliffe. Some had friends or brothers who had been told not to apply to graduate school because they would not be able to get an academic job. Those from modest families lacked such high expectations and, unlike Yezierska, usually emphasized the satisfactions of being in college.[19]

In contrast to black undergraduates, Catholics and Jews were present in urban colleges in sufficient numbers to form intimate small "crowds." Yet some students of all backgrounds wore their ethnic and religious identities lightly. Those who went to religious services together still associated comfortably with friends of other faiths. In fact, some students welcomed friendships with those different from themselves. The ideal of "well-roundedness" became a value for life. To study, to play, to grow as a person, to meet obligations to society, to have men and women friends, all these motives and desires filled the consciousness of modern females. These college women, like those earlier in the century, received a significant portion of their education outside the classroom. At all types of institutions in the twenties and thirties, cultural activities, from literary magazines to glee clubs to theatricals and other performing arts, bloomed. Whether at Vassar or Spelman, Berkeley or Howard and Fisk, students relished these experiences. Graduates of schools as different as Radcliffe and Bennett found that participation in activities like choral singing and dramatics actually helped them get jobs after graduation.

Women's athletics, first initiated in the oldest women's colleges, became routine. Yet they did not inspire the same fervor they had from the pioneers in the late nineteenth and early twentieth centuries. Athletic competition in team sports did not have as much appeal for women as for men, nor did women's sports receive the same kind of public attention. Still, intercollegiate tennis, field hockey, swimming, and basketball had moderate vogues, with the approval and encouragement of educators who saw organized sports as safe outlets for their charges.[20]

As in the prewar decades social clubs offered students important ways to develop leadership and peer group loyalties. Only Catholic colleges did not permit the Greek letter societies. Elsewhere fraternities and sororities continued to expand and serve a variety of needs in providing residences, eating facilities, and general sociability. Their growth and influence peaked during the great expansion of the state universities and the advancement of black schools in the 1920s. During the 1930s, however, when the expenses of membership could be met by fewer, these societies had less influence.[21]

Membership in sororities and fraternities became as much a badge of social status on black campuses as it was on so many mainstream ones. Black student leaders also emphasized scholarship and "finer womanhood" for their membership. The four black sororities, Alpha Kappa Alpha, Delta Sigma Theta, Zeta Phi Beta, and Sigma Gamma Rho, gained a national following to which they provided support. Not only while undergraduates, but for the rest of their lives, members would share this identity. In addition, under the prodding of women deans in the 1930s, black colleges increasingly established student government associations, which became another avenue of female student leadership. Again this advance followed the pattern of the older women's colleges; only the Catholic schools held back longer before permitting student government. Ironically, at this time older colleges found students apathetic about self-government.[22]

In the twenties students of all backgrounds and of both sexes bore the stereotype of being self-centered and disinterested in service and of keeping their distance from social and political systems. Their successors during the Depression carried instead the label of being too serious about their studies with future vocations in mind. As in earlier generations the collegians did not form a monolith, and even those who fit the prototypical flapper image had other concerns as well. While rejecting some values of their elders, students also reflected their upbringing. The nation's general political mood of isolationism in domestic and international affairs infected the campuses. The grownups seemed caught up in making and spending money, and most ignored the needs of poorer citizens. Not surprisingly daughters and sons of the affluent reacted with detachment to issues not of immediate relevance to their own lives.

But there were always small clusters of students concerned with social change and issues they connected with their interests. Some students expressed conventional concerns by helping the poor and the ill, at settlements, hospitals, and other caretaking institutions. Even though the student YMCAS and YWCAS declined in the twenties and thirties, they included 594 groups with a total membership of 51,350. Also, Catholic clubs and Menorah societies developed wherever there was a sufficient number of interested students. Black and Catholic colleges had a similar array of service organizations, often mandatory, where students were introduced to their obligations to local communities. Under the guidance of Dr. Charles Johnson, for example, Fisk students participated in communal projects like the People's College and a children's institute. In these organizations students performed conventional forms of social work. However, there was the potential for more innovative and radical undertakings. On many campuses students identified with public protests, some against compulsory military training (for men), others promulgating free speech. Some causes were purely campus concerns, such as the matter of religious observances in evangelical Protestant schools. Increasingly, as a matter of principle, students at various colleges objected to required chapel attendance. This opposition to compulsory chapel-going represented a serious level of rebellion, causing intense conflicts at institutions of evangelical origin, whether predominantly white or black. Students at Trinity (later Duke University) had their way after considerable protest. More quietly Vassar College also gave up required chapel in 1926.[23]

Other times students' protests were clearly tied to larger social movements. Black students influenced by intellectuals at Howard boycotted classes to protest having to sing spirituals. The image of the "new Negro" was at stake, and the students wanted freedom to make their own selections of music.[24]

Certain current issues sparked sporadic action and received media coverage. As a result President Calvin Coolidge claimed in 1922 that the well-known eastern women's colleges were fostering political radicalism. Coolidge based his suspicions on the few anti-war protesters at Vassar, Barnard, and Bryn Mawr. Even during this period of relative indifference to problems of the larger world, a minority of students continued to express interest in questions relating to liberal principles such as academic freedom and civil liberties. The *New Student* became a forum for their concerns. Dominated by undergraduate intellectuals like Justine Wise at Barnard (a future judge) and Talcott Parsons at Amherst (the future sociologist), the publication received guidance from Barnard alumna Freda Kirchwey ('15), a *Nation* editor. Radical and liberal professors at the Seven Sister colleges also drew students into the protests against the execution of Nicola Sacco and Bartolomeo Vanzetti in 1927.[25]

Although not gaining wide student interest, the principle of international cooperation of nations did receive some attention when there was still hope of bringing the United States into the League of Nations. The National Student Federation, representing a broad coalition of student government associations, held an intercollegiate conference to discuss foreign relations. The representatives, from many colleges, included three women, but the presence of Mabel Holloway, a black student at Howard University, brought the domestic race question to the fore. Holloway's attendance caused a delegate from Georgia to threaten to leave the conference, *The Crisis* reported. The students, however, resolved the problem of representation of white and black Georgia by appointing two delegates from the South. Holloway reported without rancor: "There was no discrimination whatsoever" and took hope that students were learning that "through education, personal contact, and love these problems will be solved."[26]

Yet relatively few students took unconventional stands regarding the complex social questions troubling American society. Thus, some students at Vassar, Barnard, Radcliffe, and California worked in 1928 for Democratic presidential nominee Catholic Al Smith, a foe of Prohibition, but a straw poll in the election showed that female collegians favored Hoover two to one. Such voting patterns did not change appreciably in the 1930s; according to college polls most students supported "the Republican and Democratic candidates of their fathers' choice," and Republican fathers predominated.[27]

In the early thirties students were accused of political apathy, whereas later in the decade some were suspected of being Communists. The reality was less polarized, however. The onset and duration of the Depression changed irreversibly the expectations of all Americans. Unemployment and increasing poverty cut deeply into the middle class and brought deprivation to people who had lived protected lives.

The young who managed to stay in college remained insulated in part from the worst of the crisis. At a time of desperate poverty for millions of Americans, college students were privileged, even though many worked their way through. The Depression sparked social consciousness among the educated—undergraduates as well as graduates. After four desolate years following the 1929 crash, the social experimentation of the New Deal brought many academics and reformers into the government, men and women. Meanwhile, students sought political alternatives, a minority taking a radical direction.[28]

The University of California at Berkeley, City College of New York, and Hunter College, as well as prestigious white women's colleges, all had their share of radicals, from old-fashioned socialists to Trotskyites and Leninists. Off campus, national recruitment of students began with the forming of the Student League for Industrial Democracy (SLID) in 1932 and the National Student League in 1931; from their merger in 1935 came the American Student Union. The ASU became a forum for

liberal and radical students on campuses across the country, from Vassar
to Hunter to the University of California, Los Angeles and Wayne State
University.[29]

Students, especially those influenced by faculty liberals and radicals,
debated fiercely such topics as unionism, fascism, and pacifism. In 1936
Vassar still had a reputation for "daisy chain" radicalism. Students who
picketed factories and lobbied to kill the Nunan bill making student loyalty oaths compulsory received media coverage. Although they generally
ignored any consideration of feminism, they engaged in a variety of hu-
manitarian and political activities, including some concerned with race
relations. In 1939 a group of Vassar students invited Walter White from
the National Association for the Advancement of Colored People to participate in a conference about the South. Following this conference student leaders asked why they had no black classmates. Economics professor Ruby Turner Norris asserted that "Vassar should take steps to
attract Negro students," by establishing freshman scholarships for them.
Although many students held popular prejudices—anti-Catholic, anti-
Negro, and anti-Semitic—others moved to more enlightened views.[30]

Black students in particular, female as well as male, became more as-
sertive wherever they attended college in reacting against the unequal
treatment of their race. Some leaders in the NAACP who were college
professors stimulated interest among the undergraduates. One example of the rising consciousness on black campuses was that of Bennett
students prominent in leading a boycott of downtown theaters in
Greensboro in protest against Hollywood stereotyping of black people.
Nor were black institutions the only places generating protest. Pauli
Murray, a graduate of Hunter and a WPA teacher, protested openly
when denied admission to the University of North Carolina Law School.
In a letter to Eleanor Roosevelt, she put it bluntly: "Do you feel as we do
that the ultimate test of democracy in the United States will be the way in
which it solves its Negro problem?" In 1934, when black organizations
supported an anti-lynching bill and protested against racial discrimination in the House and Senate restaurants, the National Association of
College Women expressed its approval. The Association, referring to a
symposium of students from Spelman, Clark, and Morehouse, rejoiced
that "students no longer had a blind acceptance of things as they are."
Yet probably only a minority of black students dared to think so aggres-
sively. Two Atlanta alumnae remembered that they had never questioned segregation when they were undergraduates in the 1930s.[31]

Just as blacks were beginning to protest unequal treatment of their
race, the rise of Nazism in Germany made Jewish students more self-
conscious about anti-Semitism. Several Radcliffe students organized a

fund-raising committee for the purpose of bringing refugees to the college.[32]

Above all, the cause of peace in the mid-thirties united students of different backgrounds. Anti-militarism appealed to many collegians with the approach of World War II, as it had at the onset of World War I. In 1935 Smith College held an anti-war week, and elsewhere pacifism picked up momentum. The student Peace Strike of 1936 attracted some half a million undergraduates. Stimulus for the youth protests for peace emerged in a range of religious and reform groups. Midwestern Protestant students most often belonged to the Methodist churches, whereas Northeastern students more often belonged to the Episcopalian and Congregational denominations. Several traditional service groups, including the YMCAs and YWCAs and the Menorah Societies, joined with radical groups in the cause of peace from 1934 to 1936. Black students and Catholics participated less often, in the latter instance because of the Church's opposition. Throughout the period the chapters of the American Student Union also played a big part in the agitation for pacifism. The ASU, in which socialist and communist groups dominated, sought to broaden its constituency to include liberals and progressives. Later, as Hitler overran Europe, the students, like other Americans, became increasingly divided on pacifism. By 1940, to the majority of the public, this form of dissent smacked of cowardice and disloyalty.[33]

Committed activists in all causes, whether leaders or close followers, comprised only small groups on campuses. The more radical-liberal students could find inspiration in a few faculty members or a president like Vassar's Henry McCracken, who led the peace parade in Poughkeepsie. Black students also had stimulus from NAACP faculty members, and the emerging Catholic Worker movement was just starting to awaken a few students in the 1930s. But clearly, conservative students were in the majority everywhere and had support from many educators.[34]

What was the role of women students as a group in activist undertakings? Only at women's colleges did students work in single-sex groups. Elsewhere female collegians, accustomed to associating with males, often joined them in off-campus causes. Although they usually participated as subordinates, sometimes they were regarded as equals in political efforts. Collegians, female as well as male, were defending freedom of the individual irrespective of sex. Women figured far more conspicuously in the peace movement in the 1930s than they did in the 1920s. Although the movement did not have a feminist focus in the way that the prewar suffrage movement had, Eileen Egan suggests that pacifism among undergraduates was stimulated by contact with older women reformers in the Women's International League for Peace and Freedom.[35]

In addition, for some students women professors and prominent public figures provided inspiration. Magnetic personalities like Eleanor Roosevelt, Marian Anderson, Dorothy Thompson, Henrietta Szold, Willa Player, Lucy Slowe, Mary Molloy, and Dorothy Day imparted to students a new sense of womanhood and of service. Although students only rarely identified personally with such extraordinary examples in the modern sense of role model, they nonetheless grasped "a certain largeness of mind."[36]

The collegiate experience as well as the collegian herself had changed over time. The student body had become open to newcomers from a greater variety of backgrounds, and the substance and form of undergraduate life differed tremendously from earlier days. Events like the Great War, the granting of suffrage, and the changes in sexual expectations had particular implications for the female student and influenced her outlook and options. The world and women's place in it became more and more complex. The first modern generations of college graduates had different life-styles from earlier ones. And yet for all these differences, continuities and similarities remained.

The flapper and the post-flapper, like their predecessors, felt a sense of accomplishment in being undergraduates. The four years of college included a richness of studies and introduced them to a variety of non-academic adventures. Each generation carried away important legacies that affected their lives long after college.

For collegians of the twenties and thirties, whatever the difficulties—exclusionary admissions policies in the elite institutions, conflicts with authorities, the economic hardships of the Depression years, limited institutional aid—college represented a time of learning, growth, and hope. More than their educators knew, students absorbed the serious values of the academic enterprise and developed mature and well-rounded personalities.

Women graduating in this era felt very conscious of the possibilities, explored or not, for their lives. The Depression left an additional legacy, never forgotten, that every individual should be prepared for the eventuality of employment of some type in case of financial need. Students were acutely aware that their lives were not necessarily set; they might choose a well-traveled path, but it was not the only road to the future.

The young college graduate had confidence in her capabilities as a woman and as an individual. Yet many of her educators, along with historians, wondered what had happened to activism on behalf of the sex. Few students thought of themselves as oppressed or perceived feminism as a special cause. Even though they had flouted the prescribed rules of behavior, alumnae recalled that they absorbed gentility and manners while at college. Many doubtless would have agreed with 1935 Fisk alumna Mary L. Martin, who explained: "Our college professors taught us to be *women* with all the social graces and these alone prepared us for leadership in our communities." Radcliffe alumna Diana Trilling ('25), although critical of her college's failure to encourage professionalism, remembered with appreciation that "we learned together how to become ladies." Strong and capable herself, the graduate felt that a woman probably could have it all, whatever she wanted; she took for granted her feminist legacy and no longer took up her sex as her cause.[37]

E·L·E·V·E·N

A Public Debate for
College Women: 1920–1944

Can a woman successfully carry on a career and
marriage simultaneously?

Can she if she has children?
Radcliffe Alumnae Information, 1928

Unlike women graduates of earlier generations, those of the 1920s and
1930s knew that they would either take a job or pursue further study in
preparation for professional work. Moreover, women in the classes of
1916–20 and later married in ever larger proportions. Still, they did not
abandon other interests and responsibilities. Those graduating in the
twenties carried an awareness of expanding options in post-war, post-
suffrage America. Even the Depression in the thirties did not completely
extinguish younger women's belief that many things were possible, although perhaps not immediately. For a variety of reasons the more education a woman had the more she determined to use it in gainful employment and in voluntary service.

The interwar generations did not obtain an education in order to sit
idly at home afterward. A considerable proportion worked or continued
their education. Contrary to the fears and misgivings of their educators,
students demonstrated in their post-collegiate pursuits seriousness of
purpose and commitment to usefulness. A sign of this spirit was the
increasing number of women who enrolled in graduate programs
throughout the period. Although many scholars have emphasized the
peak in 1930, in fact, the high proportion of female doctoral recipients
held (within one or two percentage points) throughout the 1940s and
fell off significantly only in the early 1950s. Not until the 1970s would
they match earlier levels.[1]

The twenties also witnessed a steady rise in the number of college graduates eager to enter the work force. Various colleges and universities noted that a majority, often a substantial one, reported rates of 90 percent or greater; between 89 and 92 percent of alumnae who graduated from Wellesley between 1921 and 1940 took paid employment. Large-scale surveys at Radcliffe in 1928 and 1944 recorded similarly high rates: as many as 75 to 80 percent of the respondents worked full-time at some point after college, with another 5 to 7 percent having engaged in part-time work. The norm, then, was employment for at least a short time after college for these generations of educated women.[2]

Whether graduates worked or not depended on several factors, including individual wishes, families, and situations. As might be expected, one factor with significant effect on employment rates was marriage. A 1929 survey of twelve hundred single graduates from a variety of schools found that only 4.4 percent had never been employed; another group surveyed in this study included a thousand married women (of whom over three-quarters had attended college), and found that 40 percent had never worked outside the home. Unmistakably marital status affected work status. Moreover, this survey and others implied that the division between marriage and paid employment was complete. Yet there were small groups in every generaton of the educated who married and continued to work. Thus, although marriage influenced the decision of whether or not to seek gainful employment, the two were not necessarily mutually exclusive.[3]

In the late nineteenth century some educated women had successfully introduced an option for the woman who chose not to marry. In the third decade of the twentieth century a relatively small number of educated women pioneered yet another alternative path, combining marriage and career. This chapter focuses on the critically important question that emerged in the post–World War I period: Should a woman be both a wife and a professional? Or stated differently, should women who wanted families be denied careers?

Although individuals had posed the question before, and some had put the idea into practice, for the first time it became a matter of public debate. Whereas previously most educated women had perceived two distinct life paths—marriage or career—now women started thinking about a third choice—marriage *and* career. The debate over the advisability of this path began among college women, because it was harder for them to abandon a career for which they had been trained. At the same time society decreed that a married woman should work only out of necessity. Always the problem persisted of justifying women's new options.

That women wanted to discuss the issue publicly signified that this generation had reached a new stage in the evolution of the educated woman. At long last a substantial number openly acknowledged ambitions as well as ambivalence in the light of their varied options. Moreover, a few astute educators—not only M. Carey Thomas, but Virginia Gildersleeve, Ada L. Comstock, and William Neilson among others—agreed that if all talented students married, society might never benefit from their potential scholarship, teaching, and other contributions.[4]

While colleges were still being criticized, as they had been in the nineteenth century, for "prejudicing students against marriage in favor of careers," it was obvious from statistics that the college graduate would no longer renounce marriage for her work. In fact, marrying within a few years of graduation became the choice of most. A *Fortune* inquiry of college men and women in 1936 stated that three-fifths of the women wanted to marry within one or two years of graduation; in addition, however, two-fifths reported a desire to work after marriage. The real dilemmas of modern women began, not after college, but after marriage. For an increasing number, finding a way to have lifelong work as well as marriage and motherhood became a goal.[5]

In this vein editors of the *Smith College Weekly* in December 1919 questioned the assumption that it was "fixed in the nature of things that a woman must choose between a home and her work, when a man may have both." With a sense of purpose, the students asserted: "There must be a way out, and it is the problem of our generation to find the way." More timid was the conclusion of a poll in 1923, in which the large majority of Vassar undergraduates said they would choose marriage over career if a choice had to be made. These two reactions highlight both the priority of marriage and the magnetic appeal of career. Both examples convey the ambivalence of students who had yet to make these choices.[6]

Corroborating this interest in the problems of the married college graduate, a *New York Times* article in April 1933 discussed the results of an informal study at fourteen campuses on the future aspirations of college women. Entitled "The College Girl Puts Marriage First," Eunice Fuller Barnard cited statistics showing that 83 percent of those at professionally oriented Bryn Mawr preferred marriage to career, and that 94 percent would sacrifice career if it posed a problem. Yet the title of the piece is misleading; the majority interviewed thought the two roles compatible, and nearly all felt "troubled" if they had "no vocational aim." An almost universal wish to marry was accompanied by an equally strong wish to hold a job. The women interviewed meant to have husband, children, and paid work. To facilitate the combination of roles, they consciously sought jobs with flexible hours, such as interior decorating and writing.[7]

Graduates coming out of the colleges during and immediately after World War I took advantage of the increased opportunities with a sense of euphoria that there were no limits to what they could do. At the same time, social scientists, journalists, educators, and college women generated a public dialogue about the genuine dilemma of these trained women. Those wanting to believe that feminism was dead often contrasted the graduates of the twenties with their publicly active predecessors, whereas others maintained that the new generation simply had a different style from the older feminists—an individualistic style difficult to stereotype. The new-style feminist might still be eager to accept and meet the challenges of forging a new path for her sex; but, as Dorothy Dunbar Bromley argued, she was not "hard-hitting" like the earlier generations who had fought for women's rights. Although this new feminist professed no loyalty to women en masse, she believed in individual women and cheered their successes. The new element in the approach of young college graduates in the 1920s was freedom of choice; whether to marry or not, whether to have children or not, were matters to be decided by the individual, and no judgment was passed on these various options. But if she was not strong-minded about women's rights, she was adamant about the value of work: it was essential to her well-being.[8]

College, of course, was not the only route to the work force for women. Some working-class wives had always held jobs, and their numbers, along with the numbers of virtually every type of female worker, old and young, married and single, professional and unskilled, rose throughout the twentieth century. In 1920 there were about two million married women gainfully employed. That figure represented almost four times as many as in 1890. Similarly, in 1910, only 12 percent of professional women married, but by 1930, 24 percent were marrying. By 1940, 15.2 percent of all married women were working, and throughout World War II the trend accelerated, so that in 1945 nearly one-quarter of all married women worked, representing well over one-third of the female labor pool.[9]

Despite women's participation in the work force at all levels, the American public, including most women reformers, still opposed the employment of wives and mothers of all classes. It was deplored that industrial and domestic workers were forced to work out of financial necessity, for every wife and mother should be at home with her family. Equally it was assumed that college graduates should leave the work force when they had children. Many academic and professional women who presumably made the personal choice to renounce outside responsibilities believed that other wives and mothers should also do so. Supportive of this view was a rash of magazine articles featuring a type of young woman who had decided that work and marriage was too much; one provocative title was "An Autobiography of an Ex-feminist," in which the author says: "At twenty . . . I was a feminist," believing there was "no sex to the mind! There should be no sex in education," but at thirty she thought "this whole business of educating the middle class girl a tragic mistake."[10]

In fact, the majority of college graduates did not work for long after marriage. Still, the small numbers who did received much attention. Indeed, they represented the vanguard of a new trend for educated women. These pioneers had support from a few educators, parents, and husbands who believed that this experiment needed encouragement. The progressive University of Chicago philosopher George Herbert Mead wrote in 1920 to his daughter-in-law that she must go on with her medical training and continue her preparation for a career as well as carry out her family responsibilities. "Being a wife and mother," he wrote her, is "no longer a calling in itself"; such a trained woman, he avowed, must "exercise" her intelligence. Part-time study and employment were his solutions for the educated mother during the years of responsibility for a young family.[11]

In sympathy, realistic educators understood that changes in public attitudes were needed to permit the combination of marriage and career to be effective. One of the oldest supporters of the new pattern spoke bluntly from a woman's perspective about the problems involved. Ethel Puffer Howes, Smith '91 (who had received a certificate for her work in fulfillment of Ph.D. requirements at Harvard before the granting of the degree to women), taught philosophy and psychology at several colleges. Wife, mother, and academic, she wrote feelingly about the struggles of the woman who wanted to have love, home, motherhood, and her special work. According to Howes, educators fostered "'self-deception" in women students by giving them neither guidance nor guidelines to help them live in the two spheres, those of family and profession. As Director of the Institute for the Coordination of Women's Interests at Smith College in the twenties, Howes set out to remedy this situation.[12]

It was not that educators had not been following what happened to their students after graduation. The effects of a college education on females had long preoccupied the educated public. Social analysts studied health, marriage, births, longevity, and work patterns but did not correlate all these factors. Early surveys of colleges like Oberlin, Mount Holyoke, and Wisconsin—as well as Mary Van Kleeck's well-known intercollegiate study (1918)—focused on rates of marriage, numbers of children, rates of employment, and voluntary activities. Results showed that most educated women were gainfully employed at one or more points in their lives, and the analyses ended there.

Virginia Collier's popular account in 1926 of a hundred successful career women in New York City gave favorable publicity to the experiment of combining work and marriage. Collier's conclusion was positive: "Happiness is the chief result from this extra-activity of woman; happi-

ness for herself and hence happiness for those she loves and cherishes."
Collier documented the need many women felt for assuming greater responsibilities in public life.[13]

Collier's report on the successes of a self-selected group was the first
of many surveys on this theme. A number of colleges provided data on
alumnae for studies of the career–marriage combination. Some investigations focused on a small group, others surveyed all students. Several
studies both published and unpublished, based primarily on evidence
from private women's colleges, both white and black, highlight the range
of contemporary perspectives and viewpoints revealed by the graduates
themselves. The first important trend documented both in small college
surveys and in more comprehensive studies was that a growing proportion of women worked not only before marriage but after. One of the
largest AAUW studies (1928), representing a cross-section of six thousand of its members, recorded 11.7 percent of the respondents as working wives. Moreover, a large sampling of land-grant college alumnae
showed that 19.5 percent of those who had married held paid jobs. Individual college surveys confirmed these findings, with figures ranging
from 10 to 28 percent of alumnae at different institutions. All the studies were interested in motives for working and the factors that helped or
hindered successful combinations of marriage and career. Some investigations measured the extent of approval or disapproval of this pattern;
others wanted to assess the financial value of collegiate education for the
married as well as the single graduate.[14]

Three studies of particular interest—Anne Byrd Kennon's 1927 AAUW
study, Ethel Puffer Howes's unpublished study of Smith alumnae in
1926, and Chase Woodhouse's 1929 study, also for the AAUW—stressed
the factors that either promoted or impeded the individual's success.
Kennon reported on 243 working wives from three colleges: Radcliffe,
Boston University, and Simmons. Her findings were consistent with
other studies of the time. Nearly all (231) had worked before as well as
during marriage. Approximately one-fifth (47) worked with their husbands. Significantly, over half (139) were childless; the others averaged
2.1 children.[15]

The Howes data on Smith College alumnae showed again that many
women worked with their husbands. Howes divided the respondents
into two groups, self-defined as "more successful" and "less successful."
Again most of the women had worked before marriage, many had no
children, and among those who had, the number varied from one to
three. Of interest is the number of women who made premarital agree-
ments to carry on their careers (although not always successfully). Notably, the majority of the successful ones worked at home or, if out of the
home, in an occupation that did not require set hours. Many were writ-

ers, journalists, painters, musicians, or in real estate. Of the few academic types, the scientists were working with their husbands. [16]

Among the Howes respondents the issue of children created the biggest difference for the "less successful." The personal stress that the unsuccessful expressed reinforced "confessions" in popular magazines about why married women gave up careers. The respondents acknowledged the complexity of their situations and took note of the elements necessary for an individual's success. The most frequently mentioned factors related to the presence, age, and number of children; the type and flexibility of job—full- or part-time, at home or out of the home, its relation to the husband's work when first employed; the attitude, cooperation, and understanding of the husband; and the effectiveness of her household help. More important, however, was the general agreement that above all, success depended upon the individual woman—upon her health, energy, efficiency, talent, and ability to carry on her work and family responsibilities without detriment to either.

Chase Woodhouse's 1929 study covered a cross-section, predominantly of college alumnae described as "ordinary" professional women. Her analysis indicated overwhelming practicality in the reasons respondents gave for working after marriage. A total of 336 women responded, of whom 198 had children (59 percent), 138 not (41 percent). Asked to rank, in order of importance, their reasons for working, 58.8 percent gave economic ones as the most important. Desire for work was noted less often, with only one out of three listing it first (33 percent). The rest gave personal and familial reasons primacy. The differences between those with and without children were noteworthy. Two-fifths, 39.1 percent, without children listed desire to work as a motive, as compared with 30.3 percent with children, for whom economics played a larger role. A small group referred to the demand for their services as a reason for working. Woodhouse made the important point on behalf of educated women, that many, like industrial workers, were contributing during this period of inflation to family incomes, albeit at a different economic level. Woodhouse concluded that "the day of the old-style feminist is passing and that that of the trained woman who works as a matter of course is arriving."[17]

Indeed, some of the respondents declared that they were far from militant, insisting though there were principles involved in working, they were not feminist. Most women who answered the AAUW questionnaire in 1929 did not give reasons associated with old or new feminism as the main justification for being working wives and mothers; enjoyment of work based on their training seemed to be a secondary consideration. Similarly, the two Radcliffe surveys to be discussed later in the chapter also reported that economic factors were critical in a woman's decision to combine marriage and work.

Of course some groups of college-bred women, who shared the same values about family and community, did not have the option of making a choice about working, before or after marriage. Black women, as Dr. Willa Player said, "work after college not so much because of their thirst for economic independence as out of sheer necessity."[18]

Black women faced many of the same issues as white graduates, but with different emphasis. Both worried about financial rewards, vocational training, social graces, occupational choice, marriageability, and family–career dilemmas, but these concerns had different implications for black women. As we have already noted, education added to the isolation of black women. They constituted the majority of the educated of their race, a fact that in part accounts for the very high proportion of unmarried black alumnae. In the early 1930s, a time when the marital rate and age for educated women overall approached that of her uneducated peers, a study of 1,994 black female graduates found that nearly three-fifths (58.5 percent) were unmarried. Whether black women chose to remain single due to a personal decision or to a dearth of "suitable" (meaning equally well-educated) black men, or whether black men avoided choosing "superior" (educated) black wives is unclear. For whatever reasons, many black female graduates stayed single at this time. Other differences between black and white women were noted in the levels of divorce and separation. The nonwhite population, both the educated and uneducated, had a consistently higher divorce rate throughout this period.[19]

Certainly single black women had to rely on themselves for financial support, and few married black graduates had the privilege of choice which characterized their white counterparts. Many bore some or all of the responsibility for supporting a family. An inquiry sent by racially distinct Bennett College to its alumnae in 1946 resembled the Woodhouse questionnaire of 1929. Results showed that the Bennett graduates took for granted the habit of work; moreover, the study accentuated the economic necessity of employment for educated black women. Less than half of the 317 respondents were married, and approximately half of these worked full-time, a substantially higher proportion than for educated white working wives. Black women, both married and single, worked after college in much larger proportions than white women.[20]

The handful of black graduates at Radcliffe College followed patterns similar to those found at Bennett; the twelve alumnae, only two of whom were married, not only worked, but gave approval to those who tried combining work and marriage. A very small sample of wives from the

Fisk class of 1935, responding to an informal personal inquiry in 1977, confirmed the necessity of employment. All had married professional men, and all but one had children. Every one of the nine had continued working after marriage, and seven had done so after having children.[21]

Even though fewer black than white women had a choice in deciding whether or not to continue working after marriage, both black and white graduates found themselves pulled by the ideal of domestic responsibility on the one hand and personal or professional fulfillment on the other. Marion Cuthbert's study of black college women of the 1930s found that these women experienced great stress in combining marriage and employment; they often expressed anxiety about their relationships with black men. Generally both groups wanted to contribute to homemaking and devote part of their energy to raising a family. Furthermore, careers might interfere with women's participation in religious, cultural, and service-oriented women's clubs. Black women particularly worried that they did not have enough time for community voluntary service. Several studies indicate that black college women contributed greatly to interracial projects in this period. Both black and white college women were ambivalent about their futures as wives, mothers, single adults, professionals, workers, or volunteers. Even in the 1940s, when many women looked to their colleges for training in homemaking and domestic responsibilities, they had a special concern for the economic advantages and employment opportunities derived from the period of study.[22]

Since most female students, regardless of background, worked after college, the benefits of education in financial terms were naturally of interest to students and educators. Economic reasons, which motivated many to work, justified combining work with marriage to some opponents of this growing trend. Particularly during the Depression, the need for family income from any source contributed to the legitimation of paid work for individuals. At the same time, of course, public opposition to a woman's taking a job away from a man certainly limited a woman's choices and opportunities. For whites as well as blacks, various surveys and studies showed that college increased a woman's chances to become a professional and thereby enhance her earning power. Although in every occupation women earned less than their male counterparts, women with a high level of education earned more than noncollege females. The 1933 American Woman's Association survey of 1,350 women found a median income of $2,400 among white-collar, relatively highly educated women, at a time when a large number of American families earned less than $1,000. Female-dominated fields paid less than male-dominated ones, but the few professional fields in which women were found paid higher than other female occupations.[23]

College women were engaged mostly in white-collar work, and thus their salaries were above average. The 1937 Women's Bureau study of women in the economy outlined a range of incomes for working women; professionals earned the highest salaries, followed by clerical workers, then manufacturing and sales workers, and lastly domestic servants. Only a small minority of all working women entered professional or clerical occupations, whereas the overwhelming majority of college-educated women did. This difference in occupation suggests that college provided women with the means to secure a professional job, and consequently, to command a higher salary. The implications are borne out by a comparison of graduates' salaries and national family income data from the same period. In 1929 the median family income was approximately $1,800, which contrasts with the 1928 Radcliffe sample of individual women whose median was close to $2,100. These women were probably the main or sole support of their household, since the majority were single. Some, however, lived in a household with other wage-earners and thus contributed only a portion of the family income. It must be remembered that these single women needed the incomes they earned. A 1939 AAUW study of 8,800 women found that two-fifths (41 percent) had partial or full responsibility for one or more dependents. Such findings conclusively undermine the "pin-money" theory, which assumed that women's income was used solely for frivolous luxuries.[24]

The same AAUW survey on the economic status of university women found that 97 percent of the respondents were either in educational, clerical, social service, or health work. Significantly, the study also showed that further training tended to increase salaries, with M.A. holders earning more on the average than those with only a B.A., and Ph.D.s for the most part at the top of the scale.

The situation of educated black women contrasted with that of white women. The salaries of black college women rarely approached those of the white college-bred. Willa Player's 1948 study comparing black women graduates with white women from land-grant colleges found that the former earned only 58.8 percent as much as the latter on the average; the occupations were primarily professional for both groups, with greatest equitability among social workers. Earlier, in 1937, the median annual income for these black graduates was slightly under $1,000, which contrasts sharply with the median of nearly $2,000 reported in Susan Kingsbury's large-scale survey of female graduates in 1939.[25]

Nevertheless, most of the college-trained accepted the inequities in salaries between black and white women, and again between white women and white men, and considered their educations as providing them with some economic advantages. The traditional economic motive for a woman's working to help her family still informed the educated woman's view, for it was socially the most acceptable. One wonders whether the educated woman felt constrained to minimize the satisfactions she might receive outside the domestic sphere, like the married industrial worker who often did not inform the census-taker that she was working. Although various surveys of college women revealed the importance of paid employment for the educated, both married and single, few explored graduates' opinions of the increasingly popular marriage–career pattern. What did educated women really think about combining marriage with paid employment?[26]

Two Radcliffe Alumnae Association surveys, in 1928 and 1944, stand as unusual investigations of alumnae attitudes toward marriage and career. The 1928 study of 3,362 A.B.s, nongraduates, special students, and M.A. and Ph.D. candidates, married, single, employed, and unemployed, gave varying perspectives from a range of Radcliffe women educated between 1883 and 1928. The questionnaire asked its alumnae whether or not they really believed that a woman could "successfully" combine marriage and career, and whether she could do so if she had children. Over two thousand women (approximately two-thirds) answered these questions. Nearly three-quarters of these answered affirmatively that a woman could combine marriage and career; fully one-third of the group gave unequivocal, positive answers, whereas another 40 percent qualified their positive answers. Only 15 percent expressed negative attitudes, including a small group, 5.4 percent, who were adamantly opposed and another 9.6 percent who were doubtful. In the remaining category were 11.8 percent who said that they did not know.[27]

The more difficult question for these respondents concerned the feasibility of combining marriage, career, and children. Nevertheless, a rather large percentage, 49.3 percent, answered either affirmatively or hopefully; only 14.1 percent were absolutely certain that career, marriage, and children could be combined, whereas 35.1 percent believed in the possibility with qualifications. In contrast to these, two-fifths of the sample believed that in the presence of children women could not combine marriage and career: the negative answers were almost evenly divided between the 18.4 percent totally opposed and the 21.8 percent expressing doubts. Again a small minority, 10.5 percent, answered that they simply did not know whether or not women could combine careers with marriage and motherhood.

Overall the Radcliffe study conveyed a high level of optimism. The breakdown of the answers according to marital status and presence or absence of children reveals interesting patterns. Significantly, more of the married (75 percent) than the unmarried (70.1 percent) held positive views. In the smaller categories of widow, remarried, separated, and divorced, responses were generally more positive than the norm. Of those holding negative views, the percentages of the unmarried and of the married without children were slightly higher than the percentages in this category of the married with children. We speculate that this uneven distribution of negative replies may indicate that those for whom the issue was not personally relevant were the least likely to imagine a successful combination. Also, some may have felt that they had had no choice and therefore begrudged others the freedom to choose.

When responses were sorted according to employment status the results were not entirely unexpected. Those who were never employed for pay or who only worked part-time tended to be more negative than those working full-time. Those who had once worked full-time were also a bit more negative than those employed currently, and, interestingly, were overrepresented in the "I don't know" category. Those working at the present time, especially married women, had a significantly higher percentage of positive answers. This finding is not surprising, since this group knew firsthand what the demands of the workplace were; it is very significant that they felt so positively.

Another comparison involved the responses of students who pursued graduate study and those of other types of students. Of the first group, 75 percent, slightly above the norm, answered in the categories of "yes" or "hopeful." Among the negative responses the graduates accounted for a disproportionately smaller percentage. But more grads than nongrads gave the "unsure" answers (12.5 percent as contrasted with 8.4). On the whole, more grads were unmarried, and those that were married had fewer children. The graduate students apparently wanted to believe that it could be done even if they were not impelled to try at that point; perhaps they were expressing personal hope that women would have the option.

A striking fact culled from the Radcliffe data was that 166 out of 178 working wives were positive about the combination (93.3 percent), and that 121 (68 percent) remained positive when the factor of children was taken into account. Both figures were far higher than the average. The July 1928 *Radcliffe Quarterly* registered its surprise at the optimistic opinions of the possibility of combining marriage and career. The next year President Ada L. Comstock, without alluding to the questionnaire, said: "We are coming to see, I believe, that marriage is essentially far more compatible with the continuation of a woman's career than has been assumed."[28]

The Radcliffe study has significance beyond its alumnae constituency. This college in 1928 was a coordinate school (with Harvard) whose student body was socially and economically mixed. Radcliffe was the least fashionable of the Seven Sister colleges; 25 percent of the students were working their way through college, and half were commuters. From this substantial sampling of college women it appears that some educators misjudged the attitudes of highly educated women. Sociologist Ernest Groves saw the time as a hopeful age of transition but admitted that prejudice "built upon the tradition of masculine dominance" still persisted.[29]

Public interest in this issue continued in the 1930s. Prejudice did not erode with the onset of the Depression, and neither college women nor society agreed that married women should have careers. Yet heightened expectations for female employment grew again when World War II created a new demand for women, including those who were married, in the work force. At this time Radcliffe again sent out a questionnaire that included a question on the critical issue of combining marriage and career.

The 1944 study was sent to a random sample of 1,000 A.B. holders out of 5,549 graduates from 1888 to 1944; 482 answers were returned. The wording of the question was slightly different from what it had been in the 1928 survey: "From your experience, do you advise combining work with marriage?" In contrast to the 1928 question, it asked the respondent to rely on her own experience, rather than to make a general judgment. Significantly the proportions of those who answered affirmatively (only 18.0 percent) and of those who were hopeful (39.3 percent) represented a considerable drop as compared with the responses to the 1928 questionnaire. The total on the positive side in 1944 reached only 57.3 percent, in contrast to 73.2 percent in 1928. The negative responses, totaling 32.3 percent for the 1944 group, represented quite a change from the optimism in the 1928 sample, when only 15.5 percent expressed such doubts.

How do we explain the shift in attitudes? It should be noted that, perhaps due to wartime, there was a lower yield of responses to the later questionnaire. More important, the difference in the form of the questions in the 1928 and 1944 surveys makes direct comparison of the answers difficult. The marked difference in support for the marriage–career combination may suggest that in 1944 women were more wary of this larger commitment. We may speculate that there were three contributing factors: first, the Depression, which curbed the expansive hopefulness of the twenties; second, disappointment that suffrage had not led, as hoped, to greater strides toward equality in professional opportunity; and third, the impact of World War II, which made some women—even those who worked while their husbands were overseas— eager to devote their full attention to domestic responsibilities. Still, a majority in this survey (though smaller than in 1928) thought a woman who wanted to combine marriage and career should try, and that she could succeed. Whereas those who were wary stressed the joys of full-time devotion to the home, the daring suggested that such devotion was harmful, not only to the woman, but to her marriage and her children. This divergence of opinion typified the contradictions in the thinking of women who wanted to assume that they could choose whether or not to work outside the home and whether or not to marry. All the available evidence points to only provisional acceptance of careers for married women, with the presence of children representing the largest impediment and financial need the most frequent justification.[30]

Nonetheless, Radcliffe president W. K. Jordan's responses to the information in the 1944 survey were prophetic. He divided the graduates into three groups: those who did not marry and had careers; those who reared families and found satisfaction in the activities of the home and community; and those who though married continued, perhaps with interruptions, with a paid occupation. Jordan believed that this third group was "probably the largest" and emphasized that these women had "special and difficult problems, which have never been carefully assessed." With sensitivity, this historian commented: "These women must display an unusual degree of adaptability; they are often limited to part-time employment, and, since their professional life is characteristically interrupted by childbearing and child-rearing, they have often engaged in work of extraordinarily dissimilar types when one examines the pattern of their whole career." Perhaps with some surprise, Jordan counted this group of Radcliffe alumnae as representative of "a most interesting and significant social group which may very possibly typify the college woman of the future."[31]

Women as individuals made choices and struggled with them. Anne Byrd Kennon observed in 1927 that, "while discussion rages this way and that, here and there wives are quietly combining homes and occupations." Yet it was only a rare graduate who understood that society must intervene to help educated women make full use of their training. In 1943, at a gathering to remember the struggle of women suffragists, Vera Micheles Dean (Radcliffe '25), a modern professional, wife and mother, declared that "no woman should have to make a choice between home and career." For many women of her generation and the next, that claim was impossible to accept. The Radcliffe questionnaires of 1928 and 1944 document how complex the choice of combining marriage and work was in the minds of most educated women. Just as the issue of woman suffrage before 1920 had seemed to portend a redefinition of women's roles in American society, so the idea of women's multiple identities in combining marriage, motherhood, and career seemed radical. Affirmation of this choice by a majority of graduates, whether married or unmarried, represented a giant step in the thinking of educated women.[32]

T·W·E·L·V·E

The Promises of
Liberal Education
—Forgotten and Fulfilled

What we need and, in peacetime, did not have, is the conviction that,
if we want to, we shall have the same opportunities as men for
using our special skills and creative abilities. . . . Without it,
the education of women, no matter how perfected or expanded, will
remain in essence a finishing-school process . . . lacking in that
strong incentive that gives form and purpose to
the education of men.

Vera Micheles Dean, *The Radcliffe Quarterly* 27 (1943), 13

We cultivate conformity even while we deplore it.
What if a few escape the trend and devote their lives to
some professions, and perhaps do not even marry?

Professor Emeritus Mabel Newcomer, *A Century of Higher Education*
(1959), 147

By 1940 some educated women believed that it was up to the individual
to make her own choices at her own risk on the critical matters in her
life—to marry or not, to work or not, and even to combine marriage and
career or not. Yet psychoanalyst Clara Thompson judged accurately that
even though women in America were "probably freer" to live their own
lives than those "in any other patriarchal country in the world," they
were still an "underprivileged group." Although they could make more
choices than most European or Asian or African women, even the educated among American women were still in the process of finding their
way in new roles. More women in the United States had gained access to
higher education at the start of World War II than in other modern
countries, yet this access did not ensure that they could use that education as fully as men could. Liberal education had made a real difference
in women's lives, but their choices were still limited by personal inhibi-

tions as well as public barriers. The course of development of the educated woman did not become any simpler in the next four decades. Although World War II offered to more women varied types of advanced training and professional opportunities, peacetime brought setbacks and changes. Would women be able to sustain their progress? No clear answers existed, because women were still pioneering in men's territory. Women as a group experienced gains and losses in rapid succession; but even when their general advancement seemed at a standstill, some individuals took advantage of educational possibilities.[1]

The close of World War II brought an end to long years of struggle, and most Americans felt expansive about the future. Those who had lived through the Depression welcomed military victories and looked forward to economic growth, technological advances, and social stability. Men and women anticipated with confidence a new era in which democracy would prevail at home and abroad. Meanwhile, educators and public leaders devised plans to ensure a harmonious adjustment for the soldiers and their families in peacetime. To some observers the prospect of millions of young men returning to the work force evoked fearful memories of the massive unemployment of the thirties. How would the economy accommodate these men as well as the large numbers of women who had entered the work force in their absence?

Older professional women foresaw "the inevitable recoil" from women's advances at all levels and exhorted educators to keep a watchful guard. Some proposed that women's history courses be instituted in the curriculum to sustain the aspirations of younger women. The immediate future, however, was not in the hands of feminist-minded advocates. The prospects of expanding higher education brought reconsideration of the purposes of educating men and women. Just as the war encouraged women to enter the labor force, peace made their place in it debatable. Should women keep the jobs when men needed them? Educators and economists alike perceived the immediate problem as one of wives who had taken men's jobs during the war; in colleges the old line reemerged that women should be educated primarily for domesticity. All kinds of social experts sought to discourage women from combining marriage and motherhood with jobs or careers. Nevertheless, revolutionary changes in women's work patterns continued to contradict the pervasive rhetoric. Each census from 1920 on revealed a higher proportion of married women in the work force. Public opinion had not fully stopped the trend in the Depression; neither did it hold back all women in the postwar era.[2]

Moreover, in other crucial respects the post–World War II college woman differed markedly from her predecessors: she was not only an eager candidate for matrimony, likely to be married by age twenty-two, but marriage no longer removed her from the work force. Even more than in previous decades, the more education a woman had, the more likely she was to be gainfully employed. By the early sixties almost three-fifths of college women worked, as compared to two-fifths of high school graduates. Paradoxically, at a time when more college-educated wives worked, their educators were upholding the primacy of women's roles as wife and homemaker. Neither academic institutions nor society at large helped solve the increasing dilemmas of these women.

In this chapter we will examine women's paths in higher education from World War II to the present. During this period women dealt with an array of conflicting demands that affected their aspirations in an accelerating, shifting sequence of events that finally produced an explosion and revitalized feminism. Thus, in the 1970s women of several generations initiated demands for female equality and challenged educational institutions to fulfill the promises of liberal education.

At the outset of this forty-year period sweeping changes in opportunities during World War II fed the educated woman's sense of new choices within her grasp, waiting to be seized. As earlier, women, when needed in the public sphere, received encouragement to enter "male" fields of training for future employment. For the short time of national emergency the curriculum provided women with opportunities that seemed to belie sex labels. Whereas women students in the 1930s rarely entered fields like engineering and the hard sciences, the war overturned this educational block at the training level. With coeducational schools lacking male students, professors paid more attention to talented women at the undergraduate and graduate levels in all fields. At women's colleges like Vassar the proportion of students majoring in the sciences peaked at 26 percent in the early 1940s; at Barnard women began to receive training in meteorology and electronics.[3]

Even Harvard University started to open its doors to undergraduate women in 1943 through the new Harvard/Radcliffe agreement. In addition, two years later twelve women were admitted to the Medical School, and in the fall of 1950 a handful entered the Law School. Clearly the war-time crisis, in stimulating plans for future admission of women, also affirmed confidence in their abilities. Appropriately in these years of relative openness the United States Armed Services had offered women places in eight branches, although women had to meet somewhat higher admission standards than men.[4]

All the advances enacted in World War II were real; but predictably at war's end both women's opportunities and interests diminished. Mabel Newcomer's evidence shows that the percentage of physics and chemistry majors at Vassar dropped by more than 50 percent in the decade following the war. Similarly, across the nation fewer women received doctorates in physics. It was more common for the Vassar graduate to give up the possibility of a good research job or the pursuit of a Ph.D. if it appeared to threaten her chances of marrying. The rapid decline in numbers of candidates in the medical profession was striking: in 1949 women comprised 12 percent of medical school graduates; but by the mid-fifties the proportion had slid to 5 percent, even lower than that in 1941. Although the early 1940s were peak years for women's representation among academic personnel, the next twenty saw their decline, from 27.7 percent in 1940 to 24.5 percent in 1950, dropping even more—to 22 percent—by 1960 (see table 6). The postwar years thus became a time of reduced options and expectations; yet individuals who had been able to exploit the opportunities of the early forties had distinct advantages in sustaining or developing careers further. Some college graduates who got jobs during the war in banks or filled vacancies on newspapers managed to hold on to them afterward, even if they did not advance as swiftly as men. Professional women who had responsible positions in the armed forces continued in government, academia, or business.[5]

Whatever impediments professional women—Ph.D.s, M.D.s, or L.L.D.s— experienced after the war, their situation was better than that of the most talented women in industry, where union rules and lower rates of peacetime production ousted almost all skilled workers. Yet Rosie the riveter, the doctor of philosophy, the lawyer, and the physician still had something fundamental in common: in peacetime American women lacked clout at the highest levels everywhere—in the industrial labor force, in academia, and in the professions. Only the fortunate were employed; many more found that returning veterans, who had priorities by law, regained old positions. Women did not begrudge the former soldiers, now mature men, their ambitions and special opportunities; few young women realized that their own access to undergraduate education and professional schools lessened as a result of the expanding opportunities for veterans. Due to a general acceptance of male priority, the memory of the versatilely employed woman soon faded as it had after World War I.

Women suffered a large setback when the operation of the GI bill reduced female access to higher education. Under the federal program the millions of veterans had an opportunity for further education. Governmental subsidies to the colleges ensured a warm welcome to the returning soldiers; even women's colleges, including Vassar, Finch, and Sarah Lawrence, admitted males. Men flooded campuses to take all kinds of degrees, especially at the well-known public and private schools. In 1947 veterans comprised 49 percent of the total college enrollment and 69 percent of college men. As a result of veterans' benefits black colleges found males temporarily outpacing females in enrollments by several thousands; at the end of the decade the 6,467 bachelor's degrees earned by men constituted almost half of the 13,198 conferred. Women as veterans were among the eligible everywhere, but they represented less than 3 percent of those in the armed services. By 1956, 2,232,000 veterans had been educated under the GI bill, of whom 64,728 were women.[6]

During their takeover veterans changed the character of higher education and enhanced the larger public's respect for schooling. Intellectual excitement and the professional (or vocational) purpose of mature young men electrified the campuses. At least 20 percent of the veterans, among them some who were black, would not have attended college without this federal support. The development then of various educational institutions, including community colleges and adult education programs, would ultimately attract many more women; but in this critical period between 1945 and 1956, women as a group were handicapped by the male influx into academia.[7]

Just as GIs transmitted their seriousness about the business of education, so they also established new patterns of collegiate domesticity; almost half the veterans returning to school were married. The presence of domestic couples on campuses was contagious, with female undergraduates seeking to "catch" a husband. To some the immediate goal of matrimony outstripped the value of a college degree. Although colleges increasingly permitted wives to enroll as undergraduates, those who were married (often to veterans) tended to leave school.

This pattern started during the war, when students took defense jobs instead of finishing college, with a resulting decline in female enrollments of 25,000 between 1940 and 1944. The trend accelerated in 1946 when increasing numbers of the undergraduate female student body dropped out to marry. If more young females seemed indifferent to higher aspirations then, their mood matched society's eroding expectations for them quite well.[8]

Those who pursued serious academic studies, especially in relation to careers in the prestigious "male" fields of medicine, law, the ministry, or academia, took lonely paths. Graduate education became more competitive, due to the vast numbers of men entering and the priority given to veterans. Graduate women had to be far better qualified than men to gain admission; and married women desiring to enroll part-time found it very difficult. Women as potential graduate students and professional trainees often found themselves rejected, due in part to the discriminatory quotas favoring veterans. Although later studies blamed women for not pursuing professional goals, manifestly they had severely limited access to institutions in this period.[9]

Nonetheless, the smaller percentages of women who obtained Ph.D.s in 1950 and 1960 (10–12 percent), as compared to 1930 (16–18 percent) need careful interpretation. Percentages declined (see table 6), but absolute numbers increased. Similarly, at the undergraduate level, women students lost ground relative to men; the proportion of women among college students decreased from 47.3 percent in 1920 to 35.2 percent in 1958. Once again, however, in actual numbers women advanced. They received 55,000 of the B.A.s in 1930, and 139,000 in 1960; the number of M.A.s quadrupled, from less than 6,000 in 1930 to 24,000 in 1960; and the number of Ph.D.s tripled, from 350 in 1930 to 1,030 in 1960.[10]

The postwar generations of college-educated women also became more diverse in religious and ethnic representation. By 1960 the enrollment included larger numbers of Catholics, Jews, and the smaller Protestant sects. Nonetheless, this greater religious representation did not signify greater class diversity. Christopher Jencks and David Riesman, in generalizing on the post-college enrollments of both men and women, noted that, contrary to the authors' expectations, the increase among the upper-middle classes "seems to have been greater" than the increase in lower-middle and working-class enrollments. In applying this observation to women students it is assumed that female representation from poorer families remained even less; most parents were more disposed to make an educational investment in a son rather than a daughter, with the exception of black families.[11]

Irrespective of social class, marital status, and economic need, the college woman made a swift transition from student to paid worker in the expanding economy of the 1950s and 1960s. Women had a substantial place in the labor force because there were more jobs than men could fill. By the mid-twentieth century women's participation belied or contradicted the stereotyped view of their functioning exclusively as wives and mothers. That educated women with or without children worked for most or a good part of their adult lives became increasingly the norm and not the exception, despite expectations to the contrary. Still the common belief held that collegiate instruction should somehow prepare women for female roles and foster their aspirations strictly within bounds. Wherever the potential diversity of women's lives became fulfilled, the liberal education of women became the main target of attack.[12]

Women's liberal education in the late forties became the focus of a backlash in which the old disagreement over the purposes of educating women was rekindled. Fearful of the continuing changes in work patterns and in expectations of women trained during and after the war, educators, relying on studies in psychology from a Freudian perspective, again succumbed to curricular arguments for a feminine education. The

proponents cited wartime and postwar surveys of college women to justify making liberal education for women different from that for men.
Such studies reported confusion and discontent among many graduates;
they felt unprepared for the overwhelming domesticity that they confronted after marriage. A 1942 study by Robert Foster and Pauline Park
Wilson claimed to document attitudes of 1930s graduates regretting
their lack of preparation for domestic roles. Such surveys gave further
evidence that women in a wide spectrum of colleges wanted courses on
family life. Both Willa Player's report (1948) on students of Bennett
College in 1947 and Jeanne Noble's study of black sorority women in
1953 showed that "preparation for marriage and family life was important." Although students when queried expressed interest in domestic
courses, often their intention was to supplement, not to replace, regular
academic subjects. In view of anticipated early matrimony it was reason-
able for women to seek more information about marriage, birth control,
and psychology; interestingly, their male classmates often joined
them.[13]

Overreacting educators interpreted these responses to mean that
women wanted solely a domesticity for which higher education unfitted
them. Lynn White, Mills's president, shrewdly exploited the results of
the surveys to call for a "feminine" liberal education to counteract "our
present peculiar habit" of educating our daughters "as if they were
men." With a view reminiscent of nineteenth-century educator
Catharine Beecher, White recommended enlarging the female professoriat for the education of women in their primary role, that of enriching
home and community. Although he admitted that females needed to be
prepared to hold jobs before marriage, he opposed their taking advanced degrees. White pontificated that feminine studies would include
"the theory and preparation of a Basque paella, or a well-marinated
shish kabob." Even anthropologist Margaret Mead, herself a professional and wife and mother, seemed to give support to White's views by
asking; "Have we cut women off from their natural closeness to their
children, taught them to look for a job instead of the touch of a child's
hand, for status in a competitive world rather than a unique place by a
glowing hearth?" Notions of domesticity with some variation intruded
wherever women were educated. Even at Radcliffe, identified as a Blue-
stocking haven, the president, W. K. Jordan, informed entering freshmen throughout the fifties that their education would prepare them to
be splendid wives and mothers, and their reward might be to marry
Harvard men.[14]

Though few educators, if asked directly, would have moved to the
curricular extremes advocated by White, most felt obliged to review
their own thinking on the purposes of educating women. The campaign

for "feminine" education put the proponents of rigorous study in the arts and sciences on the defensive. Rarely did they examine the potentially radical implications of liberal education for women. An exception, Harold Taylor, president of Sarah Lawrence, stood out in declaring that education should help women "find their own fulfillment" without making their needs subservient to the "needs of men." Renaissance scholar Rosemond Tuve, a professor at Connecticut College for Women, went further, stating that women were "never taught by this society to see that being a success as a woman is inextricably connected with being a success as a human being." Tuve knew the enemy: Lynn White's "feminine" curriculum and the early marriages that accompanied the education. She posed an essential question: Why should women be told that "they had to choose between marrying and caring intensely about scholarship?"[15]

Too often educators made accommodations to the advocates of domesticity. Even those who objected to the closing off of careers for women expressed themselves with such restraint that real encouragement seemed wanting. Barnard's president Millicent McIntosh, for example, asserted that "a girl does not need courses in baby tending to prepare her for motherhood, but she does need a philosophy which does not belittle the home as a place unworthy of her best, and does not glorify the job as important beyond everything else." This answer, while upholding the liberal values in education, also upheld the domestic ones. McIntosh was not alone in giving ambiguous signals to students. Bryn Mawr's president Katharine McBride, a trained psychologist, believed in fundamental role differences for men and women but was also impressed with the range in abilities among women. This range, she wrote, should influence their training: "If women are to go beyond their function as wife and mother, then this fact of wide diversity has great significance for education." Who knew what McBride meant?[16]

Barnard professor of sociology Mirra Komarovsky wrote more discerningly about the conflicts of undergraduate women dealing with two roles: first, the feminine, whatever the variants—whether the "good sport," the "glamour girl," the "young lady," or the "domestic home girl"—which were always described with reference to differences between men and women; and second, the so-called modern, which "demands of the woman much of the same virtues, patterns of behavior, and attitudes that it does of the men of a corressponding age." Neither role could be overlooked, and therein lay the dilemmas of the young, which Komarovsky analyzed very clearly.[17]

It took intellectual courage to question the premises of "feminine" education. Its exponents were anti-feminists who rested their claims not only on the old religious beliefs about woman's place and her duties but also on the Freudian gospel that decreed anatomy as destiny for women.

This so-called "scientific" rationale rendered public judgments against careers for women all the more powerful. An influential Freudian, Helene Deutsch, in her *The Psychology of Women* (1944) condemned "the more masculine women's interests which turned toward aims in the pursuit of which femininity is felt as troublesome and is rejected." Psychoanalyst Deutsch, in fact a devoted wife and mother, described the overwhelming conflicts of the professional mother: "After each success she achieves in her professional activity, instead of feeling satisfaction she is tormented by guilt feelings with regard to her children." In *Modern Woman: The Lost Sex* (1947), Ferdinand Lundberg and Maryna Farnham concluded that "contemporary women in large numbers are psychologically disordered" by the strivings to be both wife and mother and professional.[18]

A working mother who escaped the guilt implicit in such analyses had still to answer to the popular child guidance expert Dr. Benjamin Spock, who in the fifties made child-centeredness basic to good family life. Mothers who adhered to his viewpoint took full responsibility for the successes and failures of children. At a time when motherhood might have been considered a part-time occupation—though a lifetime commitment—these combined influences demanded from women more than full-time attention to the young. Motherhood was the primary function that no real woman would deny; and in the fifties women felt the burden of demonstrating their fitness for the maternal role.[19]

How were students to make choices given the array of advice? One student editor commented on the difficult choices: "The future of the Barnard graduate may be a professional or more routine career, marriage or a combination. We don't come to college to learn the finer points of motherhood, but our education should be sufficiently broad and faceted to give sure preparation for all the possibilities we face." This student understood the essence of the liberal education: that with it one could go on into any of the roles of an educated woman—wife, mother, careerist. What uses she made of her liberal education were still up to the individual. Nonetheless, for most female undergraduates in these postwar decades, it was not easy to admit personal ambition privately, let alone expresss it openly. The idea of stating that one would become a writer, a doctor, or a professor would have sounded absurd. What even the most brilliant heard, as Sylvia Plath showed in *The Bell Jar*, was that they must want, above all, to be married. From all sides came pressure for the American college girl to prove herself as a wife and mother.[20]

A diamond ring on the fourth finger was the sign of success most valued in one's senior year at Vassar in 1949. Too often college resembled a marriage market, with peers and professors reinforcing the public mood of conformity. Women's residential colleges especially became five-day enterprises, with weekends given over to trips off campus or to male invasions. In one Radcliffe alumna's first novel, *The Best of Everything* (1958), the heroine's mother insisted that her daughter go to Radcliffe to be near Harvard boys. Another graduate corroborates the idea that "the unwritten history of most Radcliffe careers is an involvement with a Harvard man, not with John Donne or a grandfatherly professor." What in fact was involved was another stage of the sexual revolution. While early marriages were encouraged, intimacy between the unmarried was officially prohibited. Students' conflicts with authorities over parietals were symptomatic of a deeper social problem. Administrators' hypocrisy about sexual relations between male and female college youth intensified the pressure to wed. Women now learned from psychologists that they had sexual needs that should be fulfilled; early marriages had great appeal. The "single" woman—whether unattached or involved in a heterosexual or lesbian relationship—was categorized as deviant in this time of social conformity.[21]

The college graduate, even if she had no strong "career ambitions," assumed that she would get a job until marriage. But in the 1950s, if college women had to make a choice between marriage and career, the large majority chose marriage unquestioningly. In a poll of Vassar undergraduates in 1956, very few indicated that they would continue with a career if it interfered with the family, and a demanding career like medicine had virtually no appeal.

Female graduates expected to marry within one to three years of graduation. Some women rushed into matrimony without going to college, and the numbers dropping out increased as well. In 1957 the average woman in the United States married at age twenty; the typical college woman, if she graduated, married somewhat later, at the age of twenty-two or twenty-three. Like the women who had grown up in the Depression and lived through the war years, younger women were ready to have families—the larger the better. The baby boom had begun. Childbearing and childrearing, however, did not preclude the now well-established pattern of college women working before and after marriage. Indeed, what is striking in the period in which the feminine mystique held sway was that ever-increasing numbers of educated women chose to work after marriage, and that a growing percentage worked after the children came. The 1960 census showed, as Alice Rossi noted, that "women accounted for 65 percent of the increase in the labor force between 1950 and 1960." College women formed an integral part of this trend.[22]

Even though the swing to domesticity was stronger than ever in rhetoric, paradoxically more and more married women held jobs. Public attitudes toward paid employment for married women did not stop individuals in some circumstances: contributing payment to the family's mortgage or the children's tuition helped certain wives legitimate employment outside the home. *Life* magazine in 1956 went further in an issue on "The American Woman—Her Achievements and Troubles." A leading article included a picture of a beautifully groomed working mother, with a baby in her arms and an approving husband in the background. No longer was this pattern atypical.[23]

Educated wives and mothers held many kinds of jobs, but most were employed in those fields regarded as traditional for females: teaching, nursing, social work, and low-level management. Still, Mabel Newcomer's analysis of women in selected professions in 1956 demonstrates some slight progress in breaking down monopolies in nine "men's" professions (engineering, dentistry, forestry, law, architecture, the ministry, medicine, veterinary medicine, and pharmacology). More substantially, by 1950 women comprised one-third of editors and reporters. Over all, however, there was no profound shift in the occupational structure; prestigious fields were still dominated by men.[24]

What kinds of women ignored or resisted the pressures to conform to the dominant vogue of limiting one's horizons to those of the cultivated lady, the supportive wife and mother? In earlier chapters I have addressed this question as it applied to those who went to college in the nineteenth and early twentieth centuries. I make a broad analogy between the earlier "first" women, who pioneered in going to college, and those who finished graduate and professional programs in the competitive decades after World War II. These were very bright students, determined, persistent in study and work habits, undeterred by setbacks, and impervious to conventional expectations. Again a combination of factors explained the aspirations of some women competing for the highly valued places. Personal traits as well as familial and environmental influences shaped their ambitions.

Often family support strengthened these nonconformists. A father or mother, or both, proved the most critical influence, although a grandparent or sibling might be important as well. Some fathers believed that all their children should be professionally educated, and others, who had no sons, could see their daughters in professional roles. Mothers could provide support for daughters in a variety of ways. Those mothers who held jobs, whether or not they were professionals, set impressive examples if they handled their responsibilities comfortably. And some mothers (though not all) who did not choose expanded roles for themselves approved of achieving daughters.[25]

The socioeconomic backgrounds of the students affected their ambitions. Retrospectively, many of the well-to-do believed that parents had discouraged them from pursuing professional goals and that teachers had remained too neutral. These were parents who could not imagine their daughters as nurses, let alone lawyers, doctors, or professors. In many monied families, there were those who felt self-conscious about their ethnic or racial origins, and consequently their highest expectation was for their daughter to be an American lady, which still meant leisure, companionship with her husband, visible devotion as a mother—all the ingredients of the feminine mystique.

By contrast, for another type of woman of modest or poor economic circumstances, graduate education became a recognized part of her route to social mobility, in which working her way through graduate school added one further step after a similar pattern in college. Although such a young woman could not expect financial support from her parents, she might get their approval of this new academic path. A girl whose mother worked in a factory or as a domestic and yet managed to give her children love and security might convey better than an upper-class leisured mother that work need not be debilitating to family life. The intelligent, hardworking parent whose lack of education limited her choices might well take pride in a daughter's professional interests in training at college and beyond.[26]

Such daughters from socially mobile or poorer families were indifferent to the pressures of the feminine mystique, for they felt the even stronger pressures to escape ghetto poverty or to move up in the middle class. Thus James Davis's study of college seniors in 1961 showed that the small group of college women concerned with earning money were the ones likely to seek graduate training in physics. The experience of Mildred Dresselhaus, who graduated from college in the 1940s, provides one example of such student motivation. As a young woman Dresselhaus believed that only education would remove her from the grind of factory work. No one in her junior high school had been admitted to Hunter High School, yet ambition took Mildred from an inadequate school in the Bronx to Hunter High School and Hunter College. There a teacher saw the talent of this girl who had planned to be an elementary schoolteacher. Instead Dresselhaus made her way to graduate studies in physics; she is now a professor at M.I.T., as well as a wife and mother.[27]

Some parents, whether white or black, gave daughters as well as sons the sense of purpose and the backing that made a difference in nurturing ambition. A black mother in Boston who saw to it that her daughter got on the college preparatory track when she had been assigned against her wishes to the home economics program knew what counted for her offspring. That daughter, Gertrude Texeira Hunter, went on to Boston University and Howard University and became a pediatrician. It was not that in girlhood such an individual envisioned specific goals; rather, that she learned early in life to take herself seriously. For ambitious women in all walks of life, education from primary school to high school to college and post-college became a continuous process. Such women appeared less worried about marrying and thus, unlike most of their peers, foreshadowed later trends.[28]

By the mid-fifties educators had become alarmed about the early marriages of undergraduates. Nevitt Sanford complained that too few wanted to prepare for professional careers. Older women professors like Smith College's Mary Ellen Chase blamed married graduates for not having ambitions, and criticism centered on the lack of seriousness of women about their education, specifically as reflected in the dropout rate and the lack of productivity of Ph.D. holders. A report of the American Council on Education identified the lack of aspirations among women as a social problem. The investigation noted "discrepancies between their education and society's expectations of women" and the "contradictions of a society that opens doors . . . but translates their vocational success as damaging to the happiness of both men and women."[29]

But this period of relative dearth in women's professional training lasted only about a decade, from 1946 to 1956. Whether or not a coincidence, the departure of the veterans signaled the turning of the tide and a renewal in women's strivings and achievements. Direct and indirect influences gradually encouraged new ambitions and initiatives for women.

In the next period two important factors affected women as well as men students: first, the launching of Sputnik by the Russians precipitated a national review of all levels of American education; second, subsequent legislation, from the National Defense Act of 1958 to other education-related acts in the mid-1960s, was intended to recruit a wider spectrum of students, including women. One study noted that, among the top 10 percent of high school seniors in 1957, almost twice as many females as males did not attend college. Since the training of future scientists started at the high school level, the investigations of the National Science Foundation focused on the recruitment of younger students, both male and female, for all academic fields. The national legislation in 1958 provided aid to needy students of ability to pursue studies in the humanities as well as the sciences. Within a decade the federal government expanded its financial support for students as part of the realization of President Johnson's Great Society; the pool of the college-bound, particularly from poorer white and black families, was greatly enlarged. Renewed enthusiasm for education spurred the development of community colleges and continuing education programs; both would have importance for women later, in the 1970s and 1980s.[30]

The Russians' scientific success corroborated the complaints of educators that the United States was not utilizing the potential of its trained men and women. New studies sought to determine why female college undergraduates in particular were "wasting" their privileged education. James Davis studied the aspirations of 1961 college seniors, male and female, from a wide range of about a hundred and forty-five colleges: public, private, coed, women's, and Catholic. (Although no black colleges were surveyed, black students were represented in the sample.) These students came mainly from middle- to upper-middle-class families. Davis's findings revealed predictable elements but also showed the complexities in the responses of the women. His data confirmed other evidence presented earlier in this chapter; over 95 percent of these college women expected to work. Most of them did not expect to marry in the next year, but neither did they plan to attend graduate school at once. Davis found that only 24 percent of the women, in contrast to 39 percent of the men, expected to enter graduate school immediately. Moreover, high academic ability was not a sure predicter of women's plans: 68.4 percent of men in the top fifth of their class would go on to graduate school in the next year, while only 36.3 percent of the women would. These statistics were more discouraging, because a higher proportion of women than men placed in the top 50 percent of their class, as measured by the Academic Performance Index.[31]

Although overall, women's aspirations at the highest level did not equal men's in the Davis study, there were positive hints. Many—42.6 percent—of the women expressed the intent to continue their education later. These answers were projections, not guarantees of future direction. Yet the majority respected the career choices that only a minority of them made. Reexamining the data from the Davis survey, Alice Rossi astutely noted that most of these educated women (close to four out of five) expressed admiration above all for those achieving scientific and scholarly recognition, and next for those attaining artistic or literary distinction. While for themselves most wanted to be mothers of "highly accomplished children" and wives of "prominent" men, they served as a "sympathetic, admiring audience for the small female minority" who were entering the masculine fields and winning acclaim for their accomplishments.[32] No one group could speak for the whole student population of women. It is evident that both discrimination and lack of incentives contributed to the slower pace of women's professional advancement. Obtaining the M.A., Ph.D., or L.L.D. required many difficult decisions for a woman. Some women, as always, pursued advanced degrees irrespective of traditional marital aspirations. Others, influenced by contemporary views advocating early marriage, took jobs while renouncing career ambitions. Both groups, as each census revealed, contributed to the increasing proportion of women in the work force.[33]

Some occupations became more open to the married. For example,

most states dropped traditional restrictions on marriage for schoolteachers (because of a shortage of single schoolteachers). By 1956 the large
majority of schoolteachers were married women. Moreover, at one institution of higher learning, Barnard College, 52 percent of the female faculty were married by 1950, as opposed to only 12 percent in 1930.[34]

Increasingly, by the late fifties individuals questioned their complex
situations. Movie scenarios presented the so-called happy ending in store
for the high-powered career woman, played by Katharine Hepburn or
Rosalind Russell, who renounced her work to ensure the success of her
marriage. In real life women who had careers had no support from the
culture, especially when they combined marriage, career, and motherhood.

Thus, in contrast to the minority of women who combined marriage
and career or who chose to work and not marry, others gave up graduate training midway because of family pressures and demands. Few institutions permitted part-time graduate study or employment; even
those women who completed their studies and had careers often did
so with a great deal of difficulty. It was to redress this lack of institutional support that President Mary I. Bunting in 1960 founded the Radcliffe Institute for Independent Study, to provide a place for women of
talent to renew scholarly and artistic interests. It was assumed that the
typical candidate was likely to be "a married woman in her middle thirties" who had abandoned her academic or creative work for domestic
responsibilities.[35]

After World War II women who continued professional and academic
training despite lack of encouragement did not have the support of
large numbers of peers or of a public women's movement, and in time
visible and invisible barriers became increasingly oppressive. Although
the breaking point came only during a convergence of public crises, the
seeds of the new feminism were being planted throughout the postwar
era. The women's movement was reborn at the end of the 1960s.

Many educated women graduating during and after World War II
were more or less happily absorbed in their private lives, and some studies in the fifties emphasized women's contentment with their domestic
roles. It was not then recognized that unfulfilled aspirations haunted
others. In an informal analysis of her 1942 Smith College classmates,
Betty Friedan in 1957 uncovered the dissatisfaction of well over one-half
of her respondents, who reported that the role of wife and mother did
not "sufficiently" utilize their "creative abilities." Her publication of *The
Feminine Mystique* in 1963 brought responses from around the world; individual women experiencing shocks of recognition learned that they
were not alone. Friedan's exposure of the pervasive cult of femininity, "the
problem that had no name," did not create the new wave of the women's

movement but provided one leader for it. At the same time that Friedan wrote, sociologist Alice Rossi illuminated professional women's dilemmas in her memorable address entitled "The Equality of the Sexes: An Immodest Proposal," presented in 1963 at a *Daedalus* conference in Cambridge, Massachusetts.[36]

Even while living out the "feminine mystique," more women questioned their life patterns; Friedan's analysis pointed to the negative role models that one generation of college-educated women may have provided for their daughters, who reclaimed from their mothers' disappointments a new set of feminist aspirations. Expectations of several generations laid the groundwork for the new explosion in the late 1960s, with consequences for educated and uneducated alike.

Although the resurgence of the women's movement did not begin on college campuses, within a few years colleges were transformed by it, as well as by other aspects of social awakening that escalated in the 1960s. Of critical importance was the forging of a new civil rights movement by black Americans. Moreover, a young president of the United States at the start of the decade symbolized heightening expectations throughout American society.

Older women graduates from the 1920s to the early 1940s welcomed the 1960 Commission on the Status of Women established by President John F. Kennedy and chaired by Eleanor Roosevelt. These women were professional and club women, long concerned with women's economic and political rights under the law. Some believed in the equal rights amendment advocated by the National Women's Party and the National Federation of Business and Professional Women's Clubs; but more women, the constituency of the League of Women Voters, opposed the ERA. The *Report of the Commission on the Status of Women* in 1963 deliberately ignored the issue, but with the continuing pressure from women's groups the long-sought Equal Pay Act passed that year. An even greater triumph followed in 1964 with the inclusion of Title Seven in the Civil Rights Act, making sexual, racial, and religious discrimination illegal. But although an Equal Employment Opportunity Commission was established in 1965 to implement this legislation, it refused to consider cases of economic discrimination against women. The EEOC faced formidable opponents in the leadership of state commissions on the status of women, which had been started to carry on the work of the national commission. Frustrated by the EEOC's failure to respond, these leaders, including Betty Friedan, founded a female civil rights organization, the National Organization for Women (NOW). By 1968 women who earlier had not thought about the ERA now made it their political goal. Thus one branch of the modern women's movement came into being.[37]

Women's consciousness was catapulted to a new level by black people's demands for equality. The Supreme Court decision in *Brown* v. *the Board of Education* in 1954 transformed the civil rights movement for black people of several generations. Rosa Parks's refusal to sit at the back of a Montgomery bus augured other actions, and before long the younger generation of the black elite reacted with new tactics. The 1959 Woolworth sit-ins in Greensboro represented undercurrents that created a tidal wave among educated young black men and women that was not feminist but racial in its purpose. These students, in creating new forces of social activism, had either direct or indirect support of their families, communities, and colleges. As the movement expanded, women of Bennett, Spelman, Fisk, and Tougalou colleges, among others, were soon protesting, picketing, and being jailed along with men.[38]

Quite separately southern white college women found their way into the civil rights cause, but without family or institutional support. Sara Evans has described movingly their responses to the Christian doctrines they had heard since childhood. Such women students gathered in small groups at colleges from the University of Texas to Duke and Vanderbilt universities, in local YWCAS, Methodist churches, and other voluntary religious organizations.[39]

Student meetings and protests not only launched an interacial movement, but black and white women discovered in various activities bonds of womanhood. Not through college courses on women's needs, but out of concern with the ideals of democracy came the unexpected awakening of feminist consciousness. Black women were the first to rebel against their subordinate roles in the civil rights movement, in 1964; soon white women protested against similar treatment. Out of their group discussions and position papers came another shock of recognition concerning discrimination against women by male colleagues. In each cause of the sixties, from Free Speech and civil rights to anti-war protests, women worked with men without being allowed to share in the policy making and critical decisions. At a convention of the National Conference on New Politics in Chicago, Shulamith Firestone was told to "cool down, little girl" when she demanded a discussion of women's roles in the politics of the New Left. Black and white women alike learned what female activists had faced a century earlier in anti-slavery, temperance, and other causes; most men considered women's opinions as secondary.[40]

The younger liberationist branch of the women's movement was born of the recognition that participation of females was not acknowledged as equal to that of males. The first black and white women activists shared the need to be valued as persons and so rediscovered what it meant to be a woman and to gain strength from a group. In their spontaneous discussions the younger women addressed the more private aspects of women's lives and formulated demands that transformed the questions women asked themselves. The various constituencies among the liberationists, in attacking the modern patriarchal society, stirred the aspirations of diverse groups of American women. It was not coincidental that the resurgence of the women's movement occurred when there were millions of women in the work force and thousands in the professions who had experienced discrimination in wages and salaries and who were all the more ready to respond to feminist demands. The outpouring of protest, anger, and questions about the place of women came from all directions—colleges, work force, professions, and voluntary organizations—and brought women of different ages and groups into the women's movement.[41]

From the beginning the movement had different meanings for different generations and for women of diverse social backgrounds. Whatever the motive, they learned to value women's group support. Organizations like NOW identified with the liberal rights tradition to effect changes in the laws; the liberationist principles strengthened the resolve of individuals to make personal choices, whether conventional or not. Women who had attended college in the fifties and sixties became leaders in the liberationist wing. Often they had been drawn together through civil rights activism, and already they were working women—journalists, writers, and scholars. Thousands of women all over the country discovered in consciousness raising that they need not be alone in resolving conflicts of work, study, creativity, and personal relationships.

For undergraduate women in the seventies the women's movement became connected with the general student politicization of the late sixties. The demands of both sexes had a wide impact on the liberal arts colleges, in the classroom and beyond. Undergraduates gained representation on some faculty committees and made their opinions count on curricular as well as social matters. Moreover, educators at men's colleges, already concerned with rising costs and declining applicant pools, acknowledged their students' preference to have women enrolled with them. Reluctantly, in the early seventies, resistant colleges like the University of Virginia, Yale, and Princeton gave up the battle and admitted women. Wesleyan once again received females and moved to co-residential living. By 1983, when Columbia opened its door to women undergraduates, there were only a handful of all-male colleges left (see table 1). Many women's colleges, notably Vassar, found it similarly expedient to admit men. Others, like Wellesley, Bryn Mawr, and Mills denied calls for coeducation but affiliated informally with nearby coeducational institutions. Thus, the women's colleges of the 1980s bore little resemblance to the nineteenth-century models, where men were hardly allowed to walk across campus. Both male and female students generally

demanded an end to parietal restrictions. Rules that had been difficult
to enforce crumbled everywhere. Essential to the new permissiveness on
campuses were the advances in birth control technology and its availability. An important consequence of the new freedom, particularly for
women, was the removal of one incentive for early marriages.

The feminist movement affected the education of women and men in
all kinds of institutions, both undergraduate and professional. As a result of federal legislation and accompanying affirmative action regulations, public efforts to reduce and eliminate discrimination against
women in academia, as well as in the work place, helped individuals to
assert themselves, to reject age-old prejudices.

Women's collegiate athletics was one area revolutionized in the 1970s
as a result of the women's movement and an inclusion in the 1972 education amendment of Title IX that prohibits sexual discrimination by
schools that receive federal financial assistance. Before Title IX there
were no women's collegiate championships; in 1984, there were thirty
national contests. Similarly, where once there had been no athletic scholarships for women, by 1984 ten thousand were available (although men
still had far more). For the decade between 1972 and 1982 the gains in
female athletics were great. Yet these may be threatened by the 1984 Supreme Court decision in the *Grove City College* case that interprets Title
IX narrowly. Moreover, female athletic directors caution that women
still receive mixed messages about their participation in athletics: the
sportswoman has yet to reconcile her femininity with her athletic
prowess.[42]

The women's movement not only invigorated extracurricular athletics, but challenged the liberal arts curriculum. All institutions were
forced to address the legacy of the sixties—an awakened feminist consciousness—and one result was an enlargement of the curriculum to include courses relating to women. Many disciplines have been affected by
women's interest in their roles and their past. The remarkable convergence of interested scholars and students created an extraordinary climate for productive scholarship. The new questions posed by scholars
who give women a central place in their investigations enrich and alter
perspectives in every field. Just as women take their identities from
many roles and activities, so does the study of women lend itself to interdisciplinary approaches, what we call women's studies. Many schools
offer B.A., M.A. and Ph.D. programs either in women's history or in
women's studies. At other institutions that give little encouragement
departmentally, individual faculty members transmit the excitement of
these new approaches. Students who make even small excursion into
this terrain are rewarded by innovative viewpoints on traditional materials of study. Though women scholars predominate in this area, men are

also making contributions. The interest of general readers as well remains strong in the 1980s.[43]

Not only in the classroom, but also in the public sphere, female consciousness raising grew, with the result that more and more middle- and working-class women looked to education for training in the professions and in politics. Finally, community colleges, supported primarily by government funding, made it possible for poor women to consider the option of higher education.

In my opinion the women's movement became, indirectly, a catalyst for the enormous increase of women students at two-year colleges. Such institutions had existed earlier; what was exciting in the seventies, however, was the rising number of women of all ages entering community colleges. Not all were feminists, but in the high tide of the women's movement consciousness of the importance of education for women caught on. As in the past women studied for different reasons: the vocational motive, the desire for a better job, was paramount; many older women, who had never gone to college or who had dropped out to marry and have babies, also found that they were now ready to study in order to have something of "one's own." Of course, the reasons often overlapped.[44]

Observers caution against too optimistic a view of the vast enrollments of women at two-year institutions. While the majority apparently do not continue to four-year schools, a proportion do enroll at liberal arts colleges. I maintain that, as in earlier times, these individuals, attending for many different, personal reasons, even with the irregularity of their course enrollment, could gain what they wanted and discover more than they had anticipated.[45]

Three older women, one native black, one white from a rural background, one a Spanish immigrant, who attended community colleges, were asked informally to comment on their education. Each indicated that her studies meant more to her than subject matter and training. When asked what difference attending college had made, all said that they had gained self-confidence. The first who was bored in high school and did not attend college until she was in her late forties remembered that earlier in her education no one had "pushed" her. She was grateful that the community college teachers had made demands on her. Before this, she said, "I did not know that I was creative." The second woman said of her education, "It's given me the freedom that it is okay to be a woman." The third went furthest, saying, "I could not have survived without it." This woman, who has completed a B.A., an M.A., and is finishing a Ph.D. while working full-time, added, "It has allowed me to become a model for my daughters." Asked about feminism, the black alumna remarked, "We're not into that. We've got it." By contrast, the third answered, "I could have gone all of my life being a feminist without knowing it." She underlined the importance of women's studies in making women aware of the potentialities offered to them by their education. By becoming students these women gained self-knowledge as well as academic knowledge. They and many others are the beneficiaries of the tradition of higher education for women.[46]

The community college graduates were part of a trend, in which older women increasingly became students. By 1980 approximately one-third of collegians were twenty-five years of age or older, and most of these were women (see table 3). Moreover, the proportion of those who were thirty-five years or older rose to 12.3 percent in 1979. We recall that a few eighteenth-century matrons, who had been denied liberal study, recognized the need for educating the younger generation. Two hundred years later the circle of history is complete; older women now seek the education that younger ones take for granted.[47]

In retrospect the period from World War II began at a low point in women's enrollments. In the context of the whole twentieth century, however, this appears to have been an aberration: the proportion of women among college students is higher today than ever. More important, the late twentieth century sees changes in women's attitudes, expectations, and demands. Earlier, women's advancement seemed to rest entirely on individuals' achievements, but both women and the society perceived these achievements as exceptions. To move beyond exceptions, women by the 1970s increasingly realized the necessity of public recognition and governmental response to blatant and less obvious inequities. Thus, women rediscovered the importance of working together. In the 1980s the momentum of the women's movement still provides consciousness and impetus. How can women sustain this momentum? Will they?

A·F·T·E·R·T·H·O·U·G·H·T·S

"If the college woman is a mistake, Nature will eliminate her." So evolutionist David Starr Jordan, Stanford University's president, answered skeptics in 1906. Yet those who supported women's education did not anticipate the rich evolution of the educated female throughout the century. Now the future belongs to young women, many of whom start with a level of choice they did not struggle to attain. What can new generations learn from the history of educated women?[1]

What I found most striking in my exploration was how few generalizations hold. Collegiate education was never static at private, public, single-sex, or coeducational schools. Whereas at the turn of the century 60 percent of American students were educated in private institutions, in the 1980s public higher education is the dominant mode, with only 20 percent of students enrolled in private schools. Morever, less than 5 percent attend single-sex colleges, and of that minority most are at women's schools. In a reversal of history, women have more collegiate options than men.[2]

A century ago separate private colleges for either men or women constituted an economic luxury. Only men's colleges that could afford it kept women out. Today only the few women's colleges that have large enough endowments and sufficient alumnae support can remain single-sex. But increasingly since World War II such schools have drawn on a diminishing pool of applicants. Most women prefer coeducation. Since the 1970s, when one male school after another converted to coeducation, women's colleges have found themselves competing still more fiercely for the brightest students.[3]

Ironically, even though coeducation has become the unmistakable norm, recent historical studies influenced by the women's movement have focused on the value of separate collegiate instruction for women. Some note that an inordinate proportion of female achievers (defined in various kinds of *Who's Whos*) took baccalaureate degrees at women's colleges. Scholars disagree on how to assess and interpret this evidence. Some regard the all-female college environment with female role models as a critical influence for the achievers. Others emphasize the importance of the socioeconomic origins of these students and point out that in large part these female alumnae achievers were congregated in the Seven Sister colleges. I would add that such students, whether or not they came from privileged backgrounds, gained advantages and connections once they attended these elite schools.[4]

Undoubtedly women's institutions, in the absence of men, provide more certain opportunities for female student leadership. Yet the assumption that women's colleges consistently offered female role models is an oversimplification. I found in my research that mentors of women students might be female or male, and unreserved support came from relatively few professors, whatever their gender. Most faculty revealed conscious and unconscious ambivalence toward women's professional aspirations. Indeed, many of the most talented graduates of women's colleges, as far back as the 1910s and afterward, have complained of limited encouragement and direction. Although studies thus far are not conclusive, they convey the complexities involved in evaluating collegiate influences. In my view evaluations should also consider how the criteria for female achievement have changed for different groups over time. What constitutes successs? What measurements are valid?

For present and future students the debate over the advantages of the separate college environment is largely anachronistic. The relatively few attending women's institutions have a different, diluted female collegiate experience, not comparable to that of earlier periods. Women are no longer educated in complete isolation from men. Thus, the most pertinent concern in the late twentieth century should be how to enlarge the coeducational environment and ensure that women are always taken as seriously as men.

Liberal arts education for women has entered a new stage; but it should be remembered that although in the 1980s collegiate access is greater than ever, women are still the second sex in most of academia. Although the number of females surpasses that of males overall, men predominate in four-year liberal arts colleges and in graduate and professional schools. Even equity in numbers would not assure equality. The real challenge lies in developing new ways to create an internal acceptance of women students. In the past coeducation has taken many forms, in which women's status varied; often women were far from equal members of the community. I view the coeducational campus as a

microcosm of the larger society, where young men and women can engage in the process of understanding one another. This aspect of education is as important as the liberal arts study and the personal growth of
individuals. In addition, as in separate colleges, so in coeducational
schools, there should be space and time for both women and men to
bond with members of their own sex and enjoy the group affinities that
gender strengthens.

Adrienne Rich has eloquently declared that we are in need of "woman-centered" universities. Since male perspectives and values are so
deeply embedded in academic disciplines, it is essential to incorporate
the innovative insights of women's studies into the main curriculum and
thereby extend its range for all students. Currently, the subject of
women in most courses, regardless of field, is treated as fringe matter.
Furthermore, until undergraduates, male and female, can take for
granted that a class will just as likely be taught by a woman as by a man,
one element in the male academic orientation remains intact. On the extracurricular level also, it will take time to alter the male traditions, especially in newly coeducational schools. It would be all too easy for women
to slip into existing deferential patterns. Instead, men and women together should forge new traditions; imaginative changes in extracurricular activities are the responsibility of students.[5]

I like to think that an ideal coeducational environment would counteract the negative, restrictive messages of the popular culture. Whether
through television or movies, newspapers or storybooks, children early
imbibe the male and female stereotypes that higher education should
dispel. Even the young men at college who express belief in the principles of the women's movement have difficulty in applying these to their
personal lives; often they prefer traditional wives. Sustaining the expectations and choices of both sexes, whether conventional or nonconforming, needs to be an ongoing enterprise.[6]

I am startled by the quality of déjà vu in media accounts of women's
lives in the 1980s. Just as the 1920s and 1930s witnessed a plethora of
"confessions" by "ex-feminists," so newspaper surveys today emphasize a
retreat from career aspirations on the part of young women. It helps, to
some extent, that we have strong feminist publications as well as those
that are blandly neutral and anti-feminist. Nevertheless, sometimes we
hear that young women are burdened by too many choices. The wom-
en's movement, it is said, puts undue pressure on females to achieve.
Undoubtedly, with increased options, women like men have to think
more and to understand that choices have consequences. Individual
choices to meet personal needs will inevitably affect one's commitments
to family, work, and society. Yet I disagree with those who tell young
women not to aim too high, not to think they can be "superwomen."

Such advice only adds to students' own uncertainties and conflicts.[7]

Rather, students should be made aware of many kinds of achievement and not regard certain conventional paths as signs of failure. Not every woman will become a wife or mother, nor will every mother have a career. Some women will remain single or become single through divorce or widowhood, while others will have female partners. For individual women independence will have different meanings, with self-definition extending over a lifetime. Although some commitments have to be made early in life—to be a scientist or mathematician, for example—the historical evidence of women's changing vocations and avocations in the course of their lives justifies expansive expectations in the young.[8]

Adult women express faith in their abilities and assert their right to serve as leaders in all spheres of society. In the nineteenth century the female writer, schoolteacher, doctor, minister, lawyer, or professor was a pioneer; in the late twentieth century, the arrival of America's first woman in space is a fitting symbol of the expanded female sphere. Women's entrance into the full range of occupations and professions has soared. The miniscule female presence in the judiciary of the United States has ended; significantly, a president who opposes the equal rights amendment appointed the first woman to the Supreme Court in 1981. Also, without precedence, females seek to become not only ministers, but rabbis and priests. Overcoming resistance, Protestant and Jewish women are being ordained in liberal congregations. Even the Catholic Church is being pressed by women, both lay and religious, for admission to the priesthood. Although we applaud female pioneering, we also hope to see an end to "firsts" and "exceptions" in all fields.[9]

The widening of access in so many fields should not blind us to its incompleteness. In the academic professoriat, for example, recent expansion in the hiring of able female faculty was long overdue. As a result of affirmative action, distinguished women have received professorships and younger women are on the academic ladder. Still, with the best of will, equity in faculty appointments cannot be achieved rapidly. Many problematic elements impede this process, including internal prejudices and the general crisis in academia because of changes in the economy and the national demography. In uncertain times, how will the progress of women in academia be affected? It remains to be shown how deep or genuine their acceptance is.

Pathbreakers in the professions today have a high level of education and training, which should be critical to the dissolution of traditional barriers in the occupations. Achievers in this era, whether or not they consider themselves feminists, are beneficiaries of the women's movement, their efforts kindled in some way either by the ethos or the practical results of feminism. Some individuals refuse to credit the women's movement with their advancement. True, exceptional women made their way before the resurgence of the movement. But they did not succeed on their own. As we have seen in this history, family, teachers, mentors, timing, and luck all made a difference. For others without such advantages, a vocal women's movement is needed to lend encouragement and support. Despite the traditional American wariness of ideology, we should respect the "shrillness" of activists, for their integrity in speaking out is necessary to sustain consciousness and to promote requisite legislation.

Those who gained from the women's movement need to remain active on behalf of others who have not yet benefited. The importance of education for social mobility of individuals appears throughout this book. Apart from such examples, we do not have sufficient data to chart the extent and the effects of upward mobility on women in particular groups. But since the 1950s we have moved into a new era in the rise in numbers of those who are moving out of deprived groups through college study. Community colleges, adult education programs, special opportunities in liberal arts colleges—all reach more than ever before those who had been left out of such opportunities. Education clearly creates its own peculiar elite from individuals of different social groups and backgrounds.

But there are valid reasons for pessimism amid optimistic visions. Since educated women are not a monolithic group, it should not be surprising that there is disagreement about unfinished work for the sex. There is genuine conflict on fundamental issues: abortion, day care, and sexual harassment. Deeply disturbing are the divisions of women by race and class. One cannot deny that thus far the women's movement has appealed primarily to middle- and upper-class educated women. Throughout the history of women's education, as I have noted, efforts to cross racial and class lines have been inadequate. Yet some feminists do want to respect pluralism in the women's movement of the late twentieth century and know that such a goal requires much work, self-honesty, and and coalition building. Dialogue, however painful, will be essential in making the women's movement more representative of all kinds of women.

We can no longer think of women's lives as set from youth to old age. Family, career, and voluntary activities will have different functions at various points in their lives. The variety of choices for women makes education increasingly important. And at each level it is up to educated women to take some measure of responsibility for the well-being of society. Eleanor Roosevelt's advice in the 1930s is still compelling and relevant fifty years later. She wanted women to ask no favors of men—rather, to earn recognition. Clearly she believed in a meritocracy that included women. At the same time she urged that they not forget each other but act in groups. This perspective is empowering for women in the 1980s. Many recognize that they must respect and retain the sense of woman's consciousness and at the same time must not permit society to limit their aspirations as individuals and as womankind. Ultimately the well-being of American women will mean the well-being of the whole society. The means to this end then is the challenge of the next generations of educated women.[10]

Notes

Chapter I

1. Quoted in Linda K. Kerber, *Women of the Republic: Intellect and Ideology in Revolutionary America* (Chapel Hill, 1980), 196.
2. Lawrence A. Cremin, *American Education: The Colonial Experience, 1607–1783* (New York, 1980); Bernard Bailyn, *Education in the Forming of American Society* (Chapel Hill, 1960).
3. Oscar and Mary F. Handlin, *The American College and American Culture: Socialization as a Function of Higher Education* (New York, 1970), 5. Kenneth Silverman, *A Cultural History of the American Revolution: Painting, Music, Literature, and the Theatre in the Colonies and the United States from the Treaty of Paris to the Inauguration of George Washington, 1763–1789* (New York, 1976), 218. Yale was so named in 1718.
4. Robert Wells, "Women's Lives Transformed: Demographic and Family Patterns in America, 1600–1970," in *Women of America: A History*, eds. Carol Berkin and Mary Beth Norton (Boston, 1974), 17–33.
5. Linda K. Kerber offers a discriminating analysis of the legal limitations and ramifications for the available sources in *Women of the Republic*. See also Nancy F. Cott, "Divorce and the Changing Status of Women in Eighteenth-Century Massachusetts," *William and Mary Quarterly*, 3d ser. 33 (October 1976): 586–614; Joseph Tomson, in *Handkerchiefs from Paul*, ed. Kenneth B. Murdock (Cambridge, Mass., 1927), 3. For other expressions of marital love see Julia Cherry Spruill, *Women's Life and Work in the Southern Colonies* (New York, 1972); also Jeannine Hensley, ed., *The Works of Anne Bradstreet* (Cambridge, Mass., 1967), 225.
6. Edith Abbott, *Women in Industry: A Study in American Economic History* (New York, 1909); Elisabeth A. Dexter, *Colonial Women of Affairs* (Boston, 1924); Mary Beth Norton, *Liberty's Daughters: The Revolutionary Experiences of American Women, 1750–1800* (Boston, 1980), 46; Catherine M. Scholten, "On the Importance of the Obstetrick Art: Changing Customs of Childbirth in America, 1760–1825," *William and Mary Quarterly*, 3d ser. 34 (July 1977): 426–45. See also Laurel T. Ulrich, *Good Wives: Image and Reality in Northern New England, 1650–1750* (New York, 1982), 126–45.
7. Kenneth Lockridge, *Literacy in Colonial New England: An Inquiry into the Social Context in the Early Modern West* (New York, 1974), 38–44. See also discussion of literacy in Linda K. Kerber, *Women of the Republic*, 192–93.
8. David D. Hall, *The Antinomian Controversy, 1636–1638: A Documentary History* (Middletown, Conn., 1968). See also Lyle Koehler, "The Case of the American Jezebels: Anne Hutchinson and Female Agitation During the Years of the Antinomian Turmoil,

213

1636–1640," *William and Mary Quarterly*, 3d ser. 31 (1974): 55–78. Koehler includes excellent documentation of previous analyses of historians.

9. S. E. Dwight, *The Life of President Edwards* (New York, 1830), 131; Jonathan Edwards, *A Narrative of Many Surprising Conversions . . . 1736 Together with Some Thoughts on the Revival of New England . . . 1740* (Worcester, 1832). See also Keith Melder, "The Beginnings of the Women's Rights Movement in the United States, 1800–1840" (Ph.D. diss., Yale, 1963), and *The Beginnings of Sisterhood: The American Women's Rights Movement, 1800–1850* (New York, 1977). Cedric B. Cowing, "Sex and Preaching in the Great Awakening," *American Quarterly* 20 (Fall 1968): 624–44, shows the complexity of the Awakening with its impact on "white males outside the major towns" as well as its appeal to "women, children, adolescents, Indians, and Negroes." On Sarah Osborne's remark, see Mary Beth Norton, *Liberty's Daughters*, 131.

10. Sydney V. James, *A People Among Peoples: Quaker Benevolence in Eighteenth-Century America* (Cambridge, Mass., 1963).

11. See Mary Mapes Dunn's insightful speculation, "Women of Light," in *Women of America*, ed. Berkin and Norton, 115–36.

12. Melissa A. Butler, "Early Liberal Roots of Feminism: John Locke and the Attack on Patriarchy," *American Political Science Review* 72 (1978).

13. On the South Carolinian parent, see Anne Firor Scott, "Self-Portraits: Three Women," in *Uprooted Americans: Essays to Honor Oscar Handlin*, ed. Richard Bushman et al. (Boston, 1979). Phillis Wheatley quote is from *Poems on Various Subjects, Religious and Moral* (1786; repr. New York, 1976). See also Saunders Redding, "Phillis Wheatley," in *Notable American Women*, III, 573–74.

14. See Benjamin Coleman to daughter Jane, August 10, 1725, in Ebenezer Turrell, ed., *Memoirs of the Life and Death of the Pious and Ingenious Mrs. Jane Turrell* (London, 1741), 14–15, 24. Jeannine Hensley, *Anne Bradstreet*, 16.

15. Margaret Rossiter, *Women Scientists in America: Struggles and Strategies to 1940* (Baltimore, 1983), 2–3.

16. John Witherspoon [Epaminondas], "Reflections on Marriage," *Pennsylvania Magazine* 1 (December 1775), 546. For full citations on the etiquette books mentioned, see Mary S. Benson, *Women in Eighteenth-Century America: A Study of Opinion and Social Usage* (New York, 1935). For a good excerpt from George Savile, Marquis of Halifax, see *The Lady's New Year Gift, or, Advice to a Daughter* in *Root of Bitterness: Documents of the Social History of American Women*, ed. Nancy F. Cott (New York, 1972), 77–82. Although Linda K. Kerber's *Women of the Republic* provides a more subtle interpretation, Benson is a very important source.

17. For comments of American women on *Pamela*, see Josephine Fisher, "The Journal of Esther Burr," *New England Quarterly* 3 (1930): 297–99. See also Laurel T. Ulrich, *Good Wives*, for an excellent interpretation of Pamela's strategy in fainting. Charles W. Akers, *Abigail Adams: An American Woman* (Boston, 1980) conveys well Adams' interest in the prescriptive literature and novels of her time, as well as the inconsistency in her reponses to women's issues. On the importance of reading and rereading *Clarissa*, see Judith Murray, *The Gleaner* (Boston, 1798). For responses to *Clarissa*, see also Cynthia Griffin Wolff, "The Problem of Eighteenth-Century Heroine-ism," *Modern Language Studies* 4 (1974), which clarifies the social contradictions.

18. Elise Pinckney, "Eliza Lucas Pinckney," in *Notable American Women*, III; Anne Firor Scott, "Self-Portraits: Three Women," 43–76. Eliza Pinckney quoted in Harriott H. Ravenal, *Eliza Lucas Pinckney* (New York, 1896), 100.

19. Mary Beth Norton, *Liberty's Daughters*, especially chapters 6 and 7. For a contrasting interpretation of the role of women in the Revolution, see Joan Hoff Wilson, "The Illusion of Change: Women and the American Revolution," in *The American Revolution:*

Explorations in the History of American Radicalism, ed. Alfred Young (DeKalb, 1976).

20. Robert A. Feer, "Mercy Otis Warren," in *Notable American Women*, III, and Lyman Butterfield, "Abigail Smith Adams," in *Notable American Women*, I, offer excellent biographical introductions. Mercy Warren to Abigail Adams, January 18, 1774, in *Adams Family Correspondence*, II, 92. Abigail Adams to Isaac Smith, Jr., April 20, 1771, in *Adams Family Correspondence*, I, 76. See Mary Beth Norton, *Liberty's Daughters*, 121ff., Linda K. Kerber, *Women of the Republic*, which convey different insights about Mercy Warren's feminist thinking. For her sardonic feminist expression, see Mercy Warren, *Poems, Dramatic and Miscellaneous* (Boston, 1790), 114.

21. Mercy Warren's satiric poem against the Clarissa type of woman appeared in the *Royal American Magazine* (June 1774).

22. On her curiosity about Mrs. Macaulay, see Abigail Adams to Isaac Smith, Jr., April 20, 1771 in *Adams Family Correspondence*, I, 77.

23. Abigail Adams to John Adams, March 31, 1776, in *Adams Family Correspondence*, I, 369–70; Abigail Adams to John Adams, August 14, 1776, in *Adams Family Correspondence*, II, 94.

24. Janet W. James, "Judith Sargent Murray," in *Notable American Women*, II, 603.

25. Judith Murray, *The Gleaner*, III, 189; Judith Murray, "Desultory Thoughts upon the Utility of Encouraging a Degree of Self-Complacency, Especially in Female Bosoms," in *Gentleman and Lady's Town and Country Magazine* 1 (1784): 252.

26. Judith Murray, "Desultory Thoughts," 253.

27. Judith Murray, *The Gleaner*, I, 168.

28. Mary Wollstonecraft, *A Vindication of the Rights of Woman*, ed. Carol H. Poston (New York, 1975). The quotation is from the introduction to the first edition, which appeared in 1791. Note that the second edition was issued later that year; it is the preferred edition and the one that Carol Poston used.

29. Susan Bull Tracy to James Morris, January 25, 1794, in *The Diary of Elihu Hubbard Smith*, ed. James E. Cronin (Philadelphia, 1973), 110. (I am indebted to Lynn T. Brickley for alerting me to this reference.) Charles Brockden Brown, *Alcuin: A Dialogue* (New York, 1798; repr. New Haven, 1935).

30. Elizabeth Drinker, quoted in Anne Firor Scott, "Self Portraits." John Adams to Abigail Adams, January 24, 1794, referred to in David Musto, "The Youth of John Quincy Adams," *Proceedings of the American Philosophical Society* 113 (August 1969): 273; on Abigail Adams's reactions, see Charles W. Akers, *Abigail Adams*, 116. See also Janet W. James, *Changing Ideas about Women in the United States, 1776–1825* (New York, 1981; reprint of Ph.D. diss., Harvard University, 1954, with new introduction. In chapter 2, we will see that the positive reactions to Wollstonecraft diminished because of her religious views and her personal life.

31. David Ramsay, *Memoirs of the Life of Martha Laurens Ramsay* (South Carolina, 1812).

32. Oscar and Mary F. Handlin, *The Dimensions of Liberty* (Cambridge, Mass., 1961); Edward Raymond Turner, "Women's Suffrage in New Jersey," *Smith College Studies in History* 1, no. 4 (Northampton, Mass., 1916), 165–87; and Mary Beth Norton, *Liberty's Daughters*, 191–93. See also Lois Carr, "Margaret Brent," in *Notable American Women*, I, 236–37. In the best-known episode in the colonial era involving women's suffrage, Dame Margaret Brent's request for the vote as a reward for her services to the colony was flatly refused by the Maryland legislature.

33. James McLachlan, "The American College in the Nineteenth Century: Toward a Reappraisal," *Teachers College Record* 80 (1978). On the significance of republican motherhood, see Linda K. Kerber, *Women of the Republic*. Benjamin Rush, *Thoughts Upon Female Education Accommodated to the Present State of Society, Manners, and the Government in the United States of America* (Philadelphia, 1787).

34. Thomas Jefferson to François Barbé-Marbois, December 5, 1783, in *The Papers of Thomas Jefferson: Volume 6, 21 May 1781 to 1 March 1784*, ed. Julian P. Boyd (Princeton, 1952), 374. John Adams to daughter Abigail Adams, April 18, 1776, in *Adams Family Correspondence*, I, 387–88.

35. Mercy Otis Warren to Rebecca Otis, n.d. 1776, in Mercy Otis Warren's unpublished Letterbook, at Massachusetts Historical Society, quoted in Linda K. Kerber, *Women of the Republic*, 252. See also Katharine Anthony, *First Lady of the Revolution: The Life of Mercy Otis Warren* (Garden City, N.Y., 1958), 188–89. Judith Murray, *The Gleaner*, II, 6.

36. Susan Bull Tracy quoted in James E. Cronin, ed., *The Diary of Elihu Hubbard Smith*, 109. "Female Advoate," quoted in Linda K. Kerber, *Women of the Republic*, 209–10.

Chapter II

1. See Samuel Knox, "An Essay on the Best System of Liberal Education, Adapted to the Genius of the Government of the United States . . . ," in Frederick Rudolph, ed., *Essays on Education in the Early Republic* (Cambridge, Mass., 1965); see Samuel H. Smith, "Remarks on Education: Illustrating the Close Connection Between Virtue and Wisdom . . . ," ibid., p. 217.

2. On these schools see Nancy F. Cott, *The Bonds of Womanhood: "Woman's Sphere" in New England, 1780–1835* (New Haven, 1977), and Mary Beth Norton, *Liberty's Daughters: The Revolutionary Experience of American Women, 1750–1800* (Boston, 1980), chapter 9.

3. Timothy Dwight, quoted in *Travels in New England and New York*, ed. Barbara M. Solomon (Cambridge, Mass., 1969), I, Introduction, and IV, 336. See also Thomas Woody, *A History of Women's Education in the United States* (New York, 1929), 2 vols.

4. Theodore R. Sizer, ed., *The Age of the Academies* (New York, 1964). See also Lynn T. Brickley, " 'Female Academies are Everywhere Establishing' the Beginnings of Secondary Education for Women in the United States, 1790–1830: A Review of the Literature" (qualifying paper, Harvard University School of Education, 1983).

5. On the Second Great Awakening, as a start, see Sydney E. Ahlstrom, *A Religious History of the American People* (New Haven, 1972); Donald G. Matthews, "The Second Great Awakening as an Organizing Hypothesis," *American Quarterly* 21 (1969).

6. Lawrence A. Cremin, *American Education: The National Experience 1783–1876* (New York, 1980); Hannah More, *Strictures on the Modern System of Female Education* (London, 1799); see Janet W. James's analysis of More in *Changing Ideas about Women in the United States, 1776–1825* (New York, 1981), reprint of Ph.D. diss., Radcliffe College, 1954, with new introduction. An example of the backlash against Wollstonecraft is Benjamin Silliman [pseud.], *Letters of Shahcoolen, a Hindu Philosopher Residing in Philadelphia, to His Friend El Hassan, an Inhabitant of Delhi* (Boston, 1802).

7. On the class differences in domestic functions of the American girl, see Nancy F. Cott, *Bonds of Womanhood*.

8. On the freedom of American girls see J. P. de Warville, *New Travels in the United States of America: 1788*, ed. Durand Echeverria (Cambridge, Mass., 1964), as well as Alexis de Tocqueville, *Democracy in America*, ed. Phillips Bradley (New York, 1945), 2 vols.

9. On the men teachers, see Lawrence A. Cremin, *American Education: The National Experience*, and Ann D. Gordon, "The Young Ladies Academy of Philadelphia," in *Women of America: A History*, ed. Carol Ruth Berkin and Mary Beth Norton (Boston, 1979).

10. On the concept of the "self-made woman," see Anne Firor Scott's major interpretations of Willard and Phelps, reprinted in *Making the Invisible Woman Visible* (Urbana, Ill., 1984).

11. Catherine Fennelly, "Sarah Pierce," in *Notable American Women*, III; and Lynn T. Brickley's unpublished work on Pierce. See also Emily N. Vanderpoel, *Chronicles of a Pioneer School from 1792 to 1833* (Cambridge, Mass., 1903).

12. John Lord, *The Life of Emma Willard* (New York, 1873); Frederick Rudolph, "Emma Willard," in *Notable American Women*, III; and Anne Firor Scott, "What, Then, Is the American: This New Woman?" *The Journal of American History* 65 (1978): 679–703.

13. Emma Hart Willard, *An Address to the Public* (Middlebury, Vt., 1819).

14. On Almira Hart Lincoln Phelps, see Frederick Rudolph, in *Notable American Women*, III; Emma Lydia Bolzau, *Almira Hart Lincoln Phelps, Her Life and Work* (Philadelphia, 1936); Ann Firor Scott, "What, Then, is the American."

15. See Kathryn Kish Sklar, *Catharine Beecher: A Study in Domesticity* (New Haven, 1973), and Barbara Cross, ed., *The Educated Woman in America* (New York, 1965).

16. Sydney R. Maclean, "Zilpah Polly Grant," and "Mary Lyon," in *Notable American Women*, II.

17. Joseph Emerson, *Female Education: A Discourse Delivered at the Dedication of the Seminary Hall in Saugus, January 15, 1822* (Boston, 1822), 27.

18. Mary Lyon quoted in Edward Hitchcock, *The Power of Christian Benevolence Illustrated in the Life and Labors of Mary Lyon* (Northampton, Mass., 1851), 186.

19. Kathryn Kish Sklar, "The Founding of Mount Holyoke College," in *Women of America*, ed. Carol Ruth Berkin and Mary Beth Norton, 15.

20. See Donald G. Matthews, "The Second Great Awakening as an Organizing Hypothesis."

21. On academy development in the South, see Isabel M. Blandin, *History of Higher Eduation of Women in the South Prior to 1870* (New York, 1909); Lynn T. Brickley, " 'Female Academies are Everywhere Establishing' "; and Elizabeth L. Ellis, "Educating Daughters of the Patriarchy: Female Academies in the American South, 1830–1860" (Honors thesis, Harvard College, 1982). On the networks, see Anne Firor Scott, "The Ever Widening Circle: The Diffusion of Feminist Values from the Troy Female Seminary, 1822–1872," *History of Education Quarterly* 19 (Spring 1979). See also Fletcher Green, "Higher Education of Women in the South," in *Democracy in the Old South and Other Essays*, ed. Isaac Copeland (Nashville, Tenn., 1969).

22. Robert Fletcher, *A History of Oberlin College from its Foundation Through the Civil War* (Oberlin, 1943), 2 vols.; Lori Ginzburg, "Women in an Evangelical Community: Oberlin, 1835–1850," *Ohio History* 89 (Winter 1980).

23. Lawrence A. Cremin, *American Education: The National Experience*, and James McLachlan, "The American College in the Nineteenth Century: Toward a Reappraisal," *Teachers College Record* 80 (1978). See especially a recent challenging interpretation of the antebellum colleges in Colin B. Burke, *American Collegiate Populations: A Test of the Traditional View* (New York, 1982).

24. Discussions of pedagogy by these educators imply more than they state about their superiority on some matters. In this context, see letter of Emma Willard to her brother, October 9, 1832, comparing female seminaries to men's colleges, in John Lord, *The Life of Emma Willard* (New York, 1873), 155–59. For her remark about Vermont, see ibid., 157.

25. David F. Allmendinger, "Mount Holyoke Students Encounter the Need for Life-Planning, 1837–1850," *History of Education Quarterly* 19 (Spring 1979). On ages of academy students, see Lynn T. Brickley, " 'Female Academies are Everywhere Establishing.' "

26. See *Catalogue of the Female Collegiate Institute of Georgetown Kentucky* (1839); *Catalogue of the Richmond Female Institute of Richmond Virginia* (1856); Robert Fletcher, *A History of Oberlin*; and Elizabeth L. Ellis, "Educating Daughters of the Patriarchy."

27. On the use of *The Federalist Papers* at Elizabeth Academy, Mississippi, see I. M. Blandin, *History of Higher Education of Women*. See also Margaret W. Rossiter, *Women Scientists in America: Struggles and Strategies to 1940* (Baltimore, 1982).

28. Elizabeth Alden Green, *Mary Lyon and Mount Holyoke: Opening the Gates* (Hanover, 1979), 221, checked Thomas Woody's original analysis and proved its reliability.

29. In the South academies were often called colleges. See discussion in Thomas Woody, *A History of Women's Education.*

30. David F. Allmendinger, "Mount Holyoke Students."

31. Anne Firor Scott, "The Ever Widening Circle"; Mary P. Ryan, *The Cradle of the Middle Class: The Family in Oneida County, New York, 1790–1865* (Cambridge, Mass., 1981), 209–10. See also the correspondence of southern educators Reverend Milo Jewett of Judson Academy and Reverend Manly of Richmond Female Institute on raising funds to help "poor young ladies of promising talents," in Elizabeth L. Ellis, "Educating Daughters of the Patriarchy." Utica's principal, Urania Sheldon, who encouraged Chubbuck, was a Troy graduate.

32. See Kathryn Kish Sklar, *Catharine Beecher*, 76; Almira Phelps, *The Educator: Or Hours With My Pupils* (New York, 1872), 189; Emma Willard to A. W. Holden, September 5, 1846, in John Lord, *Life of Emma Willard*, 223. On other educators who gained a reputation for providing a good secondary education, see, for example, Mary Johnson, "Madame Rivardi's Seminary in the Gothic Mansion," *Pennsylvania Magazine of History and Biography* 104 (January 1980); see also idem, "Antoinette Brevost: A Schoolmistress in Early Pittsburgh," *Wintherthur Portfolio* 15 (Summer 1980). On a school of great intellectual and social distinction whose head opposed collegiate education for women, see Louise L. Stevenson, "Sarah Porter Educates Useful Ladies, 1847–1900," *Winterthur Portfolio* 18 (Spring 1983).

33. Almira Phelps, *Lectures to Young Ladies: Comprising Outlines and Applications of the Different Branches of Female Education. Delivered to the Pupils of the Troy Female Seminary* (Boston, 1833), 304–05. Mary Lyon quoted in Fidelia Fisk, *Recollections of Mary Lyon with Selections From Her Instructions to the Pupils in Mount Holyoke Female Seminary* (Boston, 1866), 43.

34. For Mary Lyon quote, see Keith Melder, "Masks of Oppression: The Female Seminary Movement in the United States," *New York History* 55 (July 1974): 270. For Zilpah P. Grant quote, see Linda T. Guilford, *The Uses of a Life: A Memorial of Mrs. Z. P. G. Bannister* (New York, 1885), 254, 216.

35. Emma Hart Willard, *An Address to the Public*, 3, 22.

Chapter III

1. Barbara Welter, "The Cult of True Womanhood," *American Quarterly* 18 (1966).

2. Ann D. Gordon, "The Young Ladies Academy of Philadelphia," in *Women of America: A History*, ed. Carol Ruth Berkin and Mary Beth Norton (Boston, 1979); Susanna Rowson, *A Present For Young Ladies: Containing Poems, Dialogues, Addresses, etc. as Recited by the Pupils of Mrs. Rowson's Academy at the Annual Exhibitions* (Boston, 1811). For more personal reflections of an academy student, see *A Girl's Life Eighty Years Ago: Selections from the Letters of Mrs. Eliza Southgate Bowne* (New York, 1887).

3. *Pastoral Letter of the Massachusetts Congregationalist Clergy* (1837), quoted in Aileen S. Kraditor, *Up from the Pedestal: Selected Writings in the History of American Feminism* (Chicago, 1968), 56. S. and A. Grimké, excerpts, ibid., 53ff.

4. On the Oread Institute, see Martha Elizabeth Wright, ed., *History of the Oread Collegiate Institute, Worcester, Mass., 1849–1881 with Biographical Sketches* (New Haven, 1905); Louis Filler, "Lucy Stone," in *Notable American Women*, III, and Robert Fletcher, *A History of Oberlin From Its Foundation Through the Civil War* (Oberlin, 1943), 2 vols.

5. For Euphorsine Schmidt at Nazareth Academy, see Elizabeth L. Ellis, "Educating Daughters of the Patriarchy: Female Academies in the American South, 1830–1860" (Honors thesis, Harvard College, 1982). Anna Gale quoted in Edward A. Hoyt and Loriman S. Brigham, "Glimpses of Margaret Fuller: The Greene Street School and

Florence," *New England Quarterly* 29 (1956): 88. Mary Ann Adams quoted in Robert Fletcher, *A History of Oberlin*, I, 460–61.

6. Ralph Waldo Emerson, "Heroism," in *The Complete Works of Ralph Waldo Emerson* (Boston, 1904), II, 259–60; see also "The American Scholar," and "An Address Delivered Before the Senior Class in Divinity College," ibid., I.

7. On the Yankee mill girl, see especially Thomas Dublin, *Women at Work* (New York, 1979).

8. Caroline Lee Hentz, *Marcus Warland* (Philadelphia, 1852), 131. Ellen K. Rothman provides new examples of individuals' concerns about the seriousness of marriage in *Hands and Hearts: A History of Courtship in America* (New York, 1984).

9. David F. Allmendinger, "Mount Holyoke Students Encounter the Need for Life Planning, 1837–1850," *History of Education Quarterly* 19 (Spring 1979); Anne Firor Scott, "The Ever Widening Circle: The Diffusion of Feminist Values from the Troy Female Seminary, 1833–1872," *History of Education Quarterly* 19 (Spring 1979).

10. David F. Allmendinger, "Mount Holyoke Students"; Anne Firor Scott, "The Ever Widening Circle." For the Oberlin marriage pattern, see James H. Fairchild, *Oberlin: The Colony and the College, 1833–1883* (Oberlin, 1883).

11. Passage from Almira Phelps's *Ida Norman* quoted in Emma L. Bolzau, *Almira Hart Lincoln Phelps: Her Life and Work* (Philadelphia, 1936), 316. Theodore Stanton and Harriot Stanton Blatch, eds., *Elizabeth Cady Stanton as Revealed in Her Letters, Diary, and Reminiscences* (New York, 1922), I, 49ff. Betty L. Fladeland, "Sarah Moore Grimké and Angelina Emily Grimké," in *Notable American Women*, II.

12. Horace Mann exalted the woman as schoolteacher in his *Second* and *Seventh Annual Reports to the Massachusetts Board of Education* (Boston, 1837 and 1848). Quoted in Thomas Woody, *A History of Women's Education in the United States* (New York, 1929), I, 463, and Lawrence A. Cremin, *American Education: The National Experience, 1783–1876* (New York, 1980), 146ff.

13. Quoted from Catharine Beecher's *True Remedy* by Thomas Woody, *A History of Women's Education* (New York, 1929), I, 462.

14. Almira Hart quoted in Emma L. Bolzau, *Almira Hart Lincoln Phelps*, 38; excerpt from Arozina Perkins's diary, 1848–1854, quoted in Polly Kaufman, *Women Teachers on the Frontier* (New Haven, 1983); Antoinette Brown to Lucy Stone [Rochester, Michigan], October 9, 1846, in Carol Lasser and Marlene Merrill, eds., *Soul Mates: The Oberlin Correspondence of Lucy Stone and Antoinette Brown, 1846–1850* (Oberlin, 1983); Richard M. Bernard and Maris A. Vinovskis, "The Female School Teacher in Ante-Bellum Massachusetts," *Journal of Social History* 10 (March 1977): 3.

15. See Keith E. Melder, "Betsey Mix Cowles," in *Notable American Women*, I; Jill Kerr Conway, "Anna Peck Sill," in *Notable American Women*, III; and, on Barhamville, Anne Firor Scott, "The Ever Widening Circle."

16. Geraldine Clifford, "The Female Teacher and the Feminist Movement" (paper delivered at Mount Holyoke conference, 1982).

17. Barbara Welter, "She Hath Done What She Could: Protestant Women's Missionary Careers in Nineteenth-Century America," in *Women in American Religion*, ed. Janet W. James (Philadelphia, 1976); Earl E. Lewis, "Anne Hasseltine Judson," in *Notable American Women*, II; R. Pierce Beaver, "Cynthia Farrar," in *Notable American Women*, I; Mary Sumner Benson, "Fidelia Fiske," in *Notable American Women*, I; Nancy F. Cott, "Young Women in the Second Great Awakening in New England," *Feminist Studies* 3 (Fall 1975).

18. Statistics on the life patterns of individuals and the role of schoolteaching were prepared by Barbara M. Solomon with the assistance of Patricia Hill and Carol Lasser. Alma Lutz, "Susan B. Anthony," in *Notable American Women*, I; Keith E. Melder, "Abi-

gail Kelley Foster," in *Notable American Women*, I; Barbara M. Solomon, "Antoinette Brown Blackwell," in *Notable American Women*, I. For women listed as lecturers, see *Notable American Women*, III, 718.

19. Alice Felt Tyler, "Harriot Kezia Hunt," in *Notable American Women*, II; Elizabeth H. Thomson, "Elizabeth Blackwell," in *Notable American Women*, I; see also Mary Roth Walsh, *Doctors Wanted: No Women Need Apply* (New Haven, 1977); Regina Markell Morantz, "Feminism, Professionalism. and Germs: The Thought of Mary Putnam Jacobi and Elizabeth Blackwell," *American Quarterly* 34 (1982). Also important in this context is Gerda Lerner, "The Lady and the Mill Girl: Changes in the Status of Women in the Age of Jackson," in *The Majority Finds Its Past: Placing Women in History* (New York, 1979).

20. Elizabeth Palmer Peabody, *Reminiscences of William Ellery Channing* (Boston, 1880); Margaret Fuller's 1845 essay, "Woman in the Nineteenth Century," reprinted in *Margaret Fuller: Essays on American Life and Letters*, ed. Joel Myerson (New Haven, 1978); Barbara M. Solomon, introduction to *Margaret Fuller Ossoli*, by Thomas Wentworth Higginson (Boston: Houghton Mifflin, 1884; repr. New York, 1981), xiv; Bell Gale Chevigny, "The Long Arm of Censorship: Mythmaking in Margaret Fuller's Time and Our Own," *Journal of Women in Culture and Society* 2 (Winter 1976); also, Susan P. Conrad, *Perish the Thought: Intellectual Women in Romantic America, 1830–1860* (New York, 1976), provides an excellent introduction to this subject. For an example in her study, see Lydia Maria Child, ibid., 104–16.

21. The emergence of women writers has received considerable attention lately. See Nina Baym, *Woman's Fiction: A Guide to Novels by and about Women in America, 1820–1870* (Ithaca, N.Y., 1978); Mary Kelley, *Private Women, Public Stage: Literary Domesticity in Nineteenth-Century America* (New York, 1983). For an excellent summary and critique of recent historical analysis of the popular women writers, see Mary Kelley, "The Sentimentalists: Promise and Betrayal in the Home," *Signs: Journal of Women in Culture and Society* 4 (Spring 1979), footnote 4.

22. Sarah J. Hale, ed., *Ladies Magazine* 1 (March 1828): 121.

23. Maria Cummins, *Mabel Vaughn* (Boston, 1857), 18. See also Merrit Cross, "Mary Virginia Hawes Terhune," in *Notable American Women*, III.

24. Barbara Welter, "Sara Jane Clarke Lippincott" [Grace Greenwood], in *Notable American Women*, II. See Mary Kelley, *Private Women, Public Stage*.

25. Joel Myerson, ed., *Margaret Fuller: Essays*, 82; Ralph Waldo Emerson, "Lecture on the Times," in *The Complete Works*, I. Lucy Stone to Antoinette Brown [West Brookfield, Massachusetts], 1849, in *Soul Mates*, ed. Carol Lasser and Marlene Merrill, 51. See also Ellen K. Rothman, *Hands and Hearts*.

26. Lucy Stone to Antoinette Brown [West Brookfield, Massachusetts], June 9, 1850, in *Soul Mates*, ed. Carol Lasser and Marlene Merrill, 71; on these Quaker women doctors, see Barbara M. Solomon, "Historical Determinants in Individual Life Experiences of Successful Professional Women," *Annals of the New York Academy of Sciences* 208 (1973).

27. Leonard Sweet, *The Minister's Wife: Her Role in Nineteeth-Century American Evangelicalism* (Philadelphia, 1983); Donald G. Matthews, *Religion in the Old South* (Chicago, 1977). For biographical information on the wives of Charles Finney, see Oberlin College Archives.

28. Mrs. A. W. Fairbanks, *Mrs. Emma Willard and Her Pupils, or Fifty Years of the Troy Female Seminary, 1822–1872* (New York, 1898); Arthur C. Cole, *A Hundred Years of Mount Holyoke: The Evolution of an Educational Ideal* (New Haven, 1940). See also Louise Porter Thomas, *Seminary Militant: An Account of the Missionary Movement at Mount Holyoke Seminary and College* (South Hadley, Mass., 1937).

29. Jane Gray Swisshelm, *Half a Century* (Chicago, 1880).

30. Paul S. Boyer, "Julia Ward Howe," in *Notable American Women*, II; Alma Lutz, "Elizabeth Cady Stanton," in *Notable American Women*, III; see also Mary Kelley, "At War With Herself: Harriet Beecher Stowe as Woman in Conflict Within the Home," reprinted in *Woman's Being, Woman's Place: Female Identity and Vocation in American History* (Boston, 1979).

31. Elizabeth Cady Stanton, "Address on the Divorce Bill, 1881," in Daniel J. Boorstin, ed., *An American Primer* (Chicago, 1966). Also note that Antoinette Brown Blackwell, for example, disagreed with Stanton on divorce.

32. On Lucy Stone's inquiry and the answers, see Andrew Sinclair, *The Better Half: The Emancipation of the American Woman* (New York, 1965), 67ff.; Mary Kelley, "At War With Herself."

33. On the influence of the mother, see Mary P. Ryan, *The Cradle of the Middle Class: The Family in Oneida County, New York, 1790–1865* (Cambridge, Mass., 1981), chapter 4.

34. Fletcher, *A History of Oberlin College*, I; Mary P. Ryan, "The Power of Women's Networks: A Case Study of Female Moral Reform in Antebellum America," *Feminist Studies* 5 (Spring 1979); Estelle Freedman, *Their Sisters' Keepers: Women's Prison Reform in America, 1830–1930* (Ann Arbor, 1981); Barbara Epstein, *The Politics of Domesticity: Women, Evangelism, and Temperance in Nineteenth-Century America* (Middletown, Conn., 1981).

35. See Alma Lutz, "Maria Weston Chapman," in *Notable American Women*, I; see especially Gerda Lerner, "The Political Activities of Anti-Slavery Women," in *The Majority Finds Its Past* (New York, 1979); Alma Lutz, *Crusade for Freedom: Women in the Antislavery Movement* (Boston, 1968); Blanche Glassman Hersh, *The Slavery of Sex: Feminist Abolitionists in America* (Chicago, 1978).

36. Eleanor Flexner, "Maria W. Miller Stewart," in *Notable American Women*, III; Gerda Lerner, "Sarah Mapps Douglass," in *Notable American Women*, I.

37. Thomas E. Drake, "Prudence Crandall," in *Notable American Women*, I.

38. "Declaration of Sentiments" (Seneca Falls, 1848) in Linda Kerber and Jane De Hart Matthews, eds., *Women's America: Reforming the Past* (New York, 1962), 431.

Chapter IV

1. Lucy Stone's address quoted in *The Concise History of Woman Suffrage: Selections from the Classic Work of Stanton, Anthony, Gage, and Harper*, ed. Mari Jo and Paul Buhle (Urbana, Ill., 1978), 158. Caroline Sturgis (Tappan)'s expressed envy of "the boys" quoted in Eugenia Kaledin, *The Education of Mrs. Henry Adams* (Philadelphia, 1981).

2. Allan Nevins, *The State Universities and Democracy* (Urbana, Ill., 1962). See also Mabel Newcomer, *A Century of Higher Education for American Women* (New York, 1959), 29–30, on the impact of the legislation. On the mixed consequences for black higher education of the Morrill Act of 1890, see Jane E. Smith Browning and John B. Williams, "History and Goals of Black Institutions of Higher Learning," in *Black Colleges in America: Challenge, Development, Survival*, ed. Charles V. Willie and Ronald R. Edmunds (New York, 1978).

3. On the effects of the Civil War on women's education and employment, see Mabel Newcomer, *A Century of Higher Education*, 11–15, 17, 23. See also Gloria Melnick Moldow, "The Gilded Age, Promise and Disillusionment: Women Doctors and the Emergence of the Professional Middle Class, Washington, D.C., 1870–1900" (Ph.D. diss., University of Maryland, 1980).

4. On black and white schoolteachers, see James M. McPherson, *The Abolitionist Legacy: From Reconstruction to the NAACP* (Princeton, 1975). See A. D. Mayo, *Southern Women in the Recent Educational Movement in the South*, ed. Dan. T. Carter and Amy Friedlander (Baton Rouge, 1978).

5. Eleanor Flexner, *Century of Struggle* (Cambridge, Mass., 1959; rev. ed., 1975). Karen Blair, *The Clubwoman as Feminist: True Womanhood Redefined, 1868–1914* (New York, 1980).

6. Susan B. Carter's penetrating interpretation concludes that coeducation in the late nineteenth century "meant as much to women's economic prospects" as "the opening of the frontier" had meant to men half a century earlier. See her "Women's Educational History: A Labor Market Perspective," *Academy Notes* 13, 2 (Winter 1983). See also Charles William Dabney, *Universal Education in the South* (New York, 1969), I, 356, 324–26; and A. D. Mayo, *Southern Women.*

7. Matthew Vassar's comments appear in his manuscript autobiography and diary, Special Collections, Vassar College. See Matthew Vassar, *The Autobiography and Letters of Matthew Vassar*, ed. Elizabeth M. Haight (New York, 1916), 4.

8. Henry F. Durant quoted in Florence Kingsley, *The Life of Henry F. Durant* (New York, 1924).

9. For Sophia Smith's will, see Smith College Archives. See also Margaret Storrs Grierson, "Sophia Smith," in *Notable American Women*, III.

10. Joseph Taylor quoted in Edith Finch, *Carey Thomas of Bryn Mawr* (New York, 1947). Lawrence Veysey, "M. Carey Thomas," in *Notable American Women*, III. See especially Barbara Cross, ed., *The Educated Woman in America* (New York, 1965).

11. Thomas Woody, *A History of Women's Education in the United States* (New York, 1929), II, 142ff., 186ff., 314ff. See also Elizabeth B. Young, *A Study of the Curricula of Seven Selected Women's Colleges of the Southern States* (New York, 1932).

12. L. Clark Seelye's often quoted statement appears in Jacqueline Van Voris, ed., *College: A Smith Mosaic* (West Springfield, Mass., 1975), 1. Seelye left room for the individual to interpret his meaning freely.

13. Edward J. Power, *A History of Catholic Higher Education in the United States* (Milwaukee, 1958).

14. On Oberlin's influence on other colleges, see Robert Fletcher, *A History of Oberlin College*, I, 188, 202, passim; on black colleges see ibid., II, 909ff.

15. On the development of Quaker colleges, see Dorothy Thorne, *Guilford: A Quaker College* (Guilford, N.C., 1937). On the history of Swarthmore, see Frederick B. Tolles (1961) and Rebecca Stamm (1979), manuscripts in Swarthmore College Archives. See also Frederick B. Tolles, "Lucretia Coffin Mott," in *Notable American Women*, II. On the influence of Oberlin on Swarthmore, see Edward H. Magill, *An Address Upon the Co-Education of the Sexes* (Philadelphia, 1873).

16. Warren O. Ault, *Boston University: The College of Liberal Arts, 1873–1973* (Boston, 1973). For an excellent overview, see Patricia M. King, "The Campaign for Higher Education for Women in Nineteenth-Century Boston," *Proceedings of the Massachusetts Historical Society* 93 (1982).

17. See especially Hugh Hawkins, *Between Harvard and America: The Educational Leadership of Charles W. Eliot* (New York, 1972).

18. See Carl L. Becker, *Cornell University: Founders and the Founding* (Ithaca, N.Y., 1943); and Morris Bishop, *A History of Cornell* (Ithaca, N.Y., 1962).

19. See Andrew Dixon White to Gerrit Smith, July 21, 1874, copy in Cornell University Archives, original in Gerrit Smith Collection, George Arents Research Library for Special Collections at Syracuse University; also quoted in Morris Bishop, *A History of Cornell*, 76; on Jenny Spencer, see 145.

20. For information on the municipal institutions, I am indebted to Lyle Koehler, "Urban Higher Education and Service" (unpublished paper).

21. On the opposition to admission of women, see Merle Curti and Vernon Carstensen,

The University of Wisconsin: A History, 1848–1925 (Madison, Wis., 1949); J. F. A. Pyre, *Wisconsin* (New York, 1920). Also Howard H. Peckham, *The Making of the University of Michigan, 1917–1967* (Ann Arbor, 1967); Dorothy G. McGuigan, *A Dangerous Experiment: One Hundred Years at the University of Michigan* (Ann Arbor, 1970); Elizabeth M. Ferrand, *History of the University of Michigan* (Ann Arbor, 1885). On the admission of women to the University of Iowa, see J. L. Pickard, "Historical Sketch of the University of Iowa," *Annals of Iowa* 3 (1899). The early reports of the institution suggest that women were admitted without design and managed to stay.

22. See Merle Curti and Vernon Carstensen, *The University of Wisconsin*, I, 115–19, 370ff. See also Helen R. Olin, *The Women of a State University: An Illustration of the Working of Coeducation in the Middle West* (New York, 1909).

23. Frank F. Stephens, *A History of the University of Missouri* (Columbia, Mo., 1962). See also Jonas Viles, *The University of Missouri: A Centennial History* (Columbia, Mo., 1939), especially 132–33 on the southern influence.

24. Mabel Newcomer, *A Century of Higher Education*, 14.

25. Charles William Dabney, *Universal Education in the South*.

26. Timothy Dwight, "Education for Women at Yale," *The Forum* 13 (June 1982); Patricia A. Graham, *Community and Class in American Education, 1865–1918* (New York, 1974), 181–203. See Edward Potts Cheyney, *History of the University of Pennsylvania, 1740–1940* (Philadelphia, 1940), 28, 305, 408.

27. Maria Mitchell to Ezra Cornell, March 10, 1868, quoted in Morris Bishop, *A History of Cornell*, 143; for the pressure on Harvard to admit women, see Patricia M. King, "Higher Education for Women in Boston."

28. On Charles W. Eliot and the founding of Radcliffe, see Hugh Hawkins, *Between Harvard and America*, 195–96. Patricia M. King, "Higher Education for Women in Boston"; Paul Buck, "Harvard Attitudes Toward Radcliffe in the Early Years," *Massachusetts Historical Society* 74 (May 1962); Hugh Hawkins, "Elizabeth Cary Cabot Agassiz," in *Notable American Women*, I.

29. On Barnard College, see Mabel Newcomer, *A Century of Higher Education*, 40–42; Marion C. White, *A History of Barnard College* (New York, 1954); Annette K. Baxter, "Ella Weed," in *Notable American Women*, III; Rosalind Rosenberg, *Beyond Separate Spheres: Intellectual Roots of Modern Feminism* (New Haven, 1982), 148–49; and W. LeConte Stevens, "University Education for Women," *North American Review* 136 (January 1883).

30. Hiram C. Haydn quoted in Mabel Newcomer, *A Century of Higher Education*; see also Adele Simmons, "Education and Ideology in Nineteenth-Century America: The Response of Educational Institutions to the Changing Role of Women," in *Liberating Women's History*, ed. Berenice A. Carroll (Urbana, Ill., 1976), 115–26; see also James Orton, ed., *The Liberal Education and Women*. Russell Miller, *Light on the Hill: A History of Tufts College, 1852–1952* (Boston, 1966).

31. L. E. Zimmerman, "Josephine Louise Le Monnier Newcomb," in *Notable American Women*, II. On the limits of coeducation in the South, see Thomas Woody, *A History of Women's Education*; on Mary Munford, see Mary Gathright Newell, "Mary Munford and Higher Education for Women in Virginia," in *Stepping Off the Pedestal: Academic Women in the South*, ed. Patricia A. Stringer and Irene Thompson (New York, 1982); see also Mabel Newcomer, *A Century of Higher Education*, 50–51, note 6. Stanley I. Kutler, "Mary Eno Bassett Munford," in *Notable American Women*, II.

32. Rosalind Rosenberg, *Beyond Separate Spheres*, 7–9.

33. Edward H. Clarke, *Sex in Education; Or, a Fair Chance for the Girls* (Boston, 1873), 18, 23, 63, 69, 116, 129.

34. Julia Ward Howe, ed., *Sex and Education: A Reply to Dr. Clarke's "Sex in Education"* (Boston, Mass., 1874). See also Eliza B. Duffey, *No Sex in Education; Or, An Equal Chance for Both Girls and Boys* (Philadelphia, 1874).

35. Annie G. Howes, *Health Statistics of Women College Graduates* (Boston, 1885). See the excellent analysis of this report in Rosalind Rosenberg, *Beyond Separate Spheres,* 20–22.

36. On William R. Harper, see Lawrence R. Veysey, *The Emergence of the American University* (Chicago, 1965), 367–80; Daniel C. Gilman address in "The Inauguration of Benjamin I. Wheeler," *The University Chronicle* 2 (October 1899).

37. Mabel Newcomer, *A Century of Higher Education,* 46.

38. On the coeducational controversy, see Rosalind Rosenberg, *Beyond Separate Spheres,* 43–44. Thomas Woody, *History of Women's Education,* 295–303.

39. See Richard J. Storr, *Harper's University: The Beginnings* (Chicago, 1966), 323–27. See also William R. Harper, *Annual Report of the President* (Chicago, 1903).

40. Madeleine Wallin's opposition to segregation of women students appears in a manuscript fragment, Special Collections, Regenstein Library, University of Chicago. For public discussion of this issue, see "Segregated Chicago," *The Independent* 61 (October 1906). Richard J. Storr, *Harper's University,* 337–38; Rosalind Rosenberg, *Beyond Separate Spheres,* 44–48; Marion Talbot, *More Than Lore* (Chicago, 1936), 170–75.

41. C. W. Elliot, *Stanford University: The First Twenty-Five Years* (Stanford, 1937); Oberlin alumni expressed similar concerns but did not succeed in changing Oberlin's open policy. See Sydney D. Strong and Merritt Starr, *Proportions of Men and Women Enrolled as Students at Oberlin College: A Report to the Trustees* (Oberlin, 1904).

42. Benjamin I. Wheeler, *Annual Report of the President,* University of California (Berkeley, 1912), 5; Warren O. Ault, *Boston University,* 68–69, 74.

43. Charles Van Hise, "Educational Tendencies in the State Universities," *Educational Review* 34 (December 1907).

44. Helen R. Olin, *Shall Wisconsin University Remain a Coeducational Institution?* (Madison Wis., 1908). On the uproar that followed Van Hise's and Olin's statements, see Merle Curti and Vernon Carstensen, *The University of Wisconsin,* 81ff.

45. For further elaboration of Van Hise's sex repulsion theory, see Helen R. Olin, *The Women of a State University* (New York, 1909).

46. G. Stanley Hall, *Adolescence: Its Psychology and Its Relation to Physiology, Anthropology, Sociology, Sex, Crime, Religion, and Education* (New York, 1908), chapter 2.

47. Studies for and against coeducation abounded; see W. T. Harris, "Reports of the Mosely Education Commission," in *Report of the Commissioner of Education for the Year Ended June 30, 1905* (Washington, 1907), I; W. Le Conte Stevens, *The Admission of Women to Universities* (New York, 1883). Significantly, in 1920 both Ada Comstock (dean of Smith College) and M. Carey Thomas (president of Bryn Mawr) urged the International Federation of University Women to support coeducation. See Thomas Woody, *A History of Women's Education,* II, 264.

48. On James B. Angell's faith in women and coeducation, see *Reminiscences* (New York, 1912), 240–41.

Chapter V

1. Mabel Newcomer, *A Century of Higher Education for American Women* (New York, 1959), 45.

2. On the expanding middle class, see Robert H. Wiebe, *The Search for Order, 1877–1920* (New York, 1967), chapter 5.

3. Association of Collegiate Alumnae, *A Preliminary Statistical Study of Certain Women College Graduates* (Bryn Mawr, Pa., 1917), 24–25.

It is important to note that 745 of the 3,636 graduates surveyed (20 percent) did not state their parents' income. The ACA study speculates that many women did not know this figure and that others did not wish to disclose such information. In any case, the results of the survey must be interpreted with this caveat in mind. We have no way of knowing from which families (and income levels) the women who did not answer this question came.

The survey was conducted by mailing "schedules" to women at twenty-two colleges across the country. Women then returned the figures to the ACA. Some schools show a much higher rate of participation in the study than others. Particularly noteworthy is the relatively low percentage of returns from midwestern and western schools (p. 9), lending an eastern bias to the study's results. The presence of such a bias reinforces my interpretation of the ACA survey. The midwestern and western institutions graduated more women from families with lower income levels than the eastern schools—44 percent of all women came from families whose incomes were below $1,200, whereas only 29 percent of the eastern school graduates were from this income level (p. 25). If more western graduates had responded to the ACA "schedule," it is safe to conjecture that more women from poorer families would have been included in the data, decreasing the average income levels for graduates' families and backing up the conclusion that the wealthiest American families were not, contrary to popular opinion, sending their daughters to school in large numbers.

U.S. Department of Commerce, *Historical Statistics of the United States, Colonial Times to the Present* (Washington, 1970), F 1–9.

The average annual incomes in 1869 and 1890 are computed for a family of four. The two figures cited were calculated by multiplying the per capita gross national product for those years by four. All the figures in the chapter represent current dollar amounts, except as otherwise noted. This income calculation was used because GNP tabulation in the nineteenth century was relatively reliable. These two figures approximate impressions of income levels conveyed in letters and literature of those decades. I am indebted to Nancy Koehn for her valuable assistance in analyzing the data.

4. Charles B. Spahr, *An Essay on the Present Distribution of Wealth in the United States* (New York, 1896), 104. Information in the Wellesley College Archives indicates that the $350 figure included room, board, and tuition. Tuition alone was $150.

On professional salaries, see William Clyde DeVane, *Higher Education in Twentieth-Century America* (Cambridge, Mass., 1965). The salary range cited is an average for American institutions. It reflects what seems to be a general trend in faculty salaries throughout this period; collegiate faculty salaries, relative to those of other professions in the 1860s, were high. Mabel Newcomer, *A Century of Higher Education*, 162–63, cites the average faculty salary for male professors at private schools as $2,000 in 1867. Thereafter, professional salaries did not rise significantly. By 1905 they were even with or below doctors' earnings, and they continued to fall in relative terms through the twentieth century. The reasons behind this relative decline are beyond the scope of this study. What is important is that few professors earned enough money to make sending a daughter to college an easy undertaking, and that the few female professors earned less than their male counterparts. In 1867, when Vassar was paying its male professors $2,000 a year, the distinguished female astronomer Maria Mitchell earned $800 "plus living for her and her father." For proof of discrimination, see ibid., 163.

5. On the University of Illinois, see Winton V. Solberg, *The University of Illinois, 1867–1894* (Urbana, Ill., 1968), 98; on Boston University, see Warren O. Ault, *Boston University: The College of Liberal Arts, 1873–1973* (Boston, 1973), 21; on Michigan, Smith, and Mount Holyoke, see Mary Caroline Crawford, *The College Girl of America* (Boston, 1905); on Cornell, see Morris Bishop, *A History of Cornell* (Ithaca, N.Y., 1962), 355. For

other tuition figures, see Mary Caroline Crawford, *The College Girl*, school catalogues, and other institutional histories.

College costs at some institutions rose as much as 160 percent over the years from 1860 to 1920. Most of this increase occurred between 1910 and World War I, when the general price level in the United States rose 100 percent. College cost inflation thus followed the general inflation. It is important to note that wages and salaries also rose in this period. Analyzing the (rough) income and price averages from these years, one can conclude that the real cost of college at most institutions stayed fairly constant over this period—that is, wages kept pace with inflation. (All income and price figures appear in U.S. Department of Commerce, *Historical Statistics of the United States*.)

6. Mabel Newcomer, *A Century of Higher Eduation*, 25. See Sophonisba Breckinridge, "Memoir," written in her eighties, in Special Collections, Regenstein Library, University of Chicago (microfilm courtesy of Ellen Fitzpatrick); on Breckinridge's social work career, see Christopher Lasch, "Sophonisba Preston Breckinridge," in *Notable American Women*, I; Helen Lefkowitz Horowitz, "A Nineteenth-Century Father to his Daughter," *Wellesley Alumnae Magazine* 65 (Fall 1980).

7. Barbara Sicherman, "Alice Hamilton," in *Notable American Women*, IV (Cambridge, Mass., 1980); see also Alice Hamilton, *Exploring the Dangerous Trades* (Boston, 1943). Helen H. Bacon, "Edith Hamilton," in *Notable American Women*, II; Barbara M. Solomon, "Ada Louise Comstock," in *Notable American Women*, IV.

8. Charles Franklin Emerick, "College Women and Race Suicide," *Political Science Quarterly* 24 (June 1909); Patricia A. Palmieri, "Here was Fellowship: A Social Portrait of Academic Women at Wellesley College, 1880–1920," *History of Education Quarterly* 23 (Summer 1983). Palmieri's findings correspond with my own. Othman Abbott, "Recollections of a Pioneer Lawyer," *Nebraska History Magazine* 11 (1928); Jill Kerr Conway, "Grace Abbott," in *Notable American Women*, I; Lela B. Costin, "Edith Abbott," in *Notable American Women: The Modern Period*, IV.

9. Rosalind Rosenberg, *Beyond Separate Spheres: Intellectual Roots of Modern Feminism* (New Haven, 1982), 2–4; Richard J. Storr, "Marion Talbot," in *Notable American Women*, III.

10. Louise C. Wade, "Florence Kelley," in *Notable American Women*, II; see also Kelley's articles about her youth in *Survey* 57 (October 1926); 58 (February, April, and June 1927).

11. Marjorie H. Dobkin, ed., *The Making of a Feminist: Early Journals and Letters of M. Carey Thomas* (Kent, Ohio, 1979), 101; Laurence R. Veysey, "Martha Carey Thomas," in *Notable American Women*, III.

12. Leon Edel, "Willa Silbert Cather," in *Notable American Women*, I; see Annette K. Baxter, "Virginia Crocheron Gildersleeve," in *Notable American Women*, IV; see also Virginia Gildersleeve, *Many a Good Crusade* (New York, 1954), 39–40; Theresa Corcoran, "Vida Scudder," in *Notable American Women*, IV; on Hilda Smith, see her unpublished manuscript autobiography, Schlesinger Library, Radcliffe College; Thurman Wilkins, "Mary Hunter Austin," in *Notable American Women*, I; Elizabeth Wallace, *The Unending Journey* (Minneapolis, 1952).

13. Ida H. Washington, "Dorothy Canfield Fisher," in *Notable American Women*, IV; Donald Fleming, "Ruth Fulton Benedict," in *Notable American Women*, I.

14. Anne Firor Scott, "Jane Addams," in *Notable American Women*, I.

15. For statistics on Wisconsin students from farm families, see Merle Curti and Vernon Carstensen, *The University of Wisconsin: A History, 1848–1925* (Madison, Wis., 1949), vol. I 661. For analogous statistics on Michigan, see Laurence R. Veysey, *The Emergence of the American University* (Chicago, 1965), 291–92. For similar material on Chicago, see James Haydn Tufts, "The Senior Colleges," in *The Decennial Publications of the University of Chicago: The President's Report, 1892–1902* (Chicago, 1903), 83. Regarding Jennie

Field (Bashford), see memoir and biographical information, University of Wisconsin Archives; see also Amy Hague, " 'Give Us a Little Time to Find Our Places,' University of Wisconsin Alumnae, 1875–1900" (M.A. thesis, University of Wisconsin, 1983).

16. Barbara M. Solomon, "Alice Freeman," in *Notable American Women*, III.

17. Eleanor Flexner, "Carrie Clinton Lane Chapman Catt," in *Notable American Women*, I; idem, "Anna Howard Shaw," in *Notable American Women*, III.

18. Gerda Lerner, ed., *The Female Experience: An American Documentary* (Indianapolis, 1977), 247–51; U.S. Department of Agriculture, *Social and Labor Needs of Farm Women*, report 103 (Washington, 1915), 51.

19. Clelia Mosher, "A Study of the Ages of 4,170 Women who Entered Stanford from 1891–92 through 1920–22," in Clelia Mosher Papers, box 1, folder 3, Stanford University Archives. For information on the ages of Radcliffe women, see Barbara M. Solomon's unpublished analysis of Alumnae Questionnaire of 1928. On the ages of Smith women, see Sarah H. Gordon, "Smith College Students: The First Ten Classes, 1879–1888," *History of Education Quarterly* 15 (Summer 1975).

20. Several studies were conducted during the 1920s on self-help and self-supporting students. Such studies reinforce my conclusion that the number of self-supporting students was growing during this time, as well as was interest in them. See especially Walter J. Greenleaf, *Self-Help for Students*, U.S. Bureau of Education bulletin no. 2 (Washington, 1929). Lucy W. Stebbins's "Report of the Dean of Women," in *Annual Report of the President*, University of California, 1916–24. See also Gertrude Martin, "Report of the Advisor of Women," in *Annual Report of the President*, Cornell University (Ithaca, N.Y., 1912–13).

21. On the frugal Minnesota collegian, see Mary Caroline Crawford, *The College Girl in America*, 249–52. The information regarding Clara Beyer was gleaned in a telephone interview in 1981.

22. Although there is much indirect evidence of the growing presence of wealthier students at a variety of institutions during this period, few comprehensive socioeconomic surveys were made of the female collegiate population in the late 1800s and early 1900s. Lacking such data, I have drawn my inferences on this trend from a variety of magazine articles, dean's reports, and academic publications. See Charles F. Emerick, "College Women and Race Suicide," *Political Science Quarterly* 24 (June 1909). See also Alice Walmsley, "The Cost of Wellesley College Life," *The Wellesley Magazine* 16 (November 1907), and Ada L. Comstock, "Scholarships in Relation to Student Aid," typescript, 1915 or 1916, in Smith College Archives.

23. Alice Walmsley, "The Cost of Wellesley"; Ada L. Comstock, "Scholarships in Relation to Student Aid"; Lucy W. Stebbins, "Report of the Dean of Women," in *Annual Report of the President*, University of California (1916). Anonymous graduate of Smith College, "Earning a College Course: Setting Forth the Experiences of a Young Woman who Worked her Way through College," *McCall's* 43 (September 1915).

24. Lucy W. Stebbins, "Report of the Dean of Women," in *Annual Report of the President*, University of California (1917); Ada L. Comstock, "Scholarships in Relation to Student Aid"; Ann Miller, ed., *A College in Dispersion: Women of Bryn Mawr, 1896–1975* (Boulder, 1976), 7. I made use of Betty Lou Marple's informal study of Radcliffe scholarship holders (1975). The percentage figures on aid recipients reflect extensive research on scholarship distribution at numerous colleges across the country. It is important to note that the figures are general averages. There was great diversity among schools in the proportion of students that received aid. For a historical perspective on scholarships, see Seymour Harris, *The Economics of Harvard* (New York, 1970).

25. The Morrill Land Grant acts, discussed in chapter 4, grew out of the general belief that industrious men and women should have access to education. See also Mary Ellen

Martin, "An Historical Analysis of Financial Aid at Wellesley College" (Honors thesis, Wellesley College 1973). For an administrator's view of the importance of colleges' accessibility to the industrious poor, see University of Wisconsin president Charles Van Hise's "Inaugural Address," *Science* 20 (1901).

26. Kate Austin Tuttle, "A Plea for Scholarships for the Young Women of the South," *Journal of the Association of Collegiate Alumnae*, 3d ser. 13 (1906). On Boston University, see Warren O. Ault, *Boston University: The College of Liberal Arts, 1873–1973*); on Chicago, see Richard J. Storr, *Harper's University: The Beginnings* (Chicago, 1966), 4. In contrast to Stanford, the University of California (Berkeley) had several scholarships for women at this time. However, archivist Marie C. Thornton, in a letter of April 3, 1984, pointed out that "no information on scholarships was printed in the register or catalogue of courses. Emphasis was placed on how easy it was to support oneself by working twenty-five hours a week."

27. "Undergraduate Scholarships Offered to Women by the Nineteen Colleges of the Association of Collegiate Alumnae," *Journal of the Association of Collegiate Alumnae*, 3d ser. 2 (1899); University of Wisconsin, "Minutes of the Board of Regents, F" (1903–07), University of Wisconsin Archives.

28. Papers of the Massachusetts Society for the University Education of Women, 1877–1897. On deposit, Special Collections, Boston University Library.

29. Alice Hayes, "Can a Poor Girl Go to College?" *North American Review* 152 (1891).

30. See *The Ladies Home Journal* 7 (March 1890), 11, and 7 (October 1890), 9, advertising the contest. Of more than four hundred girls who competed for the prize, the winner was Grace Patterson, a teacher in Beaver Falls, Pennsylvania. The April 1891 *Journal* included Grace Patterson's article "How I Won the Prize"; as a teacher she was earning $35 a month. I am grateful to Maida E. Solomon who found this material.

31. Maria Mitchell, "The Collegiate Education of Girls" (paper read before the Association for the Advancement of Women [1880]), Schlesinger Library, Radcliffe College.

32. Rodman Wilson Paul, "Phoebe Apperson Hearst," in *Notable American Women* II. Mrs. Hearst's views on scholarships are quoted in William W. Ferrier, *Origin and Development of the University of California* (Berkeley, 1930), 437–38.

33. Ada L. Comstock, "Scholarships in Relation to Student Aid."

34. Sarah Pleis Miller, "Have Women's Salaries Been Increased by Higher University Training?" *The Journal of the Association of Collegiate Alumnae* 8 (April 1915); see also Walter J. Greenleaf, *Self-Help for Students*. See *Notes Concerning Financial Aid*, Harvard University, Office of Financial Aid (1982).

35. Timothy Smith, "Immigrant Social Aspirations and American Education, 1880–1930," *American Quarterly* 21 (Fall 1969).

36. Fannie Hurst, *Anatomoy of Me* (Garden City, N.Y., 1958); see also Antoinette Frederick, "Fannie Hurst," in *Notable American Women*, IV.

37. See frontispiece and author's comments in Emily Greene Balch, *Our Slavic Fellow Citizens* (New York, 1910); Oscar Handlin, "Mary Antin," in *Notable American Women: The Modern Period*; Mary Antin, *The Promised Land* (Boston, 1912); Jules Chametszky, "Anzia Yezierska," in *Notable American Women*, IV. Anzia Yezierska's collection of short stories *Hungry Hearts* (Boston, 1920) documents the immigrant experience.

38. For an example of a German immigrant, Rose Schuster, who worked her way through the University of Wisconsin, see Amy Hague, " 'Give Us a Little Time to Find Our Places'." Because Schuster was too poor to pay the $5 diploma fee, university president Bascom paid it for her. William Marshall Warren, "Dean's Report," in *Report of the President*, Boston University (Boston, 1907); Roland P. Faulkner, *Reports of the Immigration Commission: The Children of Immigrants in Schools* (Washington, 1911).

39. Roland P. Faulkner, *Reports of the Immigration Commission*; Ellen Henle and Marlene Merrill, "Antebellum Black Coeds at Oberlin College," *Oberlin College Alumni Magazine* 75 (January–February, 1980). Leona Gabel, "Anna Julia Haywood Cooper," in *Notable American Women*, IV; Anna Julia Haywood Cooper, *A Voice from the South by a Black Woman of the South* (New York, 1892), 79.

40. On Oberlin graduates, see Ellen Henle and Marlene Merrill, "Antebellum Black Coeds." Lynn R. Holmes called to my attention replies from the deans of Vassar, Mount Holyoke, and Bryn Mawr to inquiries regarding admission of black students from dean of Smith College Ada L. Comstock, in Ada Comstock Papers, Smith College Archives. Cheryl A. Wall, "Jessie Redman Fauset," in *Notable American Women*, IV.

41. Alice Katharine Fallows, "Undergraduate Life at Smith College," *Scribner's Magazine* 24 (July 1898). For the influence of *The Ladies Home Journal* on one girl, see Ruth Sapin Hurwitz, "Coming of Age at Wellesley," *Menorah Journal* 38 (Autumn 1950).

Chapter VI

1. Frederick Rudolph, *Curriculum: A History of the American Undergraduate Course of Study Since 1636* (San Francisco, 1977), 122–23; for Harvard and Cornell electives, see especially chapter 5.

2. For President Eliot's view of electives, see Hugh Hawkins, *Between Harvard and America: The Educational Leadership of Charles W. Eliot* (New York, 1972), chapter 3. See Burton J. Bledstein, *The Culture of Professionalism: The Middle Class and the Development of Higher Education in America* (New York, 1976). Also Willis Rudy, *The Evolving Liberal Arts Curriculum: A Historical Review of Basic Themes* (New York, 1960).

3. See Phyllis Keller, *Getting at the Core: Curriculum Reform at Harvard* (Cambridge, Mass., 1982), chapter 1.

4. Mabel Newcomer, *A Century of Higher Education for American Women* (New York, 1959); see especially chapter 5.

5. On the South, see Elizabeth B. Young, *A Study of the Curricula of Seven Selected Women's Colleges of the Southern States* (New York, 1932).

6. For examples of changes in requirements at various colleges, see college catalogues in the 1870s, 1880s, and 1890s. On theories of sex differences, see Rosalind Rosenberg, *Beyond Separate Spheres: Intellectual Roots of Modern Feminism* (New Haven, 1982). For a modern study of Wisconsin, see Amy Hague, " 'Give Us a Little Time to Find Our Places,' University of Wisconsin Alumnae, Classes of 1875–1900" (M.A. thesis, University of Wisconsin, 1983). See also Helen R. Olin, *The Women of a State University: An Illustration of the Working of Coeducation in the Middle West* (New York, 1909). On the "traditional" choices of women at Grinnell, see Jan G. Zimmerman, "Daughters of Main Street: Culture and the Female Community at Grinnell, 1884–1917," in *Woman's Being, Woman's Place: Female Identity and Vocation in American History*, ed. Mary Kelley (Boston, 1979).

7. Marion Talbot, "Report of the Dean of Women," in *President's Report*, University of Chicago (1902). The Boston University statistics were prepared for me from data in Boston University catalogues. My informal study of the ten most popular courses among Harvard and Radcliffe students between 1899 and 1905 showed little difference in the electives of men and women. The only difference, and that a slight one, was that men took a little bit more science than women did.

8. On the evolution of the social sciences, see Frederick Rudolph, *Curriculum*, 139, 157, 177, 219. On social sciences at Oberlin, see John Barnard, *From Evangelicalism to Progressivism at Oberlin College, 1866–1917* (Columbus, Ohio, 1969), chapter 3.

9. University of California, Berkeley, statistics were prepared for me from data in California catalogues by Betty Wolf. Women at Berkeley surpassed men in the Social Science and Letters divisions, accounting for from 55 to 75 percent of the enrollments betwen 1898 and 1913. Moreover, they often comprised over half the enrollment in the Natural Sciences division during this period when only 40 percent of the students were women. The professional schools and vocationally oriented departments were consistently over 80 percent male and most ranged from 90 to 100 percent male. That women opted for liberal arts, including the natural sciences, may be understood in light of the male movement into professional courses and the resulting room for women in the liberal arts. Some men bypassed undergraduate liberal arts completely or took only two years of liberal study before professional training. Caroline W. Latimer, quoted in a discussion of college curriculum in *Publications of the Association of Collegiate Alumnae* 3:1 (December 1898). See also James Burt Miner, "A Vocational Census of College Students," *Educational Review* 50 (September 1915). On the college woman's choice of electives in preparation to teach the subjects such as Latin and German, see Helen R. Olin, *The Women of a State University*, 204–05.
10. Margaret W. Rossiter, *Women Scientists in America: Struggles and Strategies to 1940* (Baltimore, 1982), chapter 1.
11. Mary Van Kleeck, "A Census of College Women," *Journal of the Association of Collegiate Alumnae* 11 (May 1918), 569. Vnn Kleeck hit on the essential inconsistency of these institutions in denying that their liberal arts courses prepared women for teaching, when most graduates had skills to do only that—whether or not this occupation was "best suited to their tastes or their abilities." Mabel L. Robinson, *Curriculum of the Woman's College*, U.S. Bureau of Education bulletin 6 (Washington, 1918), 128–29, 131.
12. Catalogues of Wellesley, Barnard, Mount Holyoke, and Bryn Mawr announced these innovations; see Caroline Hazard, *President's Report*, Wellesley College (1899). For an eloquent defense of the "old-fashioned" curriculum and its intellectual discipline, see M. Carey Thomas, "The Curriculum of the Woman's College," *Journal of the Association of Collegiate Alumnae* 10 (1916–17); see also Mary E. Woolley, "The College Curriculum as a Preparation for Life," *Journal of the Association of Collegiate Alumnae* 10 (1916–17). A history of Randolph-Macon shows the same kind of occasional professional orientation in courses. See Roberta D. Cornelius, *The History of Randolph-Macon Woman's College: From the Founding in 1891 through 1949–50* (Chapel Hill, 1951), 52–53.
13. Winton V. Solberg, *The University of Illinois, 1867–1894: An Intellectual and Cultural History* (Urbana, Ill., 1968). See also Margaret W. Rossiter, *Women Scientists in America*, 64–65, 70, 182. On the beginnings of home economies at the University of Illinois, see Isabel Bevier, "Recollections and Impressions of the Beginnings of the Department of Home Economics at the University of Illinois," *Journal of Home Economics* 32 (1940).
14. Janet W. James, "Ellen Swallow Richards," in *Notable American Women*, III. Marion Talbot, "Report of the Dean of Women," in *President's Report*, University of Chicago (1903). Marie Dye, ed., *History of the Department of Home Economics at the University of Chicago* (Chicago, 1972) describes the separate department of home economics in the School of Education, which was different from Talbot's Department of Household Aministration. On home economics at Wisconsin, see J. F. A. Pyre, *Wisconsin* (New York, 1920), 33; see also Margaret W. Rossiter, " 'Women's Work' in Science, 1880–1910," *Isis* 71 (1980); finally, see Elizabeth B. Young, *A Study of the Curricula of Seven Selected Women's Colleges*, 170, and table following.
15. Alexis Lange, "The Problem of Professional Training For Women," *School and Society* 3 (April 1916), 480. "The Higher Education of Women by Another of Them," *The Stanford Sequoia* 18 (May 1909), 272–73. See ibid. *The Stanford Sequoia* 18 (April 1909), 242–44 for an opposing view. This student literary magazine had female and male editors.

16. Ruth Okey, Barbara K. Johnson, and Gordon MacKinney, "Agnes Fay Morgan, 1884–1968. In Memoriam" (Berkeley, Calif., 1969). See also I. D. Raacke, "Agnes Fay Morgan," in *Notable American Women*, IV.

17. Isabel Bevier, *Home Economics in Education* (Philadelphia, 1924).

18. On Florence Robinson's will and on Beloit's refusal to let her teach history though she had a Wisconsin Ph.D., see Merle Curti's oral history interview with Donna S. Taylor (Madison, Wis., 1975), University of Wiscosin Archives. Wisconsin finally carried out Robinson's instructions. The professorship of history in her name is now held, most appropriately, by Gerda Lerner.

19. Sociology courses on the family at Stanford (1894), Wisconsin (1900s), and Vassar (1916) were of interest to men as well as women students. See Mabel Newcomer, *A Century of Higher Education*, 99. College catalogues and private papers of Sophonisba Breckinridge, Emily Greene Balch, and Dr. Lillian Welsh described their courses. I have found Florence Howe's discussion of the precursors of women's studies courses helpful. Theresa McMahon's papers are in the University of Washington Archives.

20. On the "snap course," see Lois Kimball Matthews, "Raising the Standards of Intellectual Life," *Journal of the Association of Collegiate Alumnae* 9 (May 1916). On the popularity or value of various liberal arts courses, I have drawn on alumnae reports, interviews, and memoirs. For example, see *The Prytaneans: An Oral History of the Prytanean Society, Its Members and Their University, 1901–1920*, 2 vols. (Berkeley, Calif., 1970); Jacqueline Van Voris, ed., *College: A Smith Mosaic* (West Springfield, Mass., 1975); and correspondence with former students in Lucy M. Salmon Papers, Vassar College, Special Collections. Edith R. Mirrielees, ed., *Stanford Mosaic: Reminiscences of the First Seventy Years at Stanford University* (Stanford, 1962), provides interesting examples of the lasting influence of teachers upon achieving alumnae and alumni.

21. On Franklin Giddings as mentor, see Barbara M. Solomon, "Emily Greene Balch," in *Notable American Women*, IV; see also Paul Boyer, "Elsie Clews Parsons," in *Notable American Women*, III. On Giddings's inconsistencies, see Rosalind Rosenberg, *Beyond Separate Spheres*, 152–53. As another example of a mentor relationship, sociology professor Robert Brooks at Swarthmore arranged for Alice Paul to have a Columbia settlement fellowship in New York City.

22. Woodrow Wilson's ambivalence about teaching women is well known. A penetrating letter from Lucy M. Salmon to Ray Stannard Baker, January 6, 1926, describes Wilson's attitude toward graduate students at Bryn Mawr: "Not only did teaching not satisfy Woodrow Wilson, but he was singularly ill adapted to teaching women. He had apparently never had any normal relationships of life with women, he assumed that women were quite different from men, and he made, I felt, no effort to understand them." I am grateful to John Milton Cooper, Jr., for sharing his copy of this letter from the Collections of the Manuscript Division, Library of Congress. Lucy Salmon's remarks in a letter to Mr. Smith, April 4, 1922, related her experience with Professor Charles Kendall Adams; Lucy M. Salmon Papers, Vassar College, Special Collections. In her undergraduate letters home Lucy Salmon was much more enthusiastic about her professors at Michigan.

23. During the early part of the period, women professors were not that much older than the students themselves.

24. On Vassar experiences, see Sally Gregory Kohlstedt, "Maria Mitchell: The Advancement of Women in Science," *New England Quarterly* 51 (March 1978). See also Margaret W. Rossiter's illuminating discussion of women scientists and their student protégées in *Women Scientists in America*.

25. Lucille Addison Pollard, *Women on College and University Faculties: A Historical Survey and Study of their Present Academic Status* (New York, 1977).

26. See "Lady Professors," *The Beacon* 7 (1881); Katharine C. Felton, "The Next Step in the Development of the Western State University," *The Berkeleyan* 3 (February 1, 1894).
27. On Mary Jordan's impact, see Jacqueline Van Voris, ed., *College: A Smith Mosaic*. I have found similar attitudes in conversations with Smith alumnae. See Lucy M. Salmon to her stepmother Mrs. George Salmon, 1875; Lucy M. Salmon Papers, Vassar College, Special Collections.
28. In 1872, Mount Holyoke professor Lydia Shattuck discussed Darwinism privately with her "best natural history students," according to Elaine Kendall, *"Peculiar Institutions": An Informal History of the Seven Sister Colleges* (New York, 1975), 110. On Darwinism at Wisconsin, see Merle Curti and Vernon Carstensen, *The University of Wisconsin: A History, 1848–1925* (Madison, Wis., 1949), I. See also Richard Hofstadter, *Social Darwinism in American Thought* (Boston, 1945). On liberal culture, see Laurence R. Veysey, *The Emergence of the American University* (Chicago, 1965), 180–97.
29. Merle Curti and Vernon Carstensen, *The University of Wisconsin*, 278. On Jordan, see Lois Kimball Matthews, "Raising the Standards of Intellectual Life," *Journal of the Association of Collegiate Alumnae* 9 (May 1916). On the popularity of Harris and Inez Wilder, see Jacqueline Van Voris, ed., *College: A Smith Mosaic*, 8, 30, 60–61, 68.
30. On the wrestling of these individuals with religious conflicts, see Eleanor Flexner, "Carrie Lane Chapman Catt," in *Notable American Women*, I; Marjorie H. Dobkin, *The Making of A Feminist: Early Journals and Letters of M. Carey Thomas* (Kent, Ohio, 1979).
31. On the influence of Jessica Peixotto, see oral interviews with Emily Huntington, August, 1971, at Bancroft Library, University of California, Berkeley; see also *The Prytaneans*. Information on the influence of Jessica Peixotto was obtained from my telephone conversation with Clara Beyer.
32. On the influence of Charles Eliot Norton, see Lucy Allen Paton (Radcliffe '92), "Annex Memories," written in 1943, Radcliffe College Archives. On the Wellesley experience, see Ruth Sapin Hurwitz, "Coming of Age at Wellesley," *Menorah Journal* 38 (Autumn 1950).
33. The chapel crisis caused each institution to move in its own way subject to the pressures of its constituencies. See Merle Curti and Vernon Carstensen, *The University of Wisconsin*; Morris Bishop, *A History of Cornell* (Ithaca, N.Y., 1962); Hugh Hawkins, *Between Harvard and America*. See discussions in Laurence R. Veysey, *The Emergence of the American University*. Whereas before World War I, chapel attendance at Smith College was compulsory, it was not enforced, according to Richard P. Unsworth, "A Century of Religion at Smith College" (1975), Smith College Archives.
34. On the "whole" or "well-rounded" man, see George E. Peterson, *The New England College in the Age of the University* (Amherst, Mass., 1964), chapter 2; and Laurence R. Veysey, *The Emergence of the American University*, 197ff.

Chapter VII

1. For excellent examples of family involvement, see Patricia A. Palmieri, "Patterns of Achievement of Single Academic Women at Wellesley College, 1880–1920," *Frontiers* 5 (Spring 1980).
2. "The American College Girl: By a European University Girl," *The Outlook* 76 (January 16, 1904), 172. Ruth Sapin Hurwitz, "Coming of Age at Wellesley," *Menorah Journal* 38 (Autumn 1950). Esther Cloudman Dunn, *Pursuit of Understanding* (New York, 1945), 132. Dunn became a professor of English literature at Smith College.
3. Letter from Helen L. Miller to "Maurina," October 21, 1877, Smith College Archives. See *The Wellesley Magazine* 5 (April 1897), 399. See also anonymous discussion of marks in *The Wellesley Magazine* 5 (March 1897); *The Wellesley Magazine* 5 (May 1897), 446–48.

Louise Kingsley, "The Advantage of a System of Public Graded Marks at Smith College," *Smith College Monthly* 12 (November 1904); Anna Whitaker, "A Plea for the Knowledge of One's Own Standing in College," *Smith College Monthly* 15 (May 1908). I benefited from reading the family correspondence of two Berkeley undergraduates, Esther and Louise Phillips, papers in the possession of Dr. Mary Eldred. Until 1915 Vassar students learned of their grades only at graduation. Colton Johnson, in a letter to Barbara M. Solomon, December 1, 1982. On increasing concern about the less serious type of student, see Marion Talbot, *More Than Lore: Reminiscences of Marion Talbot, Dean of Women, the University of Chicago, 1892–1925* (Chicago, 1936), 22, and Emily Greene Balch, "What's Hecuba to me or I to Hecuba?' ' *The Wellesley Magazine* 15 (1907).

4. Radcliffe song, written by Mildred Clark in 1916; see *Radcliffe College Song Book* (1916), 157.

5. See files of *Scribner's Magazine* and *The Ladies Home Journal* from 1898 on. See also examples in Elaine Kendall, *"Peculiar Institutions:" An Informal History of the Seven Sister Colleges* (New York, 1976).

6. Mabel Newcomer, "Values Which Last," in *Stanford Mosaic: Reminiscences of the First Seventy Years at Stanford University*, ed. Edith R. Mirrielees (Stanford, 1962), 80–81.

7. College memoirs abound in references to the value of college friendships. For example, see interviews with California, Berkeley, alumnae in *The Prytaneans: An Oral History of the Prytanean Society, Its Members and Their University, 1901–1920* (Berkeley, 1970), 2 vols.

8. Madeleine Wallin to her mother, May 1894, Smith College Archives; "On the Train," *The Beacon* 5 (March 15, 1880): 107.

9. Laura Scales, unpublished memoir, courtesy of Laura Scales, now at the Smith College Archives; Marguerite Wells, "A Tramp through the Berkshire Hills by Four College Girls," *The Symposium* 1 (October 1896); Ada Comstock quoted in Jacqueline Van Voris, ed., *College: A Smith Mosaic* (West Springfield, Mass., 1975), 3. See also interview with Alice W. Porterfield, California '08, in *The Prytaneans*, 78.

10. See Carroll Smith Rosenberg, "The Female World of Love and Ritual: Relations Between Women in Nineteenth-Century America," *Signs: Journal of Women in Culture and Society* 1 (Autumn, 1975). Also Nancy Sahli, "Smashing: Women's Relationships Before the Fall," *Chrysalis* 17 (Summer 1979). On the lifelong friendship of two Wellesley professors, see Judith Schwarz, "Yellow Clover: Katharine Lee Bates and Katharine Coman," *Frontiers* 4 (1979). See also Elaine Kendall, *"Peculiar Institutions,"* on dancing, 147ff.; on passionate friendships, 142–43.

11. Eliza W. McFarland, "Diary at Swarthmore College in 1902," courtesy of Corona Machemer.

12. Quoted in Warren O. Ault, *Boston University: The College of Liberal Arts, 1873–1973* (Boston, 1973), 75–76.

13. On females dancing together, see anonymous memoir of Vassar student of 1889, Vassar College, Special Collections. See also letters of Madeleine Wallin to her mother in the 1890s, Smith College Archives. On walking rather than dancing, see Elaine Kendall, *" Peculiar Institutions."* On the initial waltzing with men at Smith, see Alice Katharine Fallows, "Undergraduate Life at Smith College," *Scribner's Magazine* 24 (July 1898). Alice Duer Miller and Susan Myers, *Barnard College: The First Fifty Years* (New York, 1939). See anonymous letter from male graduate student to Marion Talbot, 1912, Talbot Papers, Regenstein Library, University of Chicago, Special Collections. Clara Beyer's remark is from a telephone conversation I had with her; see also transcript of an oral interview with Kathryn Kish Sklar, in Sklar's possession.

14. Marjorie H. Dobkin, ed., *The Making of a Feminist: Early Journals and Letters of M. Carey*

Thomas (Kent, Ohio, 1979), 142–43. Women physicians employed at the colleges often became instructors in hygiene courses. Young women's ignorance of sex is stressed in Margaret Sanger's pamphlet "What Every Girl Should Know," initially published in the socialist weekly, *The Call*, in 1912–13. See also Ada L. Comstock, "Report of the Dean of Women," in *The President's Report*, University of Minnesota (1912). On the general mood, see Agnes Repplier, "The Repeal of Reticence," *Atlantic Monthly* 113 (1914); "Sex O'Clock in America," *Current Opinion* 55 (March/August 1913). James McGovern, "The American Woman's Pre–World War I Freedom in Manners and Morals," *Journal of American History* 55 (1960), gives excellent coverage of these issues.

15. Marjorie H. Dobkin, ed., *The Making of a Feminist*, 103, 121. Since M. Carey Thomas came from a very protected background, her reaction to male students may not have been typical. Others, from simple rural families, did not react this way. See Patricia F. Haines, "For Honor and Alma Mater: Perspectives on Coeducation at Cornell University, 1868–1885," *Journal of Education* 159 (August 1977); also Charlotte W. Conable, *Women at Cornell: The Myth of Equal Education* (Ithaca, N.Y., 1977). Lillian Moller (Gilbreth) in Irving Stoner, ed., *There Was Light: Autobiography of a University, Berkeley, 1868–1968* (Garden City, N.Y., 1970).

16. Lucy Sprague (Mitchell) became the first dean of women at California in 1906; she introduced the eastern women's college pattern. See Lynn D. Gordon, "Co-Education on Two Campuses: Berkeley and Chicago, 1890–1912," in *Woman's Being, Woman's Place: Female Identity and Vocation in American History*, ed. Mary Kelley (Boston, 1979). See also Joyce Antler, "Feminism as Life-Process: The Life and Career of Lucy Sprague Mitchell," *Feminist Studies* 7 (Spring 1981).

17. For Mosher's address, see Clelia Mosher Papers, Stanford College Archives. Undergraduate writing frequently referred to the Gibson girl. For a detailed study of the image of the "natural woman," and of the influence of the Gibson girl, see Lois W. Banner, *American Beauty* (New York, 1983), especially 154–59.

18. Florence Kelley, "When Co-Education Was Young," *Survey* 58 (February 1, 1927); Rodman W. Paul, "Phoebe Apperson Hearst," in *Notable American Women*, II; William W. Ferrier, *Origin and Development of the University of California* (Berkeley, Calif., 1930); Demia Butler, manuscript diary, entry for September 2, 1892, Regenstein Library, University of Chicago, Special Collections.

19. Lucy Salmon to mother, May 1873, Lucy M. Salmon Papers, Vassar College, Special Collections. For the achievement and interest of these and other women in sports, see college yearbooks and personal papers. Roberta Wilson pointed out to me that on November 13, 1983, the Harvard women's swim team held an intramural meet in celebration of the first recorded such competition at Radcliffe, in 1901. Included in the 1901 meet were "graceful" swims: the sidestroke and breaststroke.

20. One California alumna spoke for the majority in valuing extracurricular activities: "They gave us something—the ability to speak on our feet." Interview with Alice W. Porterfield, in *The Prytaneans*, I, 76.

21. College archives have records of student organizations, though they are far from complete. Marianne Moore quoted from an interview with Donald Hall, *Paris Review* 7 (Winter 1961), 43. Editorial, *The Californian* (September 2, 1908). Undergraduate writing expressed the insecurities in the relations of young men and women. See for example *The Occident* 29 (University of California, Berkeley, 1900).

22. Arthur C. Cole, *A Hundred Years of Mt. Holyoke College: The Evolution of an Educational Ideal* (New Haven, 1940). This quotation in the *Blue and Gold* yearbook (1911) continued as follows: "It was also to settle with all masculinity the account which began with the phrase 'the Infernal Question.' Masculinity triumphed, but not before weak, clinging beautiful women had delivered some hard blows at the infernal men." The Radcliffe Idlers became the most important organization at this semicommuter

college, starting in the 1890s. Some college thespians went on to careers in theater: Radcliffe's Josephine Sherwood Hull became famous on Broadway; Beulah Marie Dix, who wrote, produced, and acted in plays at Radcliffe had a distinguished career as a Hollywood playwright.

23. Elizabeth Wilson, *Fifty Years of Association Work Among Young Women, 1866–1916: A History of Young Women's Christian Associations in the United States of America* (New York, 1916). On the importance of the YWCAs for undergraduate vocational development, see Cynthia Requardt, "Alternative Professions for Goucher College Graduates, 1892–1910," *Maryland Historical Magazine* 74 (September 1979). Membership in the YWCA reassured mothers like Lucy M. Salmon's; see letter of Mrs. George Salmon to Lucy, April 7, 1874; Lucy M. Salmon Papers, Vassar College, Special Collections. On the willingness of the young men to admit women to their Christian associations, see Corey G. Austin *A Century of Religion at the University of Michigan* (Ann Arbor, 1957).

24. On Catholic student associations at Chicago, see *Chicago University Record* 10 (October 1905). I am indebted to Elinor Grumet for sharing with me her work on the history of the Menorah societies. See also John W. Evans, *The Newman Movement: Roman Catholics in American Higher Education, 1883–1971* (Notre Dame, Ind., 1980), 39.

25. At some institutions—for example, Wisconsin—women were permitted separate student government before men. For an informative discussion, see Mabel Newcomer, *A Century of Higher Education*, 116–20. On Berkeley and Chicago, see Lynn D. Gordon, "Co-education on Two Campuses."

26. Ruth Sapin Hurwitz, "Coming of Age at Wellesley," *Menorah Journal* 38 (Fall 1950).

27. Material on sororities is diffuse. For particular organizations, see Elinor S. Davis, *A Centennial History of Alpha Phi Fraternity , 1872–1972* (Hannibal, Mo., 1972); Rebecca Rogosa et al., eds., *Gamma Delta History, 1876–1919* (Boston, 1930). For useful information, see Lynn D. Gordon, "Co-education on Two Campuses," and Mabel Newcomer, *A Century of Higher Education*, 115, 154, and 159. Marion Talbot was opposed to sororities and, when they could not be prevented, restricted their influence; Talbot Papers. Two black sororities started in this period, but the major development of black sororities came later; see chapter X. Amy Hague offers a good account of sororities at Wisconsin in " 'Give Us a Little Time to Find Our Places,' University of Wisconsin Alumnae, Classes of 1875–1900" (M.S. thesis, University of Wisconsin, 1983).

28. Dorothy Canfield Fisher, *The Bent Twig* (New York, 1917). On the protest of one senior against sororities at Western Reserve University, see Florence Allen, *To Do Justly* (Cleveland, Ohio, 1965).

29. The *Wellesley College News* reported at length on the "Society Question" and on the congress. See especially volume 9, nos. 7 (November 24, 1909), 15 (February 9, 1910), 16 (February 16, 1910), 19 (March 9, 1910), 20 (March 16, 1910), 21 (March 23, 1910). Katharine Coman quoted in no. 15, p. 7.

30. Barnard College, *Report of the Dean* (1913), 5; M. C. White, *A History of Barnard College* (New York, 1954), 89–90.

31. Mary Church Terrell, *A Colored Woman in a White World* (Washington, D.C., 1940). On another black student's painful experience at the University of Cincinnati (1913), see Susie W. Jones, oral interview with Merze Tate (July 11, 1977), The Black Women Oral History Project, Schlesinger Library, Radcliffe College. On the deteriorating situation at Oberlin, see W. E. Bigglestone, "Oberlin College and the Negro Student, 1865–1940," *Journal of Negro History* 56 (July 1971). Ida Jackson "Memoir" in *There Was Light*, ed. Irving Stone. Also at Berkeley, Agnes Smedley, briefly enrolled, remembered a discussion of Negro inferiority in an anthropology class in which the professor was amused until talk turned to interracial marriage. See Agnes Smedley's fictional account in *Daughter of Earth* (New York, 1929).

32. On Catholic experiences, I read the correspondence of Esther and Louise Phillips with their mother, 1907–09, courtesy of Dr. Mary Eldred. For Charlotte Atwood, see Wellesley yearbooks and other documents, Wellesley College Archives. Later Atwood accompanied Professor Emily Balch to Haiti to interview natives for a research project; see Emily Greene Balch, *Occupied Haiti* (New York, 1927).

33. On the college dormitory in the ghetto, see Sheila Rothman, *Woman's Proper Place: A History of Changing Ideals and Practices, 1870 to the Present* (New York, 1978), chapter 3.

34. Vida Scudder quoted in Arthur Mann, *Yankee Reformers in an Urban Age* (Cambridge, Mass., 1954). See Jane Addams, *Twenty Years at Hull House* (New York, 1910; repr. 1960), especially chapter 6. For a comprehensive overview, see Allen F. Davis, *Spearheads for Reform: The Social Settlements and the Progressive Movement, 1890–1914* (New York, 1967).

35. It is difficult to assess the number of students who participated at settlements. Debra Herman, "College and After: The Vassar Experiment in Women's Education, 1861–1924" (Ph.D. diss., Stanford University, 1979), has supplied some statistics for Vassar: 9.6 percent of the students were members of the College Settlement Association in 1891, 42.5 percent in 1899. It is my impression that the settlement movement peaked around 1915. The colleges supported the settlements through joint fellowships. See Eleanor H. Johnson, "An Account of the Anniversary Celebration," in *College Settlements Association, The Anniversary Report* (1914). Records of Denison House, Boston, at the Schlesinger Library, Radcliffe College, have interesting material. See also the University of Chicago settlement material in *University of Chicago Record* 12 (January 1908), and 10 (October 1905), and other issues. Also, see an excellent article by Anne Thorp, Vassar '17, "The Social Side of Domestic Service at Vassar College," *Wellesley College Magazine* 24 (January 1916).

36. Lynn Gordon referred to one Vassar student's prejudice in a paper presented at Mount Holyoke in 1980. On the Radcliffe reactions, see correspondence of Katharine Dummer to her mother, Dummer Papers, Schlesinger Library. Amy Brooks, "College Settlement Work at Radcliffe," *Radcliffe Magazine* 8 (December 1905). Alice Hamilton quoted in Allen F. Davis and Mary Lynn McCree, eds., *Eighty Years at Hull House* (Chicago, 1969), 100–02, especially 102. Originally in Hamilton's autobiography *Exploring the Dangerous Trades* (Boston, 1943), 72.

37. On a radical suffragist exponent of free love and socialism, see Geoffrey Blodgett, "Victoria Woodhull," in *Notable American Women*, III. On Vassar's ban on suffrage activities, see Mabel Newcomer, *A Century of Higher Education*. Anne Firor Scott and Andrew M. Scott, *One Half the People: The Fight for Woman Suffrage* (Philadelphia, 1976), 166–68, lists the state constitutional amendments from 1890 up to the federal Nineteenth Amendment in 1920.

38. The Maud Wood Park Papers of the Woman Rights Collection and Inez Haynes Irwin Papers, both at Schlesinger Library, thoroughly document lifetime devotion to the suffrage cause. College Equal Suffrage League Papers are also at the Schlesinger Library.

39. On Minnesota and California, see the Maud Wood Park Papers. Also on Minnesota, see Clarke A. Chambers, "Clara Hampson Ueland," in *Notable American Women*, III. On California, see *The Californian* during Parks's visits: for example, the issues of February 10, 1909; February 15, 1911; and September 13, 1911. The Equal Suffrage League at Lynchburg, Virginia, gave support to the equivalent group on campus in 1915. See Roberta D. Cornelius, *The History of Randolph-Macon Woman's College: From the Founding in 1891 through 1949–1950* (Lynchburg, Va., 1951), 187; I am indebted to Lucy Somerville Howorth for information on Randolph-Macon in correspondence and conversation, October–November, 1983. A set of books that belonged to the College Equal Suffrage League's traveling library is at the Schlesinger Library. The

contest is mentioned in Sally G. Kohlstedt, "Single-Sex Ecuation and Leadership: The Early Years of Simmons College," in *Women and Educational Leadership*, ed. Sari Knopp Biklen annd Marilyn B. Branigan (Lexington, Mass., 1980).

40. In contrast to Mabel Newcomer, Arthur C. Cole, in *A Hundred Years of Mt. Holyoke College*, found scant positive response to suffrage. Cole's view is supported by Mount Holyoke alumnae of 1907 at their seventieth reunion. See Jean Caldwell, "Seven Attend 70th Reunion at Mt. Holyoke," *The Boston Globe* (May 30, 1977). For the opposition to suffrage at Wellesley, see *Wellesley College News*, 1910–11, especially February 15, 1911. On the conforming attitudes of her Wellesley classmates, I found Myra Morgan McNally's letter to me of November 9, 1982, very illuminating. She summed up arguments that the anti-suffrage students accepted, as follows: "1. Women were not as intelligent as Men. 2. They would lose their femininity . . . 3. Women's votes would just duplicate men's, for they would vote like their fathers or sons etc. 4. Women's place was the home." Quote appears in John W. Evans, *The Newman Movement*. Adelia Hunt Logan, "Colored Women as Voters," *The Crisis* 3–4 (1911–12), 242–43.

41. On Vassar, see Mabel Newcomer, *A Century of Higher Education*, 18. I am appreciative of information from the Vassar College Archives supplied by Barbara Page (letter of December 29, 1980), who pointed out to me that the new president, McCracken, who took office in 1915, favored suffrage. Apparently, there was no anti-suffrage club at Vassar. On Howard women undergraduates marching in 1913, see Mary E. Vroman, *Shaped to Its Purpose: Delta Sigma Theta, The First Fifty Years* (New York, 1965).

42. Lorna R. F. Birtwell, "The Point at Issue," *Radcliffe Magazine* 13 (June 1911), 166.

43. See pamphlet of the Oberlin Suffrage Club "To Which Class Do You Belong?" (1908), Oberlin College Archives, courtesy of Carol Lasser. On a vocational-minded southern student's inhibitions about supporting suffrage, see Lib and Virginia Wiley, "R-MWC a Lifetime Ago," *Randolph-Macon Woman's College Alumnae Bulletin* (Fall 1983).

44. On suffrage at Radcliffe, see "The Difficult Question—An Argument," *Radcliffe Magazine* 13, 3 (April 1911). See also editorial, *Radcliffe Magazine* 16 (February 1914), 81. On the enthusiasm of Hunter students, see editorial, *Hunter College Bulletin* 3, 5 (October 26, 1915). League chapters invited opponents of suffrage to attend meetings. I have not found an organized anti-suffrage club except at Radcliffe.

45. Marian Parris, "Non-Teaching Positions Open to Students of Economics, Politics, and Sociology," *Association of Collegiate Alumnae Journal* 21 (April 1910), 64.

Chapter VIII

1. Jane Addams quoted in Allen F. Davis, *American Heroine: The Life and Legend of Jane Addams* (New York, 1973), 22–23; Marion Talbot, "A Modern Problem" (graduating thesis, June 2, 1880), Marion Talbot Papers, Boston University, Special Collections Library. Goucher senior quoted in Cynthia Requardt, "Alternative Professions for Goucher College Graduates, 1892–1910," *Maryland Historical Magazine* 74 (1979), 276.

2. On Jane Addams and the "family claim," see Jane Addams, *Democracy and Social Ethics*, ed. Anne Firor Scott (Cambridge, Mass., 1964), 85–86. For a penetrating modern analysis, see Joyce Antler, " 'After College, What?': New Graduates and the Family Claim," *American Quarterly* 32 (Fall 1980).

3. Mary Church Terrell, *A Colored Woman in a White World* (Washington, D.C., 1940). See Mary Coe's discussion with other administrators, *Journal of the Association of Collegiate Alumnae* 4 (January 1911), 24, on the dilemmas of the college graduate "who is not obliged to be self-supporting." About how this person may "best utilize her time," Coe asked, "What is the right proportion to be put into a 'career' as against the simple living at home to make the best whole of family life?"

4. Helen Ekin Starrett, *After College What? For Girls* (New York, 1896); quoted in Elizabeth Wallace, *The Unending Journey* (Minneapolis, 1952), 219.

5. Madeleine Wallin, "Points of View from a Bicycle" (daily theme, May 22,1894), Special Collections, Regenstein Library, University of Chicago.

6. Smith College Archives provided information about Madeleine Wallin. On the neutral attitudes toward marrying of so many college women, see Katherine Bement Davis, "Why They Failed to Marry," *Harper's Monthly Magazine* 157 (March 1928). A letter I received from Dorothea de Schweinitz, June 21, 1977, confirms Davis's point. De Schweinitz quoted in Jacqueline Van Voris, ed., *College: A Smith Mosaic* (West Springfield, Mass., 1975), 28.

7. John Raymond quoted in Debra Herman, "College and After: The Vassar Experiment in Women's Education, 1861–1924" (Ph.D. diss., Stanford University, 1979); on single professional women, see Karen Blair, *The Clubwoman as Feminist: True Womanhood Redefined, 1868–1914* (New York, 1980), 50–51.

8. See discussion of women's friendships and endnotes 8 and 11 in chapter seven; Helen Howe, *The Gentle Americans, 1864–1960: Biography of a Breed* (New York, 1965).

9. Anne Firor Scott, "The Ever Widening Circle: The Diffusion of Feminist Values From the Troy Female Seminary, 1822–1872," *History of Education Quarterly* 19 (Spring 1979); Mary Van Kleeck, "A Census of College Women," *Journal of the Association of Collegiate Alumnae* 11 (May 1918), 577; Helen R. Olin, *The Women of a State University: An Illustration of the Working of Coeducation in the Middle West* (New York, 1909). Although, in the nation as a whole, 10 percent of native-born white women remained single, in some regions this figure was considerably higher (for example, in Massachusetts, the percentage of unmarried women reached 18 percent in 1870). See Peter Uhlenberg, "Cohort Variations in Family Life Cycle Experience of United States Females," *Journal of Marriage and the Family* 16 (May 1975).

10. On race suicide, see Barbara M. Solomon, *Ancestors and Immigrants: A Changing New England Tradition* (Cambridge, Mass., 1956). On the college bachelor problem, see G. Stanley Hall and Theodore L. Smith, "Marriage and Fecundity of College Men and Women," *The Pedagogical Seminary* 10 (September 1903); see Charles Franklin Emerick, "College Women and Race Suicide," *Political Science Quarterly* 24 (June 1909).

11. See Association of Collegiate Alumnae, *A Preliminary Statistical Study of Certain Women College Graduates* (Bryn Mawr, Pa., 1917), 132–33; see also Millicent Washburn Shinn, "The Marriage Rate of College Women," *The Century Magazine* 50 (October 1895).

12. Quoted in Mabel Newcomer and Evelyn S. Gibson, "Vital Statistics from Vassar College," *American Journal of Sociology* 29 (January 1924), 442.

13. Roberta Frankfort, *Collegiate Women: Domesticity and Career in Turn-of-the-Century America* (New York, 1977), 73. Marriage rates for Bryn Mawr graduates rose between 1889 and 1918, from 47 percent married (of those surveyed) to 67 percent married (of those responding). For a recent study of old Wellesley data, see Janet Z. Giele, "Cohort Variation in Life Patterns of Educated Women, 1911–1960," *Western Sociological Review* 133 (1982), table 2; also see Ann Miller, ed., *A College in Dispersion: Women of Bryn Mawr, 1896–1975* (Boulder, 1976), 11, 106.

14. Charles Eliot quoted by Dorothy Kenyon at a Smith College commencement of 1908, in Jacqueline Van Voris, ed., *College: A Smith Mosaic*, 16; on Ellis Abbott, see a son's interpretation in Ring Lardner, Jr., *The Lardners: My Family Remembered* (New York, 1976); anonymous Wellesley graduate quoted in her article "What I Got Out of College," *Woman's Home Companion* 39 (October 1912); James Hoopes, *Van Wyck Brooks: In Search of American Culture* (Amherst, 1977), 84–85, 263. Elsie Frederickson, quoted in Smith College class report, 1912. I am indebted to Maida H. Solomon for access to her copy of the report. On ambivalence of graduates, see Edith Rickert, "What

has the College Done For Girls: A Personal Canvass of Hundreds of Graduates of Sixty Colleges," *Ladies Home Journal* 29 (January–April 1912).

15. Alumnae reported on the membership in various clubs and on their participation in many voluntary activities. Early studies of college graduates focused on employment statistics. We are in need of quantitative analyses to evalute the level of commitment to organizations.

16. The Chicago Kindergarten Training Schools published Elizabeth Harrison's book; by 1914 it had gone through forty-five editions.

17. Emily Greene Balch, "The Effect of War and Militarism on the Status of Women," *American Sociological Society Publications* 10 (1915).

18. Robert Sklar, "Mary Morton Kehew," in *Notable American Women*, II; Mary Earhart Dillon, "Frances Elizabeth Caroline Willard," in *Notable American Women*, III. See Ruth Bordin, *Woman and Temperance: The Quest for Power and Liberty, 1873–1900* (Philadelphia, 1981), for excellent recent scholarship on this issue.

19. Karen Blair, *The Clubwoman as Feminist: True Womanhood Redefined, 1868–1914* (New York, 1980). For a penetrating study of the professionalization of the women's missionary movement, see Patricia R. Hill's book, *The World Their Household: The American Woman's Foreign Missionary Movement and Cultural Transformation, 1870–1920* (Ann Arbor, 1984).

20. Joan Hoff Wilson, "Jeanette Pickering Rankin," in *Notable American Women*, IV; Anne Firor Scott, "Nellie Nugent Somerville," in *Notable American Women*, IV; Eleanor Flexner, "Carrie Clinton Lane Chapman Catt," in *Notable American Women*, I; Sharon Hartman Strom, "Maud May Wood Park," in *Notable American Women*, IV; Adelaide Washburn, "Helen Hamilton Gardener," in *Notable American Women*, II; on Alice Paul, see oral interviews with Amelia Frye, 1972 and 1973, in Regional Oral History Office, University of California, Berkeley. Two papers delivered at the Berkshire Conference, Vassar, 1981, were useful: Sidney Bland, "Stormy Petrel of Suffragism: Lucy Burns, the Other Leader of the National Women's Party," and Pamela Elam, "The Militant State of Mind: Alice Paul, Lucy Burns, and the Militant Woman Suffrage Movement in the United States, 1916–1920." For evidence of the growing professionalism of the suffrage movement, see Anne Firor Scott and Andrew M. Scott, *One Half the People: The Fight for Woman Suffrage* (Philadelphia, 1975).

21. See Alice Kessler-Harris, *Out to Work: A History of Wage-Earning Women in the United States* (New York, 1982); on the "semi" professions, see Amitai Etzione, *The Semi-Professions and Their Organization* (New York, 1969); Dee Garrison, "The Tender Technicians: The Feminization of Public Librarianship, 1875–1905," *Journal of Social History* 6 (1972–73).

22. Roy Lubove, *The Professional Altruist: The Emergence of Social Work as a Career, 1880–1930* (Cambridge, Mass., 1965), see especially chapter 5. See also Edward Devine and Mary Van Kleeck, *Positions in Social Work* (New York, 1916).

23. A recent economic analysis emphasizes that teaching was a good job for women. See Susan B. Carter and Mark Prus, "The Labor Market and the American High School Girl, 1890–1928," *Journal of Economic History* 42 (March 1982). Percentages of women cited in *Notable American Women* are based on my own unpublished analysis; Mary Van Kleeck, "A Census of College Women"; Alba M. Edwards, *Sixteenth Census of the United States, 1940, Comparative Occupation Statistics for the United States, 1870 to 1940, a Comparison of the 1930 and the 1940 Census Occupation and Industry Classifications and Statistics; A Comparable Series of Occupation Statistics, 1870 to 1920; and a Social-Economic Grouping of the Labor Force, 1910 to 1940*. U.S. Bureau of the Census (Washington, D.C., 1943).

24. On different views of college women toward schoolteaching, see Lucy Salmon to Emily Balch in Mercedes Randall, *Improper Bostonian: Emily Greene Balch* (New York, 1964),

86; see also Clotilde Grunsky, "College Women as Teachers," *The California Alumni Fortnightly* 9 (February 5, 1916); see Sophonisba P. Breckinridge, "Political Equality for Women and Women's Wages," *Annals of the American Academy of Political and Social Science* 56 (November 1914), on the limited opportunities for women in teaching. Additionally, many states witnessed controversy over the issue of permitting a married woman to teach in public schools. For an illuminating personal account of what school-teaching was like for a black woman, see Mamie Garvin Fields with Karen Fields, *Yellow Swamp and Other Places: A Carolina Memoir* (New York, 1983), especially page 40 and chapter 7.

25. See biographical information on these authors in *Notable American Women*, I–IV.

26. Adela Rogers St. Johns quoted in *The Good Housekeeping Woman's Almanac* (New York, 1977), 264–65; a precise comparison of numbers of men and women in the field is not available. According to U.S. Bureau of the Census, Historical Statistics, part I (New York, 1975), 140, there were a total of 32,000 editors and reporters by 1900. Joseph Hill, in *Women in Gainful Occupations, 1870–1920*, Census Monograph 9 (Washington, D.C., 1929), 42, indicates the rise in numbers of women editors and reporters from 35 in 1870 to 2,193 in 1900 and 5,730 in 1920.

27. See biographical information for these artists in *Notable American Women*, I–IV.

28. On the increase in women as clerical workers, see Alice Kessler-Harris, *Out to Work*. The college woman's participation in this force is referred to in records of college appointment bureaus. Barbara Sicherman and Carol Hurd Green in their introduction to *Notable American Women: The Modern Period*, IV, noted that many women took temporary employment as secretaries or clerical workers rather than as teachers.

29. See biographical information on these women in *Notable American Women*, I–IV.

30. Morton Keller, *Affairs of State: Public Life in Late Nineteenth-Century America* (Cambridge, Mass., 1977), 353, notes that in 1895, "twenty-four states required from one to four years of study (or a college degree) before a candidate could take the bar examination." Of 350 women lawyers in 1902, about one-third had graduated from law schools. On the historical background of women's struggles to enter law schools and the legal profession, see Elva Hulburd Young, "Law as a Profession for Women," *Publications of the Association of Collegiate Alumnae*, 3d ser. 5 (February 1902). See biographical essays on lawyers in *Notable American Women*, I–IV. Cynthia F. Epstein, *Women in Law* (New York, 1981), refers to her doctoral study of a group of immigrant women lawyers in New York City. On Portia Law School graduates, see Ronald Chester, "Women Lawyers in the Urban Bar: An Oral History," *New England Law Review* 18 (1983).

31. *Notable American Women*, I–IV, includes essays on these women. In all, thirty-four lawyers were included in these volumes.

32. See biographical information in *Notable American Women*, I–IV; for an excellent historical summary of women and medicine, see introduction to *In Her Own Words: Oral Histories of Women Physicians*, ed. Regina M. Morantz (Westport, Conn., 1982); see also Regina M. Morantz, "Feminism, Professionalism, and Germs: The Thought of Mary Putnam Jacobi and Elizabeth Blackwell," *American Quarterly* 34 (1982).

33. See Jeanette Cheek, oral history interview with Dr. Martha Eliot, Schlesinger Library, Radcliffe College; also Mary Roth Walsh, *Doctors Wanted: No Women Need Apply* (New Haven, 1977).

34. Regina M. Morantz, ed., *In Her Own Words*.

35. Walter Crosby Eells, "Earned Doctorates for Women in the Nineteenth Century," *Bulletin of the American Association of University Professors* 42, 4 (Winter 1956).

36. Margaret W. Rossiter, *Women Scientists in America: Struggles and Strategies to 1940* (Baltimore, 1982).

37. Ibid., 644–51; Laurel Furumoto, "Mary Whiton Calkins (1863–1930), Fourteenth

President of the American Psychological Association," *Journal of the History of the Behavioral Sciences* 15 (1979); see also Virginia Onderdonk, "Mary Whiton Calkins," in *Notable American Women*, I.

38. M. Carey Thomas, "Present Tendencies in Women's College and University Education," *Journal of the Association of Collegiate Alumnae*, 3d ser. 17 (February 1908), 62. On the obstacles for the "woman of genius," see Anna Garlin Spencer, *Woman's Share in Social Culture* (New York, 1912).

39. On the history of fellowships for women, see Ruth W. Tryon, *Investment in Creative Scholarship* (Washington, D.C., 1957); see also Emilie J. Hutchinson, "Women and the Ph.D.," *Journal of the American Association of University Women* 22 (October 1928).

40. On these two scientists, see Hans Ris, "Nettie Maria Stevens," in *Notable American Women*, III, and Ingrith J. Deyrup, "Ida Henrietta Hyde," in *Notable American Women*, II. Hyde's diaries are in the archives of the American Association of University Women, Washington, D.C. See Ida H. Hyde, "Before Women Were Human Beings: Adventures of an American Fellow in the German Universities of the '90s," *Journal of the American Association of University Women* 31–32 (1937–39).

41. See Cheryl A. Wall, "Jessie Redmon Fauset," in *Notable American Women*, IV. For a moving recollection of Jessie Fauset at Cornell, see letter from Charlotte Holmes Crawford to Edith Fox, university archivist, in 1966; she recalls that "Jessie came out of his office in great agitation. I went in, Professor Bristol was standing by the window and motioned to me. I looked out and saw Jessie, face down under a tree, sobbing her heart out. Prof. Bristol was very pale and much moved. 'What could I do?' he said. 'I had to advise her not to take a classics course. What future could there be for her teaching the classics?' " I am indebted to Patricia Haines for alerting me to this correspondence. On the first three doctoral awards to black women, see Jeanne L. Noble, *The Negro Woman's College Education* (New York, 1956).

42. See Margaret W. Rossiter, *Women Scientists in America*. On the classical and literary scholars, see essays in *Notable American Women*: Ann Townsend Zwart, "Abby Leach," in II; Theodore H. Erck, "Grace Harriet Macurdy," in II; Emily Vermeule, "Mary Hamilton Swindler," in *The Modern Period*, IV; Agnes Kirsopp Michels, "Lily Ross Taylor," in *The Modern Period*, IV; Helen C. White, "Myra Reynolds," in III; Earl Leslie Griggs, "Alice D. Snyder," in III; Kenneth S. Lynn, "Constance Mayfield Rourke," in III; James W. Halporn is currently doing an interesting study of women scholars in classical studies.

43. On Lois Kimball Matthews, see University of Wisconsin Archives, Madison, Wisconsin; in addition to her scholarly work, Matthews wrote *The Dean of Women* (Boston, 1915). See also endnote 19 in chapter six.

44. See Ruth M. Tryon, *Investment in Creative Scholarship*.

45. David Riesman's mother was one who declined a fellowship; see his article, "The Two Generations," *Daedalus* 93 (Spring 1964). I have found other examples of this in conversations with several older alumnae.

46. Edith Abbott, *Women in Industry: A Study in American Economic History* (New York, 1918), 322. On the segregated patterns of women's work, see Margaret W. Rossiter, " 'Women's Work' in Science, 1880–1910," *Isis* 71 (1980); see also Ellen Richards, "Desirable Tendencies in Professional and Technical Education for Women," *Journal of the Association of Collegiate Alumnae*, 3d ser. 17 (February 1908).

47. See Barbara M. Solomon, "Emily Greene Balch," in *Notable American Women*, IV; Blanche Wiesen Cook, ed., *Crystal Eastman: On Women and Revolution* (New York, 1978).

48. See Barbara Sicherman, "Alice Hamilton," in *Notable American Women*, IV; Isabel M. Stewart, *The Education of Nurses* (New York, 1943).

Chapter IX

1. Mabel Newcomer, *A Century of Higher Education for American Women* (New York, 1959). Also William C. Devane, *Higher Education in Twentieth-Century America* (Cambridge, Mass., 1965), 59.

2. Frank Holt, "Are We Sending Too Many to College?" *Wisconsin Alumni Magazine* 30 (1929–30), is representative of many articles by college graduates questioning the numerical influx. On black enrollments in predominantly white colleges, see Raymond Wolters, *The New Negro on Campus* (Princeton, 1975), 313. It is difficult to be precise on the percentages of black students in these schools. I received various estimates about black enrollment at Hunter College: Ernestine Friedl, class of '35, on the basis of her class yearbook, gave an estimate of 3 percent of her classmates; according to a letter of January 26, 1984, that I received from Renée Créange, Hunter administrators suggested "between 2 and 3 percent as a fair estimate."

3. On discrimination at men's colleges, see Marcia Graham Synott, *The Half-Opened Door: Discrimination and Admissions at Harvard, Yale, and Princeton, 1900–1970* (Westport, Conn., 1979). See Harold S. Wechsler, *The Qualified Student: A History of Selective College Admission in America* (New York, 1977). See also David O. Levine, "The Functions of Higher Education in American Society Between World War I and World War II" (Ph.D. diss., Harvard University, 1981).

4. Discrimination at comparable women's colleges has not been studied systematically, but both Marcia Synott and I have found some evidence of discrimination in college records. I know from conversations with alumnae of various schools that they were aware of these exclusionary practices. Female students learned from high school teachers that there were Jewish quotas at elite private institutions. On discrimination at Stanford University, see J. Michael Korff, "Student Control and University Government at Stanford: The Evolving Student–University Relationship" (Ph.D. diss., Stanford University, 1975). Korff shows that, for the first time in 1933, Stanford eliminated the five hundred restriction on women's admisson because of the economic crisis.

5. Conversations with Andrew Greeley and Mary Oates have been helpful to me. Mabel Newcomer, *A Century of Higher Education*, 37, has some material.

6. Raymond Wolters, *The New Negro on Campus*; W. E. B. DuBois, "Negroes in College," *The Nation* 122 (March 3,1926), 229. On Oberlin, see Ellen Henle and Marlene Merrill, "Antebellum Black Coeds at Oberlin College," *Oberlin College Alumni Magazine* 75 (January–February 1980). On the percentage of Jewish women in Ivy League women's colleges, see "Admissions: The Jewish Problem, Admissions Office, November 1, 1937," Ada Comstock Presidential Papers, Radcliffe College.

7. See Jeanne Noble, *The Negro Woman's College Education* (New York, 1956), Appendix D. See Raymond Wolters, *The New Negro*; see also E. Horace Fitchett, "The Role of Claflin College in Negro Life in South Carolina," *Journal of Negro Education* 12 (Winter 1943), and Martin D. Jenkins, "Enrollment in Negro Colleges and Universities, 1939–40," *Journal of Negro Education* 7 (April 1938). Susan Hill of the U.S. Department of Education reviewed available historical statistics and informed me that, depending on which source is used, the shift to the predominance of women among black college students took place between 1929 and 1933 at black institutions. See table 2 in Henry G. Badger, *Statistics of Negro Colleges and Universities: Students, Staff, and Finances, 1900–1950* , U.S. Office of Education, statistical circular 293 (April 1951).

8. I. J. Semper, "The Church and Higher Education for Girls," *Catholic Educational Review* 29 (April 1931). Mary M. Bowler, *A History of Catholic Colleges for Women in the United States* (Washington, D.C., 1933). Karen Kennelly, "Mary Molloy: Women's College Founder," in *Women of Minnesota: Selected Biographical Essays*, ed. Barbara

Stuhler and Gretchen Kreuter (St. Paul, Minn., 1977). Mary Friel, "The History of Emmanuel College, 1919–1974" (Ph.D. diss., Boston College, 1979). Karen Kennelly, "The Dynamic Sister Antonia and the College of St. Catherine," *Ramsey County History* 14 (Fall–Winter 1978).

9. Edgar Reynolds, *The Social and Economic Status of College Students* (New York, 1927), 23. On the lower middle class economic level of students in normal schools and teachers colleges, see 24–25.

10. Helen Bertha Goetsch, *Parental Income and College Opportunities* (New York, 1940), 85. This study of Milwaukee youth showed that 64 percent of Jewish parents, 57 percent of Scandinavians, 34 percent of native-born parents, and 18 percent of French, Italian, and Greek parents sent their children to college, 141.

11. Quoted in Jeanne Westin, *Making Do: How Women Survived the '30s* (Chicago, 1976), 101, 113.

12. Professor Margaret Rawley of Atlanta University confirmed my impression of the movement of black parents out of the South to gain a better education for their children. See Ida Jackson's memoir in *There was Light: Autobiography of a University, Berkeley, 1868–1948*, ed. Irving Stone (Garden City, N.Y., 1970).

13. Quoted in Jeanne Westin, *Making Do*, 93.

14. Charles S. Johnson, *The Negro College Graduate* (Chapel Hill, 1938). On Howard students, see Charles H. Thompson, "The Socio-Economic Status of the Negro College Student," *Journal of Negro Education* 2 (January, 1933); Thompson's study shows that one-third of the Howard male students were wholly self-supporting, whereas only one-tenth of the females were. Most black students depended on parental help combined with varying degrees of self-help. On Fisk students, see Ambrose Caliver, *A Background Study of Negro College Students*, U.S. Office of Education Bulletin 8 (1933). On the "enigma," see Marion V. Cuthbert, *Education and Marginality: A Study of the Negro Woman College Graduate* (New York, 1942), 15.

15. Helen Tredway Graham et al., "The Expenses of Women College Students, A Survey of 114 Colleges and Universities." Prepared for the American Association of University Women by the College Club of St. Louis (May 1923); see also Thyrsa W. Amos, "Self-Help for Women College Students," *Journal of the American Association of University Women* 20 (October 1926).

16. Walter J. Greenleaf, *Self-Help for College Students*, U. S. Bureau of Education bulletin 2 (1929); see table 2 for a breakdown of self-help in women's colleges and universities. Variations are evident; for example, public Hunter College had 50 percent of its students reporting self-help, Radcliffe had 28 percent, Vassar 21.8 percent, St. Catherine's 21 percent, Agnes Scott 17 percent, Wheaton 15 percent, Skidmore 19.1 percent, Mills 16 percent, and the University of Chicago 25 percent. Table 4 in Greenleaf, on "Negro Institutions," gives figures that are incomplete and usually not broken down by sex. See also a cumulative study apparently reflecting the onset of the Depression: Floyd Reeves and John D. Russell, *The Alumni of the Colleges* (Chicago, 1933). For further citations that reflect particular schools, see Paula S. Fass, *The Damned and the Beautiful: American Youth in the 1920s* (New York, 1977), including the endnotes for chapter 3.

17. Quoted in Walter J. Greenleaf, *Self-Help*, 55. Self-help students availed themselves of less expensive residential on-campus living in cooperative houses where available; see Greenleaf, 5. See also "College and University Cooperative Houses for Women Students," *Journal of the American Association of University Women* 18 (March 1925). Greenleaf included letters from college girls who were working their way at Alabama College, Utah Agricultural College, Wellesley, Radcliffe, Shurtleff College, University of Iowa, Fairmount College, Piedmont College, and Syracuse University.

18. Susan Ware, *Holding Their Own: American Women in the 1930s* (Boston, 1982), 57. David

O. Levine, in the "The Functions of Higher Education," noted that of 1,700 colleges eligible for NYA funds, only about 1,466 availed themselves. Vandenberg quoted in Jeanne Westin, *Making Do*, 90.

19. Elaine M. Smith, "Mary McLeod Bethune and the National Youth Administration," in *Clio Was a Woman: Studies in the History of American Women*, ed. Mabel E. Deutrich and Virginia C. Purdy (Washington, D.C., 1980), 166. Idem, "Mary McLeod Bethune," in *Notable American Women*, IV.

20. See William C. DeVane, *Higher Eduation*, chapter 4, and Frederick Rudolph, *Curriculum: A History of the American Undergraduate Course of Study Since 1636* (San Francisco, 1977), 230ff. Alexander Meicklejohn, "The Wisconsin Experimental College," *Journal of American Association of University Women* 22 (October 1928).

21. Henry McCracken, "Flexner and the Woman's College," *Journal of Higher Education* 2 (October 1931). See also Mary McCarthy's praise of the college course "The Vassar Girl," in *On the Contrary* (New York, 1961). See Muriel S. Snowden, Radcliffe '38, "Reflections from an Overseer," Harvard University *Gazette*, June 4, 1982, on the intellectual and personal impact of a young "section man," Robert Merton. William C. DeVane, *Higher Education*, and Frederick Rudolph, *Curriculum*.

22. Ada Comstock's inaugural address quoted in *Radcliffe News* (October 26,1923). See also Ada Comstock to Grace R. Foster, November 23, 1932, Ada Comstock Papers, Radcliffe College Archives. Clara M. Brown, "New Problems and a New Curriculum," *Journal of the American Association of University Women* 23 (January 1930), 74–75, 79.

23. On euthenics at Vassar, see Elizabeth Elliott Wellington, "Re-Routing Woman's Education," *Journal of the American Association of University Woman* 19 (June 1926). Smith College student quoted in Ethel Puffer Howes, "The Women's Orientation Course—What Shall Be Its Basic Concept?" *Journal of the American Association of Collegiate Alumnae* 20 (June 1927), 108.

24. See Lucy Stebbins's annual reports as dean of women at the University of California, and notably her report to the president in the *Annual Report of the President*, University of California (1930).

25. See James M. McPherson, *The Abolitionist Legacy: From Reconstruction to the NAACP* (Princeton, 1975), 205, on the academic levels of black colleges before 1910. The papers of the National Association of College Women are at Howard University.

26. See Lucy D. Slowe, "Higher Education of Negro Women," *Journal of Negro Education* 2 (July 1933). See Marion Thompson Wright, "Lucy Diggs Slowe," in *Notable American Women*, III. See also Lucy D. Slowe, "The Colored Girl Enters College: What Shall She Expect?" *Opportunity* 15 (September 1937); Slowe's questionnaire, sent to deans of 76 institutions, of which 44 answered with 14,843 students replying, showed that in the 1920s and early 1930s most black female undergraduates had not had the full breadth of a liberal arts curriculum.

27. On the history of Spelman, see Beverly Guy-Sheftall and Jo Moore Stewart, *Spelman: A Centennial Celebration, 1881–1981* (Charlotte, N.C., 1981). On the 1930s, see Florence M. Read, "The Place of the Women's College in the Pattern of Negro Education," *Opportunity* 15 (September 1937). See also idem, *The Story of Spelman College* (Atlanta, 1961).

28. David D. Jones, "The War and the Higher Education of Negro Women," *Journal of Negro Education* 12 (April 1942), 333–34. On the history of Bennett College, see Constance H. Marteena, "A College For Girls," *Opportunity* 16 (October 1938).

29. See Willa Player, "Improving College Education for Women at Bennett College: A Report of a Type A Project" (Ed.D. diss., Columbia Teachers College, 1948).

30. Marion V. Cuthbert, *Education and Marginality*, found alumnae most concerned with

better vocational guidance. See also Ina Bolton, "Problems of Negro College Women Graduates" (Ph.D. diss., University of California, 1946).

31. Mabel Newcomer, *A Century of Higher Education*, 97–98; she notes the heavy concentration of philosophy and psychology as well as classics in Catholic colleges in the sample years of 1931–32 and 1956–57. The classics had declined in non-Catholic colleges while remaining strong in Catholic institutions. Latin courses were important for women who would teach in Catholic high schools.

32. See John Lancaster Spalding, *Opportunity and Other Essays* (Chicago, 1903), 58; see also idem, *Means and Ends of Education* (Chicago, 1895).

33. On a reactionary view, see I. J. Semper, "The Church and Higher Education," 220. On Katherine Conway, see Karen Kennelly, "Philosophy of Women's Higher Education, 1875–1900" (paper delivered at the Berkshire Conference at Vassar, 1980).

34. On Sister Mary Molloy, see Karen Kennelly, "Mary Molloy: Women's College Founder," in *Women of Minnesota*, ed. Barbara Stuhler and Gretchen Kreuter. On Sister Antonia McHugh, see Karen Kennelly, "The Dynamic Sister Antonia and the College of St. Catherine," *Ramsey County History* 14 (Fall–Winter 1978). On Sister Helen Madeleine Ingraham, see Mary Friel, "History of Emmanuel College." Another important Catholic educator was Sister Mary Madeleva Wolff, president of St. Mary's College at Notre Dame; see Karen Kennelly, "Sister Madeleva Wolff," in *Notable American Women*, IV.

35. Mary Molloy quoted in Karen Kennelly, "Mary Molloy: Women's College Founder," 127, 126.

36. See Abigail McCarthy, *Private Faces, Public Places* (New York, 1972).

37. Mary Friel, "History of Emmanuel," is very informative about the Boston situation; Ann Drinan is quoted here, 85.

38. Deans of women, on the defensive, insisted that the presence of women in coeducational schools had not had negative effects on the moral or intellectual climate. See Lois K. M. Rosenberry, "Have Women Students Affected the Standards of Coeducational Institutions?" *Journal of the American Association of University Women* 20 (January 1927). By contrast, one father suggested that his daughter's education "smacked of vacation rather than vocation," in I. M. Rubinow, "The Revolt of a Middle-Aged Father," *Atlantic Monthly* 139 (May 1927), 593. I am indebted to Allen Weinstein for alerting me to this article.

Chapter X

1. I have been struck by the evidence in Laurence R. Veysey, *The Emergence of the American University* (Chicago, 1965), of the conflicts between male students and faculty in the late nineteenth and early twentieth centuries, at a time when women undergraduates appeared quite deferential to their professors.

2. On the flapper, see Paula S. Fass, *The Damned and the Beautiful* (New York, 1977), 21, 25.

3. Although F. Scott Fitzgerald, in *This Side of Paradise* (1920), created the literary stereotype of the college man, he made no female counterpart. His wife Zelda, however, created her own flapper style and stated her views in "What became of Our Flappers and Sheiks," an interview originally reported in *McCall's* (October 1925) and subsequently reprinted in *The Romantic Egoists: Scott and Zelda Fitzgerald*, ed. Matthew J. Bruccoli, Scottie Fitzgerald Smith, and Joan P. Kerr (New York, 1974). Daniel J. Kevles, *The Physicists: The History of a Scientific Community in Modern America* (New York, 1971), 205, points out the anti-careerist stand of Zelda Fitzgerald. Her creed of personal independence, however, places her in the broader feminist spectrum. On the

public fear of flappers, see Clemence Dane, "When They Are Grandmothers," *Forum* 71 (May 1927).

4. Marita Bonner, "On Being Young, A Woman, and Colored," *The Crisis* 31 (December 1925). Bonner, a graduate of Radcliffe, class of '22, taught English in a Washington, D.C., high school and later in Chicago.

5. Lucy Slowe, "The Colored Girl Enters College: What Shall She Expect?" *Opportunity* 15 (September 1937).

6. Paula S. Fass, *The Damned and the Beautiful*, 194–95, 331–32.

7. Radcliffe students in the 1930s, myself included, were told never to appear in Harvard Square without hat and gloves. On a similar rule in Nebraska sororities, see Jeanne Westin, *Making Do: How Women Survived the '30s* (Chicago, 1976), 117. Mary Friel refers to the "white glove syndrome" in "The History of Emmanuel College, 1919–1974" (Ph.D., diss., Boston College, 1979).

8. Abigail Jackson quoted in Raymond Wolters, *The New Negro on Campus* (Princeton, 1975), 37. Wolters gives an excellent description of the discipline in black colleges.

9. On college drinking at Berkeley, see Minnie Selvin Crutcher, "Remembering the Class of 1927," *California Living Magazine* (October 30, 1977), 41. Paula Fass gives excellent coverage to the various responses of students to rules prohibiting drinking on and off campuses. The University of Wisconsin issued a pamphlet entitled "If I were a Freshman Again." Its "code for Wisconsin Women" suggested that they "refuse to associate with men who have been drinking"; University of Wisconsin Archives.

10. The suspicious father is quoted in Jeanne Westin, *Making Do*, 255. On similar views of deans, as well as on Mary Woolley and Marion Park, see Paula S. Fass, *The Damned and the Beautiful*. President Ellen Pendelton is quoted in an oral interview with Margaret Clapp (then head of student government and later president of Wellesley) in June 1972, Wellesley College Archives. Mary Friel, in "History of Emmanuel," describes a student's rebuke for probable smoking off campus. Cornelia Meigs, *What Makes a College? A History of Bryn Mawr* (New York, 1956).

11. Freda Kirchwey, ed., *Our Changing Morality: A Symposium* (New York, 1924). On the popular level of social etiquette, Emily Post no longer sufficed. See Alice Leone Moats, *No Nice Girl Swears* (New York, 1933), which became a best-seller; see discussion of reprint in *New York Times*, January 4, 1984. For insights on the diverse sex patterns of educated women, Katherine Bement Davis's work is indispensable; see *Factors in the Sex Life of Twenty-Two Hundred Women* (New York, 1929) and "Why They Failed to Marry," *Harper's Monthly Magazine*, 156 (March 1928).

12. For a good presentation of younger women's attitudes toward sex, see Susan Ware, *Holding Their Own: American Women in the 1930s* (Boston, 1982), 63–64. On their fear of pregnancy and horror of abortion, see Jeanne Westin, *Making Do*, 90. Paula S. Fass, *The Damned and the Beautiful*, 267–68, 272–73, gives an example of an anti-petting league at the University of California. Fass also shows that every time students were asked (in surveys at various colleges, from the University of Chicago to North Carolina), they indicated a desire for more information on contraceptives. On the new ways of youth, see Robert S. Lynd and Helen Merrell Lynd, *Middletown: A Study of Modern American Culture* (New York, 1929), especially Chapter 11.

13. See YMCA pamphlet of 1922 in Marion Talbot Papers, box II, folder 2, Regenstein Library, University of Chicago, Special Collections.

14. On the reactions of the older generation, see Jane Addams, *The Second Twenty Years at Hull House* (New York, 1930), 197; and Charlotte Perkins Gilman, "A New Generation of Women," *Current History* 18 (August 1923). For contrast, see Freda Kirchwey, ed., *Our Changing Morality: A Symposium* (New York, 1924).

15. The ambiguity of older educators in judging women's friendships appears in the YWCA

pamphlet from the early 1920s, in which the question was asked, "If a girl finds herself falling in love with another woman, should she restrict all expression of that love?" I remember when two Radcliffe students were called in and warned that their behavior was unacceptable. For an excellent analysis of the changed attitudes toward women's friendships, see Christina Simmons, "Companionate Marriage and the Lesbian Threat," *Frontiers* 4 (1979).

16. On conventional patterns of friendship, Minnie Selvin Crutcher is quoted, "Remembering the Class of 1927." Mary McCarthy, *The Group* (New York, 1954), especially 385ff. Helen Vendler informed me that this character was modeled after the poet Elizabeth Bishop, another Vassar alumna.

17. This impression is based on personal experience and on conversations with Catholic alumnae of Radcliffe. On the conflicts of black college women within their communities, see Marion V. Cuthbert, *Education and Marginality: A Study of the Negro Woman College Graduate* (New York, 1942). See also Marita Bonner, "On Being Young, a Woman, and Colored," *The Crisis* 31 (December 1925), 63.

18. Zora Hurston, "How it Feels to be Colored Me," *The World Tomorrow* 11 (May 1928), 216. Edythe Hargrave, "How I Feel as a Negro at a White College," *Journal of Negro Education* 2 (October 1942), 485, 486. See Muriel S. Snowden, "Reflections from an Overseer," Harvard University *Gazette*, June 4, 1982.

19. Quoted in Alice Kessler-Harris's introduction to Anzia Yezierska, *Bread Givers: A Struggle Between a Father of the Old World and a Daughter of the New* (repr. New York, 1975), xiv; see also chapter 16. Barbara Wertheim Tuchman (Radcliffe '33) informed me of her experience at Swarthmore, where she was not admitted to a sorority because she was Jewish.

20. According to a *Fortune* poll in 1936, "Athletics do not bulk large in the girl student's life. She may do a little swimming, play a little tennis. A very few go in for golf." *Fortune* 13 (June 1936), 102. W. Carson Ryan, Jr., "What Do We Know About Women's College Athletics," *Journal of the American Association of University Women* 23 (June 1930), noted the discouragement of intercollegiate athletics at women's colleges. Anzia Yezierska, in *Bread Givers*, 215–17, describes an immigrant student's reaction to the college gymnastics requirement: considering her work in a steam laundry exercise enough, one day in frustration she seized a jumping hurdle and "smashed it to pieces."

21. Old sororities and new boomed in the 1920s. Histories of particular ones do not provide historical analyses. While Paula Fass, in *The Damned and the Beautiful*, refers to many Greek letter societies, usually she treats the fraternities and sororities together. On the power of these organizations to control student's dating, behavior, and appearance, see pp. 199, 202. On the impact of sororities on individuals, see Jeanne Westin, *Making Do*, 91, 109, 110.

22. On the importance of sororities for black women, see Jeanne Noble, *The Negro Woman's College Education* (New York, 1956), 10–11, and Marion V. Cuthbert, *Education and Marginality*. See also Mayford W. Logan, *Howard University: The First Hundred Years* (New York, 1969), 119. Raymond Wolters, *The New Negro*, shows black students identifying social status with these affiliations. See Mary E. Vroman, *Shaped to Its Purpose: Delta Sigma Theta, the First Fifty Years* (New York, 1965). On introducing student government at black colleges, see Lucy D. Slowe, "The Colored Girl Enters College." Women at the older women's colleges appeared indifferent to student government, except on personal issues like smoking. Women students confronted Mary Yost at Stanford in 1920, where they objected to social regulations that men students did not have. J. Michael Korff, "Student Control and University Government at Stanford: The Evolving Student–University Relationship" (Ph.D. diss., Stanford University, 1975).

23. Figures on the declining YWCAS appear in Eileen Egan, *Class, Culture, and the Classroom:*

The Student Peace Movement of the 1930s (Philadelphia, 1981), 157–58. See also Mary S. Sims, *The Natural History of a Social Institution: The Young Women's Christian Association* (New York, 1936). Paula Fass, in *The Damned and the Beautiful*, observes that freshman and sophomores were more likely to join the ywcas and then drop them for other interests. On the greater importance of the ywcas for black students, see Gerda Lerner, ed., *Black Women in White America: A Documentary History* (New York, 1972), 479–97.

24. On resistance to chapel-going, see Paula Fass, *The Damned and the Beautiful*, 42–46, 136–39. Surprisingly, in the 1920s and 1930s there were some demands for reinstituting compulsory chapel. See student newspapers, Smith College Archives. Raymond Wolters, *The New Negro*, deals well with the rebelliousness of black collegians on the chapel requirement; see especially 73, 75.

25. See Eileen Egan, *Class, Culture, and the Classroom*, 36–37, and Paula Fass, *The Damned and the Beautiful*, who notes that some student radicalism emerged through the ywcas and ymcas and through Methodist groups, 334–35. On the support of intellectuals and academics for Sacco and Vanzetti, see G. Louis Joughin and Edmund M. Morgan, *The Legacy of Sacco and Vanzetti* (New York, 1948); see also Barbara M. Solomon, "Brahmins and the Conscience of the Community," and Daniel Aaron, "The Idea of Boston: Some Literary Responses to the Sacco-Vanzetti Case," in *Sacco-Vanzetti: Developments and Reconsiderations—1979* (Boston, 1982).

26. See Mabel Holloway, "At Princeton: A Student World Court Conference," *The Crisis* 31 (February 1926).

27. Paula Fass, in *The Damned and the Beautiful*, notes that Barnard students in 1924 supported LaFollette over Coolidge far more than did students at other eastern colleges. Again, some women students under the influence of deans Virginia Gildersleeve at Barnard and Lucy Stebbins at California, Berkeley, supported Al Smith in 1928.

28. Caroline Bird, *The Invisible Scar* (New York, 1966), gives an insider's recollections of Vassar during the Depression and conveys well the guilt of the privileged, 138ff. In contrast, see William H. Hale, "A Dirge for Liberalism," *The New Republic* 66 (May 13, 1931). See Susan Ware, *Beyond Suffrage: Women in the New Deal* (Cambridge, Mass., 1981) for historical background on educated women's participation in the New Deal.

29. See Susan Ware's excellent presentation in *Holding Their Own: American Women in the 1930s* (Boston, 1982); see also Eileen Egan, *Class, Culture, and the Classroom*. Egan discusses both the origins of slid, and its role as the predecessor of the Students for a Democratic Society (sds) of the 1960s.

30. *Vassar Miscellany News*, November 8, 1939, included an article on Professor Ruby T. Norris's proposal to establish freshman scholarhips for Negroes. See in addition the letter of student Nancy McIrney of the *Vassar Miscellany News* to Walter White of the naacp on the issue of bringing black students to Vassar. I am indebted to Marcia Synott for making this material available to me. See Susan Ware, *Holding their Own*, 60.

31. William H. Chafe, *Civilities and Civil Rights: Greensboro, North Carolina, and the Struggle for Black Freedom* (New York, 1980), 20–21, describes the Bennett students' role in the boycott of movie theaters. On conservatism among black students, see LaFayette Harris, "Problems Before the College Negro," *The Crisis* 44 (August 1937), and Edward Warner Brice, "How Radical are College Students?" *The Crisis* 44 (October 1937). Pauli Murray is quoted in Joseph P. Lash, *Franklin and Eleanor* (New York, 1971), 682. The National Association of College Women in 1934 praised the attitudes of black students at a local symposium. Contrast the recollections of two Atlanta students regarding acceptance of segregation, in Jeanne Westin, *Making Do*, 94.

32. On renewed Jewish consciousness, see, for example, *The Radcliffe College News* in the 1920s and 1930s. There were a few Zionists at the elite women's colleges, but more, probably, at Hunter college.

33. Eileen Egan, *Class, Culture, and the Classroom*, gives coverage to student participation in the peace movement and shows the diversity in the movement as well.
34. Eileen Egan, *Class, Culture, and the Classroom*, 116. For an excellent introduction to the Catholic Worker movement, see Mel Piehl, *Breaking Bread: The Catholic Worker and the Origin of Catholic Radicalism in America* (Philadelphia, 1982). For information about Emmanuel students (including one student's visit to a Catholic Worker "house of hospitality"), see Mary Friel, "History of Emmanuel College," 93–97. Another student at Emmanuel, Evangeline Mercier, daughter of a Harvard professor, started the St. Thomas More bookshop in Harvard Square with a group of classmates. The store was meant to be a link between Catholic and Protestant intellectual worlds, ibid., 106.
35. Eileen Egan, *Class, Culture, and the Classroom*, notes that two officers of the ASU were women: Molly Yard, a Swarthmore graduate, and Mary Fox, of SLID. In fact, a flyer of the ASU (sent to me by Marcia Synott) shows that women comprised ten out of twenty-five members of the New National Executive Committee of the ASU.
36. See Mary McCarthy, "The Vassar Girl," in *On the Contrary* (New York, 1961), 63, for the impact of great teachers on one alumna of the 1930s; they had "a certain largeness of mind" and conveyed "the idea of excellence, the zest for adventure, the fastidiousness of mind, and humanistic breadth of feeling." Student publications reported on the visits of famous women. Fisk graduates of the class of '35 also described the influence of teachers. Deborah Pinckney West recalled to me in 1977 that "Dr. Lorenzo Turner encouraged me to earn a graduate degree . . . and Dr. James Weldon Johnson urged me to continue creative writing."
37. Mary L. Martin, Mrs. Wilbur Martin, class of '35 in response to questionnaire of mine. Another alumna of Fisk described the Fisk tradition of womanhood, explaining the early strictness and welcoming the "new freedom" of the 1920s and 1930s which had "not lowered the standards of conduct"; see Mayme Upshaw Foster, "Fisk Women— Today and Yesterday," Fisk *News* (January–February 1938). Diana Trilling, *We Must March, My Darlings* (New York, 1977), 245.

Chapter XI

1. The overall percentages of women receiving doctorates from 1920 to 1945 are fairly constant, ranging from 15.3 to 13.4 percent (and according to Patricia S. Graham, peaked at 18.0 percent). Nevertheless, most scholars relied on Jessie Bernard's study, *Academic Women* (University Park, 1964), which seemed to stress the leveling off. I have utilized Susan Carter's path-breaking study, which confirmed my own skepticism about earlier interpretations. For specific trends, see Susan B. Carter, "Academic Women Revisited: An Empirical Study of Changing Patterns in Women's Employment as College and University Faculty, 1890–1963," *Journal of Social History* 14 (Summer 1981).
2. Hélène Kazanjian Sargeant, "Genus: Alumnae, Species: Wellesley, A Summary of the 16,662 Replies to the Recent Alumnae Questionnaire," *Wellesley Alumnae Magazine* 49 (November 1964). Radcliffe Alumnae Questionnaires of 1928 and 1944 form a major source in this chapter. The analyses are based on my research conducted under the auspices of the Henry A. Murray Center, Radcliffe College. Responses to the Radcliffe questionnaire did not provide clear information showing when in their life cycles women worked.
3. Katherine Bement Davis, *Factors in the Sex Life of Twenty-Two Hundred Women* (New York, 1929).
4. Dean Virginia Gildersleeve at Barnard approved the inevitable rise in the number of alumnae who would combine marriage and paid work in the world; see *Barnard College*

Alumnae Monthly 24 (June 1935). President Neilson at Smith College supported Ethel Puffer Howes's project discussed later in this chapter.

5. Mary Anna Nettleton, "A Survey of Hollins Graduates," *The Hollins Alumnae Quarterly* 10 (Summer 1935). Idem, "Youth in College," *Fortune Magazine* 13 (June 1936).

6. Quoted in Peter G. Filene, *Him/Her Self: Sex Roles in Modern America* (New York, 1975), 128. On the Vassar poll, see William H. Chafe, *The American Woman: Her Changing Social, Economic, and Political Roles, 1920–1970* (New York, 1972), 102.

7. Eunice Fuller Barnard, "The College Girl Puts Marriage First," *New York Times Magazine*, April 2, 1933.

8. Dorothy Dunbar Bromley, "Feminist—New Style," *Harper's Magazine* 155 (1927), 552, 556.

9. Frank Stricker, "Cookbooks and Law Books: The Hidden History of Career Women in Twentieth-Century America," *Journal of Social History* 10 (Fall 1976). William H. Chafe, *The American Woman*, 56.

10. Worth Tuttle quoted in "Autobiogaphy of an Ex-Feminist," *Atlantic Monthly* 152 (December, 1933), 641. For other examples see Peter G. Filene, *Him/Her Self*; and Frank Stricker, "Cookbooks and Law Books." On the tensions of successful married career women, see also *These Modern Women*, ed. Elaine Showalter (New York, 1978).

11. Steven J. Diner, "George Herbert Mead's Ideas on Women and Careers: A Letter to His Daughter-in-Law, 1920," *Signs: Journal of Women in Culture and Society* 4 (Winter 1978), 409.

12. Ethel Puffer Howes, "The Meaning of Progress in the Woman Movement," in *Women in the Modern World, The Annals of the American Academy of Political and Social Science* 143 (1929), 16.

13. Virginia M. Collier, *Marriage and Careers* (New York, 1926). The book used data from the Bureau of Vocational Information.

14. Chase Going Woodhouse wrote two articles exploring the material made available by the AAUW study that started in 1926: "The Occupations of Members of the American Association of University Women," *Journal of the American Association of University Women* 21, 4 (1928); and "Married College Women in Business and the Professions," *The Annals of the American Academy of Political and Social Science* 143 (1929). For statistics on the land-grant college graduates, see idem, *After College, What? A Study of 6,665 Land-Grant College Women, their Occupations, Earnings, Families, and some Undergraduate and Vocational Problems, Bulletin of the Institute of Women's Professional Relations* (Greensboro, N.C., 1932).

15. Anne Byrd Kennon, "College Wives Who Work," *Journal of the American Association of University Women* 20, 4 (1927).

16. Ethel Puffer Howes's unpublished study of married and unmarried Smith alumnae (1926), Smith College Archives. This study apparently remained in draft; I have found no completed analysis of the material. The college cohorts in the Howes as well as the Kennon study include graduates from the classes of the 1880s on to the early 1920s; but neither analyzed the statistics by birth cohort or year of college graduation.

17. Chase Going Woodhouse, "Married College Women."

18. Willa Player, "Improving College Education for Women at Bennett College" (Ed.D. diss., Columbia Teachers College, 1948).

19. Charles S. Johhnson, *The Negro College Graduate* (Chapel Hill, 1938). His study is based on material collected in the early 1930s. He found that 29.1 percent of the male graduates were unmarried.

20. Willa Player, "Improving College Education."

21. Information on black Radcliffe alumnae is derived from my analysis of the responses to the 1928 Radcliffe questionnaire. On Fisk women class of 1935, I refer to responses to my questionnaire. See note 26 below.

22. See Marion V. Cuthbert, *Education and Marginality: A Study of the Negro Woman College Graduate* (New York, 1942), on the strains of combining marriage and employment.

23. Lorine Pruette, *Women Workers Through the Depression* (New York, 1934), 17.

24. Mary Elizabeth Pidgeon, *Women in the Economy of the United States of America*. A Summary Report. Bulletin of the Women's Bureau (1937). Susan Kingsbury, "Economic Status of University Women in the United States," *Journal of the American Association of University Women* 32 (June 1939), 38ff.

25. Susan Kingsbury, "Economic Status of University Women."

26. Nine individuals from the Fisk class of 1935 responded to an informal personal inquiry that I sent out in 1977, confirming the necessity of employment. All had married professional men and all but one had children. I thank Aurelia W. Franklin for this information.

27. Questionnaires were sent out to 6,400 former students of Radcliffe College (including 2,112 special students). By June 1928, 3,567 women had responded.

28. See letter from Tamblyn and Brown to John Lowes, June 13, 1928, Radcliffe College Archives. Ada L. Comstock, in her last years as dean of Smith College, had been aware of the new questioning of restrictions on opportunities for the married college women. She backed Ethel Puffer Howes's Institute for the Coordination of Women's Interests at Smith College. Ada L. Comstock, "The Fourth R For Women," *Century Magazine* 142 (1929), 413.

29. Ernest R. Groves, "The Personality of the Wage Employment of Women Outside the Home and Their Social Consequences," *The Annals of the American Academy of Political and Social Science* 143 (May 1929), 339ff.

30. Agnes Rogers made an informal study among Vassar alumnae of 1937 that showed the same patterns and differences as at Radcliffe, with one group insisting that homemaking was sufficient and another group managing to combine homemaking with an outside career. On the debate, see Agnes Rogers, *Vassar Women: An Informal Study* (Poughkeepsie, N.Y., 1940). W. K. Jordan, *General Education at Radcliffe College* (Cambridge, Mass., 1945).

31. W. K. Jordan, *President's Report* (1946–47), 8–9, Radcliffe College Archives.

32. Anne Byrd Kennon, "College Wives Who Work," 100. Vera M. Dean, "Woman's Responsibilities in the Postwar World," *Radcliffe Quarterly* 27 (November 1943).

Chapter XII

1. Clara M. Thompson quoted in Jean Strouse, ed., *Women and Analysis: Dialogues on Psychoanalytic Views of Femininity* (New York, 1974), 266.

2. On "the recoil," see Alice C. Lloyd, "Women in the Postwar College," *The Journal of the American Association of University Women* 39 (Spring 1946), 132. See also Professor Margery Bailey, urging students to prepare for independence, *Stanford Daily* (January 13, 1947). Pro- and anti-ERA advocates wanted to introduce female undergraduates to their history. See Alma Lutz, "Women's History—Background for Citizenship," *The Journal of the American Association of University Women* 40 (Fall 1946). On Mary Beard's frustrated efforts to introduce college women to this history, see Ann Lane, ed., *Mary Ritter Beard: A Sourcebook* (New York, 1977), especially chapter 6. Maud Wood Park approached Radcliffe president W. K. Jordan about endowing a chair in women's history at Harvard and of course was rebuffed. See especially Janet Wilson James, *Changing Ideas About Women in the United States, 1776–1825* (New York, 1981), the introduction to which evokes very well the climate of opinion toward feminism and women's history in academia from the 1930s to the 1960s.

3. Susan M. Hartmann, *The Home Front and Beyond: American Women in the 1940s* (New York, 1982), 110; Barnard College, *President's Report* (1942).

4. For a discerning discussion, see Dorothy Schaffter, "Educational Implications of Women's Military Training," in *The Annals of the American Academy of Political and Social Sciences* 251, ed. Louise Young (May 1947). Susan M. Hartmann, *The Home Front*, 103–04. The Harvard/Radcliffe agreement of 1943 did not result in complete coeducational instruction until 1950.

5. Mabel Newcomer, *A Century of Higher Education*, 93. On academic personnel, see Susan M. Hartmann, *The Home Front*, 108. See also Daniel J. Kevles, *The Physicists: The History of a Scientific Community in Modern America* (New York, 1971), for a discussion of the limitations of women in the academic world of the late 1940s; see especially 370–71. I know that many of my classmates gained access to journalism and banking at low levels during the war, and some were able to sustain their positions afterward. On a different level, I cite the accomplishments of Mina Rees, a Hunter graduate of 1923, who obtained a Ph.D. from the University of Chicago in 1931 and went from a faculty position at Hunter College into the Office of Naval Research, where she headed the Mathematics branch and coordinated research on computers. After the war she rose to president of the graduate school of New York University. Anthropologist Ruth Benedict was called to Washington to work in the Office of War Information from 1943 to 1945; her work on race and culture was so highly valued by the government that in 1947 she received a grant from the Office of Naval Research to head a program of "Research in Contemporary Cultures." One result of this grant, made technically to Columbia, was that Benedict belatedly received a full professorship.

6. Susan M. Hartmann, *The Home Front*, chapter 6. See also Keith W. Olson, *The GI Bill, the Veterans and the Colleges* (Lexington, Ky., 1974), 104.

7. Susan M. Hartmann, *The Home Front*, 106–08, points out the effects of the GI bill on male black attendance. See also Jean W. Campbell, "Women Drop Back In: Educational Innovation in the Sixties," in *Academic Women on the Move*, ed. Alice S. Rossi and Ann Calderwood (New York, 1973).

8. See Susan M. Hartmann, *The Home Front*, on women dropouts in wartime.

9. As a graduate student starting in the forties and finishing in the early fifties, I observed the increasing restrictions on the admissions of women at Harvard and Radcliffe.

10. For graduate degree statistics, see table 6. For more detailed figures, see Pamela Roby, "Institutional Barriers to Women in Higher Education," in *Academic Women on the Move*, ed. Alice S. Rossi and Ann Calderwood, 40. On college enrollments, see Mabel Newcomer, *A Century of Higher Education*, 46. For a recent penetrating analysis of the data, see Susan Carter, "Academic Women Revisited," *Journal of Social History* 14 (Summer 1981). The numbers are cited in Eli Ginzberg, *Life-Styles of Educated Women* (New York, 1966), 10.

11. Christopher Jencks and David Riesman, *The Academic Revolution* (New York, 1969), 95, concluded that almost half of black undergraduates were attending predominantly white colleges by 1965.

12. Because of the smaller proportion of babies born during the Depression, there were fewer males to fill jobs in the expanding economy. Thus, women were needed in the labor force.

13. Robert Foster and Pauline Park Wilson, *Women After College: A Study of the Effectiveness of Their Education* (New York, 1942), 48–50, passim. See also the results of Barnard alumnae questionnaires of 1948. Willa Player, "Improving College Education for Women at Bennett College" (Ed.D. diss., Columbia Teachers College, 1948). Jeanne L. Noble, *The Negro Woman's College Education* (New York, 1956).

14. Lynn White, *Educating Our Daughters* (New York, 1950), 10, 48, 78. Margaret Mead, *Male and Female: A Study of the Sexes in a Changing World* (New York, 1949), 35. Several

Radcliffe alumnae, independently of each other, recalled President Jordan's remarks on their marrying of Harvard men.

15. Harold Taylor is quoted in Mabel Newcomer, *A Century of Higher Education*, 61–62. Rosemund Tuve, "AAUW Fellows and Their Survival," *Journal of the American Association of University Women* 44 (Summer 1951), 106.

16. Millicent McIntosh is quoted in *Newsweek* (October 5, 1951), 7. See Katharine McBride, "What is Women's Education?" in *The Annals of the American Academy* 251, ed. Louise M. Young (May 1947), 148. Although McBride stated that "where women go beyond the home at all, their education can no more follow a single pattern than can education for men," her essay has a tone of carefulness and avoidance of a strong stand.

17. Mirra Komarovsky, *Women in the Modern World: Their Education and Their Dilemmas* (Boston, 1953), 12.

18. Helene Deutsch is quoted in Katharine McBride, "What is Women's Education?" Ferdinand Lundberg and Maryna Farnham, *Modern Woman: The Lost Sex* (New York, 1947).

19. Nancy P. Weiss, "Mother, The Invention of Necessity: Dr. Benjamin Spock's *Baby and Child Care*," *American Quarterly* 29 (Winter 1977). Benjamin Spock, *Baby and Child Care* (New York, 1957). Ironically, throughout the period another critic of women, Philip Wylie, attacked momism in *A Generation of Vipers* (New York, 1942).

20. *Barnard Bulletin* (January 11, 1951), 2, quoted in Susan Romer Kaplan, "Roots of Ambivalence: College-Educated Women, 1945–1963" (seminar paper for Professor Paula S. Fass, University of California, Berkeley), courtesy of Professor Fass. See Judith Kroll, "Sylvia Plath," in *Notable American Women*, IV, on Plath's desire to appear "the well-rounded American girl." Sylvia Plath (pseudonym Victoria Lucas) wrote about her years at Smith College in the 1950s in *The Bell Jar* (London, 1963).

21. Rona Jaffee, *The Best of Everything* (New York, 1958). Anonymous comments of a Radcliffe alumna, "The Flat Fifties," Radcliffe College Archives. For other examples of the educated young woman, see Herman Wouk, *Marjorie Morningstar* (New York, 1955), and Phillip Roth, *Good-Bye, Columbus* (New York, 1959). The place of women in the novels of the 1950s is beginning to attract attention as a subject of analysis. On the negative view of the single woman, see David Riesman's perceptive comment mentioned in Mervin B. Freedman, "Studies of College Alumni," in *The American College: A Psychological and Social Interpretation of Education*, ed. Nevitt Sanford (New York, 1962), 878.

22. On the age of marrying and on college dropouts, see Mabel Newcomer, *A Century of Higher Education*, 214–15. Mervin B. Freedman, "Studies of College Alumni." Alice S. Rossi, "Barriers to the Career Choice of Engineering, Medicine, or Science Among American Women," in *Women and the Scientific Professions*, ed. Jacqueline Mattfield and Carol Van Aken (Cambridge, Mass., 1965), 57.

23. "My Wife Works and I Like It," *Life* 41 (December 1956). In contrast to this feature, *Life* more often included articles promoting domesticty.

24. Mabel Newcomer, *A Century of Higher Education*, 179.

25. See Eli Ginzberg and Alice M. Yohalem, *Educated American Women: Self-Portraits* (New York, 1966), on the social origins of academic women achievers and the fellowships they received. See also Eli Ginzberg, *Life-Styles of Educated Women* (New York, 1966). In the same context see Cynthia Fuchs Epstein, "Positive Effects of the Multiple Negative: Explaining the Success of Black Professional Women," in *Changing Women in a Changing Society*, ed. Joan Huber (Chicago, 1973).

26. On family influences on achieving women in the fifties and early sixties, see Diana Grossman Kahn, "Lessons of Their Mothers' Lives: Imitation and Avoidance by Contemporary College Women," *International Journal of Women's Studies* 5 (January–

February 1982). Kahn makes points about both positive and negative role models mothers can offer, as well as the way in which mothers can be positive influences even when they are not role models.

27. Mildred Dresselhaus, "Electrical Engineer" in *Successful Women in the Sciences: An Analysis of Determinants*, ed. Ruth Kundsin (New York, 1973).

28. Gertrude Texeira Hunter, "Pediatrician," in *Successful Women*, ed. Ruth Kundsin.

29. Nevitt Sanford, "Is College Education Wasted on Women?" *Ladies Home Journal* 74 (May 1957), noted with approval that feminism was dead, at the same time that he deplored the limited intellectual interests of Vassar students. On Mary Ellen Chase, see "The American Woman: Her Achievements and Her Troubles." For intelligent recognition of the problem, see American Council on Education, *How Fare American Women* (Washington, D.C., 1955); also the National Manpower Council, *Womanpower* (New York, 1957).

30. James A. Davis, *Great Aspirations: The Graduate School Plans of American College Seniors* (Chicago, 1964).

31. Ibid.

32. Alice S. Rossi, "Barriers to the Career Choice," see especially 126–27.

33. U.S. Department of Labor, *College Women: Seven Years After Graduation* (1964). See discussion of this survey in Caroline Bird, *Born Female: The High Cost of Keeping Women Down* (New York, 1968), 188–89. The 1964 survey of 1957 college graduates contrasted with a 1958 survey of college women graduating in that year; the 1958 graduates expressed little interest in long-range plans to work. Women's Bureau, *First Jobs of College Women*, bulletin 268 (Washington, D.C., 1959), 41, 44, quoted in Valerie K. Oppenheimer, *The Female Labor Force in the United States: Demographic and Economic Factors Governing Its Growth and Changing Composition* (Westport, Conn., 1970), 112. On the doctorate, see Helen Astin, *The Woman Doctorate in America* (New York, 1969).

34. On schoolteachers, see Valerie K. Oppenheimer, *The Female Labor Force*, 131. On Barnard College, see Robert McCaughey, *A Statistical Profile of the Barnard Faculty 1900–1974*, cited in Patricia A. Graham, "Expansion and Exclusion." Moreover, a biographical survey of women doctors by Regina Morantz shows that the percentage who married rose between 1900 and 1960, sometimes to as much as 50 percent. See discussion by Joan Jacobs Brumberg and Nancy Tomes, "Women in the Professions: A Research Agenda for American Historians," *Reviews in American History* 5 (June 1982), which likewise shows that the marital rate of women doctors rose substantially between 1900 and 1960. Similarly, Cynthia Fuchs Epstein, *Women's Place: Options and Limits in Professional Careers* (Berkeley, 1970), documents this rising percentage; see Epstein's table on the marital status of women lawyers, scientists, engineers and doctors, 97. Frank Stricker speculates on this changing trend in "Cookbooks and Law Books: The Hidden History of Career Women in Twentieth-Century America," *Journal of Social History* 10 (Fall 1976). In 1940, only a small number of women over thirty-five worked; but by 1960, as much as 37 percent of the female labor force was over thirty-five; see Valerie K. Oppenheimer, *The Female Labor Force*, 19.

35. On the founding of the Radcliffe Institute for Independent Study, see *New York Times Magazine*, November 20, 1960; *Harvard Crimson*, November 21, 1960; and "The Radcliffe Institute for Independent Study," brochure (November 1960). Significantly, institute fellowships were part-time appointments that carried $3,000 stipends, and it was acceptable to use these for child-care expenses.

36. Betty Friedan's Notes in analysis of interviews with Smith College class of 1942, in Friedan Papers, Schlesinger Library (Radcliffe). Betty Friedan, *The Feminine Mystique* (New York, 1963). Alice S. Rossi in *The Woman in America*, ed. Robert Lifton (Boston, 1965).

37. On these national women's organizations, see William H. Chafe, *The American Woman:*

Her Changing Social, Economic, and Political Roles, 1920–1970 (New York, 1972). On the increasing momentum for the ERA in the 1950s, I benefited from Blanche Linden's paper at the 1981 Berkshire conference. It is well known that the President's Commission on the Status of Women was intended to divert attention from the ERA. See the report and recommendations of the commission in *American Women: The Report of the President's Commission on the Status of Women*, ed. Margaret Mead and Frances Kaplan (New York, 1965). On NOW's adoption of the ERA in 1968 and not earlier, my source is Frances Kolb, who is writing a history on NOW's early years.

38. On the civil rights movement, see William H. Chafe, *Civilities and Civil Rights: Greensboro, North Carolina, and the Black Struggle for Freedom* (New York, 1980). When no one else would give Reverend Martin Luther King a place to speak, Bennett's president Willa Player did not hesitate to open the school's chapel to him. Bennett students again participated in a live civil rights tradition. I am grateful to William Chafe for sharing his oral interview with Willa Player. See William H. Chafe, *Civilities and Civil Rights*, 80.

39. Sara Evans provides an important account in *Personal Politics: The Roots of Women's Liberation in the Civil Rights Movement and the New Left* (New York, 1979). Jo Freeman, *The Politics of Women's Liberation* (New York, 1975), elaborates on her excellent article "The Origins of the Women's Liberation Movement" in *Changing Women in a Changing Society*, ed. Joan Huber (Chicago, 1973).

40. There are several accounts of the rising resentments expressed by black and white women; in addition to Jo Freeman, *The Politics of Women's Liberation*, and Sara Evans, *Personal Politics*, see Clayborne Carson, *In Struggle: SNNC and the Black Awakening of the 1960s* (Cambridge, Mass., 1981), 148.

41. For an excellent example of shared consciousness raising, see Sara Ruddick and Pamela Daniels, eds., *Working it Out: 23 Women Writers, Artists, Scientists, and Scholars Talk About Their Lives and Work* (New York, 1977).

42. Newspapers like the *New York Times* have documented the coeducational movements in the 1970s. See Bob Packard, "Discrimination Aided," *New York Times*, April 20, 1984. Patricia S. Griffin, " 'But She's So Feminine': Changing Mixed Messages We Give to Girls and Women in Sports," *Journal of the National Association for Women Deans, Administrators, and Counselors* 47 (Winter 1984).

43. From the wealth of material on women's studies, see Hunter College Women's Studies Collective, *Women's Realities, Women's Choices: An Introduction to Women's Studies* (New York, 1983). Walter Goodman, "Women's Studies: The Debate Continues," *New York Times*, April 22, 1984, notes that 150 colleges offer B.A.s in women's studies, 60 have M.A. programs, and 12 have Ph.D. programs in women's studies.

44. On the historical background of the community college, see Arthur M. Cohen and Florence B. Brawer, *The American Community College* (San Francisco, 1982), 6–10, 204.

45. Mary Lou Randour, Georgia L. Strasbourg, and Jean Lipman-Blumen, "Women in Higher Education: Trends in Enrollments and Degrees Earned," *Harvard Educational Review* 52 (1982).

46. Marcia René, oral interview with Barbara M. Solomon (July 19, 1983); Barbara Murphy and Victoria Viera, oral interviews with Maida E. Solomon (June 5 and June 23, 1983, respectively). I benefited from conversations with Brunetta Wolfman (president) and William Thompson of Roxbury Community College, as well as with Erna Koch, a graduate of Cape Cod Community College. It is of interest that Smith College is recruiting older women to be undergraduates; see Janice Castro, "Cultivating Late Bloomers," *Time* 122 (November 21, 1983).

47. National Center for Education Statistics, *Digest of Education Statistics*, 1982.

Afterthoughts

1. David Starr Jordan, "The Question of Coeducation," *Munsey's Magazine* 34 (March 1906).
2. Noted in Alice S. Rossi, "Educating Women and Men Together: Coeducation in a Gender-Stratified Society," keynote address to the National Conference on Coeducation: Past, Present, and Future. Sesquicentennial celebration at Oberlin College, Ohio, March 11–13, 1983.
3. Carnegie Commission on Higher Education, *Priorities for Action. Final Report* (New York, 1973), 52.
4. See M. Elizabeth Tidball, "Perspective on Academic Women and Affirmative Action," *Educational Record* 54 (Spring 1973), and other related papers cited in Mary Oates and Susan Williamson, "Women's Colleges and Women Achievers," *Signs: Journal of Women in Culture and Society* 3 (Summer 1978). See also response to Oates and Williamson in M. Elizabeth Tidball, "Women's Colleges and Women Achievers Revisited," *Signs* 5 (Spring 1980). See Mary Oates and Susan Williamson, "Comment on Tidball's 'Women's Colleges and Women Achievers Revisited,' " *Signs* 6 (Winter 1980). Finally, see the important article of M. Elizabeth Tidball and Vera Kistiakowsky, "Baccalaureate Origins of American Scientists and Scholars," *Science* 193 (August 20, 1976).
5. Adrienne Rich, "Toward a Woman-Centered University," in *On Lies, Secrets, and Silences: Selected Prose 1966–1978* (New York, 1979), 125–55.
6. Mirra Komarovsky, "Cultural Contradictions and Sex Roles: The Masculine Case," *Changing Women in a Changing Society*, ed. Joan Huber (Chicago, 1973).
7. There is an enormous array of newspaper articles trying to assess the attitudes of young college-educated women and offering advice to them. See, for example, Barnard president Ellen Futter and opera singer Beverly Sills speaking to commencing seniors, in the *New York Times*, May 14, 1981. See the results of contradictory polls; "Many Young Women Now Say They'd Pick Family Over Career," *New York Times*, December 28, 1980, and "Many Women in Poll Equate Values of Job and Family Life," *New York Times*, December 4, 1983. See also the *Boston Globe*, January 3, 1981, in which Burton L. White, expert in educational psychology and a "skeptic on substitute baby care," refers to a recent survey of three thousand college students at Barnard, Brown, Dartmouth, Princeton, Wellesley, and the State University of Stony Brook which shows that "77 percent of the women (and 84 percent of the men) believed mother should not work at all or only work part-time until their children are five."
8. University of Chicago president Hanna Holborn Gray has spoken discriminatingly about the choices and constraints of college women of the seventies and eighties; see "What About Women at Yale," in *The Radcliffe Quarterly* 62, 3 (September 1976). For an excellent presentation on the different choices women make over the course of their lives, see Pamela J. Perun and Janet Giele, "Life After College: The Historical Links Between Education and Women's Work," in *The Undergraduate Women: Issues in Educational Equity*, ed. Pamela J. Perun (Lexington, Mass., 1982).
9. On Sally Ride's academic background, see the *New York Times*, June 18, 1983. Ms. Ride received a Ph.D. in astrophysics in 1977 and started astronaut training in 1978. On Sandra Day O'Connor's appointment as a Supreme Court Justice, see *New York Times* July 7 and September 22, 1981. See Theodore H. White's commentary on women in politics, "New Powers, New Politics," *New York Times Magazine*, Feburary 5, 1984.
10. Eleanor Roosevelt, "Women in Politics," *Good Housekeeping Magazine* 110 (January, March, and April 1940).

Note on Sources

The 1980s have witnessed a renaissance in women's educational history; but when I started research for this book, the subject attracted few scholars. It was not that the history of education was an untrodden field; rather that the many volumes usually ignored the presence of women in higher education. Barbara Cross's introduction to an anthology of selected writings *The Educated Woman in America* (1965) was a harbinger of the greater interest soon to come of scholars viewing female education within the contexts of feminist consciousness and women's history. Exploring women's education in the 1970s, I found stimulus in Patricia Graham's "So Much To Do: Guides for Historical Research on Women in Higher Education," and Jill Conway's "Perspectives on the History of Women's Education in the United States."

My book builds on Thomas Woody's pioneering work (1929) and Mabel Newcomer's study for the Vassar centennial (1959). Woody's two massive volumes covered the founding of institutions—from dame schools to colleges—and offered a richness of detail not provided elsewhere. Newcomer gave an economist's statistical presentation focusing on women's colleges and concluded with a thoughtful discussion of women's education in the 1950s.

While Woody and Newcomer emphasized institutional perspectives, I place women, as students and graduates, at the center of my book. The recent studies of Linda Kerber, Mary Beth Norton, Anne Firor Scott, and Kathryn Kish Sklar were crucial in reviewing the origins of women's access to liberal arts education. Their work reinforced my belief in the importance of academy education for nineteenth-century female students. By the end of my project, I had unearthed institutional records of academies which deserve utilization by scholars.

Institutional histories of colleges and universities were, of course, essential sources; even anecdotal or unsystematic accounts conveyed what mattered to a particular institution at a given time. Among the most solid in this category are Arthur C. Cole on Mount Holyoke, Robert Fletcher on Oberlin, Winton Solberg on the University of Illinois, and Merle Curti and Vernon Carstensen on the University of Wisconsin. As early as 1909 Helen Olin set out to redress the male bias in educational history with a lively account of women at the state University of Wisconsin. Similarly, contemporary academic studies by Dorothy McGuigan on Michigan and Charlotte Conable on Cornell provide needed emphasis on women's experience at coeducational institutions. However, recent intellectual and social interpretations in studies of men's higher education proved germane for comparative purposes. Although women are marginal in the writings of Laurence Veysey, Frederick Rudolph, Hugh Hawkins, and George Peterson, their work provides historical background on the academic environments that affected women students directly or indirectly. In a different category, Peter Filene's *Him/Her Self* offers an innovative introduction to the study of sex roles in modern America.

College archives provided varied sources of published and unpublished material for the exploration of student and graduate perspectives. I made use as much as possible of autobiographies, memoirs, letters, and diaries, as well as novels and films. While poking about in institutional records, I was also fortunate in locating personal accounts of social, religious, ethnic, and racial groups largely overlooked in histories of women's education.

A wealth of periodical literature proved relevant. I found the *New York Times* a helpful indicator of shifts in public opinion in the late twentieth century. And in following educational trends, government documents, as indicated in the endnotes, provided critical information. I consulted the files of many college magazines. Also essential were the publications of the Association of Collegiate Alumnae, and the American Association of University Women.

Especially informative were *Crisis Magazine* and the papers and journal of the National Association of College Women, an organization of black college alumnae active in the 1920s and 1930s; its files are in the archives at Howard University. On the place of black women in higher education, earlier doctoral studies of Marion Cuthbert, Willa Player, and Jeanne Noble remain valuable. In additon, the *Journal of Negro Education* is an important resource. The latter journal devoted its summer 1983 issue to "The Impact of Black Women in Education."

On higher education in the South for white and black women, the appendix to *Stepping Off the Pedestal* (1982), edited by Patricia Stringer and Irene Thompson, lists important sources for research. A selected bibliography on black women prepared by Janet L. Sims at the Moorland-Spingarn Research Center is useful.

Historical scholarship on Catholic women's colleges is under way as well. Good starting points on this subject are the doctoral thesis of Mary Friel and recent publications by Karen Kennelly. In addition, Mary Oates's study of Catholic sisters in Massachusetts introduces another dimension for understanding Catholic women's education.

For twentieth-century women of diverse backgrounds, I found oral history interviews rewarding; excellent collections are available at the Bancroft Library, University of California; the Schlesinger Library, Radcliffe College; the University of Wisconsin; Fisk University; and Wellesley College. In addition to interviews cited in the endnotes of this book, I conducted personal, informal interviews with friends and strangers, with students and graduates, all educated in different generations.

As this book was evolving, I made several investigations that are incorporated in particular chapters: namely, an analysis of the role of schoolteaching in the lives of women achievers in the first three volumes of *Notable Amerian Women,* analyses of Radcliffe Alumnae Questionnaires of 1928 and 1944, and a study based on an informal questionnaire sent in 1977 to women graduates of Fisk University, class of 1935. These and other materials relating to Radcliffe/ Harvard students will be made available to qualified researchers at the Schlesinger Library, Radcliffe College.

My commments would be incomplete without taking note of younger scholars who are breaking new ground in the educational history of women. I was well along in my work when Rosalind Rosenberg's *Beyond Separate Spheres* appeared. This brilliant monograph on the origins of the modern study of sex differences captures the intellectual climate at the research universities that women attended at the turn of the century. Another original scholarly work is Margaret W. Rossiter's *Women Scientists in America*. These books and others referred to in my book have important bibliographies. Several excellent doctoral theses cited in my bibliography foreshadow a rich harvest of future scholarship.

The following bibliography does not begin to cover the multiple sources that have shaped my understanding of this subject over years of research, thinking, and writing about American social and intellectual history.

Selected Bibliography

Books and Dissertations

Abbott, Edith. *Women in Industry: A Study in American Economic History*. New York: D. Appleton, 1918.

Addams, Jane. *Democracy and Social Ethics*. Edited by Anne Firor Scott. Cambridge, Mass.: Harvard University Press, 1964.

———. *The Second Twenty Years of Hull House*. New York: Macmillan, 1930.

———. *Twenty Years at Hull House*. New York: Macmillan, 1910. Reprint, 1960.

Ahlstrom, Sydney E. *A Religious History of the American People*. New Haven: Yale University Press, 1972.

Akers, Charles W. *Abigail Adams: An American Woman*. Boston: Little, Brown, 1980.

Allen, Florence. *To Do Justly*. Cleveland, Ohio: The Press of Western Reserve University, 1965.

Angell, James B. *Reminiscences*. New York: Longmans, Green, 1912.

Anthony, Susan B. et al. *History of Woman Suffrage*. Rochester: Fowler and Wells, 1881.

Antin, Mary. *The Promised Land*. Boston: Houghton Mifflin, 1912.

———. *From Plotzk to Boston*. Boston: W. B. Clarke, 1899.

Antler, Joyce. "The Educated Woman and Professionalization: The Struggle for a New Feminine Identity, 1890–1920." Ph.D. dissertation, State University of New York, Stony Brook, 1977.

Association of Collegiate Alumnae. *A Preliminary Statistical Study of Certain Women College Graduates: Dealing With the Health, Marriage, Children, Occupations of Women Graduating Between 1869 and 1898 And Their Sisters and Brothers*. Bryn Mawr, Pa., 1917.

Astin, Helen. *The Woman Doctorate in America*. New York: Russell Sage Foundation, 1969.

Ault, Warren O. *Boston University: The College of Liberal Arts, 1873–1973*. Boston: Trustees of Boston University, 1973.

Austin, Corey G. *A Century of Religion at the University of Michigan.* Ann Arbor: University of Michigan Press, 1957.

Bailyn, Bernard. *Education in the Forming of American Society.* Chapel Hill: University of North Carolina Press, 1960.

Baker, Liva. *I'm Radcliffe! Fly Me!* New York: Macmillan, 1976.

Balch, Emily Greene. *Occupied Haiti.* New York: Writers Publishing Co., 1927.

———. *Our Slavic Fellow Citizens.* New York: Charities Publication Committee, 1910.

Banner, Lois W. *American Beauty: A Social History . . . through Two Centuries of the American Idea, Ideal, and Image of the Beautiful Woman.* New York: Random House, 1983.

Barnard, John. *From Evangelicalism to Progressivism at Oberlin College, 1866–1917.* Columbus: Ohio State University Press, 1969.

Baym, Nina. *Woman's Fiction: A Guide to Novels by and about Women in America, 1820–1870.* Ithaca, N.Y.: Cornell University Press, 1978.

Becker, Carl L. *Cornell University: Founders and the Founding.* Ithaca, N.Y.: Cornell University Press, 1943.

Benson, Mary S. *Women in Eighteenth-Century America: A Study of Opinion and Social Usage.* New York: Columbia University, 1935.

Berkin, Carol Ruth, and Norton, Mary Beth, eds. *Women of America: A History.* Boston: Houghton Mifflin, 1979.

Bernard, Jessie. *Academic Women.* University Park: Pennsylvania State University Press, 1964.

Bevier, Isabel. *Home Economics in Education.* Philadelphia: Lippincott, 1924.

Biklen, Sari Knopp, and Branigan, Marilyn B., eds. *Women and Educational Leadership.* Lexington, Mass.: Lexington Books, 1980.

Bird, Caroline. *Born Female: The High Cost of Keeping Women Down.* New York: D. McKay, 1968.

———. *The Invisible Scar.* New York: D. McKay, 1966.

Birney, Catherine H. *The Grimké Sisters: Sarah and Angelina Grimké: The First American Women Advocates of Abolition and Woman's Rights.* Boston: Lee and Shepard, 1885.

Bishop, Morris. *A History of Cornell.* Ithaca, N.Y.: Cornell University Press, 1962.

Blair, Karen. *The Clubwoman as Feminist: True Womanhood Redefined, 1868–1914.* New York: Holmes and Meier, 1980.

Blandin, Isabel M. *History of Higher Education of Women in the South Prior to 1870.* New York: Neale, 1909.

Bledstein, Burton J. *The Culture of Professionalism: The Middle Class and The Development of Higher Education in America.* New York: Norton, 1976.

Boas, Louise Schultz. *Women's Education Begins: The Rise of The Women's Colleges.* Norton, Mass.: Wheaton College Press, 1935. Reprint. New York: Arno Press, 1971.

Bolton, Ina. "Problems of Negro College Women Graduates." Ph.D. dissertation, University of California, 1946.

Bolzau, Emma Lydia. *Almira Hart Lincoln Phelps, Her Life and Work.* Philadelphia: Science Press, 1936.

Boorstin, Daniel J. *The Lost World of Thomas Jefferson.* New York: Henry Holt, 1948.

Bordin, Ruth. *Woman and Temperance: The Quest for Power and Liberty, 1873–1900.* Philadelphia: Temple University Press, 1981.

Bowen, Eliza Southgate. *A Girl's Life Eighty Years Ago: Selections from the Letters of Mrs. Eliza Southgate Bowen.* New York: Arno Press, 1974.

Bowler, Mary M. *A History of Catholic Colleges for Women in the United States.* Washington, D.C.: Catholic University of America Press, 1933.

Boyd, Julian P., ed. *The Papers of Thomas Jefferson.* 21 vols. Princeton: Princeton University Press, 1950. Vol. 6, 1952.

Bradstreet, Anne. *The Works of Anne Bradstreet.* Edited by Jeannine Hensley. Cambridge, Mass.: Harvard University Press, 1967.

Brickley, Lynn T. "Female Academies Are Everywhere Establishing the Beginnings of Secondary Education for Women in the United States, 1790–1830: A Review of the Literature." Qualifying paper, Harvard University School of Education, 1983.

Brissot de Warville, Jacques Pierre. *New Travels in the United States of America: 1788.* Edited by Durand Echeverria. Cambridge, Mass.: Harvard University Press, 1964.

Brown, Charles Brockden. *Alcuin: A Dialogue.* 1798. Reprint. New Haven: C. and Margaret Rollins, 1935.

Bruccoli, Matthew J.; Smith, Scottie Fitzgerald; and Kerr, Joan P., eds. *The Romantic Egoists: Scott and Zelda Fitzgerald.* New York: Scribner, 1974.

Buhle, Mari Jo, and Buhle, Paul, eds. *The Concise History of Woman Suffrage: Selections from the Classic Work of Stanton, Anthony, Gage, and Harper.* Urbana, Ill.: University of Illinois Press, 1978.

Burke, Colin B. *American Collegiate Populations: A Test of the Traditional View.* New York: New York University Press, 1982.

Bushman, Richard et al., eds. *Uprooted Americans: Essays to Honor Oscar Handlin.* Boston: Little, Brown, 1979.

Butterfield, L. H. et al., eds. *Adams Family Correspondence.* 2 vols. Cambridge, Mass.: Harvard University Press, 1963.

Carnegie Commission on Higher Education, *Priorities for Action. Final Report.* New York, 1973.

Carroll, Berenice A., ed. *Liberating Women's History.* Urbana, Ill.: University of Illinois Press, 1976.

Carson, Clayborne. *In Struggle: SNCC and the Black Awakening of the 1960s.* Cambridge, Mass.: Harvard University Press, 1981.

Chafe, William H. *The American Woman: Her Changing Social, Economic and Political Roles, 1920–1970.* New York: Oxford University Press, 1972.

———. *Civilities and Civil Rights: Greensboro, North Carolina, and the Black Struggle for Freedom.* New York: Oxford University Press, 1980.

Cheyney, Edward Potts. *History of the University of Pennsylvania, 1740–1940.* Philadelphia: University of Pennsylvania Press, 1940.

Clarke, Edward H. *Sex in Education; Or, a Fair Chance for the Girls.* Boston: Osgood, 1873.

Cohen, Arthur M., and Brawer, Florence B. *The American Community College*. San Francisco: Josse-Bass, 1982.

Cole, Arthur C. *A Hundred Years of Mount Holyoke College: The Evolution of an Educational Ideal*. New Haven: Yale University Press, 1940.

Collier, Virginia M. *Marriage and Careers*. New York: The Channel Bookshop, 1926.

Conable, Charlotte W. *Women at Cornell: The Myth of Equal Education*. Ithaca, N.Y.: Cornell University Press, 1977.

Conrad, Susan P. *Perish the Thought: Intellectual Women in Romantic America, 1830–1860*. New York: Oxford University Press, 1976.

Cook, Blanche Wiesen, ed. *Crystal Eastman: On Women and Revolution*. New York: Oxford University Press, 1978.

Cooper, Anna Julia Haywood. *A Voice From the South by a Black Woman of the South*. New York: Negro University Press, 1892.

Cornelius, Roberta D. *The History of Randolph-Macon Woman's College: From the Founding in 1891 through 1949–50*. Chapel Hill: University of North Carolina Press, 1951.

Cott, Nancy F. *The Bonds of Womanhood: "Woman's Sphere" in New England, 1780–1835*. New Haven: Yale University Press, 1977.

Cott, Nancy F., ed. *Root of Bitterness: Documents of the Social History of American Women*. New York: E. P. Dutton, 1972.

Crawford, Mary Caroline. *The College Girl of America*. Boston: L. C. Page, 1905.

Cremin, Lawrence A. *American Education: The Colonial Experience, 1607–1783*. New York: Harper and Row, 1980.

———. *American Education: The National Experience 1783–1876*. New York: Harper and Row, 1980.

Cronin, James E., ed. *The Diary of Elihu Hubbard Smith*. Philadelphia: American Philosophical Society, 1973.

Cross, Barbara, ed. *The Educated Woman in America*. New York: Teachers College Press, Columbia University, 1965.

Cummins, Maria. *Mabel Vaughn*. Boston: Crosby, Nichols, 1857.

Curti, Merle, and Carstensen, Vernon. *The University of Wisconsin: A History, 1848–1925*. 2 vols. Madison Wis.: University of Wisconsin Press, 1949.

Cuthbert, Marion V. *Education and Marginality: A Study of The Negro Woman College Graduate*. New York: American Book-Stratford, 1942.

Dabney, Charles William. *Universal Education in the South*. 2 vols. New York: Arno Press, 1969.

Davis, Allen F. *American Heroine: The Life and Legend of Jane Addams*. New York: Oxford University Press, 1973.

———. *Spearheads for Reform: The Social Settlements and the Progressive Movement, 1890–1914*. New York: Oxford University Press, 1967.

Davis, Allen F., and McCree, Mary Lynn, eds. *Eighty Years at Hull House*. Chicago: Quadrangle Books, 1969.

Davis, James A. *Great Aspirations: The Graduate School Plans of American College Seniors*. Chicago: Aldine, 1964.

Davis, Katherine Bement. *Factors in the Sex Life of Twenty-two Hundred Women*. New York: Harper, 1929.

Deutrich, Mabel E. and Purdy, Virginia C., eds. *Clio was a Woman: Studies in the History of American Women*. Washington, D.C.: Howard University Press, 1980.

DeVane, William Clyde. *Higher Education in Twentieth Century America*. Cambridge, Mass.: Harvard University Press, 1965.

Devine, Edward, and Van Kleeck, Mary. *Positions in Social Work*. New York: The New York School of Philanthropy, 1916.

Dexter, Elisabeth A. *Colonial Women of Affairs*. Boston: Houghton Mifflin, 1924.

Dobkin, Marjorie H., ed. *The Making of a Feminist: Early Journals and Letters of M. Carey Thomas*. Kent, Ohio: Kent State University Press, 1979.

Dublin, Thomas. *Women at Work: The Transformation of Work and Community in Lowell, Massachusetts, 1826–1860*. New York: Columbia University Press, 1979.

Duffey, Eliza B. *No Sex in Education; Or, An Equal Chance for Both Girls and Boys*. Philadelphia: J. M. Stoddart, 1874.

Dunn, Esther Cloudman. *Pursuit of Understanding*. New York: Macmillan, 1945.

Dwight, S. E. *The Life of President Edwards*. New York: G. and C. and H. Carvill, 1830.

Dwight, Timothy. *Travels in New England and New York*. Edited by Barbara Miller Solomon. Cambridge, Mass.: Harvard University Press, 1969.

Dye, Marie, ed. *History of the Department of Home Economics at the University of Chicago*. Chicago, 1972.

Edwards, Jonathan. *A Narrative of Many Surprising Conversions . . . 1736 Together with Some Thoughts on the Revival of England . . . 1740*. Worcester, Mass.: Moses W. Grant, 1832.

Egan, Eileen. *Class, Culture, and the Classroom: The Student Peace Movement of the 1930s*. Philadelphia: Temple University Press, 1981.

Elliot, C. W. *Stanford University: The First Twenty-five Years*. Stanford, Calif.: Stanford University Press, 1937.

Emerson, Joseph. *Female Education: A Discourse Delivered at the Dedication of the Seminary Hall in Saugus, January 15, 1822*. Boston: S. T. Armstrong and Crocker and Brewster, 1822.

Emerson, Ralph Waldo. *The Complete Works of Ralph Waldo Emerson*. II. Boston: Houghton Mifflin, 1904.

Epstein, Barbara. *The Politics of Domesticity: Women, Evangelism, and Temperance in Nineteenth-Century America*. Middletown, Conn.: Wesleyan University Press, 1981.

Epstein, Cynthia Fuchs. *Woman's Place: Options and Limits in Professional Careers*. Berkeley: University of California Press, 1970.

———. *Women in Law*. New York: Basic Books, 1981.

Etzione, Amitai. *The Semi-Professions and Their Organizations*. New York: Free Press, 1969.

Evans, John W. *The Newman Movement: Roman Catholics in American Higher Education, 1883–1971*. Notre Dame, Ind.: University of Notre Dame Press, 1980.

Evans, Sara. *Personal Politics: The Roots of Women's Liberation in the Civil Rights Movement and the New Left*. New York: Random House, 1979.

Fairbanks, Mrs. A. W. *Mrs. Emma Willard and Her Pupils, or Fifty Years of the Troy Female Seminary, 1822–1872*. New York: Mrs. R. Sage, 1898.

Fairchild, James H. *Oberlin: The Colony and The College, 1833–1883*. Oberlin,

Ohio: E. J. Goodrich, 1883.

Fass, Paula S. *The Damned and the Beautiful: American Youth in the 1920s.* New York: Oxford University Press, 1977.

Ferrand, Elizabeth M. *History of the University of Michigan.* Ann Arbor: University of Michigan Press, 1885.

Ferrier, William W. *Origin and Development of the University of California.* Berkeley: University Press, 1930.

Fields, Mamie Garvin, and Fields, Karen. *Yellow Swamp and Other Places: A Carolina Memoir.* New York: The Free Press, 1983.

Filene, Peter G. *Him/Her Self: Sex Roles in Modern America.* New York: Harcourt, Brace, Jovanovich, 1975.

Finch, Edith. *Carey Thomas of Bryn Mawr.* New York: Harper and Row, 1947.

Fisher, Dorothy Canfield, *The Bent Twig.* New York: Grosset and Dunlap, 1917.

Fisk, Fidelia. *Recollections of Mary Lyon with Selections From Her Instructions to the Pupils in Mount Holyoke Female Seminary.* Boston: American Tract Society, 1886.

Fitzpatrick, Ellen. "Academics and Activists: Women Social Scientists and the Impulse for Reform, 1890–1920." Ph.D. dissertation, Brandeis University, 1981.

Fletcher, Robert. *A History of Oberlin College from its Foundation through the Civil War.* 2 vols. Oberlin, Ohio: Oberlin College Press, 1943.

Flexner, Eleanor. *Century of Struggle.* Cambridge, Mass.: Belknap Press of Harvard University Press, 1975.

Foster, Robert, and Wilson, Pauline Park. *Women After College: A Study of the Effectiveness of Their Education.* New York: Columbia University Press, 1942.

Frankfort, Roberta. *Collegiate Women: Domesticity and Career in Turn-of-the Century America.* New York: New York University Press, 1977.

Freedman, Estelle. *Their Sisters' Keepers: Women's Prison Reform in America, 1830–1930.* Ann Arbor: University of Michigan Press, 1981.

Freeman, Jo. *The Politics of Women's Liberation.* New York: McKay, 1975.

Friedan, Betty. *The Feminine Mystique.* New York: Norton, 1963.

Friel, Mary. "The History of Emmanuel College, 1919–1974." Ph.D. dissertation, Boston College, 1979.

Fuller, Margaret. *Essays on American Life and Letters.* Edited by Joel Myerson. New Haven: College and University Press, 1978.

Gildersleeve, Virginia. *Many A Good Crusade.* New York: Macmillan, 1954.

Ginzberg, Eli. *Life-Styles of Educated Women.* New York: Columbia University Press, 1966.

Ginzberg, Eli, and Yohalem, Alice M. *Educated American Women: Self-Portraits.* New York: Columbia University Press, 1966.

Goetsch, Helen Bertha. *Parental Income and College Opportunities.* New York: Teachers College, Columbia University, 1940.

The Good Housekeeping Woman's Almanac. Edited by Barbara McDowell and Hana Umlauf. New York: Newspaper Enterprise Association, 1977.

Graham, Patricia A. *Community and Class in American Education, 1865–1918.* New York: Wiley, 1974.

Green, Elizabeth Alden. *Mary Lyon and Mount Holyoke: Opening the Gates.* Hanover, N.H.: University Press of New England, 1979.

Green, Fletcher, M. *Democracy in the Old South and Other Essays.* Edited by J. Isaac Copeland. Kingsport, Tenn.: Vanderbilt University Press, 1969.

Guilford, Linda T. *The Uses of a Life: Memorials of Mrs. Z. P. G. Bannister.* New York: American Tract Society, 1885.

Guy-Sheftall, Beverly, and Stewart, Jo Moore. *Spelman: A Centennial Celebration, 1881–1981.* Charlotte, N.C.: Delmar, 1981.

Hague, Amy. " 'Give Us a Little Time to Find Our Places,' University of Wisconsin Alumnae, Classes of 1875–1900." M.A. thesis, University of Wisconsin, 1983.

Hall, David D. *The Antinomian Controversy, 1636–1638: A Documentary History.* Middletown, Conn.: Wesleyan University Press, 1968.

Hall, G. Stanley. *Adolescence: Its Psychology and Its Relations to Physiology, Anthropology, Sociology, Sex, Crime, Religion, and Education.* II. New York: D. Appleton, 1908.

Hamilton, Alice. *Exploring the Dangerous Trades.* Boston: Little, Brown, 1943.

Handlin, Oscar, and Handlin, Mary F. *The American College and American Culture: Socialization as a Function of Higher Education.* New York: McGraw-Hill, 1970.

————. *The Dimensions of Liberty.* Cambridge, Mass.: Harvard University Press, 1961.

Hansen, Allen O. *Liberalism and American Education in the Eighteenth Century.* New York: Macmillan, 1926.

Harris, Barbara J. *Beyond Her Sphere: Women and The Professions In American History.* Westport, Conn.: Greenwood Press, 1978.

Harris, Seymour. *The Economics of Harvard.* New York: McGraw-Hill, 1970.

Hartmann, Susan M. *The Home Front and Beyond: American Women in the 1940s.* New York: Twayne Publishers, 1982.

Hawkins, Hugh. *Between Harvard and America: The Educational Leadership of Charles W. Eliot.* New York: Oxford University Press, 1972.

Hentz, Caroline Lee. *Marcus Warland.* Philadelphia: A. Hart, 1852.

Herman, Debra. "College and After: The Vassar Experiment in Women's Education, 1861–1924." Ph.D. dissertation, Stanford University, 1979.

Hersh, Blanche Glassman. *The Slavery of Sex: Feminist Abolitionists in America.* Urbana, Ill.: University of Illinois Press, 1978.

Higginson, Thomas Wentworth. *Margaret Fuller Ossoli.* Boston: Houghton Mifflin, 1884. Reprint. New York: Chelsea House, 1981, with introduction by Barbara M. Solomon.

Hill, Patricia R. *The World Their Household: The American Woman's Foreign Missionary Movement and Cultural Transformation, 1870–1920.* Ann Arbor: University of Michigan Press, 1984.

Hitchcock, Edward. *The Power of Christian Benvolence Illustrated in the Life and Labors of Mary Lyon.* Northampton, Mass.: Hopkins, Bridgman, 1851.

Hofstadter, Richard. *Social Darwinism in American Thought.* Boston: Beacon Press, 1955.

Hoopes, James. *Van Wyck Brooks: In Search of American Culture.* Amherst: University of Massachusetts Press, 1977.

Howe, Helen. *The Gentle Americans, 1864–1960: Biography of a Breed.* New York: Harper and Row, 1965.

Howe, Julia Ward, ed. *Sex and Education: A Reply to Dr. Clarke's "Sex in Education."* Boston: Roberts, 1874.

Howes, Annie G. *Health Statistics of Women College Graduates.* Boston: Wright and Porter, 1885.

Huber, Joan, ed. *Changing Women in a Changing Society.* Chicago: University of Chicago Press, 1973.

Hunter College Women's Studies Collective. *Women's Realities, Women's Choices: An Introduction to Women's Studies.* New York: Oxford University Press, 1983.

Hurst, Fannie. *Anatomy of Me.* Garden City, N.Y.: Doubleday, 1958.

Jaffee, Rona. *The Best of Everything.* New York: Simon and Schuster, 1958.

James, Edward T., ed. *Notable American Women, 1607–1950: A Biographical Dictionary.* 3 vols. Cambridge, Mass.: Harvard University Press, 1971.

James, Janet Wilson. *Changing Ideas About Women in the United States, 1776–1825.* New York: Garland Publishers, 1981. Reprint of 1954 Ph.D. diss., Radcliffe College/Harvard University, with new introduction.

James, Janet Wilson, ed. *Women in American Religion.* Philadelphia: University of Pennsylvania Press, 1978.

James, Sydney V. *A People Among Peoples: Quaker Benevolence in Eighteenth-Century America.* Cambridge, Mass.: Harvard University Press, 1963.

Jefferson, Thomas. *The Family Letters of Thomas Jefferson.* Edited by Edwin M. Betts and James A. Bear, Jr. Columbia, Mo.: University of Missouri Press, 1966.

Jencks, Christopher, and Riesman, David. *The Academic Revolution.* Garden City, N.Y.: Doubleday, 1968.

Johnson, Charles S. *The Negro College Graduate.* Chapel Hill: University of North Carolina Press, 1938.

Jordan, W. K. *General Education at Radcliffe College.* Cambridge, Mass.: Harvard University Press, 1945.

Joughin, G. Louis, and Morgan, Edmund M. *The Legacy of Sacco and Vanzetti.* New York: Harcourt, Brace, 1948.

Kaledin, Eugenia. *The Education of Mrs. Henry Adams.* Philadelphia: Temple University Press, 1981.

Kaufman, Polly. *Women Teachers on the Frontier.* New Haven: Yale University Press, 1984.

Keller, Morton. *Affairs of the State: Public Life in Late Nineteenth-Century America.* Cambridge, Mass.: Harvard University Press, 1977.

Keller, Phyllis. *Getting at the Core: Curricular Reform at Harvard.* Cambridge, Mass.: Harvard University Press, 1982.

Kelley, Mary. *Private Woman, Public Stage: Literary Domesticity in Nineteenth-Century America.* New York: Oxford University Press, 1983.

Kelley, Mary, ed. *Woman's Being, Woman's Place: Female Identity and Vocation in American History.* Boston: Hall, 1979.

Kendall, Elaine. *"Peculiar Institutions": An Informal History of the Seven Sister Colleges.* New York: Putnam, 1976.

Kerber, Linda K. *Women of the Republic: Intellect and Ideology in Revolutionary America*. Chapel Hill: University of North Carolina Press, 1980.

Kerber, Linda K., and Matthews, Jane DeHart. *Women's America; Refocusing the Past*. New York: Oxford University Press, 1982.

Kessler-Harris, Alice. *Out to Work: A History of Wage-Earning Women in the United States*. New York: Oxford University Press, 1982.

Kevles, Daniel J. *The Physicists: The History of a Scientific Community in Modern America*. New York: Knopf, 1971.

Kingsley, Florence. *The Life of Henry F. Durant*. New York: Century, 1924.

Kirchwey, Freda, ed. *Our Changing Morality: A Symposium*. New York: Arno Press, 1924.

Komarovsky, Mirra. *Women in the Modern World: Their Education and Their Dilemmas*. Boston: Little Brown, 1953.

Korff, J. Michael. "Student Control and University Government at Stanford: The Evolving Student–University Relationship." Ph.D. dissertation, Stanford University, 1975.

Kraditor, Aileen S. *Up From the Pedestal: Selected Writings in the History of American Feminism*. Chicago: Quandrangle Books, 1968.

Kundsin, Ruth, ed. *Successful Women in the Sciences: An Analysis of Determinants*. New York: Morrow, 1973.

Lane, Ann, ed. *Mary Ritter Beard: A Sourcebook*. New York: Schocken Books, 1977.

Lardner, Ring, Jr. *The Lardners: My Family Remembered*. New York: Harper and Row, 1976.

Lash, Joseph P. *Franklin and Eleanor*. New York: Norton, 1971.

Lasser, Carol, and Merrill, Marlene, eds. *Soul Mates: The Oberlin Correspondence of Lucy Stone and Antoinette Brown, 1846–1850*. Oberlin, Ohio: Oberlin University Press, 1983.

Lerner, Gerda. *The Majority Finds Its Past*. New York: Oxford University Press, 1979.

Lerner, Gerda, ed. *Black Women in White America: A Documentary History*. New York: Pantheon Books, 1972.

———. *The Female Experience: An American Documentary*. Indianapolis: Bobbs-Merrill Educational Publishers, 1977.

Levine, David O. "The Functions of Higher Education in American Society Between World War I and World War II." Ph.D. dissertation, Harvard University, 1981.

Lifton, Robert, ed. *The Woman in America*. Boston: Houghton Mifflin, 1965.

Lockridge, Kenneth. *Literacy in Colonial New England: An Inquiry into the Social Context in the Early Modern West*. New York: Norton, 1974.

Logan, Mayford W. *Howard University: The First Hundred Years*. New York: New York University Press, 1969.

Lord, John. *The Life of Emma Willard*. New York: Appleton, 1873.

Lubove, Roy. *The Professional Altruist: The Emergence of Social Work as a Career, 1880–1930*. Cambridge, Mass.: Harvard University Press, 1965.

Lundberg, Ferdinand, and Farnham, Maryna. *Modern Woman: The Lost Sex*. New York: Harper, 1947.

Lutz, Alma. *Crusade for Freedom: Women in the Antislavery Movement.* Boston: Beacon Press, 1968.

Lynd, Robert S., and Lynd, Helen Merrell. *Middletown: A Study of Modern American Culture.* New York: Harcourt, Brace, and World, 1929.

Magill, Edward H. *An Address Upon the Co-Education of the Sexes.* Philadelphia: Swarthmore College, 1873.

Mann, Arthur. *Yankee Reformers in an Urban Age.* Cambridge, Mass.: Belknap Press of Harvard University Press, 1954.

Mattfield, Jacqueline, and Van Aken, Carol, eds. *Women and the Scientific Professions.* Cambridge, Mass.: Harvard University Press, 1965.

Matthews, Donald G. *Religion in the Old South.* Chicago: University of Chicago Press, 1977.

Matthews, Lois Kimball. *The Dean of Women.* Boston: Houghton Mifflin, 1915.

Mayo, A. D. *Southern Women in the Recent Educational Movement in the South.* Edited by Dan T. Carter and Amy Friedlander. Baton Rouge: Louisiana State University Press, 1978.

McCarthy, Abigail. *Private Faces, Public Places.* New York, Doubleday, 1972.

McCarthy, Mary. *On the Contrary.* New York: Strauss and Cudahy, 1961.

———. *The Group.* New York: Avon, 1954.

McGuigan, Dorothy G. *A Dangerous Experiment: One Hundred Years at the University of Michigan.* Ann Arbor: University of Michigan Press, 1970.

McPherson, James M. *The Abolitionist Legacy: From Reconstruction to the NAACP.* Princeton: Princeton University Press, 1975.

Mead, Margaret. *Male and Female: A Study of the Sexes in a Changing World.* New York: Morrow, 1949.

Mead, Margaret, and Kaplan, Frances, eds. *American Women: The Report of the President's Commission on the Status of Women.* New York: Scribner, 1965.

Meigs, Cornelia. *What Makes A College? A History of Bryn Mawr.* New York: Macmillan, 1956.

Melder, Keith. *The Beginnings of Sisterhood: The American Woman's Rights Movement, 1800–1850.* New York: Schocken, 1977.

———. "The Beginnings of the Women's Rights Movement in the United States, 1800–1840." Ph.D. dissertation, Yale University, 1963.

Miller, Alice Duer, and Myers, Susan. *Barnard College: The First Fifty Years.* New York: Columbia University Press, 1939.

Miller, Ann, ed. *A College in Dispersion: Women of Bryn Mawr, 1896–1975.* Boulder: Westview Press, 1976.

Miller, Russell. *Light on the Hill: A History of Tufts College 1852–1952.* Boston: Beacon Press, 1966.

Mirrielees, Edith R., ed. *Stanford Mosaic: Reminiscences of the First Seventy Years at Stanford University.* Stanford: Stanford University Press, 1962.

Moats, Alice Leone. *No Nice Girl Swears.* New York: Knopf, 1933.

Moldow, Gloria Melnick. "The Gilded Age, Promise and Disillusionment: Women Doctors and the Emergence of the Professional Middle Class, Washington, D.C., 1870–1900." Ph.D. dissertation, University of Maryland, 1980.

Morantz, Regina M., ed. *In Her Own Words: Oral Histories of Women Physicians.* Westport, Conn.: Greenwood Press, 1982.

More, Hannah. *Strictures on the Modern System of Female Education*. London: Printed for T. Cadell, Jr., and W. Davies in the Strand, 1799.

Murdock, Kenneth B., ed. *Handkerchiefs from Paul*. Cambridge, Mass.: Harvard University Press, 1927.

Murray, Judith [Constantia]. *The Gleaner: A Miscellaneous Production in Three Volumes*. Boston: Thomas and E. J. Andrews, 1798.

National Manpower Council. *Womanpower*. New York: Columbia University Press, 1957.

Nevins, Allan. *The State Universities and Democracy*. Urbana, Ill.: Illinois University Press, 1962.

Newcomer, Mabel. *A Century of Higher Education for American Women*. New York: Harper, 1959.

Noble, Jeanne L. *Beautiful, Also, Are the Souls of My Black Sisters*. Englewood Cliffs, N.J.: Prentice-Hall, 1978.

————. *The Negro Woman's College Education*. New York: Teachers College, Columbia University, 1956.

Norton, Mary Beth. *Liberty's Daughters: The Revolutionary Experiences of American Women, 1750–1800*. Boston: Little, Brown, 1980.

Olin, Helen R. *Shall Wisconsin University Remain a Coeducational Institution?* Madison, Wis.: University of Wisconsin Press, 1908.

————. *The Women of a State University: An Illustration of the Working of Coeducation in the Middle West*. New York: Putnam, 1909.

Olson, Keith W. *The GI Bill, the Veterans and the Colleges*. Lexington, Ky.: University Press of Kentucky, 1974.

Oppenheimer, Valerie K. *The Female Labor Force in the United States: Demographic and Economic Factors Governing Its Growth and Changing Composition*. Berkeley: Institute of International Studies, University of California, 1970.

Palmieri, Patricia A. "In Adamless Eden: A Social Portrait of the Academic Community at Wellesley College 1875–1920." Ed. D. thesis, Harvard Graduate School of Education, 1981.

Peabody, Elizabeth Palmer. *Reminiscences of William Ellery Channing*. Boston: Roberts, 1880.

Peckham, Howard H. *The Making of the University of Michigan, 1917–1967*. Ann Arbor: University of Michigan Press, 1967.

Perkins, Linda. "Fanny Jackson Coppin and the Institute for Colored Youth: A Model of Nineteenth-Century Black Female Educational and Community Leadership, 1837–1902." Ph.D. dissertation, University of Illinois, Urbana, 1978.

Perun, Pamela J. *The Undergraduate Woman: Issues in Educational Equity*. Lexington, Mass.: Lexington Books, 1982.

Peterson, George E. *The New England College in the Age of the University*. Amherst: Amherst College Press, 1964.

Phelps, Almira. *Lectures to Young Ladies: Comprising Outlines and Applications of the Different Branches of Female Education Delivered to the Pupils of the Troy Female Seminary*. Boston: Carter, Hendee, 1833.

————. *The Educator: or Hours With My Pupils*. New York: A. S. Barnes, 1872.

Piehl, Mel. *Breaking Bread: The Catholic Worker and the Origin of Catholic Radicalism in America*. Philadelphia: Temple University Press, 1982.

Plath, Sylvia [Victoria Lucas]. *The Bell Jar*. London: Heinemann, 1963.

Player, Willa. "Improving College Education for Women at Bennett College: A Report of a Type A Project." Ed. D. dissertation, Columbia Teachers College, 1948.

Pollard, Lucille Addison. *Women on College and University Faculties: A Historical Survey and Study of their Present Academic Status*. New York: Arno Press, 1977.

Power, Edward J. *A History of Catholic Higher Education in the United States*. Milwaukee: Bruce, 1958.

Pruette, Lorine. *Women Workers Through the Depression*. New York: Macmillan, 1934.

Prytaneans. *An Oral History of the Prytanean Society, Its Members and Their University, 1901–1920*. 2 vols. Berkeley: University of California Press, 1970.

Pyre, J. F. A. *Wisconsin*. New York: Oxford University Press, 1920.

Ramsay, David. *Memoirs of the Life of Martha Laurens Ramsay*. 3d ed. Boston: S. J. Armstrong, 1812.

Randall, Mercedes. *Improper Bostonian: Emily Greene Balch*. New York: Twayne Publishers, 1964.

Ravenal, Harriott H. *Eliza Lucas Pinckney*. New York: Scribner's, 1896.

Read, Florence M. *The Story of Spelman College*. Atlanta, Georgia: [Printed by Princeton University Press; published by Florence M. Read], 1961.

Reeves, Floyd, and Russell, John Dale. *The Alumni of the Colleges*. Chicago: University of Chicago Press, 1933.

Reynolds, O. Edgar. *The Social and Economic Status of College Students*. New York: Bureau of Publications, Teachers College, Columbia University, 1927.

Rich, Adrienne. *On Lies, Secrets, and Silences: Selected Prose 1966–1978*. New York: Norton, 1979.

Rogers, Agnes. *Vassar College: An Informal Study*. Poughkeepsie, N.Y.: Quinn and Boden, 1940.

Rosenberg, Rosalind. *Beyond Separate Spheres: Intellectual Roots of Modern Feminism*. New Haven: Yale University Press, 1982.

Rossi, Alice S., and Calderwood, Ann, eds. *Academic Women on the Move*. New York: Russell Sage Foundation, 1973.

Rossiter, Margaret W. *Women Scientists in America: Struggles and Strategies to 1940*. Baltimore: John Hopkins University Press, 1982.

Roth, Philip. *Good-Bye, Columbus*. Boston: Houghton Mifflin, 1959.

Rothman, Ellen K. *Hands and Hearts: A History of Courtship in America*. New York: Basic Books, 1984.

Rothman, Sheila. *Woman's Proper Place: A History of Changing Ideals and Practices, 1870 to the Present*. New York: Basic Books, 1978.

Rowson, Susanna. *A Present for Young Ladies: Containing Poems, Dialogues, Addresses, etc. As Recited by the Pupils of Mrs. Rowson's Academy at the Annual Exhibitions*. Boston: John West, no. 75, Cornhill, 1811.

Ruddick, Sara, and Daniels, Pamela, eds. *Working It Out: 23 Women Writers, Artists, Scientists, and Scholars Talk About Their Lives and Work*. New York: Pantheon Books, 1977.

Rudolph, Frederick. *The American College and University: A History.* New York: Knopf, 1962.

————. *Curriculum: A History of the American Undergraduate Course of Study Since 1636.* San Francisco: Josse-Bass, 1977.

Rudolph, Federick, ed. *Essays on Education in the Early Republic.* Cambridge, Mass.: The Belknap Press of Harvard University Press, 1965.

Rudy, Willis. *The Evolving Liberal Arts Curriculum: A Historical Review of Basic Themes.* New York: Bureau of Publications, Teachers College, Columbia University, 1960.

Rush, Benjamin. *Thoughts Upon Female Education Accommodated to the Present State of Society, Manners, and the Government in the United States of America.* Philadelphia: S. Hall, 1787.

Ryan, Mary P. *The Cradle of the Middle Class: The Family in Oneida County, New York, 1790–1865.* Cambridge: Cambridge University Press, 1981.

Sanford, Nevitt, ed. *The American College: A Psychological and Social Interpretation of Higher Education.* New York: Wiley, 1962.

Schwager, Sally. " 'Harvard Women': A History of the Founding of Radcliffe College." Ed. D. dissertation, Harvard University, 1982.

Scott, Anne Firor. *Making the Invisible Woman Visible.* Urbana, Ill.: University of Illinois Press, 1984.

Scott, Anne Firor, and Scott, Andrew M. *One Half the People: The Fight for Woman Suffrage.* Philadelphia: Lippincott, 1975.

Showalter, Elaine, ed. *These Modern Women: Autobiographical Essays.* Westbury, N.Y.: Feminist Press, 1978.

Sicherman, Barbara, and Green, Carol Hurd, eds. *Notable American Women: The Modern Period.* Cambridge, Mass.: Harvard University Press, 1980.

Silliman, Benjamin. *Letters of Shahcoolen, A Hindu Philosopher Residing in Philadelphia, to His Friend El Hassan, an Inhabitant of Delhi.* Boston: Russell and Cutler (Proprietors of the Work), 1802.

Silverman, Kenneth. *A Cultural History of the American Revolution; Painting, Music, Literature and the Theatre in the Colonies and the United States from the Treaty of Paris to the Inauguration of George Washington, 1763–1789.* New York: Crowell, 1976.

Sims, Mary S. *The Natural History of a Social Institution: The Young Woman's Christian Association.* New York: The Woman's Press, 1936.

Sinclair, Andrew. *The Better Half: The Emancipation of the American Woman.* New York: Harper and Row, 1965.

Sizer, Theodore R., ed. *The Age of the Academies.* New York: Bureau of Publications, Teachers College, Columbia University, 1964.

Sklar, Kathryn Kish. *Catharine Beecher: A Study in Domesticity.* New Haven: Yale University Press, 1973.

Smedley, Agnes. *Daughter of Earth.* New York: Coward-McCann, 1929.

Solberg, Winton V. *The University of Illinois, 1867–1894: An Intellectual and Cultural History.* Urbana, Ill.: University of Illinois Press, 1968.

Solomon, Barbara Miller. *Ancestors and Immigrants: A Changing New England Tradition.* Cambridge, Mass.: Harvard University Press, 1956.

Spahr, Charles B. *An Essay on the Present Distribution of Wealth in the United States.* New York: Crowell, 1896.

Spalding, John Lancaster. *Means and Ends of Education.* Chicago: McClurg, 1895.
———. *Opportunity and Other Essays.* Chicago: McClurg, 1900. 3d ed. 1903.

Spencer, Anna Garlin. *Woman's Share in Social Culture.* New York: Kennerley, 1912.

Spock, Benjamin. *Baby and Child Care.* New York: Hawthorn Books, 1957. New rev. ed., 1968.

Spruill, Julia Cherry. *Women's Life and Work in the Southern Colonies.* New York: Norton, 1972.

Stanton, Theodore, and Blatch, Harriot Stanton, eds. *Elizabeth Cady Stanton as Revealed in Her Letters, Diary, and Reminiscences.* 2 vols. New York: Harper, 1922.

Starrett, Helen Ekin. *After College What? For Girls.* New York: Crowell, 1896.

Stephens, Frank F. *A History of the University of Missouri.* Columbia, Mo.: University of Missouri Press, 1962.

Stevens, W. LeConte. *The Admission of Women to Universities.* New York: S. W. Green, 1883.

Stewart, Isabel M. *The Education of Nurses.* New York: Macmillan, 1943.

Stone, Irving, ed. *There Was Light: Autobiography of A University, Berkeley, 1868–1968.* Garden City, N.Y.: Doubleday, 1970.

Storr, Richard J. *Harper's University: The Beginnings.* Chicago: University of Chicago Press, 1966.

Stringer, Patricia A., and Thompson, Irene, eds. *Stepping Off the Pedestal: Academic Women in the South.* New York: Modern Language Association of America, 1982.

Strouse, Jean, ed. *Women and Analysis: Dialogues on Psychoanalytic Views of Femininity.* New York: Grossman, 1974.

Stuhler, Barbara, and Kreuter, Gretchen, eds. *Women of Minnesota: Selected Biographical Essays.* St. Paul, Minn.: Historical Society Press, 1977.

Sweet, Leonard. *The Minister's Wife: Her Role in Nineteenth-Century American Evangelicalism.* Philadelphia: Temple University Press, 1983.

Swisshelm, Jane Gray. *Half a Century.* Chicago: Jansen, McClurg, 1880.

Synott, Marcia Graham. *The Half-Opened Door: Discrimination and Admissions at Harvard, Yale, and Princeton, 1900–1970.* Westport, Conn.: Greenwood Press, 1979.

Talbot, Marion. *More than Lore: Reminiscences of Marion Talbot, Dean of Women, the University of Chicago, 1892–1925.* Chicago: University of Chicago Press, 1936.

Terrell, Mary Church. *A Colored Woman in a White World.* Washington, D.C.: Ransdell, 1940.

Thorne, Dorothy. *Guilford: A Quaker College.* Guilford, N.C.: Printed for Guilford College by J. J. Stone, 1937.

Tocqueville, Alexis de. *Democracy in America.* Edited by Phillips Bradley. 2 vols. New York: Knopf, 1945.

Trilling, Diana. *We Must March, My Darlings.* New York: Harcourt, Brace, and Jovanovich, 1977.

Tryon, Ruth W. *Investment in Creative Scholarship*. Washington, D.C.: American Association of University Women, 1957.

Turrell, Ebenezer, ed. *Memoirs of The Life and Death of the Pious and Ingenious Mrs. Jane Turrell*. London, 1741.

Ulrich, Laurel T. *Good Wives: Image and Reality in Northern New England, 1650–1750*. New York: Knopf, 1982.

Vanderpoel, Emily N. *Chronicles of a Pioneer School from 1792 to 1833*. Cambridge, Mass.: University Press, 1903.

———. *More Chronicles of a Pioneer School*. New York: The Cadmus Book Shop, 1927.

Van Voris, Jacqueline, ed. *College: A Smith Mosaic*. West Springfield, Mass.: Smith College Press, 1975.

Vassar, Matthew. *The Autobiography and Letters of Matthew Vassar*. Edited by Elizabeth H. Haight. New York: Oxford Press, 1916.

Veysey, Laurence R. *The Emergence of the American University*. Chicago: University of Chicago Press, 1965.

Viles, Jonas. *The University of Missouri: A Centennial History*. Columbia, Mo.: The University of Missouri Press, 1939.

Vroman, Mary E. *Shaped To Its Purpose: Delta Sigma Theta, The First Fifty Years*. New York: Random House, 1965.

Wallace, Elizabeth. *The Unending Journey*. Minneapolis: University of Minnesota Press, 1952.

Walsh, Mary Roth. *Doctors Wanted: No Women Need Apply*. New Haven: Yale University Press, 1977.

Ware, Susan. *Beyond Suffrage: Women in the New Deal*. Cambridge, Mass.: Harvard University Press, 1981.

———. *Holding Their Own: American Women in the 1930s*. Boston: Twayne Publishers, 1982.

Warren, Mercy. *Poems, Dramatic and Miscellaneous*. Boston: I. Thomas and E. T. Andrews, 1790.

Wechsler, Harold S. *The Qualified Student: A History of Selective College Admission in America*. New York: Wiley, 1977.

Westin, Jeanne. *Making Do: How Women Survived the '30s*. Chicago: Follet, 1976.

Wheatley, Phillis. *Poems on Various Subjects, Religious and Moral*. 1786. Reprint. New York: AMS Press, 1976.

White, Lynn. *Educating Our Daughters*. New York: Harper, 1950.

White, Marion Churchill. *A History of Barnard College*. New York: Columbia University Press, 1954.

Wiebe, Robert H. *The Search for Order, 1877–1920*. New York: Hill and Wang, 1967.

Willard, Emma Hart. *An Address to the Public: Particularly to the Members of the Legislature of New York, Proposing a Plan for Improving Female Education*. Middlebury, Vt.: J. W. Copeland, 1819.

Willie, Charles V., and Edmunds, Ronald R., eds. *Black Colleges in America: Challenge, Development, Survival*. New York: Teachers College Press, Columbia University, 1978.

Wilson, Elizabeth. *Fifty Years of Association Work Among Young Women, 1866–1916, A History of Young Women's Christian Associations in the United States of America.* New York: National Board of the Young Women's Christian Association, 1916.

Wollstonecraft, Mary. *A Vindication of the Rights of Woman.* Edited by Carol H. Poston. New York: Norton, 1975.

Wolters, Raymond. *The New Negro On Campus.* Princeton: Princeton University Press, 1975.

Woody, Thomas. *A History of Women's Education in the United States.* 2 vols. New York: The Science Press, 1929.

Wouk, Herman. *Marjorie Morningstar.* New York: Doubleday, 1955.

Wright, Martha Elizabeth, ed. *History of the Oread Collegiate Institute, Worcester, Mass., 1849–1881 with Biographical Sketches.* New Haven: Yale University Press, 1905.

Wylie, Philip. *A Generation of Vipers.* New York: Farrar and Rinehart, 1942.

Yezierska, Anzia. *Bread Givers: A Struggle Between a Father of the Old World and a Daughter of the New.* Reprint. New York: Persea Books, 1975.

———. *Hungry Hearts.* Boston: Houghton Mifflin, 1920. Reprint. New York: Arno Press, 1975.

Young, Elizabeth B. *A Study of the Curricula of Seven Selected Women's Colleges of the Southern States.* New York: Teachers College Press, Columbia University, 1932.

Other Published Materials

"A Flapper Has the Last Word." *The Woman Citizen* 12 (June 1927).

Aaron, Daniel. "The Idea of Boston: Some Literary Responses to the Sacco-Vanzetti Case." In *Sacco-Vanzetti: Developments and Reconsiderations—1979.* Conference Proceedings. Boston: Trustees of the Public Library of the City of Boston, 1982.

Abbott, Othman. "Recollections of a Pioneer Lawyer." *Nebraska History Magazine* 11 (1928).

Allmendinger, David F. "Mount Holyoke Students Encounter the Need for Life-Planning, 1837–1850." *History of Education Quarterly* 19 (Spring 1979).

"The American College Girl: By a European University Girl." *The Outlook* 76 (January 16, 1904).

"The American Woman: Her Achievements and her Troubles." *Life* (December 1956).

Amos, Thyrsa W. "Self-Help for Women College Students." *Journal of the American Association of University Women* 20 (October 1926).

"Another of Them." *The Stanford Sequoia* 18 (May 1909).

Antler, Joyce. " 'After College, What?': New Graduates and the Family Claim." *American Quarterly* 32 (Fall 1980).

———. "Feminism as Life-Process: The Life and Career of Lucy Sprague Mitchell." *Feminist Studies* 7 (Spring 1981).

Badger, Henry G. *Statistics of Negro Colleges and Universities: Students, Staff, and Finances, 1900–1950.* U.S. Office of Education statistical circular 293, April 1951.

Bailey, Margery. *Stanford Daily* (January 13, 1947).

Balch, Emily Greene. "The Effect of War and Militarism on the Status of Women." *American Sociological Society Publications* 10 (1915).

———. "What's Hecuba to me or I to Hecuba?" *The Wellesley Magazine* 15 (1907).

Barker, Nancy Nichols. "More Light on Early Days at Vassar." *Vassar Alumnae Magazine* 47 (February 1962).

Barnard College. *Report of the Dean.* 1895–1942.

Barnard, Eunice Fuller. "The College Girl Puts Marriage First." *New York Times Magazine,* April 2, 1933.

Bernard, Richard M., and Vinovskis, Maris A. "The Female School Teacher in Ante-Bellum Massachusetts." *Journal of Social History* 10 (March 1977).

Bevier, Isabel. "Recollections and Impressions of the Beginnings of the Department of Home Economics at the University of Illinois." *Journal of Home Economics* 32 (1940).

Bigglestone, W. E. "Oberlin College and the Negro Student, 1865–1940." *Journal of Negro History* 56 (July 1971).

Birtwell, Lorna R. F. "The Point at Issue." *Radcliffe Magazine* 13, 4 (June 1911).

Bonner, Marita. "On Being Young, A Woman, and Colored." *The Crisis* 31 (December 1925).

Breckinridge, Sophonisba P. "Political Equality for Women and Women's Wages." *The Annals of the American Academy of Political and Social Science* 56 (November 1914).

Brice, Edward Warner. "How Radical Are College Students?" *The Crisis* 44 (October 1937).

Bromley, Dorothy Dunbar. "Feminist—New Style." *Harper's Magazine* 155 (1927).

Brooks, Amy. "College Settlement Work at Radcliffe." *Radcliffe Magazine* 8, 1 (December 1905).

Brown, Clara M. "New Problems and a New Curriculum." *Journal of the American Association of University Women* 23 (January 1930).

Brumberg, Joan Jacobs, and Tomes, Nancy. "Women in the Professions: A Research Agenda for American Historians." *Reviews in American History* 5 (June 1982).

Buck, Paul. "Harvard Attitudes Toward Radcliffe in the Early Years." *Massachusetts Historical Society* 74 (May 1962).

Butler, Melissa A. "Early Liberal Roots of Feminism: John Locke and the Attack on Patriarchy." *American Political Science Review* 72 (1978).

Caldwell, Jean. "Seven Attend 70th Reunion at Mt. Holyoke." *The Boston Globe,* May 30, 1977.

Caliver, Ambrose. *A Background Study of Negro College Students.* U. S. Office of Education, bulletin 8 (1933).

Carter, Susan B. "Academic Women Revisited: An Empirical Study of Changing Patterns in Women's Employment as College and University Faculty, 1890–1963." *Journal of Social History* 14 (Summer 1981).

———. "Women's Educational History: A Labor Market Perspective," *Academy Notes* 13, 2 (Winter 1983).

Carter, Susan B., and Prus, Mark. "The Labor Market and the American High School Girl, 1890–1928." *Journal of Economic History* 42, 1 (March 1982).

Castro, Janice. "Culivating Late Bloomers." *Time* November 21, 1983.

Catalogue of the Female Collegiate Institute of Georgetown, Kentucky (1839).

Catalogue of the Richmond Female Institute of Richmond, Virginia (1856).

Chester, Ronald. "Women Lawyers in the Urban Bar: An Oral History." *New England Law Review* 18, 3 (1983).

Chevigny, Bell Gale. "The Long Arm of Censorship: Myth-making in Margaret Fuller's Time and Our Own." *Signs: Journal of Women in Culture and Society* 2 (Winter 1976).

"College and University Cooperative Houses for Women Students." *Journal of the American Association of University Women* 18 (March 1925).

Comstock, Ada L. *Annual Report of the President*. Radcliffe College, 1927.

———. "Report of the Dean of Women." In *The President's Report*. University of Minnesota, 1912.

———. "The Fourth R for Women." *Century Magazine* 142 (1929).

Conway, Jill K. "Perspectives on the History of Women's Education in the United States." *History of Education Quarterly* 14, 1 (Spring 1974).

Cott, Nancy F. "Divorce and the Changing Status of Women in Eighteenth-Century Massachusetts." *William amd Mary Quarterly*, 3d ser., 33 (October 1976).

———. "Young Women in the Second Great Awakening in New England." *Feminist Studies* 3 (Fall 1975).

Coulter, E. Merton. "The Ante-Bellum Academy Movement in Georgia." *The Georgia Historical Quarterly* 5 (December 1922).

Cowing, Cedric B. "Sex and Preaching in the Great Awakening." *American Quarterly* 20 (1968).

Crutcher, Minnie Selvin. "Remembering the Class of 1927." *California Living Magazine* October 30, 1977.

Dane, Clemence. "When They Are Grandmothers." *Forum* 71 (May 1927).

Davis, Elinor Smith. *A Centennial History of Alpha Phi Fraternity, 1872–1972*. Reprinted in *Alpha Phi Quarterly* 74 (Spring 1972).

Davis, Katherine Bement. "Why They Failed to Marry." *Harper's Monthly Magazine* 156 (March 1928).

Dean, Vera M. "Woman's Responsibilities in the Postwar World." *Radcliffe Quarterly* 27 (November 1943).

Diner, Steven J. "George Herbert Mead's Ideas on Women and Careers: A Letter to His Daughter-In-Law, 1920." *Signs: Journal of Women in Culture and Society* 4 (1978).

Dubois, W. E. B. "Negroes in College." *The Nation* 122 (March 3, 1926).

Dwight, Timothy. "Education for Women at Yale." *The Forum* 13 (June 1982).

"Earning a College Course: Setting Forth the Experiences of a Young Woman Who Worked her Way through College." *McCall's* 43 (September 1915).

"Editorial." *Hunter College Bulletin* 3, 5 (October 26, 1915).

"Editorial." *Radcliffe Magazine* 16 (February 1914).

Edwards, Alba M. *Sixteenth Census of the United States, 1940, Comparative Occupation Statistics for the United States, 1870 to 1940, a Comparison of the 1930 and the 1940 Census Occupation and Industry Classifications and Statistics; A Comparable Series of Occupation Statistics, 1870 to 1920; and a Social-Economic Grouping of the*

Labor Force, 1910 to 1940. U.S. Bureau of the Census (1943).

Eells, Walter Crosby. "Earned Doctorates for Women in the Nineteenth Century." *Bulletin of the American Association of University Professors.* 42, 4 (Winter 1956).

Emerick, Charles Franklin. "College Women and Race Suicide." *Political Science Quarterly* 24 (June 1909).

Fallows, Alice Katharine. "Undergraduate Life at Smith College." *Scribner's Magazine* 24 (July 1898).

Faulkner, Roland P. *Reports of the Immigration Commission: The Children of Immigrants in Schools.* U.S. Government Printing Office 1, 5 (1911).

Felton, Katharine C. "The Next Step in the Development of the Western State University." *The Berkeleyan* 3 (February 1, 1894).

Fisher, Josephine. "The Journal of Esther Burr." *New England Quarterly* 3 (1930).

Fitchett, E. Horace. "The Role of Claflin College in Negro Life in South Carolina." *Journal of Negro Education* 12 (Winter 1943).

"Free Press." *The Wellesley Magazine* 5 (April 1897).

Furumoto, Laurel. "Mary Whiton Calkins (1863–1930), Fourteenth President of the American Psychological Association." *Journal of the History of the Behavioral Sciences* 15 (1979).

Futter, Ellen, and Sills, Beverly. *The New York Times*, May 14, 1981, sec. B3, col. 6.

Garrison, Dee. "The Tender Technicians: The Feminization of Public Librarianship, 1875–1905." *Journal of Social History* 6 (1972–73).

Giele, Janet Z. "Cohort Variation in Life Patterns of Educated Women, 1911–1960." *Western Sociological Review* 13 (1982).

Gilman, Charlotte Perkins. "A New Generation of Women." *Current History* 18 (August 1923).

Gilman, Daniel C. "The Inauguration of Benjamin I. Wheeler." *The University of California Chronicle II* (1899).

Ginzburg, Lori. "Women in an Evangelical Community: Oberlin, 1835–1850." *Ohio History* 89 (Winter 1980).

Goodman, Walter. "Women's Studies: The Debate Continues." *New York Times Magazine*, April 22, 1984.

Gordon, Sarah H. "Smith College Students: The First Ten Classes, 1879–1888." *History of Education Quarterly* 15 (Summer 1975).

Graham, Helen Tredway et al. "The Expenses of Women College Students: A Survey of 114 Colleges and Universities." Prepared for the American Association of University Women by the College Club of St. Louis (May 1923).

Graham, Patricia A. "Expansion and Exclusion: A History of Women in American Higher Education." *Signs: Journal of Women in Culture and Society* 3 (Summer 1978).

———. "So Much to Do: Guides for Historical Research on Women in Higher Education." *Teachers College Record* 76 (February 1975).

Gray, Hanna Holborn. "What About Women at Yale?" *The Radcliffe Quarterly* 62, 3 (September 1976).

Greenleaf, Walter J. *Self-Help for College Students.* Bureau of Education, bulletin 2 (1929).

Griffin, Patricia S. " 'But She's So Feminine': Changing Mixed Messages We Give to Girls and Women in Sports." *Journal of the National Association for Women Deans, Administrators, and Counselors* 47 (Winter 1984).

Groves, Ernest R. "The Personality of the Wage Employment of Women Outside the Home and Their Social Consequences." *The Annals of the American Academy of Political and Social Science* 143 (May 1929).

Grunsky, Clotilde. "College Women as Teachers." *The California Alumni Fortnightly* 9 (February 5, 1916).

Haines, Patricia F. "For Honor and Alma Mater: Perspectives on Coeducation at Cornell University, 1868–1885." *Journal of Education* 159 (August 1977).

Hale, Sarah Josepha, ed. "Female Education." *The Ladies Magazine* 1 (1828).

Hale, William H. "A Dirge for Liberalism." *The New Republic* 66 (May 13, 1931).

Hall, Donald. "Interview with Marianne Moore." *Paris Review* 7 (Winter 1961).

Hall, G. Stanley, and Smith, Theodore L. "Marriage and Fecundity of College Men and Women." *The Pedagogical Seminary* 10 (September 1803).

Hargrave, Edythe. "How I Feel as a Negro at a White College." *Journal of Negro Education* 2 (October 1942).

Harper, William R. *Annual Report of the President.* University of Chicago, 1903.

Harris, LaFayette. "Problems before the College Negro." *The Crisis* 44 (August 1937).

Harris, W. T. "Reports of the Mosely Education Commission." In *Report of the Commissioner of Education for the Year Ended June 30, 1905, 1* (1907).

Hayes, Alice. "Can a Poor Girl Go to College?" *North American Review* 152, 5 (1891).

Hazard, Caroline. *President's Report.* Wellesley College, 1899.

Henle, Ellen, and Merrill, Marlene. "Antebellum Black Coeds at Oberlin College." *Oberlin College Alumni Magazine* 75, 4 (January–February 1980).

Hise, Charles Van. "Educational Tendencies in the State Universities." *Educational Review* 34 (December 1907).

———. "Inaugural Address." *Science* 20 (August 12, 1901).

Holloway, Mabel. "At Princeton: A Student World Court Conference." *The Crisis* 31 (February 1926).

Holt, Frank. "Are We Sending Too Many to College?" *Wisconsin Alumni Magazine* 30 (1929–30).

Horowitz, Helen Lefkowitz. "A Nineteenth-Century Father to his Daughter." *Wellesley Alumnae Magazine* 65 (Fall 1980).

Howe, Florence. "Three Missions of Higher Education for Women: Vocation, Freedom, Knowledge." *Liberal Education* 66 (Fall 1980).

Howes, Ethel Puffer. "The Meaning of Progress in the Woman Movement." *The Annals of the American Academy of Political and Social Science* 143 (1929).

———. "The Women's Orientation Course—What Shall Be Its Basic Concept." *Journal of the American Association of University Women* 20 (June 1927).

Hoyt, Edward A., and Brigham, Loriman S. "Glimpses of Margaret Fuller: The Greene Street School and Florence." *New England Quarterly* 29 (1956).

Hurston, Zora. "How It Feels to Be Colored Me." *The World Tomorrow* 11 (May 1928).

Hurwitz, Ruth Sapin. "Coming of Age at Wellesley." *Menorah Journal* 38 (Fall 1950).

Hutchinson, Emilie J. "Women and the Ph.D." *Journal of the American Association of University Women* 22 (October 1928).

Hyde, Ida H. "Before Women Were Human Beings: Adventures of an American Fellow in the German Universities of the '90s." *Journal of the American Association of University Women* 31–32 (1937–39).

Jenkins, Martin D. "Enrollment in Negro Colleges and Universities, 1939–40." *Journal of Negro Education* 7 (April 1938).

Johnson, Eleanor H. "An Account of the Anniversary Celebration." In *College Settlements Association, The Anniversary Report,* 1914.

Johnson, Mary. "Antoinette Brevost: A Schoolmistress in Early Pittsburgh." *Winterthur Portfolio* 15 (Summer 1980).

———. "Madame Rivardi's Seminary in the Gothic Mansion." *Pennsylvania Magazine of History and Biography* 104 (January 1980).

Jones, David D. "The War and the Higher Education of Negro Women." *Journal of Negro Education* 12 (April 1942).

Jordan, David Starr. "The Question of Coeducation." *Munsey's Magazine* 34 (March 1906).

Jordan, W. K. *President's Report,* 1946–47. Radcliffe College Archives.

Kahn, Diana Grossman. "Lessons of Their Mothers' Lives: Imitation and Avoidance by Contemporary College Women." *International Journal of Women's Studies* 5, 1 (January–February 1982).

Kelley, Florence. "When Co-Education Was Young," *Survey* 58 (February 1927).

Kelley, Mary. "The Sentimentalists: Promise and Betrayal in the Home." *Signs: Journal of Women in Culture and Society* 4 (Spring 1979).

Kennelly, Karen. "The Dynamic Sister Antonia and the College of St. Catherine." *Ramsey County History* 14 (Fall–Winter 1978).

Kennon, Anne Byrd. "College Wives Who Work." *Journal of the American Association of University Women* 20, 4 (1927).

King, Patricia M. "The Campaign for Higher Education for Women in Nineteenth-Century Boston." *Proceedings of the Massachusetts Historical Society* 93 (1982).

Kingsbury, Susan. "Economic Status of University Women in the United States." *Journal of the American Association of University Women* 32 (June 1939).

Kingsley, Louise. "The Advantage of a System of Public Graded Marks at Smith College." *The Smith College Monthly* 12 (November 1904).

Kleeck, Mary Van. "A Census of College Women." *Journal of the Association of Collegiate Alumnae* 11 (May 1918).

Koehler, Lyle. "The Case of the American Jezebels: Anne Hutchinson and Female Agitation during the Years of Antinomian Turmoil, 1636–1640." *William and Mary Quarterly,* 3d ser. 31 (1974).

Kohlstedt, Sally Gregory. "Maria Mitchell: The Advancement of Women in Science." *New England Quarterly* 51 (March 1978).

"Lady Professors." Boston University, *The Beacon* 7 (1881).

Lange, Alexis. "The Problem of the Professional Training for Women." *School and Society* 3 (April 1916).

Lindley, Josephine. University of California *Echo* 1 (1871).

Lloyd, Alice C. "Women in the Postwar College." *Journal of the American Associa-*

tion of University Women 39 (Spring 1946).

Logan, Adelia Hunt. "Colored Women As Voters." *The Crisis* 3–4 (1911–12).

Lutz, Alma. "Women's History—Background for Citizenship." *The Journal of the American Association of University Women* 40 (Fall 1946).

"Many Women in Poll Equate Values of Job and Family Life." *New York Times,* December 4, 1983.

"Many Young Women Now Say They'd Pick Family Over Career." *New York Times,* December 28, 1980.

Marteena, Constance H. "A College for Girls." *Opportunity* 16 (October 1938).

Martin, Gertrude. "Report of the Advisor of Women." In *Annual Report of the President.* Cornell University, 1912–1913.

Matthews, Donald G. "The Second Great Awakening as an Organizing Hypothesis." *American Quarterly* 21 (1969).

Matthews, Lois Kimball. "Raising the Standards of Intellectual Life." *Journal of the Association of Collegiate Alumnae* 9 (May 1916).

Mayo, Margaret. "Vita: Annie Jump Cannon." *Harvard Magazine* 83 (March–April 1981).

McCracken, Henry. "Flexner and the Woman's College." *Journal of Higher Education* 2 (October 1931).

McGovern, James. "The American Woman's Pre–World War I Freedom in Manners and Morals." *Journal of American History* 55 (1960).

McLachlan, James. "The American College in the Nineteenth Century: Toward a Reappraisal." *Teachers College Record* 80 (1978).

Meicklejohn, Alexander. "The Wisconsin Experimental College." *Journal of the American Association of University Women* 22 (October 1928).

Melder, Keith. "Masks of Oppression: The Female Seminary Movement in the United States." *New York History* 55 (July 1974).

Miller, Sarah Pleis. "Have Women's Salaries Been Increased by Higher University Training?" *The Journal of the Association of Collegiate Alumnae* 8 (April 1915).

Miner, James Burt. "A Vocational Census of College Students." *Educational Review* 50 (September 1915).

Morantz, Regina Markell. "Feminism, Professionalism, and Germs: The Thought of Marty Putnam Jacobi and Elizabeth Blackwell." *American Quarterly* 34 (1982).

Murray, Judith [Constantia]. "Desultory Thoughts upon the Utility of Encouraging a Degree of Self-Complacency, Especially in Female Bosoms." *The Gentleman and Lady's Town and Country Magazine* (October 1784).

Musto, David. "The Youth of John Quincy Adams." *Proceedings of the American Philosophical Society* 113 (1969).

"My Wife Works and I Like It." *Life* 41 (December, 1956).

Nettleton, Mary Anna. "A Survey of Hollins Graduates." *The Hollins Alumnae Quarterly* 10 (Summer 1935).

Newcomer, Mabel, and Gibson, Evelyn S. "Vital Statistics from Vassar College." *American Journal of Sociology* 29 (January 1924).

Notes Concerning Financial Aid. Harvard University, Office of Financial Aid, 1982.

Oates, Mary, and Williamson, Susan. "Comment on Tidball's 'Women's Colleges and Women Achievers Revisited.' " *Signs: Journal of Women in Culture and Society* 5 (Winter 1980).

———. "Women's Colleges and Women Achievers." *Signs: Journal of Women in Culture and Society* 3 (Summer 1978).

Oberlin Suffrage Club. "To Which Class Do You Belong?" Pamphlet published in 1908. Oberlin College Archives.

Okey, Ruth; Johnson, Barbara Kennedy; and MacKinney, Gordon. "Agnes Fay Morgan, 1884–1968." *In Memoriam.* Berkeley: University of California Press, 1969.

"On the Train." Boston University, *The Beacon* 5 (March 15, 1980).

"One of Them." *The Stanford Sequoia* 18 (April 1909).

Packard, Bob. "Discrimination Aided." *New York Times,* April 20, 1984.

Palmieri, Patricia A. "Here was Fellowship: A Social Portrait of Academic Women at Wellesley College, 1880–1920." *History of Education Quarterly* 23 (Summer 1983).

———. "Patterns of Achievement of Single Academic Women at Wellesley College, 1880–1920." *Frontiers* 5 (Spring 1980).

Parris, Marian. "Non-Teaching Positions Open to Students of Economics, Politics, and Sociology." *Journal of the Association of Collegiate Alumnae* 21 (April 1910).

Perkins, Linda. "Heed Life's Demands: The Educational Philosphy of Fanny Jackson Coppin." *Journal of Negro History* 51 (Summer 1982).

Pickard, J. L. "Historical Sketch of the University of Iowa." *Annals of Iowa* 3 (1899).

Pidgeon, Mary Elizabeth. *Women in the Economy of the United States of America.* A Summary Report. Bulletin of the Women's Bureau (1937).

Randour, Mary Lou; Strasbourg, Georgia L.; and Lipman-Blumen, Jean. "Women in Higher Education: Trends in Enrollments and Degrees Earned." *Harvard Educational Review* 52, 2 (1982).

Read, Florence M. "The Place of the Women's College in the Pattern of Negro Education." *Opportunity* 15 (September 1937).

Repplier, Agnes. "The Repeal of Reticence." *Atlantic Monthly* 113 (March 1914).

Requardt, Cynthia. "Alternative Professions for Goucher College Graduates, 1892–1910." *Maryland Historical Magazine* 74 (September 1979).

Richards, Ellen. "Desirable Tendencies in Professional and Technical Education for Women." *Journal of the Association of Collegiate Alumnae,* 3d ser. 17 (February, 1908).

Rickert, Edith. "What has the College Done for Girls: A Personal Canvass of Hundreds of Graduates of Sixty Colleges." *Ladies Home Journal* 29 (January–April 1912).

Robinson, Mabel L. *Curriculum of the Woman's College.* U.S. Bureau of Education Bulletin (1918).

Roosevelt, Eleanor. "Women in Politics." *Good Housekeeping Magazine* 110 (January, March, and April 1940).

Rosenberg, Carroll Smith. "The Female World of Love and Ritual: Relations Between Women in the Nineteenth-Century America." *Signs: Journal of Women in*

Culture and Society 1 (Autumn 1975).

Rosenberry, Lois K. M. "Have Women Students Affected the Standards of Co-educational Institutions?" *Journal of the American Association of University Women* 20 (January 1927).

Rossiter, Margaret W. " 'Women's Work' in Science, 1880–1910." *Isis* 71 (1980).

Rubinow, I. M. "The Revolt of a Middle-Aged Father." *Atlantic Monthly* 139 (May 1927).

Ryan, Mary P. "The Power of Women's Networks: A Case Study of Female Moral Reform in Antebellum America." *Feminist Studies* 5 (Spring 1979).

Ryan, W. Carson, Jr. "What Do We Know About Women's College Athletics." *Journal of the American Association of University Women* 23 (June 1930).

Sahli, Nancy. "Smashing: Women's Relationships Before the Fall." *Chrysalis* 17 (Summer 1979).

Sanford, Nevitt. "Is College Education Wasted on Women?" *Ladies Home Journal* 74 (May 1957).

Sanger, Margaret. "What Every Girl Should Know." *The Call* (1912–1913). Reprinted. Belvedere, New York, 1980.

Sargeant, Hélène Kazanjian. "Genus: Alumnae, Species: Wellesley, A Summary of the 16,662 Replies to the Recent Alumnae Questionnaire." *Wellesley Alumnae Magazine* 49 (November 1964).

Schaffter, Dorothy. "Educational Implications of Women's Military Training." *The Annals of the American Academy of Political and Social Sciences* 251. Edited by Louise Young (May 1947).

Scholten, Catherine M. "On the Importance of the Obstetrick Art: Changing Customs of Childbirth in America, 1760–1825." *William and Mary Quarterly* 3d ser. 34 (July 1977).

Schwarz, Judith. "Yellow Clover: Katharine Lee Bates and Katharine Coman." *Frontiers* 4 (1979).

Scott, Anne Firor. "The Ever Widening Circle: The Diffusion of Feminist Values from the Troy Female Seminary, 1822–1872." *History of Education Quarterly* 19 (Spring 1979).

———. "What, Then, Is the American: This New Woman?" *The Journal of American History* 65 (December 1978).

"Segregated Chicago." *The Independent* 61 (October 1906).

Semper, I. J. "The Church and Higher Education for Girls." *Catholic Educational Review* 29 (April 1931).

"Sex O'Clock in America." *Current Opinion* 55 (August 1913).

Shinn, Millicent Washburn. "The Marriage Rate of College Women." *The Century Magazine* 50 (October 1895).

Simmons, Christina. "Companionate Marriage and the Lesbian Threat." *Frontiers* 4 (1979).

Slowe, Lucy D. "Higher Education of Negro Women." *Journal of Negro Education* 2 (July 1933).

———. "The Colored Girl Enters College: What Shall She Expect?" *Opportunity* 15 (September 1937).

Smith College Class Report. 1912.

Smith, Timothy. "Immigrant Social Aspirations and American Education,

1880–1930." *American Quarterly* 21 (Fall 1969).

Snowden, Muriel S. "Reflections from an Overseer." Harvard University *Gazette*, June 4, 1982.

Solomon, Barbara Miller. "Brahmins and the Conscience of the Community. " In *Sacco-Vanzetti: Developments and Reconsiderations—1979*. Co nference Proceedings. Boston: Trustees of the Public Library of the City of Boston, 19 82.

Solomon, Barbara M. " Historical Determinants in Individual Life Experi ences of Successful Professional Women." *The Annals of the New York A cademy of Sciences* 208 (1973).

Stanley, Louise. "Home-Making Education in the Colleges." *The An nals of the American Academy of Political and Social Sciences* 143 (May 1929).

Stebbins, Lucy. "Report of the Dean of Women." In *Annual Report of the President*. University of California, 1913–1930.

Stevens, W. LeConte. "University Education for Women." *North Ame rican Review* 136 (January 1883).

Stevenson, Louise L. "Sarah Porter Educates Useful Ladies, 1847–1900.' ' *Winterthur Portfolio* 18 (Spring 1983).

Stricker, Frank. "Cookbooks and Law Books: The Hidden History of Career Women in Twentieth-Century America." *Journal of Social History* 10 (Fall 1976).

Strong, Sydney D., and Starr, Merritt. *Proportions of Men and Women Enrolled as Students at Oberlin College*. A report to the Trustees. Oberlin College, 1904.

Talbot, Marion. "Report of the Dean of Women." In *President's Report*. University of Chicago, 1898–1920.

Thomas, M. Carey. "Present Tendencies in Women's College and University Education." *Journal of the Association of Collegiate Alumnae*, 3d ser. 17 (February 1908).

———. "The Curriculum of the Woman's College." *Journal of the Association of Collegiate Alumnae* 10 (1916–17).

Thompson, Charles H. "The Socio-Economic Status of the Negro College Student." *Journal of Negro Education* 2 (January 1933).

Thorp, Anne. "The Social Side of Domestic Service at Vassar College." *Wellesley College Magazine* 24, 4 (January 1916).

Tidball, M. Elizabeth. "Perspectives on Academic Women and Affirmative Action." *Educational Record*. 54 (Spring 1973).

———. "Women's Colleges and Women Achievers Revisited." *Signs: Journal of Women in Culture and Society* 5 (1980).

Tidball, M. Elizabeth, and Kistiakowsky, Vera. "Baccaluareate Origins of American Scientists and Scholars." *Science* 193 (August 20, 1976).

Tufts, James Haydn. "The Senior Colleges." In *The Decennial Publications of the University of Chicago: The President's Report, 1892–1902*. University of Chicago, 1903.

Turner, Edward Raymond. "Women's Suffrage in New Jersey." *Smith College Studies in History* 1, 4 (1916).

Tuttle, Kate Austin. "A Plea for Scholarships for the Young Women of the South." *Journal of the Association of Collegiate Alumnae*, 3d ser. 13 (1906).

Tuve, Rosemond. "AAUW Fellows and Their Survival." *Journal of the American*

Association of University Women 44 (Summer 1951).

Uhlenberg, Peter. "Cohort Variations in Family Life Cycle Experience of United States Females." *Journal of Marriage and the Family* 16 (May 1975).

"Undergraduate Scholarships Offered to Women by the Nineteen Colleges of the Association of Collegiate Alumnae." *Journal of the Association of Collegiate Alumnae*, 3d ser. 2 (1899).

U.S. Bureau of the Census. *Historical Statistics.* 1975. Part I.

U.S. Department of Agriculture. *Social and Labor Needs of Farm Women.* Report 103. 1915.

U.S. Department of Commerce. *Historical Statistics of the United States, Colonial Times to the Present.* 1970.

U.S. Department of Health, Education, and Welfare, National Center for Education Statistics. *Digest of Education Statistics.* 1974, 1976, 1980, 1982.

U.S. Department of Labor. *College Women: Seven Years After Graduation.* 1964.

Walmsley, Alice. "The Cost of Wellesley College Life." *The Wellesley Magazine* 16, 2 (November 1, 1907).

Warren, William Marshall. "Dean's Report." In *Report of the President.* Boston University, 1907.

Weiss, Nancy P. "Mother, The Invention of Necessity: Dr. Benjamin Spock's *Baby and Child Care.*" *American Quarterly* 29 (Winter 1977).

Wellington, Elizabeth Elliott. "Re-Routing Woman's Education." *Journal of the American Association of University Women* 19 (June 1926).

Wells, Marguerite. "A Tramp Through the Berkshire Hills by Four College Girls." *The Symposium* 1 (October 1896).

Welter, Barbara. "The Cult of True Womanhood." *American Quarterly* 18 (1966).

"What I Got Out of College." *Woman's Home Companion* 39 (October 1912).

Wheeler, Benjamin I. *Annual Report of the President.* University of California, Berkeley, 1912.

Whitaker, Anna. "A Plea for the Knowledge of One's Standing in College." *Smith College Monthly* 15 (May 1908).

White, Theodore H. "New Powers, New Politics." *New York Times Magazine*, February 5, 1984.

Wiley, Lib, and Wiley, Virginia. "R-MWC a Lifetime Ago." *Randolph-Macon Woman's College Alumnae Bulletin* (Fall 1983).

Wilson, Joan Hoff. "The Illusion of Change: Women and the American Revolution," in *The American Revolution: Explorations in the History of American Radicalism*, ed. Alfred Young. DeKalb, Ill.: Northern Illinois University Press, 1976.

Witherspoon, John [Epaminondas]. "Reflections on Marriage." *Pennsylvania Magazine* 1 (December 1775).

Wolff, Cynthia Griffin. "The Problem of Eighteenth-Century Heroine-ism." *Modern Language Studies* 4 (1974).

Woodhouse, Chase Going. *After College, What? A Study of 6665 Land-Grant College Women, their Occupations, Earnings, Families, and some Undergraduate and Vocational Problems.* Bulletin of the Institute of Women's Professional Relations, 1932.

———. "Married College Women in Business and the Professions." *The Annals of the American Academy of Political and Social Science* 143 (1929).

————. "The Occupations of Members of the American Association of University Women." *Journal of the American Association of University Women* 21, 4 (1928).

Woolley, Mary E. "The College Curriculum as a Preparation for Life." *Journal of the Association of Collegiate Alumnae* 10 (1916–17).

Young, Elva Hulburd. "Law as a Profession for Women." *Publications of the Association of Collegiate Alumni*, 3d ser. 5 (February 1902).

Young, Louise, ed. *The Annals of the American Academy of Political and Social Sciences*, 251 (May 1947).

"Youth in College." *Fortune* 13 (June 1936).

Manuscript Sources

PAPERS AND RECORDS

Boston. Boston University. Mugar Library. Records of the Massachusetts Society for the University Education of Women.

————. Marion Talbot papers.

Cambridge. Radcliffe College Archives. Ada L. Comstock presidential papers.

Cambridge. Radcliffe College. The Arthur and Elizabeth Schlesinger Library on the History of Women in America. Ethel Sturges Dummar papers.

————. Betty Friedan papers.

————. Hilda W. Smith papers.

————. Maud Wood Park papers.

Chicago. University of Chicago. Joseph Regenstein Library. Sophonisba Breckinridge, Autobiography. MS.

————. Marion Talbot papers.

Northampton. Smith College Archives. Ada L. Comstock papers.

————. Madeleine Wallin papers.

Poughkeepsie. Vassar College Library. Lucy M. Salmon papers.

Stanford. Stanford University. Stanford College Archives. Clelia Duel Mosher papers.

Swarthmore. Swarthmore College. Peace Collection. Emily Greene Balch papers.

Washington, D.C. Howard University. Moorland-Spingarn Research Collection. Lucy Diggs Slowe papers.

INDIVIDUAL MANUSCRIPTS

Butler, Demia. Manuscript diary. Joseph Regenstein Library. University of Chicago.

Howes, Ethel Puffer. Informal Study on Married and Unmarried Smith Alumnae, 1926. Smith College Archives.

Hyde, Ida Henrietta. Diary. American Association of University Women Archives. Washington, D.C.

Irwin, Inez Haynes. Manuscript autobiography. Schlesinger Library.

Miller, Helen L. Letter to "Maurina." October 21, 1877. Smith College Archives.

Minutes of the Board of Regents. University of Wisconsin. University of Wisconsin Archives, 1903–07.

Paton, Lucy Allen. "Annex Memories," 1943. Radcliffe College Archives.

Salmon, Lucy M., to Ray Stannard Baker, January 6, 1926. Collections of the Manuscript Division, Library of Congress.

Scales, Laura. Unpublished memoir, Smith College Archives.

Stamm, Rebecca. "A History of Swarthmore College," 1979. Swarthmore College Archives.

Tolles, Frederick B. "A History of Swarthmore College." 1961. Swarthmore College Archives.

Unsworth, Richard P. "A Century of Religion at Smith College." 1975. Smith College Archives.

Wallin, Madeleine. "Points of View from a Bicycle." *Daily Theme*, May 22, 1894. Special Collections, Regenstein Library, University of Chicago.

INDEX

Abbott, Edith, 66–67
Abbott, Elizabeth Griffin, 66
Abbott, Ellis, 122
Abbott, Grace, 66
Abbott, Othman, 66
Abolition, 40–41, 45, 46
Academies: growth to *1850*, 15–16; founded by women, 17–20; sectional differences in, 20–22; curricula of, 22–23, 28; finances, goals of, 24–26; students' views of, 27; students' education at, versus their futures, 27–31; graduates as teachers at, 32–34
Adams, Abigail, 1, 7–8, 10, 11
Adams, Henry, 62
Adams, John, 1, 7, 8, 11, 13
Adams, Mary Ann, 30
Addams, Jane, 68, 91, 110, 116, 124, 131, 139
Agassiz, Elizabeth Carey, 54, 55
Agnes Scott College, 49, 80
Alger, William, 98
American Revolution: women's part in, 7–8; leaders' views of women, 11–13
American Student Union, 167–68, 169
Amherst College, 143
Angell, James, 53
Anthony, Susan B., 34, 46
Antin, Israel, 75
Antin, Mary, 75
Antioch College, 50
Association of Collegiate Alumnae, 135, 136
Athletics, women's: in academies, 23; in colleges, 103–04, 164, 247*n20*; affected

by women's movement, 204
Atwood, Charlotte, 109
Austin, Mary, 68

Balch, Emily Greene, 87, 91, 128, 139
Barnard, Frederick, 54
Barnard College, 55, 82, 84
Bascom, Florence, 89, 135
Bascom, John, 53
Bates College, 50
Baxter, Sarah, 108
Beecher, Catharine, 17, 19–20, 21, 24, 25, 32
Beecher, Lyman, 30
Benedict, Ruth, 68, 252*n5*
Bennett, Joseph, 54
Bennett College, 152–53, 168, 179
Bennington College, 150
Bethune, Mary McLeod, 148–49
Bevier, Isabel, 86
Beyer, Clara, 71, 102
Birth control. *See* Contraception
Blacks: at Oberlin, 21, 29, 108; as teachers, abolitionists, 40–41, 128; after abolition, 45, 46; colleges for, 50, 144–45; attendance in college, 76, 146–47, 148–49, 191, 242*n2*; discrimination against, in colleges, 108–09, 143–44; and women's suffrage, 112, 113; barred as secretaries, 130; in graduate schools, 136–37; and vocationalism, 151–53, 244*n26*; strict with students in twenties, 159–60; identity crises among, 163–64; organizations of, on campuses, 165, 166; protests among,